The Christian Faith

Henri de Lubac

The Christian Faith

An Essay on the Structure
Of the Apostles' Creed

Translated by
Brother Richard Arnandez, F.S.C.

Ignatius Press   San Francisco

Title of the French original:
La Foi chrétienne
Essai sur la structure
du Symbole des Apôtres
© 1969 Aubier-Montaigne
Paris, France

Cover by Victoria Hoke Lane

With ecclesiastical approval
© 1986 Ignatius Press, San Francisco
All rights reserved
ISBN 0-89870-053-1
Library of Congress catalogue number 84-80903
Printed in the United States of America

*Cordis nostri meditatio,
semper praesens custodia,
thesaurus pectoris nostri.*

> Saint Ambrose
> *Explanatio symboli*, I.

Contents

Foreword		9
Outline of the Book		17
1	History of a Legend	19
2	A Trinitarian Creed	55
3	The Economic Trinity	85
4	Belief and Faith	133
5	The Believing Church	171
6	The Believer in the Church	203
7	The Unity of the Faith	227
8	Christian Solecisms	261
9	The Dynamism of Faith	291
10	Faith and Profession of Faith	317

Foreword

This book does not pretend to impart any information to the learned historians of the creeds, save that, for better or worse, the author has often made use of their works. Nor does it deal in depth with any of the current theological problems, although it does not avoid alluding to them in passing. Nor should one seek in this book a systematic study of trinitarian doctrine or Christology. Its purpose is not even, at least not directly, pastoral. Rather, we have tried to make it a sort of introduction to catechesis, addressed to all those who, either in preparing candidates for baptism or in teaching children or in day-by-day preaching to the Christian people, are entrusted with this most beautiful of all roles: handing on the faith received from the Apostles, always and infinitely fruitful even as it was when they themselves received it from Jesus Christ.

Like everyone else, the believer is able to observe the changes, slow or sudden depending on the times, in people's mentalities and interests, the variations that occur in language. Without becoming enslaved to theories (themselves subject to so many vicissitudes) that seek to account for these changes, he does not necessarily remain insensitive to the repercussions of this historical development of culture or cultures upon theological work and even, on occasion, upon the very expression of his faith. If he himself is not conscious of it, the Magisterium guides him to make him understand that in certain circumstances renewal is necessary and that one would be condemned to wither and die if one did not ever consent to adapt or change anything. But at the same time he sees with great clarity that the treasure he has received as his inheritance is not the fruit of a perishable culture. The Christian tradition, that living force in which he shares, is rooted in the eternal. If he strives to be faithful, the newness that rejuvenates his heart is not exposed to the erosion of time. Consequently he is not in the least tempted to a certain kind of forced advance in which a number of those around him are indulging. He can only see in that, as Pascal would say, a confusion of orders. He knows in advance: in the letter of the Creed which he recites with his brothers, following so many others, there is infinitely more depth in reserve and timeliness in potential than in all the explanations and critical reductions that would affect to "go beyond" it. He knows this in advance, and experience and reflection reveal it to him a little more each day.

Above all, this Creed teaches us the mystery of the divine Trinity. It is in this mystery that our faith consists. It is for us both light and life. Nevertheless, it is very necessary for us to recognize that this is not always easy to understand and is not readily apparent to everyone. For a number of Christians, and not just those who retain only a vague, conventionalized version of their faith, this seems to be a sealed mystery. Is it proper to blame those who have the task of instructing us? It would be more just to take this blame upon ourselves. We do not always know how to embrace the most pregnant truth, which must slowly produce its fruit within us. Impatient as we are, we would like to understand immediately, or rather, in our shortsighted pragmatism, if we are not shown practical applications for it right away, we declare it to be abstract, unassimilable, "unrealistic", an "empty shell", a hollow theory with which there would be no point in burdening ourselves. This is what Faustus Socinus and his disciples thought, as witnessed by their Catechism of Racow (1605): "The dogma of the Trinity is contrary to reason. It is absurd to think that by the will of God, who is reason and who loves his creatures, men must believe something incomprehensible and useless to moral life and therefore to salvation." This was also the opinion of Jean-Jacques Rousseau, agreeing in this respect with all the Christians of his century seduced by the "lights": the Trinity, in the judgment of the Savoyard Vicar, was a part of those things that "lead to nothing useful or practical". Now we must really be convinced that, when we allow ourselves to indulge in such thoughts, it is we who are thus living superficially, outside of ourselves. The Christian who does not trust the fruitfulness of revealed truth, who consents to interest himself in it only to the degree to which he perceives the benefit in advance, who does not consent to let himself be grasped and modeled by it, such a Christian does not realize of what light and power he has deprived himself.[1] He does not see that in consenting to hear—if it may be called that—only the voices that promise him a response to his immediate questions, he is himself renouncing the opportunity to grow in

---

[1] "The life of the Church is more reliable than our own judgment. It is necessary to trust it, and experience does not hesitate to enlighten in this regard the one who lives his faith simply and profoundly": Cardinal G. M. Garrone, *Que faut-il croire?* (Paris: Desclée de Brouwer, 1967), 45.

self-understanding and depth while shutting himself up within the limits of his own narrow experience. Sometimes he even reaches the point of imagining he can no longer find any meaning in a hackneyed, "out-of-date" concept, when in fact he is dealing with a mystery he has not yet glimpsed.

The revelation of the trinitarian mystery turned the world upside down. Not after the fashion of human, political, social or, to use the current jargon, "cultural" revolutions which mark the course of history; but by opening up within man himself new depths, definitive depths, which he must thenceforth never cease to explore. By transforming totally his idea of the divinity, it at the same time transformed man's understanding of himself. More precisely, it revealed him to himself and transformed him. The transcendence of this mystery is total, and precisely for that reason its light can plumb the depths of our being. If I speak as one who believes in the Most Holy Trinity, then "I do not speak of it as I might of a constellation lost somewhere in the limitless reaches of space, but I see in it the first principle and the last end of my own existence; and my belief in this supreme mystery includes me too."[2] It includes me, it includes all of us. By this faith the Church of Jesus Christ lives.[3] If, instead of getting caught in that pathetic masochism into which so many perverse prophets work unceasingly to plunge them, Christians truly resolved to believe—I mean, to trust in their faith—this faith would in all truth make of them today the soul of the world.

---

[2] Romano Guardini, *Vie de la foi* (Paris: Éd. du Cerf, 1968), 48.

[3] Cf. Origen, *In Exodum*, hom. 9, no. 3: *"Funis triplex non rumpitur, quae est Trinitatis fides, de qua pendet et per quam sustinetur omnis Ecclesia"* (Éd. Baehrens, 239).

Our God is a living God, a God who, in himself, is sufficient unto himself. In him there is neither solitude nor egoism. In the very depths of Being there is ecstasy, the going out of self. There is, "in the unity of the Holy Spirit", the perfect circumincession of Love. Thus we can glimpse the depths of truth in St. John's remark (which is not true vice versa) that "God is love." If we exist, it is not due to chance(!) or to some blind necessity; nor is it the effect of a brutal and domineering omnipotence; it is in virtue of the omnipotence of Love. If we can recognize the God who speaks to us and wishes to link our destiny to his, this is because within himself he knows himself eternally; within his being a dialogue exists which can overflow without; he is animated by a vital movement with which he can associate us. If, even without philosophical training, we can resist those who tell us that matter is the ground of all being, and if we spontaneously go beyond the overly abstract views of those who tell us that spirit, or the "one", is the ground of being, it is because this mystery of the Trinity has opened up before us an entirely new perspective: the ground of all being is communion.[4] If we are able to overcome all the crises which might lead us to despair of the human adventure, it is because by the revelation of this mystery we know that we are loved. And at the same time we learn what the most clearsighted among men are inclined to question: we learn that we ourselves

---

[4] Jean Daniélou, *La Trinité et le mystère de l'existence* (Paris: Desclée de Brouwer, 1968), 53. "It is hard to believe that Christians who possess the ultimate secret of things, who are the only ones able to penetrate, by the light of Christ, into the abyss of the hidden mystery that envelops all things, should not be more aware of the fundamental importance of the message they have to convey."

can love; we have been made capable of doing so by the communication of divine life, that life which is love. We thereby understand also how "the fullness of personal existence coincides with the fullness of the gift", how self-realization without the gift of self is a delusion, and how, on the other hand, the gift of self goes astray into aimless activism if it is not the overflow of an inner life. We know, finally, that we must yield to this desire for bliss which no theory, no negation, no despair will ever tear out of the human heart because, far from being the pursuit of one's own interest, it blossoms under the action of God's Spirit into a hope of loving even as God loves.

If, as explained in the following pages, the mystery of the Trinity is not revealed to us first of all in itself but in the Trinity's action outside of itself, in its saving activity, it is no less true that the term of that saving action is indeed, already, the Trinity itself, glimpsed by faith in its very essence—even though always veiled in mystery, *in umbris et imaginibus*. So the "Trinity in itself" is still, even now, "the Trinity in relationship with us". Trinitarian doctrine is not the brainchild of some solitary thinker; it comes from the revelation of Jesus Christ. Nor is it a result of "high theological speculation". It is not a secret "reserved to the learned professionals, but it has an effective importance for every Christian".[5] Our inner existence, our personal relationships, our social action, our research and our efforts toward Christian unity, the entire basic orientation of our thought and life will be right and fruitful in proportion as they are in conformity with the reality of this mystery.

[5] Cf. Timothy Ware, *L'Orthodoxie*, French trans. Charité de Saint-Servais (Paris: Desclée de Brouwer, 1968), 285.

The mystery of the Trinity, which sheds light on the mystery of human existence, is wholly contained in the mystery of Christ. For this reason, as we well realize, another work would be necessary to introduce this one. It would start with the very first formulations of the Christian faith, which are Christic formulas. In Jesus Christ, God has opened his heart to us. Through him, "the Mediator of revelation and also its fullness", the Good News was proclaimed and will never cease to be heard. "A day has dawned which will know no ending. It comes to us out of the obscurity of Nazareth and reaches down to us through the centuries; it leads us on beyond all time . . . even to the very Center of truth. Hope has already begun; it can no longer end."[6]

---

[6] Jean Ladrière.

Outline of the Book

A legend attributes the composition of our "Apostles' Creed" to the twelve Apostles themselves (Chapter 1). This has the disadvantage of calling attention to a division (an artificial division) into twelve articles, whereas the structure of the Creed is tripartite because Christian faith is essentially faith in the indivisible Trinity (Chapter 2). But the Trinity did not reveal itself "as it is in itself" without any reference to man. It revealed itself through its works; as the Fathers of the Church remark, it is through the "mystery of the divine action" that we are led to the mystery of "theology" (Chapter 3). Faith in the divine Trinity is characterized in the Creed by the triple formula: *Credo in* . . . (πιστεύω εἰς . . .) which can refer to God alone. It is thereby distinguished from simple belief. But on the other hand, since the divine action and theology are joined in a single revealing act, belief and faith are inseparable in man's response to God's revelation (Chapter 4). Thus we do not say that the Christian believes "in" the Church because the Church is not God; she herself believes and is believed. Still, her role is of capital importance. As the community of believers, she brings each Christian to life, like a mother, and each one is a Christian insofar as he shares her faith (Chapter 5). The Church was first mentioned in a concluding phrase, less as an object for belief than as the locus within which faith is received and lived. The additions made to the Creed, by blurring this perspective, have given rise to involved explanations, but it has always been understood that it is in the Church and through her that "the Spirit's universal operation" is achieved (Chapter 6). So, whether we are discussing the object of faith or the body of those who believe, the Christian faith is therefore one, just as the Trinity is one; and if the dogma is developed and brought up to date, if the mystery is condensed and deepened, this will always be within the perfect circle of the Creed (Chapter 7). The characteristic formula for expressing faith, *Credo in* . . . , is one of those Christian solecisms which were necessary and spontaneously coined, prior to any reflective explanations, in order to express the new Christian reality (Chapter 8). By its dynamism it gives felicitous expression to the movement of faith which brings the believer toward God, a movement which eternal life, far from freezing into immobility, will cause to flower forth (Chapter 9). Finally, faith, which is addressed to God, must show itself exteriorly in the profession of faith. This is at the same time a testimonial offered to God (*confessio*, *martyrium*) and the bond of Christian unity (*symbolum*). The Apostles' Creed is this profession of faith (Chapter 10).

CHAPTER ONE

HISTORY OF A LEGEND

Let us reread our *Credo*, the one called the Apostles' Creed. It is the simplest and oldest of the creeds still in use in the Church, the one which even today all Christian sects in the West claim as their own,[1] the one which every Christian child learns in the catechism, the one which his godparents recited in his name the day he was baptized: "I believe in God, the Father Almighty, Creator of heaven and earth."

As we know, this venerable profession of faith goes back to remote antiquity. It did not, however, exist in its present form in the earliest days of Christianity. It was fully constituted and acquired a fixed form only at the end of a long and very complicated history which, in spite of the many critical studies devoted to it, we still cannot reconstruct in all its details. As we also know, according to an old legend, it was supposed to have been first drawn up at Jerusalem, under the inspiration of the Holy Spirit, by the twelve Apostles of Jesus Christ. It was on the eve of their dispersal. By this step the Apostles wanted to forestall any danger of diversity in the teaching of the new faith which they were preparing to bring to the ends of the earth. For this reason it would be called the "Apostles' Creed". It was already designated by this

[1] We will merely note that in their translation, the French Evangelical and Reformed Protestants adopted (rather late) the word "universal" instead of "catholic" in the article on the Church.

name in an official letter addressed by a council headed by St. Ambrose at Milan to the Pope in Rome, Siricius, in the year 390. The manner in which the Milanese bishops expressed themselves gives us to understand that neither the formula nor its designation was new at that time: *"Credatur symbolo apostolorum, quod Ecclesia romana intemeratum semper custodit et servat."*[2]

As for the explanatory legend, it is not one invented during the Middle Ages "in their ingenuous simplicity", as someone has written.[3] The Middle Ages may have improved on it but did not invent it.

As far back as the second century, mention was made of a "rule of faith", and the conviction grew up, not entirely without justification, that this rule went back to the twelve Apostles. This is what is deduced from the declarations of St. Irenaeus, who says that "if the Apostles had not left any writing behind, we would still need to follow the rule of faith which they passed on to the leaders of the Church."[4] What Tertullian also, in more than one place, calls the "rule of faith", a rule which "is immutable and irrevocable", already closely resembles our Creed (farther on we shall call attention to the differences in certain cases). Now he says that this rule of faith goes back to the very beginning, *"ab initio Evangelii"*, and claims that it was established by Christ

---

[2] St. Ambrose, *Epist.* 42, no. 5 (PL, 16:1125 B): "Let us believe the Apostles' Creed, which the Roman Church keeps and always preserves intact."

[3] Cf. Josef A. Jungmann, *La Liturgie des premiers siècles*, Lex Orandi 33 (Paris: Éd. du Cerf, 1962): 138.

[4] *Adversus haereses*, bk. 3, chap. 4, nos. 1–2; cf. bk. 1, chap. 10, no. 1 (PG, 7:549; 855–57).

himself[5] so that, when the Apostles went out preaching all over the earth, they all proclaimed "the same teaching about the same faith".[6] A little later, at the beginning of his *Peri archôn*, Origen gives a list of truths which were, he says, "obviously handed on by the preaching of the Apostles".[7] The Creed was a more or less developed expression of this rule of faith.[8] It would, therefore, seem natural enough to attribute its composition to the Twelve. This would have been little more than introducing more precise information.

When, exactly, did this attribution take place? We cannot say. We mentioned above the declaration made by the Council of Milan in 390. St. Ambrose himself is more explicit—if, as we think, he is indeed the author of a short "Explanation of the Creed" which at times has been ascribed to St. Augustine and even to St. Maximus of Turin.[9] The Reformers decided against the authorship of St. Ambrose, as did the Maurists and Dom Ceillier. Since then, the works by Fr. Probst (1843), Dom Morin

---

[5] *De praescriptione haereticorum*, chap. 13; cf. chap. 37. *Adversus Praxean*, chap. 2; *De virginibus velandis*, chap. 1 (CCL, 1:197–98; 2:1160, 1209). Cf. Oscar Cullmann, *La Foi et le culte de l'Église primitive* (Neuchâtel and Paris: Delachaux et Niestlé, 1963), 53.

[6] *De praescriptione*, chap. 20, no. 4: "*Apostoli . . . in orbem profecti, eamdem doctrinam ejusdem fidei nationibus promulgaverunt*" (CCL, 1:201–2).

[7] *De principiis*, bk. 1, preface, no. 4 (Koetschau, GCS, 22:11).

[8] The connection between the two is well brought out by Victorinus of Pettau, *In Apoc.*, 11:1: "*Haec est arundo et mensura fidei ut nemo adoret ad aram sanctam nisi qui haec confitetur, dominum et Christum ejus*" (ed. J. Haussleiter, CSEL, 49:96).

[9] So says Kattenbusch, *Das Apost. Symbolum* 1 (1894): 89–91; 2 (1900): 7–8. Cf. Th. Camelot: "Unless it was St. Maximus of Turin" (*Lumière et vie* 2 [1952]: 61).

(1928), O. Faller (1940), Dom Connolly (1942)[10] and J. H. Strawky (1950) have concluded to the contrary in favor of Ambrose; but the arguments presented were not absolutely convincing. It is true that this *Explanatio symboli* does repeat certain Ambrosian formulas, especially some from the *De sacramentis*; but the question could still be raised whether an author writing a little later might not have borrowed them, and even whether the *De sacramentis* itself was certainly authentic. We think, however, that the works of Miss Christine Mohrmann[11] and Dom Bernard Botte[12] have resolved all possibility of doubt on that score. The *Explanatio* is not exactly a sermon but "the minutes of a session on the *traditio symboli*". Its style and thought are those of St. Ambrose. One significant detail would seem to eliminate the hypothesis of a later date: "We still remain at a period when the candidates for baptism are mostly adults who must be made to learn the Creed by heart, without writing it down."[13] By the beginning of the fifth century the situation had changed, as we can see by the parallel sermons of St. Augustine.[14] In the *Explanatio*, on the

---

[10] In the edition which he brought out in 1952 (*The* Explanatio symboli ad initiandos, *a Work of Saint Ambrose*, Texts and Studies 10 (Cambridge), Dom H. R. Connolly referred to the verbal forms but without studying the development of the thought.

[11] "Le Style oral du *De sacramentis* de Saint Ambroise", in vol. 3 of his *Études sur le latin des Chrétiens* (Rome, 1965), 389–93.

[12] Introduction to Ambrose of Milan, *De sacramentis et De mysteriis*, new ed., revised and augmented with the *Explicatio Symboli* (Sources chrétiennes = SC, 25 *bis* [1961]: 7–45).

[13] Ibid., 22.

[14] *Sermo* 214, chap. 1. "*Haec sunt quae fideliter retenturi estis et memoriter reddituri.*" Or again, *Sermo* 212, chap. 2, after quoting

contrary, "the fact that the preacher insists on this point shows that we are not dealing with a mere surviving custom":

> I want you to be well aware of this: the Creed must not be written down. . . . Why not? Because we have received it in a way that was not meant to be written. What then must you do? Remember it. But, you will say, how can we remember it if we do not write it down? You will remember it all the better. . . . When you write something down, in fact, certain that you can reread it, you do not take the trouble to go over it every day, meditating on it. But, when you do not write something down, on the contrary, fearing to forget it, you do take the trouble to go over it every day. . . . Go over the Creed in your mind; I insist, in your mind. Why? So that you may not fall into the habit, by repeating it aloud to yourself, of starting to repeat it among the catechumens or the heretics.[15]

"The person who took these minutes", writes Dom Botte, "obeyed this injunction."[16] Then again, the manuscript tradition favors the authorship of St. Ambrose. The opinion of Erasmus, who did not hesitate to ascribe

---

Jeremiah 3:33: "*Hujus rei significandae causa, audiendo symbolum discitur, nec in tabulis vel in aliqua materia, sed in corde scribitur*" (PL, 38:1060 and 1058). Cf. the explanation given by Rufinus in his *Expositio symboli*, chap. 2: "*Idcirco denique haec non scribi cartulis aut membranis, sed retineri in cordibus tradiderunt, ut certum esset neminem haec ex lectione, quae interdum pervenire etiam ad infideles solet, sed ex apostolorum traditione didicisse*" (ed. Manlius Simonetti, CCL, 20:135).

[15] *Explanatio*, no. 9 (SC, 25 bis:57–59). Cf. *De Cain et Abel*, bk. 1, chap 9, 37: "*Cave ne imprudenter loquaris. . . . Cave ne incaute symboli vel dominicae orationis divulges mysteria*" (ed. C. Schenkl, CSEL, 32:370).

[16] Loc. cit., 22 and 25.

this little work to the Bishop of Milan, seems firmly established from then on. The *Explanatio symboli* should be dated about 380–390.

Thus, if we follow the great Bishop, the Creed professed by the Roman Church, which is the See of Peter, Prince of the Apostles, was composed and handed on by the Apostles themselves; they had come together to draw up as a group this summary of the faith, so that we might all easily keep this faith in our memories and recall it in full.[17] In this brief instruction, whose written style reproduces spoken language, the assertion is repeated at least six times. We find the same thing a little later, at the beginning of the commentary on the Apostles' Creed written by Rufinus of Aquilea. In this passage, which we shall discuss later on, Rufinus expressly states that he got his account from tradition.[18]

The Greeks were not responsible for spreading this legend. However, it is probably in the East that we must seek its origin. Perhaps Rufinus, whose commentary is dated some time after 400,[19] had been unduly impressed by some lines by Origen which he himself had translated a few years earlier (in 398). In the preface to the first book of his *Peri archôn*, Origen had written: "You must know

---

[17] *Explanatio fidei (a quodam excepta)*, no. 2: "*Sancti ergo apostoli in unum convenientes breviarium fidei fecerunt, ut breviter fidei totius seriem comprehendamus. Brevitas necessaria est, ut semper memoria et recordatione teneatur.*" Cf. no. 3, n. 7: "*Ergo dixi apostolos symbolum composuisse.*" "*Hoc autem est symbolum, quod Romana ecclesia tenet, ubi primus apostolorum Petrus sedit et communem sententiam eo detulit.*" (CSEL, 73: *S. Ambrosii Opera*, ed. Otto Faller [1955], pt. 7, 3–12.)

[18] *Commentarius in symbolum apostolorum*, no. 2: "*Tradunt majores nostri . . .*" (ed. Simonetti, CCL, 20:434).

[19] Date not certain; between 401 and 409. Cf. M. Villain, *Recherches de science religieuse* (1944), 130–31; M. Simonetti (1961), viii–ix.

that the holy Apostles, preaching the faith of Christ, handed down in clear words the points of doctrine which they deemed necessary", and he had then enumerated in the first place the essential truths concerning God, Christ and the Holy Spirit.[20] However, to judge from Rufinus' own translation, neither in this passage nor later on did Origen make the slightest allusion to a *compendium* in any way resembling our Creed. But at a later date (circa 399), Rufinus had translated a very different work: the Epistle of Clement to James. He considered it to be authentic.[21] But this Epistle belongs to the pseudo-Clementine writings,[22] which is precisely where we find that legend which Rufinus related. One can read it in the sixth volume of the *Apostolic Constitutions*. The author of this huge compilation, who at this point (circa 375) is adapting a passage from the *Didascalia of the Apostles* (third century), was a semi-Arian from Constantinople or Syria. He claims to be Clement of Rome but is in reality almost a contemporary of both Ambrose and Rufinus. According to him, the twelve Apostles, joined by James, the brother of the Lord, and Paul, had gathered in Jerusalem to prepare a long letter addressed to the first bishops they had appointed, defining Catholic doctrine in matters of faith and morals; and they supposedly charged Clement with delivering it.[23] The chapters of the *Didascalia of the Apostles* which contain this anecdote

---

[20] *De principiis*, bk. 1, no. 3: "*Illud autem scire oportet, quoniam sancti apostoli fidem Christi praedicantes, de quibusdam quidem quaecumque necessaria crediderunt . . . manifestissime tradiderunt*" (PG, 11:116 B).

[21] CCL, 20:282–83.

[22] Rufinus also translated in 406 the Clementine "*Recognitiones*".

[23] *Constit. apost.*, bk. 6, chap. 11: "*Nos vero . . . unum solum Deum annuntiamus*" (PG, 1:935); chap. 12: "*Congregati Hierosolymis nos duodecim*" (939 A); chap. 14: "*Nunc in unum congregati nos . . . item Jacobus*

have also been preserved for us in part in a Latin translation.[24] Rufinus, who had lived in the Orient, and who perhaps had also read this translation of the *Didascalia*, must have been familiar with the story; the same expressions are to be found in his work as in that of the pseudo-Clement. However, in the East these pages of the *Apostolic Constitutions* never had much influence. With regard to the origin of the creeds, the Greek and Syrian tradition followed rather the quite simple explanation given by St. Cyril of Jerusalem. In his fifth instruction on baptism, when the moment comes for presenting to the "illuminated", i.e., the newly baptized, "the holy and apostolic faith transmitted in view of the promise", Cyril told them:

> Remember and practice the faith which the Church hands on to you, the faith which rests on all the Scriptures. Everyone, of course, cannot read the Scriptures; some are prevented from knowing them well because of their lack of culture, and others because of their occupations. Therefore, so that the soul might not die because of its ignorance of the faith, we have summed up in these few phrases all the teachings of our faith. . . . It is not indeed by the caprice of men that these articles were put together; rather, having been selected out of all of Scripture in the

---

frater Domini . . . nec non Paulus gentium doctor . . . hanc catholicam doctrinam scripsimus vobis, ad confirmandos et corroborandos vos" (946 A–B); chap. 18: "*Vobis episcopis caeterisque sacerdotibus hanc doctrinam catholicam reliquimus . . . quam misimus per comministrum nostrum Clementem*" (962 B–C).

[24] Chap. 24: "*Convenientes nos duodecim apostoli in unum et Hierosoluma . . . placuit nobis scribere unum sentientibus catholicam (hanc doctrinam). . . .*" Chap. 25: "*Relinquentes hanc catholicam doctrinam . . . ecclesiae catholicae ad commemorationem confirmationis credentibus contestati*" (ed. H. Connolly [Oxford, 1929], 205 and 215).

most opportune way, they give the unique teaching of faith in full.[25]

We find the same explanation in the fifth century in the catechetical works of the Syrian Theodore of Mopsuestia: "Our fathers took care to state everything briefly so that it might be easy for their hearers to learn.... What they said was in full agreement with the Scriptures."[26]

Many in the Latin West were also content with that. One was St. Augustine, who seems to know nothing about what the *Explanatio* of St. Ambrose says on the subject except with regard to the role of the memory. At the beginning of his short treatise on the Creed, written for catechumens, he speaks much like Cyril and Theodore. "These words which you have just heard are scattered throughout the divine Scriptures; they have been extracted and gathered together in summarized form to spare men whose memories are slow from experiencing excessive fatigue, so that each one can say and remember what he believes."[27]

Again, in another sermon: "The teaching which you are about to receive is neither new nor incomprehensible for you. You are accustomed to hearing it expressed in

---

[25] *Cinquième Catéchèse baptismale*, chap. 12 (PG, 33:520 B; cf. 521-24). The creed given by Cyril is quite close to our Apostles' Creed in twelve articles.

[26] *Sixième Homélie catéchétique*, chap. 6, nos. 2 and 7. Cf. ninth homily, no. 1, etc.

[27] *De symbolo ad catechumenos*, chap. 1: "*Ista verba, quae audistis per divinas Scripturas sparsa sunt, sed inde collecta et ad unum redacta*" (PL, 40:627). Sermo 212, no. 2: "*Hunc igitur brevem sermonem de universo symbolo vobis debitum reddidi.... Quicquid enim in symbolo audituri estis, jam divinis sanctarum Scripturarum litteris continetur*" (Augustine of Hippo, *Sermons sur la Pâque*, ed. S. Poque, SC, 116:182).

various ways in the Holy Scriptures and in the sermons made in church. But it is going to be delivered to you in a brief form, drawn up in a certain condensed order."[28]

Neither in the *De fide et symbolo*[29] nor in the *Enchiridion*[30] is there question of anything else. Nor is there in the *De doctrina christiana*[31] where he speaks of the rule of faith; and we know that the Creed is, for him, the expression par excellence of that rule of faith. No doubt Augustine also readily attributes an apostolic origin to all that the universal Church of his time believed and practiced.[32] But in this there is still no precise and literal attribution, in the sense that we find it in St. Ambrose and in Rufinus. The *Tractatus de symbolo* by Faustus of Riez says that the Creed comes to us from the *Apostoli et Ecclesiarum*

---

[28] *Sermo* 214, chap. 1: "*Quae accepturi estis, non nova vel inaudita sunt vobis. Nam in sanctis Scripturis et sermonibus ecclesiasticis ea . . . soletis audire. Sed collecta breviter et in ordinem certum redacta . . . tradenda sunt vobis*" (PL, 38:1066). Cf. *Sermo* 59, no. 1 (38:400).

[29] Chap. 1, no. 1: "*Est autem catholica fides in symbolo nota fidelibus, memoriaeque mandata, quanta res passa est brevitate sermonis*" (Bib. aug., 9:18). Chap. 10, no. 25, *in fine*: "*Haec est fides quae paucis verbis tenenda in symbolo novellis christianis datur*" (74).

[30] Chap. 2, no. 7: "*Ecce tibi est symbolum et dominica oratio: quid brevius auditur aut legitur? Quid facilius memoriae commendatur?*" (Ibid., 110).

[31] Bk. 3, no. 2: "*Consulat regulam fidei, quam de Scripturarum planioribus locis et Ecclesiae auctoritate percepit*" (Bib. aug., 3:340).

[32] *De baptismo contra Donatistas*, bk. 2, chap. 12; bk. 4, chap. 9, no. 31; bk. 5, chap. 31. Cf. Vacandard, *Études de critique et d'histoire religieuse* (Paris: Lecoffre, 1906), 3–68, which is still useful. Augustine, then, did not laud the Creed "as though it had fallen from the very lips of God", nor did he recommend that it be recited "as though it were a sort of magical formula". Cf. F. Chaponnière, in *Encyclopédie des sciences religieuses* 1 (1877): 472.

Patres.[33] This rather vague formula might indicate that Faustus was not very confident about the story given by Rufinus. In another sermon on the Creed, part of the collection called *Collectio gallicana* which has come down to us as the work of Eusebius of Emesa,[34] we find only—if we can trust the printed text—*Ecclesiarum Patres* or *Ecclesiarum magistri*.[35] It is very probable that this "*Collectio gallicana* is a unified work whose sole author is Faustus of Riez".[36] Formulas such as these would therefore seem to indicate in Faustus' mind a certain critical resistance to the legend.[37] No allusion to it can be found in the works of St. Gregory the Great, nor, after his time, in a number of other orators and writers who commented on our Creed. Thus, even in the West the legend was never universally adopted. For a whole series of writers whom we might call the Augustinian school, the expression "Apostles' Creed" meant nothing more than the concise and authorized form given throughout

[33] Ed. C. P. Caspari, *Alte und neue Quellen* (Christiania, 1897), 263. About the author, see Gustave Weigel, *Faustus of Riez* (Philadelphia, 1938).

[34] On this enigmatic title, see L. A. Van Buchem, O.P., *L'Homélie pseudo-eusébienne de Pentecôte* (Nijmegen, 1967), 79–82: "The origin of the attribution to Eusebius".

[35] PL, Supplement (Hamman, vol. 3, cols. 541 and 577). Cf. Caspari, 263, n. 32. As is known, St. Jerome called Origen "post apostolos ecclesiarum magistrum", in *De nom. hebr.*, praef. (PL, 23:816; cf. 25:611).

[36] Abbé Jules Leroy, unpublished thesis, Strasbourg, quoted by Msgr. Élie Griffe, in *Bulletin de littérature ecclésiastique* 61 (1960): 27–38; "Les Sermons de Fauste de Riez", in *La "Collectio gallicana" du pseudo-Eusèbe*.

[37] The critical edition prepared by Jules Leroy has not been published, so these conclusions are still unconfirmed.

the churches to the teaching that had come down from the Apostles.[38]

St. Ambrose, then, used to tell his catechumens that the holy Apostles themselves had composed a "summary of the faith". Rufinus of Aquilea likewise said that they had drawn up "a brief resumé of their future preaching". In its general terms, without the specific details added by Rufinus, this same information is found in St. Jerome, who here shows himself less critical than St. Augustine; for Jerome, "the creed of our faith and our hope was handed down by the Apostles."[39] It is found again in an *Instructio ad competentes* on the Creed, by Nicetas of Remesiana (in southern Dacia), which reproduces word for word a phrase from the *Explanatio* of St. Ambrose: "The holy Apostles gathered together to draw up a summary of the faith so that we might take in at a glance the whole range of our faith."[40] Virgilius of Tapsensis in the fifth century,[41] Fulgentius of Ruspe in the sixth,[42] say no more than St. Jerome did. On the other hand, without retracting the apostolic origin of the Creed, Nicetas obviously was also inspired by the tradition represented by Cyril of Jerusalem and Augustine

---

[38] Cf. St. Augustine, *In Joannem*, tract. 37, no. 6: "*Catholica fides, veniens de doctrina apostolorum, plantata in nobis, per seriem successionis accepta, sana ad posteros transmittenda*" (CCL, 36:335). The "*Vetus missale gallicanum*" in chapter 16 contains an "*expositio symboli*" which gives Augustine's explanations but not a word about the legend.

[39] *Contra Joannem Hierosolymitanum*, chap. 28: "*In symbolo fidei et spei nostrae, quod ab apostolis traditum*" (PL, 23:396).

[40] Bk. 5, Sermo 1, no. 4: "*Sancti ergo apostoli, in unum convenientes, breviarium fidei fecerunt, ut breviter fidei totius seriem comprehendamus*": ed. Klaus Gamber (Regensburg, 1964), 103.

[41] PL, 62:119.

[42] PL, 65:822–23.

to show the practical necessity of a substantial resumé drawn from Holy Scripture. "Thus", he writes, "the illiterate or those too absorbed by the affairs of everyday life can, in learning it by heart, obtain the necessary minimum knowledge of salvation."[43] John Cassian repeats both of these declarations. Faustus of Riez, who definitely wavers a bit, does the same. These writers add to the "historical" information derived from Ambrose and Rufinus the idea derived from Cyril of Jerusalem and Augustine of a doctrinal resumé drawn from Scripture and enjoying the same authority.

Cassian takes his inspiration in the first place, as Rufinus had done,[44] from a view expressed by Origen, who had called the Creed *"verbum breviatum"*, a term derived from Isaiah and quoted by St. Paul in the Epistle to the Romans.[45] But, again like Rufinus, he attributes to the Apostles the fatherhood of this "abridged word", something that Origen had not done. The Apostles, he says, brought together here the entire Catholic faith, which was at first dispersed throughout the immense body of

---

[43] *De symbolo*, chap. 13: "*De totis enim Scripturis haec sub brevitate collecta sunt . . . ut, quoniam plures credentium litteras nesciunt, vel qui sciunt per occupationes saeculi Scripturas legere non possunt, haec corde retinentes, habeant sufficientem sibi scientiam salutarem*": in *Nicetas of Remesiana*, ed. A. R. Burn (Cambridge, 1905), 51–52. Nicetas speaks in the same way of his own instructions: *Ad competentes*, bk. 1, Sermo 1, no. 2: "*Instructiones igitur necessarias ad fidem . . . non ex proprio ingenio compositas, sed ex divinarum Scripturarum praedicatione collectas*" (Gamber, 17).

[44] *Expositio symboli*, chap. 1 (CCL, 20:133–34).

[45] Origen, *In Romanos*, bk. 7, chap. 19 (translated by Rufinus): "*Potest et 'verbum breviatum' dici fides symboli, quae credentibus traditur, in qua totius mysterii summa paucis connexa sermonibus continetur*" (PG, 14:1154 A). So too writes Eusebius (translated by Faustus) in *De symbolo* (PL, Suppl., 3:583).

the sacred volumes. Such a summary is also the work of God, for just as God had given us the Scriptures through the instrumentality of the prophets and patriarchs, so through his Apostles and priests did he frame our Creed. In both cases the authority is the same: the Creed, like Scripture, has been given to us by God through the mediation of men inspired by him.[46] Faustus of Riez is thinking perhaps of the Nicene Creed rather than of the Apostles' Creed that Cassian had in mind;[47] but that does not matter to us here. We would simply remark that in his treatise on the Holy Spirit, he also stresses the dependence of the Creed on the sacred books and mentions only in passing its apostolic origin.[48]

A homily on the handing on of the Creed, mistakenly published in the works of St. Maximus of Turin but which seems rather to be that of St. Caesarius of Arles, repeats Ambrose's declaration, adding one more highly

---

[46] John Cassian, *De incarnatione Domini contra Nestorium*, bk. 6, chaps. 3 and 4: "*Per homines enim id Deus fecit; sicut enim immensam illam Scripturarum sacrarum copiam per partiarchas et prophetas maxime suos condidit, ita symbolum per apostolos suos sacerdotesque constituit, et quidquid illic per suos larga ac redundanti copia dilatavit, idem hic per suos plenissima brevitate conclusit. Nihil ergo in symbolo deest, qui ex scriptis Dei per apostolos Dei conditis, totum in se, quantum ad auctoritatem pertinet, habet quidquid vel hominum est vel Dei*" (ed. M. Petschenig, CSEL, 17 [1888]: 327–29).

[47] This is what seems to be brought out in his Preface. Cf. Joseph de Ghellinck, "En marge de l'explication du 'Credo' par saint Albert le Grand"; *Beiträge zur Geschichte der Philosophie und Theologie des Mittelalters* (A. M. Landgraf), suppl. 4, *Studia Albertina, Festschrift für Bernhard Geyer* (H. Ostlender), 148–66.

[48] *De Spiritu sancto*, bk. 1, chaps. 1 and 2: "*Apostolica sollicitudo . . . in symboli salutare carmen mira brevitate collegit (fidem catholicam)*". "*De sacris voluminibus . . . de quorum forte symboli ipsius series derivata subsistit*" (ed. Engelbrecht, CSEL, 21:102 and 104).

anachronistic detail. It was "the blessed Apostles" who themselves "handed down to us the mystery of the Creed"; their intent, says our author, (*"ut ego reor"*) was not only to unite all those who would later believe in Christ but to distinguish them from heretics.[49] This last idea is also stressed in a letter addressed by St. Leo the Great on June 13, 449, to the Empress Pulcheria.[50] In that letter St. Leo refers to "the Catholic Creed, a brief and perfect profession of faith, which in its twelve articles bears the imprint of the twelve Apostles".[51] The formula used does not indicate whether this was to be taken in a historical sense or only a symbolic one; but a sermon by the great Pontiff removes this ambiguity by speaking of those who deny the Incarnation as being in opposition to the Creed instituted by the holy Apostles.[52] Another document of the same period, possibly written by St. Leo as well, further affirms that the text insisted on by the Apostles was "inspired by the Lord" and "dictated by the Holy Spirit".[53] This recalls to mind Cassian's exposition about the *"verbum breviatum"*. We shall find the same thing in the Gelasian sacramentary.[54]

Still, the legend had not been slow in acquiring a more precise and detailed form. For this, all that was needed

[49] *Homelia* 83 (PL, 57:433 A–B).

[50] *Epist.* 31, chap. 4 (PL, 54:794).

[51] Ibid.: *"Catholici symboli brevis et perfecta confessio quae duodecim apostolorum totidem est signata sententiis"* (194 B).

[52] *Sermo* 96, chap. 1: *"Incarnationis dominicae negatores, et instituto a sanctis apostolis symbolo repugnantes"* (PL, 54:466 C).

[53] *Praefatio symboli ad electos*.

[54] Ed. Wilson (1894), 53: *"Suscipientes evangelici symboli sacramentum a Domino inspiratum, ab apostolis institutum . . . Sanctus etenim Spiritus qui magistris Ecclesiae ista dictavit"*. (One can recognize here the formula used by Faustus in the sermon quoted above, 28f.)

was to lay more stress on an indication found in a rather vague way in St. Ambrose and emphasized a bit more by Rufinus. St. Ambrose, in fact, said toward the end of his *Explanatio*: "As there were twelve Apostles, there are also twelve articles."[55] And after having the catechumens recite the Creed, he says: "This is how the twelve articles were brought together by the twelve Apostles." Rufinus in turn declared that each of the Apostles had stated before the others "what he felt".[56] This gave rise to the more insistent version of the story according to which each of the Twelve, in turn, had pronounced one of the twelve articles of which the Creed is composed. This version, however, was not current in the fifth century. In a sermon about the Lenten fasts, toward the beginning of that century, St. Maximus of Turin hardly goes beyond what St. Ambrose and Rufinus had affirmed.[57] The same could be said of St. Leo, who in the letter already mentioned asks Pulcheria to admire "the fullness of the Creed".[58] The earliest known author to put into words the new version which would enjoy such a long history is a sixth-century preacher, probably a Gaul, whose two sermons on the Creed were attributed to

---

[55] N. 8: "*Ergo quemadmodum duodecim apostoli, et duodecim sententiae. . . . Ecce secundum duodecim apostolos, et duodecim sententiae comprehensae sunt*" (Botte, SC, 25 bis:56). The same phrase is found in Nicetas, according to Klaus Gamber's edition: *Instructio ad competentes*, bk. 5, *Sermo* 1, no. 27 (107–8).

[56] The Apostles composed the Creed "*in unum conferendo quod sentiebant unusquisque*"; "*in unum conferendo unusquisque quod sensit*": no. 2 (PL, 21:337 A–B; Manlius Simonetti, CCL, 20:134).

[57] In St. Ambrose, *Sermo* 33, chap. 17, no. 6: "*Arbitror illam (fidem) duodecim artificum operatione conflatam; duodecim enim apostolorum symbolo fides sancta concepta est*" (PL, 17:671 B).

[58] *Epist.* 31, chap. 3: "*Cujus symboli plentitudinem*" (PL, 54:794 B).

HISTORY OF A LEGEND

St. Augustine. Going beyond another of Rufinus' statements,[59] he places the scene on the very day of Pentecost and gives us a dramatic and detailed account of it.

> On the tenth day after the Ascension, the disciples, fearing the Jews, had gathered together. Then the Lord sent them the promised Paraclete. They were all on fire, like red-hot iron, and, filled with the knowledge of all languages, they composed the Creed. Peter said: I believe in God, the Father Almighty. . . . Andrew said: and in Jesus Christ his Son. . . . Thaddeus said: the resurrection of the body. . . . Matthias said: and life everlasting. Tried like gold by the fire of the Holy Spirit, the Apostles, who up to then had considered themselves unworthy, went forth boldly to preach the gospel to every creature, as the Lord had commanded them to do.[60]

A preacher's ingenious trick to make a catechism lesson more stimulating. According to this pseudo-Augustine, each Apostle not only stated his article but also gave a brief explanation of it. However, the legend thus embellished does not seem to have met with a great deal of success at first. St. Isidore of Seville knows nothing of these additional details, or else prefers to ignore them. He merely reproduces Rufinus' text, shortening it somewhat.[61] St. Ildefonsus of Toledo, who

---

[59] Op. cit., chap. 2: "When the Holy Spirit had come to rest on each of the Apostles, . . . they were given the order to disperse. . . . Before leaving each other . . ." (134).

[60] *Sermo* 240, nos. 1 and 2 (PL, 39:2189). We find the same outline, in an abbreviated form, in *Sermo* 241, no. 1 (39:2190).

[61] *De ecclesiasticis officiis*, bk. 2, chap. 23, no. 2: "*Discessuri itaque ab invicem, normam prius sibi futurae praedicationis in commune constituunt, ne, localiter ab invicem discedentes, diversum aliquid vel dissonum praedicarent his qui ad fidem Christi invitabantur. Omnes igitur in uno positi, et Spiritu sancto repleti, breve sibi praedicationis indicium conferendo in unum*

copies Isidore, is not aware of them either.[62] Nor is Venantius Fortunatus, the author of an *Expositio symboli* in the eighth century,[63] nor the great compiler Rabbanus Maurus in the ninth.[64] All four of these, directly or not, depend on Rufinus. They also follow St. Augustine[65] as well as (Fortunatus excepted) Cassian when he comments in his own fashion on the *"verbum breviatum"*. So too in the eleventh century Yves of Chartres does not know (or rejects) the imaginary story given by the pseudo-Augustine. He merely knows that the holy Apostles, who were twelve in number, have left to the Church a rule of faith in twelve articles, to serve as a symbol of unity among Christians.[66] In certain places, especially France, Germany and Hungary, a feast was instituted in the Middle Ages called the Feast of the Dispersion or Separation of the Apostles.[67] Now, in the sequence which Gottschalk of Limburg composed toward the middle of the eleventh century for the Mass on this feast day, we find no explicit allusion, even in their more restrained and ancient form, to the traditions about the

---

quod sentiebant componunt, atque hanc credentibus dandam esse regulam statuunt" (PL, 83:816 A).

[62] *De cognitione baptismi*, chaps. 32–33 (PL, 96:126).

[63] *Expositio symboli*, no. 2: *"Adhuc in uno positi, hoc inter se symbolum, unusquisque quod sensit dicendo, considerarunt, ut discedentes ab invicem hanc regulam per omnes gentes aequaliter praedicarent"* (Carmina, bk. 11, chap. 1; Monumenta Germaniae historica, A. Ant., 4:253).

[64] *De clericorum institutione*, bk. 2, chap. 56 (PL, 107:368–69).

[65] Thus Isidore in his *Sententiae*, 1:21: *"Omnis latitudo Scripturarum in eadem oratione dominica et symboli brevitate concluditur"* (PL, 83:587 A).

[66] Sermo 23, *De symbolo apostolorum* (PL, 162:604 C–D).

[67] So claims Daniel, in *Thesaurus hymnologicus*, 2:3 (PL, 141:1331 A–C). This feast is unknown in the Roman, Italian and Mozarabic liturgical books.

formation of the Creed.⁶⁸ In the following century Peter Abelard, while attributing the Creed to the Apostles themselves, also said merely that it "contains a resumé of the faith".⁶⁹

On the other hand, the pseudo-Augustine had a number of followers among other writers. A Gallican sacramentary of the seventh century, a passage in the *Scarapsus* by St. Pirminus in the eighth century,⁷⁰ the *Disputatio puerorum* by Alcuin in the ninth century,⁷¹ a German collection of the tenth century, all attribute each of the twelve articles of the Creed to one of the twelve Apostles in particular. The only occasional difference between these authors occurs in the order in which the Apostles are enumerated. Pseudo-Augustine in his sermon 240 uses the order given in the Canon of the Mass; St. Pirminus follows that found in the first chapter of the Acts of the Apostles (1:13), which was also retained in the pseudo-Augustine's sermon 241; Alcuin lists the names in the order found in chapter 10 of St. Matthew (10:2–4). The list given in Acts is the one accepted by St. Thomas Aquinas, but somewhat eclectically and without attaching any importance to it: "*sed in hoc non est magna vis*", he remarks with good sense.⁷²

The Spaniards Heterius and Beatus, in their zeal for

---

⁶⁸ Fourth sequence, *In divisione apostolorum* (PL, 141:1330–31).

⁶⁹ "Summam fidei": *Expositio symboli* (PL, 178:619 C–D).

⁷⁰ *Scarapsus de singulis libris canonicis*. Pirminus even gives the precise time on the day of Pentecost: "*hora tertia*". In August Hahn, *Bibliothek der Symbole und Glaubensregeln der alten Kirche*, ed. Ludwig Hahn (Breslau, 1897), 76–77 and 97. See also 103–4. Cf. PL, 89:1034 C–D.

⁷¹ Chap. 11 (PL, 101:1138–45).

⁷² *In 3 Sent.*, dist. 25, q. 1, a. 2. The second mentioned is "*Matthias, vel terum Thomas, ut quidam dicunt*".

orthodoxy, are not content with a general affirmation either. In 787, writing against their fellow Spaniard Elipand, they reproach him with prefiguring the Antichrist because he dares to dogmatize by himself and has done away with one of the twelve articles, even though Peter, who was the head of the Apostles, "did not dare to compose the Creed all by himself" but wanted it to be the work of the Twelve. "Twelve were the disciples of Christ and the teachers of the nations; since all of them together made only one, they composed a single Creed; each spoke his word, and these words fit together to form a single faith; and there are only twelve words or articles." This was a model of perfect unity in spite of distinct roles. This was because these twelve Apostles were like the twelve rays of daylight, ready to bring the light of the one Sun to all the extremities of the earth.[73]

In addition to the enumeration given above, Alcuin commented on the scene, adding to it a symbolic prefiguration drawn from the story of Jephthah the Gileadite.[74] This sort of pedagogical procedure was not out of place in popular preaching or in a catechism for children like the *Disputatio puerorum*. But, although devoted to a different type of work, the Scholastics went still further. They sought to give more detailed explanations which, in their ingeniousness, are not completely irrelevant. We find this in the *Summa theologica* of Alexander of Halès.[75] We find even more of it in St.

[73] *Ad Elipandum*, bk. 1, chap. 21 (PL, 96:906 C); bk. 2, chaps. 8–9, cols. 982–83; chap. 99, cols. 1026–27; cf. col. 998.

[74] Chap. 11: *Incipit de fide* (PL, 101:1136–43). Cf. *Judges* 11.

[75] Bk. 3, pt. 3, tract. 2, q. 2: *De distinctione et expositione articulorum*, chap. 1, "Qualiter in symbolo apostolorum distinguantur articuli" (ed Quaracchi, 4:1122).

HISTORY OF A LEGEND

Bonaventure, whose symbolic imagination never runs dry. In his *Breviloquium* and in his commentary on the *Sentences* of Lombard, Bonaventure relates the legendary account as it has been handed down, he says, by the Catholic Doctors.[76] But in his own commentary he does not fail to add to it some later accretions. For "the building up of the faith", he says, making use of the old expression of St. Gregory,[77] each of the twelve Apostles came to set down at the proper place his own article, like a living stone, but "firm and immutable", after having extracted it "from the depths of the Scriptures". This had been prefigured in the past by the Holy Spirit in the book of Joshua, under the form of the twelve men who, chosen by the one whose very name was a figure of Jesus Christ, took twelve stones from the bed of the Jordan to build the altar of the Lord.[78] This theme had already been outlined by Alcuin. But in one of his conferences on the *Hexameron*, in which he exalts the beauty of the faith, Bonaventure indulges in some variations which seem more personal. The twelve gates of the heavenly Jerusalem with their twelve angels, the twelve foundation stones of the city bearing the names of the twelve Apostles which

---

[76] *In 3 Sent.*, dist. 25 (ed. Quaracchi, 3:534).

[77] On the meaning and history of this expression, see my *Exégèse médiévale* 2:522–37.

[78] *Breviloquium*, pt. 5, chap. 7: "*Et quia Spiritus sanctus hos articulos fidei in Scripturarum profunditate contentos in unum conpegit per duodecim apostolos tamquam per testes firmissimos; hinc est, quod praedicti articuli in unum symbolum apostolorum collecti fuerunt. Et ideo secundum apostolos conponentes duodecim articuli dici possunt, quia quilibet apostolus in aedificationem fidei posuit unum articulum quasi lapidem unum vivum; quod Spiritus sanctus recte praefiguravit in duodecim viris, qui duodecim lapides de Jordanis alveo extraxerunt ad altare dominicum construendum*" (ed. Quaracchi, 5:261). *In 3 Sent.*, dist. 25 (3:534–37).

call to mind the twelve patriarchs, the twelve kinds of precious stones which shine on its walls, are for him the occasion for a lyrical effusion. In the twelve precious stones, to which he adds the twelve signs of the zodiac in which the infinity of the stars is included, he sees the figure, not exactly of the twelve articles of the Creed, but, in a more liberal interpretation, that of "the twelve contemplations which we can draw from the faith". All of these have God for their object, God contemplated in turn according to the diverse aspects of his being and the various forms of his action for us:

> These twelve contemplations are those which we draw from the faith: we believe in one God—who is three and one—the Exemplar of all things—who created the world—formed the soul—gave the Spirit—God united with flesh—God crucified—the remedy of our souls—the lifegiving food—the avenger of crime—the eternal reward.[79]

That leads us rather far away from the "twelve articles". . . .

In St. Albert the Great we have another witness of the survival of our legend in the thirteenth century. Apart from his scientific works, Albert drafted a treatise on the Sacrifice of the Mass, which is a popular, or more precisely a pastoral, work intended for the parish clergy. In it, he explains the Creed by using the theme found in the pseudo-Augustine's sermon as the picturesque

---

[79] *In Hexaemeron*, collatio 10, *Quae incipit agere de fidei speciositate*, nos. 1–3 (ed. Quaracchi, 5:377). "*Duodecim speculationes sunt quae habemus ex fide: credere Deum unicum—Deum trinum et unum—et exemplar rerum—et creantem mundum—et formantem animam—dantem spiritum— Deum carni unitum—Deum crucifixum—medelam mentium—vitale pabulum—ultorem scelerum—praemium aeternum.*"

framework for his commentary on each article. For attributing the different articles to the various Apostles, he follows the order given by Alcuin, i.e., that found in St. Matthew.[80] About the same time another Dominican, Raymond Martin, the author of an *Explanatio symboli* (1258), gives a rather different listing.[81] A bit of mnemonic verse attributed to St. Bernard helped to popularize the legend:

> Articuli fidei sunt bis sex corde tenendi,
> Quos Christi socii docuerunt pneumate pleni.
> Credo Deum Patrem, Petrus inquit, cuncta creantem;
> Andreas dixit: Ego credo Jesum fore Christum;
> Conceptum, natum Jacobus; passusque Joannes. . . .[82]

Later than the written texts, but following their teaching, we find the artistic representations, which are often more beautiful, more evocative in any case, than the texts themselves of a truth that is more real, since they are by nature images. Thus, in the parish church of Charlieu in the diocese of Lyons, a church which formerly belonged to a famous Cluniac priory, one can still see "above the choir stalls some beautiful paintings on wood dating back to the fifteenth century, which represent each of the twelve Apostles holding a streamer whereon is written a phrase of the Creed which bears his name".[83]

It is the common fate of legends to grow and to

---

[80] *De sacrificio missae*, bk. 2, chap. 8, no. 2 (*Opera omnia*, ed. Borgnet, 38:60–66). Cf. J. de Ghellinck, "En marge de l'explication du 'Credo' par saint Albert le Grand", 149.

[81] F. Cavallera, "L'*Explanatio symboli* de R. Martin", in *Studia mediaevalia, in honorem R. J. Martin* (Bruges, 1942), 202.

[82] In Hahn, 53.

[83] Pierre Nautin, "*Je crois à l'Esprit Saint: Étude sur l'historie de la théologie du Symbole*", Unam Sanctam (Paris: Éd. du Cerf, 1947), 7.

become more involved as they get older. After about 1300, the legend we have been discussing is found combined more closely with the ancient theme of the union of the two Testaments, for which it provides a new illustration.[84] Each Apostle now has a specific corresponding prophet, the latter reciting a verse of his prophecy which foretells the article authored by his partner. Émile Mâle noticed the first evidence of this in several miniatures from the end of the thirteenth century, and in the *Verger de Soulas*.[85] In a collection of *Sententiae*, which is a sort of catechism in verse, the Creed makes one think of the marvelous clock of Marbourg: the great prophets of the Old Testament, then the Apostles of the New Testament, each come in turn to sing a couplet on center stage. "All this unsophisticated but interesting presentation gives one food for thought", notes M. Jacques Toussaert at the end of his analysis.[86] The manuscript, preserved in the library at Bruges, dates back to the fourteenth century. Just about everywhere in Europe, in stained glass or tapestry, in frescoes or the statuary of the churches in the illuminations of Books of Hours, one can see the double series of twelve persons, arranged two by two for their "alternating song". Almost always each one carries his own streamer. So it is in the upper windows of Bourges and Riom, and again in the choir of the cathedral at Albi: each pillar of the choir screen bears a prophet facing outward and an Apostle facing in. The same thing is found on the carved wooden stalls in a

[84] We do not mention the pictures which connect the prophets and the Apostles without specifically referring to the Creed.
[85] Émile Mâle, *L'Art religieux de la fin du moyen âge en France* (Paris: Armand Colin, 1908), 261–62.
[86] *Le Sentiment religieux en Flandre à la fin du moyen âge* (1963), 76.

dozen churches located in the former possessions of the dukes of Savoy: Saint Claude, Fribourg, Romart, Aosta, Hauterive, Saint-Jean-de-Maurienne, Yverdon, Mondon, Estavayer-le-Lac. All these works of art belong to the period running from 1450 to 1525 approximately. The same motif is found in the frescoes (which have partially worn away) in the apse of the ancient cathedral of St. Valery of Sion. In the collegiate church of St. Peter and St. Ours at Aosta, it is both painted on the vaulted ceiling and sculpted on the choir stalls.[87] At the Charterhouse of Salvatorberg, the famous catalogue dating from the fifteenth century mentions a work containing "the Apostles' Creed depicted in a beautiful painting, which represents the articles as they were pronounced by each of the Apostles, with the corresponding prophets".[88] The two Testaments thus bear witness to each other in the most eloquent and well-ordered precision, in the service of our common faith.

Some works of the fourteenth century offer us new refinements. The Breviary of Belleville (circa 1345) contains a calendar in which prophets and Apostles are shown in reference to the twelve months of the year, during which the edifice of the new faith is being built.

> At the bottom of each page an Apostle is shown standing opposite a prophet. The prophet is standing near an edifice which symbolizes the Synagogue, or, if one prefers, the Old Law. The prophet has torn a stone out of this edifice and seems to be presenting it to the Apostle,

[87] Robert Berton, *Les Stalles de l'insigne collégiale de Saint-Pierre et de Saint-Ours d'Aoste* (Istituto geografico de Agostini-Novara, 1964).
[88] "*Symbolum apostolorum in quadam figura contractum pulchre per articulos ad singulos apostolorum cum correspondantia prophetarum.*" Cf. J. de Ghellinck, 160.

for these stones taken from the Temple will be the foundation stones of the Church. Each time a prophet recites one of his verses, a wall collapses, a tower crumbles; at each new page the Temple seems to be falling into ruin, and when the final word is pronounced the ruins themselves are destroyed. The Apostles, however, seem to be advancing toward the prophets and strip away the veils they wear on their heads. . . . And so that no doubt may remain, a streamer placed near the prophet bears a biblical verse which is explained by a phrase of the Creed attributed to the Apostle.[89]

This motif which also appears in the *Heures* of Jeanne de Navarre and in the *Grandes et petites heures* of the Duke of Berry, undoubtedly also goes back to the last years of the thirteenth century. It is itself accompanied by another motif. No doubt certain theologians were determined not to see St. Paul entirely excluded from the composition of the Creed. So the Apostle to the Gentiles was brought back onto the scene in a very ingenious manner—which moreover did not entail belief in another legendary tale. Let us continue examining these same pages, guided by Émile Mâle:

At the top of the page an Apostle speaks to a group of men. These latter are sometimes called Colossians and at other times Corinthians or Romans. The Apostle is therefore St. Paul, who is also teaching his Creed. Paul was not in the Cenacle on the day when the Creed was composed; nevertheless, he preached the same truths to the Gentiles. . . . A phrase drawn from his Epistles and juxtaposed to the prophetic verse and to the article of the Creed demonstrates the unity of doctrine. Moreover, the artist has made this unity of the faith visible under the

[89] Mâle, 262.

figure of the Church. We see her on every page, standing on the top of a tower. . . . She holds up a standard bearing a painted image. This image changes twelve times. Each one refers to one of the phrases of the Creed. . . . Thus the twelve escutcheons on the Church's flag sum up the teaching of the prophets, that of the Apostles and that of St. Paul.[90]

Nor is this all. Before long, through a new set of symmetrics, the choir of the Apostles and prophets will be joined by the voice of the Sybils. It was toward the end of the fifteenth century that these pagan prophetesses appeared, twelve in number, and began to invade all of Europe. The first to have placed them in relation to the twelve Apostles seems to have been the Italian Filippo Barbieri, in 1481.[91] An anonymous book dated 1505 and dedicated to Anne of France had as its title: *La Conformité, concordance et assonance des Prophètes et Sybilles aux douze articles de la foi*.[92] It was no doubt about this same time that the stalls in the cathedral of Geneva were carved; today all that remains of them are a few preserved in the right nave: of eleven panels there are five representing prophets, five others representing Apostles and one showing the Sybil of Erythrea. Each of these eleven personages carries a streamer.[93]

In 1562 Cardinal Clement Moriliani published a theology manual in which he suggested an original variation on this same theme. He established a correspondence,

[90] Ibid., 262–63.
[91] *Discordantiae nonnullae inter sanctos Hieronymum et Augustinum*.
[92] Cf. Mâle, 291–92.
[93] In the surviving order they are: the Sybil, James the Less, Amos, Thomas, Hosea, John, Zachariah, James the Greater, Isaiah, Andrew, David.

no longer through analogy, but through contrast: after quoting "Cyprian" (i.e., Rufinus of Aquilea),[94] he shows the opposition between "the tower of pride" which the sons of Noah wished to build before separating to take possession of the earth, and the "tower of the faith" which the twelve Apostles of Christ erected before separating to go and conquer the world for the gospel. Then in the twelve articles composed by the twelve Apostles he recognizes, as Alcuin and Bonaventure had done, the twelve commemorative stones which Joshua had the representatives of the twelve tribes carry according to the Lord's command.[95]

The religious dramas so common at the end of the Middle Ages and in the sixteenth century also contain more than one scene that give witness to the popularity of the legend. They also offer us several rather curious variants. Thus, in the *Assumption of Mary*, it is St. Paul who utters the second article, whereas St. Thomas does not figure in the list at all—no doubt because it was said that he had not been present at the Assumption and had doubted it. In the *Play for Corpus Christi* and in the collection of epic pieces entitled *The Old Passional*, each article is preceded by a prophecy. In the *Play of Eger* (1560), it is while Jesus is washing their feet that the Apostles declare the articles of the Creed. Peter, the first, says to Jesus: "Lord, I believe that you created all things", and so on. After the eleventh article, Jesus comes to Judas and speaks to him, but Judas does not answer; and the

---

[94] Rufinus' book was often attributed to Cyprian, sometimes to Jerome or to Pope St. Leo the Great.

[95] *Theologicarum institutionum compendium*, Clementis Mariliani Card. Arae Caeli (Fulginci, 1562), chap. 1, "De symbolo apostolorum".

twelfth article is not uttered. To avoid a profanation, the Creed remains incomplete.[96]

But while the legend was being thus enriched with new features and while, in order to place them in a specific locale, the composition of the Creed by the Apostles was localized in Jerusalem, in the substructure of the ancient peristyle of Eleona, the theory of the apostolic origin of the Creed was being more and more contested. A first shock was produced in 1438 when, during the Council of Florence (it was still at Ferrara), Mark of Ephesus declared in the name of the Greeks opposed to the union of the Churches: "We neither profess nor even know this Apostles' Creed; if it had existed, the book of Acts would have mentioned it."[97] Not long afterward, in 1443, Lorenzo Valla, being overly severe in his criticism, claimed that the Creed was a late abridgment of the Creed of Nicaea-Constantinople; but his skepticism and his irony had not won the approval even of the learned. Nor did the more serious criticism of Reginald Pecock, the English Bishop of Chichester (d. 1450).[98] Erasmus showed himself both informed and

---

[96] Examples drawn from Georges Duriez, *La Théologie dans le drame religieux en Allemagne au moyen âge* (1914), 536–660.

[97] Harduinus, *Conciliorum collectio* 9:842–43. The Orthodox respect our Creed as an ancient formula of faith and accept its teaching, but "it is never used in any liturgical service in any of the Oriental patriarchates". Timothy Ware, *L'Orthodoxie*, French trans. Charité de Saint-Servais (Paris: Desclée de Brouwer, 1968), 276.

[98] "For a whole century everybody, even the Carthusians who were as a rule more critical, remained faithful to the story of the Franciscan Antonio of Bitonto, whom Valla was trying to make ridiculous": J. de Ghellinck, 160. See idem, *Patristique et moyen âge* 1 (1949): 18–21.

prudent. We read in a note of his *Novum Testamentum*, on Matthew 11:20: "the Creed transmitted to us by the Apostles or by apostolic men". And in a preface to his *Paraphrases* he again says: "Whether the Creed called the Apostles' Creed was given to us by the Apostles themselves, I do not know; at least it bears the mark of the majesty and purity proper to the Apostles."[99] That was in 1517. The Sorbonne was upset by this, and the proposition was the subject of the eleventh censure it proposed against Erasmus.[100] The latter replied in his *Declaration* on censures and later let it be known that he had not in the least changed his opinion by entitling his own commentary on the Creed: *Delucida et pia explanatio symboli quod dicitur apostolorum*.[101] On the other hand, he drew a parallel between the attribution of each article to a given Apostle and the obviously late and arbitrary attribution of each of the four biblical meanings to a given Father.[102]

The Spanish Franciscan Luis de Carvajal nevertheless maintained that the Creed had been indeed drawn up by the Apostles themselves, "and not by the Council of Nicaea, as Erasmus, following Valla, has supposed in our day". These words are found in chapter 22 of his book *De restituta theologia* (1545), which was in fact a manifesto in favor of renewal in sacred studies.[103] The Roman Catechism would later teach that "the holy

---

[99] *Opera omnia* (Leyden, 1704), 5:92, 1136, 1178. "*Utrum Symbolum, quod apostolorum dicitur, ab ipsis apostolis proditum sit, nescio; certe majestatem ac puritatem apostolicam prae se fert.*"

[100] Du Plessis d'Argentré, *Collectio judiciorum* (1728), 2 a:60.

[101] *Opera omnia* 9:457–58, 868–70, 554–57, 1080, 1169–70.

[102] 5:1034 D.

[103] *Theologicae sententiae*, 2nd ed. (Antwerp, 1548), fol. 78. It is true that for twenty years Carvajal had been quarrelling with Erasmus.

Apostles, our masters and guides in the faith . . . thought it proper to compose a formula of Christian faith. . . . This profession of faith and hope . . . we call the Creed."[104] Baronius and Bellarmine on the Catholic side and the Centuriators of Magdeburg on the Protestant side were equally in accord in maintaining the thesis of the apostolic origin. Baronius even tried to draw an argument from the very word *symbolum*; does this word not mean the result of an important matter discussed by arbiters who have the right to judge it? And who would thus have had this right but the twelve Apostles? Suárez, going even further, claimed that the apostolic origin of the Creed was *de fide*; the Twelve, he declared, composed the Creed "before the death of James". However, eclectic as usual, he leaves each one free to choose between the idea of a collegial composition or that whereby each article was made up by a specific Apostle.[105]

Little by little, however, the truth was coming to light. Thus the celebrated Portuguese Dominican John of St. Thomas (d. 1644), although strongly attached to the old tradition and considering Erasmus to be "extremely rash", no longer dared to claim like Suárez that the theory of the strictly apostolic origin of the Creed was really *de fide*. He defended it only as being *verissima*.[106] The Protestant scholars felt freer. They had been put at ease by the position adopted by Calvin,

---

[104] First part, chap. 1.

[105] *De fide*, disputatio secunda, sectio 5: *Opera omnia* (Paris: Éd. Vivès, 1858), 12:27–28.

[106] *Cursus theologicus* (Paris: Éd. Vivès, 1886), 7:134. He implicitly refutes Baronius' argument by observing that "*ut optime notavit Cajetanus, nomen symbolum non a colligentibus sed ab ipsis rebus collectis impositum est*". For John De Lugo (1583–1660), the classical position will merely be the "*concors Patrum sententia*" embraced by the majority

which was very much the same as that of Erasmus. In his *Institution chrétienne*, Calvin had made this declaration about the Creed: "I call it 'apostolic', without concerning myself much about who its author was." It is true that he had added: "Be that as it may, I in no way doubt that, wherever it comes from, it existed from the very beginning of the Church, and even from the time of the Apostles, and was recognized as a public and certain confession of the faith."[107] But this last precision did not appear in his little *Catechisme* or *Formulaire d'instruire les enfants en la Chrestienté*; he simply speaks of "the confession of faith which all Christians make, and which is commonly called the Apostles' Creed, because it is a summary of the true belief which has always been held in Christendom and also because it is drawn from the pure apostolic doctrine".[108]

After the solid critical discussion begun in 1647 by the Anglican Bishop James Usher, one can say that there was nothing more to be added on any side.[109] Another Anglican, Bramhall, shortly afterward, simply said, in a formula that reproduces St. Augustine's position: "Scripture and the Creed are not two different rules of faith but one and the same rule—expanded in Scripture, drawn

---

of theologians, "*sive omnes apostoli communi sensu omnes symboli partes, sive singuli unam partem apponentes ex aliorum approbatione, ut alii volunt*": *Disputationes scholasticae et morales* (Paris: Éd. Vivès, 1891), 1:253.

[107] Cf. 4, *De la foy*, Belles Lettres (Paris: Éd. Jacques Pannier, 1937), 2:45.

[108] *Catechisme*, i.e., *Formulaire d'instruire les enfans en la Chrestienté, faict en manière de dialogue, ou le Ministre interrogue, et l'enfant respond*, by John Calvin (1553); ed. de Genève, 1853 ("Catéchisme de l'Église de Genève").

[109] *De Romanae ecclesiae symbolo apostolico vetere aliisque formulis Diatriba* (London, 1647).

together in the Creed."[110] And Tillemont noted that the silence of the Council of Nicaea on the subject of our Creed would be impossible to explain if the Church at that time had believed in its apostolic origin.[111]

The criticism of the legend, observed Fr. Pierre Benoit, O.P., "was a healthy and necessary reaction; but it went too far."[112] It failed to recognize, "beyond the amplifications" or the arbitrary simplifications, "the profound truth" which had found this means of expression.[113] When, for instance, a Lessing in the eighteenth century spoke of "the so-called Apostles' Creed", he was looking only at the negative side of the question. Such a manner of speaking might be understood if it had been a question of a recent discovery, or one which at that date had not yet been widely publicized. In any event, we should be mistaken if today we insisted too much on the legendary (i.e., illusory) character of the stories and representations we have been discussing. Rather, we should recognize in all this a type of historical stylization, like many others found in both profane and religious material, and not only in antiquity or in the Middle Ages but even in modern times and in the classical period: for instance, the fiction of the Platonic Academy which was supposed to have been founded at Florence by Cosimo de Medici.[114] Even though it became overly ingenious in the end, the stylized form which gave shape

---

[110] Quoted by G. Tavard in *La Poursuite de la catholicité* (1065), 74.

[111] Regarding the critical research which came later, especially that of Caspari, Hahn, Kattenbusch, Burn, etc., see J. de Ghellinck, with the bibliography.

[112] "Les Origines du symbole des apôtres dans le Nouveau Testament", in *Lumière et vie* 2 (1952): 39.

[113] Th. Camelot, O.P., *Lumière et vie* 2 (1952): 78.

[114] "The classical period, which liked to sum up every epoch in

to the conviction held by St. Ambrose and those who followed him was, and remains, the vehicle of a very important lesson, which is at all times a lesson of unity: the convergence of the Jewish world with the pagan world itself in the expectation and the foreshadowing of the one Savior; the identity of the divine revelation under its two forms throughout the two dispensations or the two successive Covenants; the unanimity of the apostolic witness; and finally, and more radically, the permanence of the Christian faith from its beginning. At all times and in all places that faith is the same; it was handed down unchanged from the first generation; and when we today recite our Creed, it is quite truly on the testimony of the first Apostles of Jesus that we rely; it is this testimony that has come down to us in an uninterrupted succession which today still evokes the response of our faith.[115]

The Protestant theologian Vossius, in 1662, closed a dissertation on the origin of our Creed with these words, which echo those of Erasmus and Calvin: "*Apostolicum*

---

one central figure and a representative group, proposed Lorenzo as the precursor of 'enlightened despots' and the gathering of Careggi as the model of modern 'Academies' ": André Chastel, *Marsile Ficin et l'art* (1954), 7–9 and 16. An historian of Italian humanism as competent as Mr. Eugène Garin has no hesitation in speaking of the flourishing "Academy" that existed in the entourage of Lorenzo the Magnificent, and of other similar academies. See *L'Education de l'homme moderne*, trans. J. Humbert (Paris: Fayard, 1968), 111–12.

[115] M. Villain, "Rufin d'Aquilée commentateur du symbole des apôtres", in *Science religieuse* (1944), 132–33: "The legend preserves and includes a capital truth, namely, that under a stereotyped form the Creed condenses the authentic and immutable belief of the Church just as it was received from Christ and handed down by the Apostles themselves."

dici potest quia compendium est apostolicae doctrinae."[116] A wise conclusion. Rev. Fr. Edmond Schillebeeckx, O.P., says the same thing today:

> By its contents and its form, the *Apostolicum* is indeed apostolic because it reproduces the tradition of the Apostles' faith. . . . It is truly the faithful reflection of the main themes in the preaching of the Apostles, in the catechesis taught by the Apostles to the first converts, in the profession of faith made by the early Christians.[117]

Harnack had already observed that all the elements it contains are to be found, word for word, in the canonical and ecclesiastical texts of the first two centuries. F. J. Badcock, historian of the ancient creeds, remarked more recently that the great resemblance that exists between the formulas expressing the faith of the various churches during the fourth century bears witness to the great antiquity of their content.[118] As St. Cyril of Jerusalem had said, long before, speaking of the baptismal creed in use in his church, which was substantially the same as the creed used in the church at Rome, one can find in it an authentic resumé of the faith transmitted by the Apostles: ἁγία καὶ ἀποστολικὴ πίστις.[119]

---

[116] *Dissertationes tres de tribus symbolis, apostolico, athanasio et constantinopolitano*, 2nd ed. (Amsterdam, 1662), 17.

[117] *Approches théologiques* 1, *Révélation et théologie* (trans. P. Bourgy, 1965): 174 and 179.

[118] *The History of the Creeds*, 2nd ed. (London, 1938), 165.

[119] *Catéchèse* 18, chap. 32 (PG, 33:1054).

CHAPTER TWO

A Trinitarian Creed

The trouble with the legendary accounts whose history we have been examining is not so much that they are legendary but that they served to ensure a division of the Creed's text into twelve articles, a division which is too often considered to be its original and basic division. "*Ecce secundum duodecim apostolos, et duodecim sententiae comprehensae sunt.*"[1] At times this was all that was remembered about the analyses made by the ancient writers. The facts, however, are different. Such a division "does not correspond with the primitive arrangement of the formula; it is a later and artificial arrangement, which obscures rather than sheds light on the relationships between the articles."[2] The pedagogical advantages (of the twelve-article division) only helped to reinforce it. But by granting this too much importance, one might be led to think that one had before him a list of twelve disconnected and juxtaposed truths to be believed. There would be no genuine unity between these twelve "articles" beyond the divine authority which serves as their guarantee and incites us to accept all of them equally. In short, our Creed would be nothing but a sort of catalogue. It would offer us a mere "collection". That word is

[1] Ambrose and Nicetas of Remesiana (cf. above, Chapter One, n. 55).
[2] Josef A. Jungmann, *La Liturgie des premiers siècles*, Lex Orandi 33 (Paris: Éd. du Cerf, 1962): 149.

found, with a slightly different connotation, in Cassian[3] and in those who quoted him later on, but it can also be found with the same meaning in the titles of certain medieval collections of "sentences" which are in fact hardly more than collections and not always very well arranged: *"compendiosa collectio"*, *"singulorum brevis comprehensio"*, as Robert of Melun says in presenting his own collection to his readers.[4] Or again, as has been said, the Creed would be a simple *credendorum series*, a list of truths to be believed. This expression is already found in St. Ambrose's text where the first state of the legend appears: *"fidei totius series"*. But the change from *fidei* to *credendorum* is not without significance.

Still, we must observe, this is not what the word "article" should suggest. Nor was this the meaning that St. Thomas gave to the twelve articles as a whole. Basing himself on the etymology of the word, which brought to mind the "contingent coaptation" of the members of a single body, he saw the truths enumerated in the Creed as linked to one another so as to make up an organic whole endowed with an internal unity.[5] But not long after, William of Mende still spoke of the "Catalogue of the Apostles".[6] The notion of interconnectedness, in line with St. Thomas' thought, was brought out again by the Roman Catechism which, following the ancient writers,

---

[3] *De incarnatione*, chap. 3 (ed. M. Petschenig, CSEL, 17 [1888]: 328).

[4] *Sententiae*, praefatio (ed. R. M. Martin, Louvain [1947], 3).

[5] *Summa theologica*, Secunda secundae, q. 1, art. 6: "*Nomen articuli . . . significat quandam coaptationem aliquarum partium distinctarum; et ideo particulae corporis sibi invicem coaptatae dicuntur membrorum articuli*".

[6] *Rationale divinorum officiorum*, bk. 4, chap. 25, no. 6.

A TRINITARIAN CREED

at first insisted on the essential division;[7] but if for instance one opens the *Catechismus major*, or *Summa doctrinae christianae* of St. Peter Canisius (1555–1565), the prototype of so many later expositions of the faith, one can see that the division into articles, which inspires the plan of the work, leaves scarcely more than an extrinsic unity.[8]

Now, if one adopts such a point of view he misses the essential characteristic of our Creed. Far from being only a list or collection or series or catalogue, it is a strongly organized whole. It has a structure. Nor is this a simple question of literary form. The very notion of the Christian faith, in its unique originality, is linked, as we shall see, to the structure of the Creed in which this faith took shape, and the consequences which follow from this for Christian thought and life are of the first importance. It is, therefore, essential for us to recognize and analyze this structure.

However, still another division has sometimes been proposed—an apparently more simple one, into two parts: the first concerning the Divinity and what refers to eternity; the other concerning Christ's humanity and his work in time. Each of these two parts could, moreover, be subdivided into seven articles, which would bring the

---

[7] First part, introduction, no. 2: "*Eas autem sententias, similitudine quadam a Patribus nostris frequenter usurpatas, articulos appellamus. Ut enim corporis membra articulis distinguuntur. . . .*"

[8] Chap. 1, *De fide et symbolo fidei*, no. 4: *Quid fidei nomine intelligitur?* "*Fides est Dei donum quo illustratus homo firmiter adhaeret et assentitur iis quae ad credendum divinitus revelantur; cujusmodi sunt: Deum esse trinum et unum, ex nihilo creari mundum. . . .*" No. 5: *Quae est simplex fidei regula et veluti summa?* "*Symbolum apostolorum in duodecim distinctum articulos.*" St. Peter Canisius, *Catechismi latini et germanici*, pt. 1.; *Catechismi latini*, 6.

total number of articles to fourteen. This is how the great Scholastics proceeded, those lovers of well-ordered classifications: Alexander of Halès,[9] St. Bonaventure[10] and St. Thomas Aquinas. They rearranged into fourteen divisions what they had at first more simply, and following the common practice, divided into twelve. St. Thomas in particular does this on two occasions: in the *Compendium theologiae* and in the *Summa theologica*. He bases his procedure on the words of St. John, "This is eternal life: that they may know thee, the one true God, and Jesus Christ whom thou hast sent" (Jn 17:3), and on this other passage: "You know where I am going, and you know the way there" (Jn 14:4). From this he concludes, following a concept dear to St. Augustine, that "the entire knowledge of the faith refers to these two objects": the divine Trinity, which is the term, and the humanity of Christ, which is the way to attain it. Concerning the Divinity, one article teaches us its unity; three others declare the Trinity of Persons, and three more tell us of its works: nature, grace and glory. This adds up to seven. The other seven articles set forth the mysteries of Christ's humanity, from the Incarnation to the Last Judgment, including the nativity, death, descent into hell, Resurrection and Ascension.[11] Such a division into two sets of seven articles does not allow us to keep the figure of the twelve stones drawn from the Jordan, but one can refer to the seven candelabras and the seven stars of Revelation, the former signifying the mysteries of the Savior's humanity and the stars, those of his

---

[9] Loc. cit., q. 2, art. 1 (1124).

[10] *In 3 Sent.*, dist. 25, art. 1 (ed. Quaracchi, 3:586); *Breviloquium*, pt. 5, chap. 7 (5:261–62).

[11] *Compendium theologiae*, chap. 1 and 190 (Éd. Vivès, 27:2 and 75). Secunda secundae, q. 1, art. 8 (3:81–82).

divinity. St. Bonaventure, who loved symbols, did not fail to do this.[12]

This, too, is a tenable division. It has the merit of organizing the entire contents of the Creed in a logical manner, and on the other hand it shows a certain detachment with respect to the legend. But especially in the work of St. Thomas, who was inspired by it more particularly in his own expositions, it has the disadvantage of introducing man's sanctification and eternal life before bringing in Jesus Christ. Further, it remains theoretical and abstract; and its altogether artificial character is shown by the fact that it upsets the natural, original and traditionally accepted order of the articles.[13] As Erasmus observed, it does not have the same pedagogical and, so to speak, mnemotechnic usefulness as the usual division into twelve articles.[14] In the seventeenth century they were still arguing over this, and John of St. Thomas, who, of course, considered the division adopted by St. Thomas "excellent", nevertheless observed on this point that the various ways of enumerating and distributing the articles that can be observed in the course of history are not to be taken "with metaphysical rigor".[15]

---

[12] *In 3 Sent.*: "*Per septem namque stellas luminosas, quae sunt de natura caelesti, intelliguntur septem articuli respicientes divinitatem; per septem autem candelabra aurea, quae sunt de terrena materia, verumtamen optima et depurata, intelliguntur septem articuli respicientes humanitatem; et ideo dicit, quod in medio illorum videt similem Filio hominis*" (3:536; *Apoc.* 1:12, 13, 16).

[13] Jungmann, 149. A similar contradiction can be found in some medieval liturgical works, mainly in England.

[14] *Explicatio in symbolum apostolorum et decalogum* (Lugduni Batavorum, 1541), 29.

[15] *Cursus theologicus*, tract. 7 ([Paris: Éd. Vivès, 1886], 129–30); *De fide*, disputatio 6, art. 4.

With certain differences, the division adopted by Melanchthon in his *Enarratio symboli Niceni* resembles that of St. Thomas, and we would reproach it for the same reason. Melanchthon divides his explanation into two parts: in the first he treats of God, the Trinity, creation, sin, the divine law (Decalogue); in the second part he puts everything which deals with the Mediator and the redemption, as well as with the Church and eternal life.[16] As we see, Melanchthon does not bring in the truths concerning salvation before having spoken of Jesus Christ, but on the other hand he separates the Holy Spirit from the entire work of sanctification. And his reconstruction of a scheme which professes to be logical is not faithful to the movement of the Creed or to the very economy of revelation.

Although much more ancient, as we have seen, and more natural, the simple division into twelve articles does not have any fundamental principle behind it either. In fact, if one overlooks a few additions or some variants that only affect details—which we shall consider later— the Creed we still recite today is the ancient profession of faith that the Church of Rome had drawn up for candidates for baptism. Now, the structure of this ancient Creed leaves no room for hesitation. It is undoubtedly ternary—because its substance is trinitarian.

---

[16] *Corpus Reformatorum* (Bruncvigae, 1855), vol. 23, col. 196, ss. col. 335: "*Secunda pars Symboli.—Hactenus dictum est fideliter de parte Symboli prima, de tribus personis, de creatione hominis, et aliarum rerum, de lapsu primorum parentum, de peccato et de lege.—Nunc accedimus ad doctrinam de Filio Mediatore et de redemptione humani generis, de restitutione justitiae et vitae aeternae, de collectione Ecclesiae aeternae, et caeteris articulis qui in Symbolo sequentur.*"

A TRINITARIAN CREED 61

"*In totis sane tribus personis una confessio*", as St. Paschasius Radbert was to say in the ninth century.[17]

It is in an *Ordo romanus* (a little book detailing the liturgical ceremonies) from the year 950 that we find the first statement of our present formula, complete and word for word. But, as far as the essential points are concerned, we can go back a lot farther. With insignificant variants it is contained in a sermon by St. Caesarius of Arles, who died in 543.[18] With some slightly more important variants, it figures in several of St. Augustine's sermons,[19] in the treatise by Rufinus of Aquilea and earlier still in the letter that Marcellus of Ancyra addressed (in Greek) to Pope Julius in the year 340, to make known to him his communion of faith with the Church of Rome.[20] Finally, with slightly different words here or there, we can read it in Hippolytus' *Tradition of the Apostles*, which takes us back to the beginning of the third century.[21] In its basic content and in its very structure, the Roman profession of faith was fixed from that period on. It constituted what we can call, with Jungmann,[22] "the most ancient catechism of Christianity".

Thanks to the apostolic prestige enjoyed by the See

---

[17] *De fide, spe et caritate*, bk. 1, chap. 6, no. 1 (PL, 120:1402).
[18] *Opera omnia*, ed. Germain Morin (Maredsous), 1:51; or PL, 39:2195.
[19] *Sermons* 212–15 (PL, 38:1058–76).
[20] In St. Epiphanius, *Adversus haereses*, bk. 3, vol. 1, Haer. 72, no. 3 (PG, 42:385–88). Cf. F. J. Badcock, 58–63.
[21] No. 21 (ed. B. Botte, SC, 11 *bis* [1968]: 84–86), under the form of the triple baptismal interrogation. Concerning the nature of this document, see the introduction, 16–17.
[22] *L'Annonce de la foi*, trans. R. Virrion (Mulhouse: Éd. Salvator, 1965), 20.

of Rome, and to the more direct authority which it exercised in the West, the Roman Creed rather quickly became the one used by all the Latin Churches.[23] At least, it provided them with a solid common foundation. In Africa, Gaul, Spain and Britain, the creeds used at baptism all issued from this *Vetus symbolum romanum*, as it was in use in the third and fourth centuries. But where did the latter itself come from?

Its origins are complex. Mr. Oscar Cullmann discerns in it traces of the teaching given to the catechumens, of the baptismal ceremonies, of the ordinary liturgy of the community, of the preaching, the exorcisms and even of the controversy with heretics.[24] To this one might add, with Fr. Pierre Benoit, the controversies with the Jews and the pagans, and also the testimonies of faith given in the course of the early persecutions. Each element in the Creed pre-exists, scattered through the writings of the New Testament, in more or less stereotyped expressions "which, without having the invariability of the formulas elaborated later on, presage these and prepare the way for them".[25] Whatever may be the truth about all these various contributions, what interests us directly here is

---

[23] Augustine insinuates "that the baptismal creed is the same in all the Churches of the *Catholica*." *Epist.*, 214, *De gestis Pelagii*, 4. See P. Battifol in "Apôtres, Symbole des", *Dictionnaire de théologie catholique*, vol. 1, col. 1028.

[24] *La Foi et le culte de l'Église primitive* (1963), 56.

[25] "Les Origines du symbole des apôtres dans le Nouveau Testament", in *Lumière et vie*, 40–55. Cf. H. Schlier, *Essais sur le Nouveau Testament*, trans. A. Liefooghe (Paris: Éd. du Cerf, 1968), 26, note: "The historical process was undoubtedly as follows: the consigning of the apostolic heritage in Scripture and in the creeds was brought about through actions that were independent but which nevertheless had an effect on one another."

A TRINITARIAN CREED

that we can easily recognize in our present Creed the development of a very old baptismal profession of faith, which someone has ventured to call "the most ancient Roman catechism"[26] and which was essentially a profession of faith in the divine Trinity—without including, naturally, the conceptual precisions that we can include today under the divine names and which were attained only little by little.[27] This baptismal creed itself made more explicit the formula transmitted to us by St. Matthew's Gospel: "Make disciples of all nations, baptizing them in the name of the Father and of the Son and of the Holy Spirit" (Mt 28:19).[28] We even find a rather close equivalent of this formula in an earlier text, the First Epistle of St. Paul to the Corinthians (1 Cor 6:11): "But you have been washed, you have been sanctified, you have been justified through the name of our Lord Jesus Christ and through the Spirit of our God."[29]

We also find, from the very beginning, the existence of another baptismal formula, no doubt even older, simpler and more purely christological. The Acts of the Apostles know only baptism "in the name of Jesus Christ" or "in the name of the Lord Jesus".[30] Peter's first Epistle contains a christological exposition, mentioning the death, the Resurrection and the Ascension, which

---

[26] Jungmann, 125.

[27] See the next chapter.

[28] Cf. the *Doctrine des apôtres*, chap. 7. Jules Lebreton, *Histoire du dogme de la Trinité*, 4th ed. (Paris: Beauchesne, 1928), 141–44.

[29] On such triple formulas in the New Testament, see Badcock, 17–19.

[30] Acts 2:38; 8:16; 10:48; 22:16. Cf. Rom 10:9. On the difference between Matthew and Acts, see St. Hilary, *De synodis* (PL, 10:537–38). On the baptismal formulas found in Acts and in Paul, see Adalbert Hamman, *Baptême et confirmation* (Paris: Desclée, 1969), 24–33.

seems to be a sort of instruction preparatory to baptism.[31] The letter of St. Ignatius of Antioch to the Trallians contains another one, separated from the baptismal context, and aimed at the Docetists: "Be deaf when someone speaks to you of anything else but Jesus Christ."[32] This was the christological formula represented by the symbol of the fish: ἰχθύς "Jesus Christ, Son of God, Savior".[33] There is every reason to think that the trinitarian text in St. Matthew does not give us the very earliest formula of Christian baptism, or consequently of the profession of Christian faith. But nothing would authorize us to suppose that the transition from a christological to a trinitarian formula constituted a mutation which would indicate a first weakening of or deviation from the early faith in the mystery of Christ. To hold as authentic and pure only the very earliest expression of the faith, with no other standard than this primitiveness itself, would be the mark of a very shortsighted positivism.[34] Appropriate here is a remark by Dom Christopher Butler concerning the very figure and being of Jesus: "It is quite possible that the evangelists and their predecessors may have understood less well what they were transmitting than did those who came after them."[35]

[31] 1 Pet 3:18–22. The passage, moreover, does not lack allusions to God the Father, and even, in a more implicit way, to the Spirit.

[32] Chap. 7, no. 1 (Camelot, SC, 10 *bis* [1950]: 118).

[33] The *Didache*, which gives the baptismal formula found in Matthew, also speaks of baptism "in the name of the Lord": 7:1–3; 9:5.

[34] In *L'Évangile selon saint Matthieu* (Neuchâtel: Delachaux et Niestlé, 1963), 19, Pierre Bonnard remarks that "we have gone beyond the stage where we instinctively give priority to the 'simplest' texts". We would add that even chronological priority should not always be automatically considered privileged.

[35] B. C. Butler, *L'Idée de l'Église*, French trans. (1965), 205: "A

A TRINITARIAN CREED

Time and reflection are required, and a certain incubation in the mind, in order that a spiritual deposit may be assimilated after the initial impact of receiving it. This is necessary in order to discern the elements included in it and to let them organize themselves with a little clarity.[36] Only a reflection that had matured slowly could enable the immediate disciples of Jesus to grasp all the implications of the mystery of his identity, which they had from the first sensed in his masterful presence. Besides, in the transition (which must have taken place very soon) from the christological to the trinitarian profession of faith, it was less a matter of a deepened understanding, properly so called, than a more explicit statement of belief, since, "in the primitive catechesis and the apostolic professions of faith, the mystery of Christ is basically viewed from the standpoint of the mystery of God, which includes all", and since, in addition, "the experience of the working of the Spirit was closely linked in the primitive Church" to faith in the mystery of Christ.[37] In any event, it is clear that the two

---

priori, it is not very likely that the collective consciousness created the Jesus of the New Testament and the Christian religion. It is much more probable that in transmitting the facts it did not succeed in doing justice to his greatness, to the brilliance of his thought. The true historical Jesus was perhaps more 'Johannine' than he appears in the synoptic tradition."

[36] Cf. Maurice Blondel, *Histoire et dogme* (1904), in *Premiers écrits* (Paris: P.U.F., 1956). One can find similar reflections in Louis Massignon, *L'Expérience mystique et les modes de stylisation littéraire* (1927), in *Opera minora* (Beirut, 1963), 2:376. See also J. H. Newman, "Christ Manifested in Remembrance", *Parochial and Plain Sermons*, vol. 4, s. 17.

[37] E. Schillebeeckx, O.P., "Symbolum" (1958), in *Révélation et théologie* (1965), 183.

sorts of formulas are already witnessed to in the New Testament, although the simple christological formula is found more frequently.

If, moreover, one does not restrict his inquiry to the immediate context of baptism, one will find that from the beginning, too, the Father and the Spirit are, even explicitly, linked to the work of the Son. "Texts abound in the New Testament which associate either the Father and the Son or the three Persons of the Trinity; and these are often expressed in formulas which, without being 'confessions of faith', nevertheless foreshadow by their stereotyped form a tradition which is really primitive and common to all."[38] See for instance the passage in the First Epistle to the Corinthians on the diversity of charisms and the unity of the One who distributes them: "the same Spirit, the same Lord . . . , the same God";[39] or the closing salutation of the Second Epistle to the Corinthians: "the grace of the Lord Jesus Christ, the love of God and the fellowship of the Holy Spirit";[40] or, again, the opening greeting in the first Epistle of St. Peter: "according to the foreknowledge of God the Father, in the sanctification of the Spirit, unto obedience to Jesus Christ".[41] So, whether they were baptismal or not, christological or trinitarian, the formulas in which the Christian faith was summed up in the various Churches did for some time follow parallel paths,[42] finally coming together in the Roman baptismal creed, at

---

[38] Benoit, 56.
[39] 1 Cor 12:4–6.
[40] 2 Cor 13:13.
[41] 1 Pet 1:2. See also Eph 2:18.
[42] Cf. Jungmann, *L'Annonce de la foi*, 21: "The resumé of the entire catechesis probably included, from the beginning, the trinitarian

least as early as the middle of the second century. This is the period in which St. Justin, in his first *Apology*, uses sometimes one, sometimes the other formula separately, and sometimes inserts the christological formula into a trinitarian one.[43] It was about this time that there came into being the liturgical formula which scholars are in the habit of calling the *forma antiquissima*, the immediate ancestor of the Roman Creed with which we are familiar.

There exist also, especially in the writings of St. Ignatius of Antioch, St. Irenaeus and Tertullian, a number of passages which are, so to speak, intermediary and include but two terms. They reproduce more or less freely certain official formulas in which the Holy Spirit is not mentioned. Thus, in the *Adversus haereses*: "*Unum Deum factorem caeli et terrae, a lege et prophetis annuntiatum, et unum Christum Filium Dei tradiderunt nobis (evangelistae).*"[44] Again, we find in the *De virginibus velandis*: "The absolutely unique rule of faith, the only immutable and unchangeable one, is to believe in one God almighty, the Creator of the world, and in his Son, Jesus Christ. . . ."[45] But it would be a mistake to see in such texts a chronologically intermediary form between the christological and the trinitarian formulas, as though they gave evidence of a state of doctrine in which faith in the Trinity had not

---

outline along with the christological message." See also A. Stenzel, *Die Taufe* (Innsbruck, 1958), 81.

[43] I *Apol.*, chaps. 13, 21, 31 and 61 (trans. L. Pautigny [Paris: Picard, 1904], 21–24, 42, 60, 128).

[44] Bk. 3, chap. 1, no. 2 (PG, 7:845 B). "The evangelists passed on to us [faith in] one sole God, the Creator of heaven and earth, announced by the law and the prophets, and [in] one sole Christ, the Son of God."

[45] Chap. 1 (PL, 2:889 A–B). Cf. *De praescriptione haereticorum*, chap. 36, no. 4 (F. Refoulé, SC, 46:138).

68   THE CHRISTIAN FAITH

yet been fully established.⁴⁶ Other texts, dated with certainty, are strictly opposed to such a theory. Besides, both Irenaeus and Tertullian also offer us trinitarian formulas,⁴⁷ as both St. Clement of Rome and St. Justin had done before. "As God lives", says the Epistle of Clement, "and as the Lord Jesus Christ lives, and the Holy Spirit, the faith and hope of the elect. . . ."⁴⁸ Speaking of baptism, Justin says: "In the name of God, the Father and Master of all things, and of Jesus Christ our Savior and of the Holy Spirit, they are then washed in the water."⁴⁹ In reality, if these texts that mention only two Persons do constitute, in one sense, professions of faith, and if they explicitly claim to be "rules of truth",⁵⁰ or "rules of the faith",⁵¹ or rather if they witness the existence of such rules without always claiming to reproduce them word for word, they are still not baptismal formulas; they are not liturgical texts; nor do they claim to be complete summaries of the teaching

⁴⁶ Cf. Cullmann, *La Foi et le culte de l'Église primitive*, 68.

⁴⁷ Irenaeus, *Demonstratio*, chap. 6, etc. Tertullian, *De praescriptione*, chap. 13, 2–5 (SC, 46:106); *Adversus Praxean*, chap. 2 (CCL, 2:1160). See below.

⁴⁸ *Epist.* chap. 58, no. 2; verse 96 (trans. H. Hemmer [1926], 119).

⁴⁹ I *Apol.*, chap. 61, no. 3 (trans. L. Pautigny [1904], 129); ibid., no. 10.

⁵⁰ Irenaeus, *Adversus haereses*, bk. 1, chap. 22, no. 1: "*Regulam veritatis, id est, quia sit unus Deus omnipotens, qui omnia condidit per Verbum suum*" (PG, 7:669 A). In his *Demonstratio*, chaps. 3 and 6 (ed. Froidevaux, 31 and 32), the rule of faith concerns the Trinity.

⁵¹ Tertullian, *De praescriptione*, chap. 36; *De virginibus velandis*, chap. 1 (see above). In his *Adversus Praxean*, chap. 2, nos. 1–2 (CCL, 2:1160), he gives a trinitarian formula as the "rule" which has been in use since the beginning of the Gospel; similarly in *De praescriptione*, chap. 13 (1:197–98).

imparted to catechumens or the newly baptized, nor do they attempt to cover all the ground of apostolic preaching. Neither Irenaeus' "rule of truth" nor Tertullian's "rule of faith" invariably has exactly the kind of relationship with the Creed that we shall find later on, for instance, in Nicetas of Remesiana[52] or St. Augustine.[53] They were not always intended to give expression to the whole mysterious reality of the faith lived by the baptized.

I think it is possible to be even more precise. At the end of a minute comparative study, basing himself on a statement by St. Irenaeus himself, Rev. Fr. Joseph Moingt recently gave a simple explanation of those "two-Person" texts which completes the one begun by Mr. René Braun with reference to Tertullian,[54] and which reinforces the one proposed by J. A. Jungmann in his exposition of the kerygma. In my opinion, this explanation merits our firm belief. "The Apostles", says Irenaeus, "preached the truth boldly; to the Jews they proclaimed that Jesus, the one whom they had crucified, was the Son of God, the Judge of the living and the dead, who had received from the Father the eternal reign over Israel. To the Greeks they proclaimed the one God who has created all things, and Jesus Christ, his

---

[52] Bk. 5, *Sermo* 3, no. 20: "*Hanc enim regulam fidei Apostoli a Domino acceperunt, ut in nomine Patris et Filii et Spiritus sancti omnes gentes credentes baptizarent*" (ed. Gamber, 118–19).

[53] *Sermo* 59, no. 1: "You first of all learned the creed, where you will find the rule of your faith, a short but great rule . . ." (*Prius symbolum didicistis, ubi est regula fidei vestrae, brevis et grandis*; PL, 38:400).

[54] René Braun, "Deus christianorum", in *Recherches sur le vocabulaire doctrinal de Tertullien* (Paris: P.U.F., 1962), 453. Cf. J. M. Restrepo-Jaramillo, "Tertuliano y la doble formula en el símbolo apostólico", in *Gregorianum* 15 (1934): 3–58.

Son."[55] Now, St. Irenaeus imitates the Apostles. Those of his formulas which speak only of God and of Jesus Christ "are not *complete* summaries of apostolic tradition, nor are they presented as such"; they are content with recording in an abbreviated form the *initial* preaching of the faith, as it was addressed at the very beginning to unbelievers, both Greeks and Jews, and as it was still being addressed to them in Irenaeus' time. "They remind us of it because of its value as a *didactic norm*, which permits one to judge doctrinal deviations; they define the Christian faith for people *outside* its fold, by showing how it *differs* from pagan and Jewish religions and by opposing it to every sort of falling back into infidelity."[56] It is only within the Church that the Christian, at the time of his initiation, learns how to profess his faith in the sanctification which he receives from the Spirit of God sent by Christ.[57] The type of use which thus accounts for

[55] *Adversus haereses*, bk. 3, chap. 12, no. 13: "*Cum omni fiducia (veritatem) praedicabant: Judaeis quidem, Jesus, eum qui ab ipsis crucifixis est, esse Filium Dei, judicem vivorum et mortuorum, a Patre accepisse aeternum regnum in Israel; Graecis vero, unum Deum, qui omnia fecit, et ejus Filium Jesum Christum annuntiantes*" (PG, 7:907 B).

[56] Cf. O. Cullmann, 72: The two-part formulas "came into existence because of the struggle against paganism"; one might add, and also against the "gnostic" heresy.

[57] Joseph Moingt, S.J., *La Théologie trinitaire de Tertullien*, Théologie (Paris: Aubier, 1966), 1:66–86. Cf. Jungmann, *La Liturgie des premiers siècles*, 139–40: "The major theme of the preaching directed to the Jews by the Apostles was the proclamation that Jesus was the Christ. Among the pagans . . . it was necessary to proclaim first of all the faith in only one God. Thus the missionary sermon to pagans contained a double theme: God and Christ. . . . Such were the two fundamental ideas embodied in the Christian kerygma, then and always."

A TRINITARIAN CREED

the two-Person texts found in Irenaeus and Tertullian is attested to as early as the time of St. Ignatius of Antioch, when he wrote to the Magnesians, "The divine prophets were inspired by the grace of Jesus Christ so that unbelievers might be fully convinced that there is only one God, manifested by Jesus Christ, his Son, who is his Word, emerging from silence."[58] This same practice is even suggested by St. Paul himself, when he declares to the first Christians at Corinth, "for even if there be so-called gods, either in the sky or on earth—and as a matter of fact there are a great number of gods and a great number of lords—yet for us there is but one God, the Father, from whom all things come and for whom we were made; and one Lord, Jesus Christ, through whom all things exist and through whom we are."[59]

So we really have no grounds for speaking of an evolution which would have led the Christian communities from an entirely christological formula of faith to a trinitarian formula, with an intermediate stage using two terms. Moreover, nowhere do we find a trace of a baptismal formula of faith limited to two Persons. On the other hand, the three-term formulas are linked, at least by their origin and very often later on, to the rite of baptism. We quoted above the final passage from St. Matthew and Paul's reminder to the Corinthians of their baptism. Everywhere in the early centuries, the documents show us that the baptismal infusion or immersion and the (trinitarian) profession of the creed are two inseparable elements of the same rite. We find this in

---

[58] *Ad Magn.*, 8:2.
[59] 1 Cor 8:5–6. Cf. 1 Tim 2:5 and 6:13.

the *Didache*,[60] in the Epistle of Clement of Rome,[61] in Justin's first *Apology*,[62] and so on. This is something which remains constant, even while the liturgical celebration expands and becomes more diversified. We find the same thing in Origen, who evokes "the regenerative power of the Triad",[63] and in Firmilianus of Caesarea.[64] On the practice of the Church at Carthage in the third century we are quite fully informed by the writings of Tertullian and St. Cyprian.[65] So also the Catecheses of St. Cyril (or perhaps of his successor, John II) give us some precise information about the Church at Jerusalem in the fourth century.[66] The *Eucology* of Serapion of Thmuis (d. 360) in Egypt contains several trinitarian prayers which were recited over the future or newly baptized: "May he be preserved for you even to the end, Creator of the universe, by your only Son, Jesus Christ, through whom honor is given thee in the power of the Holy Spirit, now and in all the ages to come."[67] At Rome, during the fourth century also,

---

[60] *Didache*, chap. 7, no. 1 (H. Hemmer [Paris: Picard, 1916], 14).

[61] Clement, 46, 5–7 (ed. Hemmer [1926], 96); Cf. Ignatius of Antioch, *Ad Magn.*, chap. 13, no. 1 (ed. Camelot, SC, 10:106).

[62] I *Apol.*, chap. 61, nos. 3 and 10 (see above).

[63] *In Joannem*, vol. 6, chap. 17 (PG, 14:257).

[64] Inter ep. Cypriani, *ep.* 75: "*Qui baptizatus est, gratiam consequi potuit, invocata Trinitate nominum Patris, et Filii, et Spiritus sancti*" (ed. Hartel, 818).

[65] Tertullian, *Traité du baptême* (ed F. Refoulé, SC, 35 [1952]), introduction, 29–53. Cf. Fr. Th. Camelot, O.P., "Le Baptême, sacrement de la foi", in *La Vie spirituelle* 76 (1947): 820–34.

[66] *Deuxième Catéchèse baptismale*, chap. 2, no. 4 (SC, 126:111).

[67] *Prières* 21, 22, 24, 25. We are quoting the twenty-fourth one, "after baptism and coming out [of the water]". In F. X. Funk, *Didascalia et Constitutiones Apostolorum* (Paderborn, 1905), 2:187.

the explanation of the Creed used to begin on the fifth Sunday of Lent, by the *traditio symboli*, i.e., the solemn delivery of the Creed to the catechumens. . . . On Holy Saturday morning the candidates gathered for a last time. . . . At the end of the ceremony the *redditio symboli* took place: those who were going to receive baptism "gave back the Creed" by reciting the trinitarian "I believe in God".[68]

Thanks to St. Augustine's sermons,[69] the same procedure, at least in its essential points, is known to us as it was carried out in the Church of Hippo in the fifth century. This is what explains the apparent anomaly: the profession of faith sung by the whole community is nevertheless entirely in the singular: *I believe*, not *we believe*.[70] The same thing is true also for the Nicene-Constantinople Creed, which we recite or sing every Sunday at Mass and which originated from the ancient baptismal creed of Jerusalem.[71]

Such then is the basic truth which Erasmus expressed in words which obviously presuppose the later explanations of the dogma: "*Trium una deitas, et tres unus Deus: hinc summa symboli distinctio.*"[72] This is the resumé of Christian faith. "We adore", says St. Justin, "the Cre-

[68] Cf. Adalbert Hamman, *Le Baptême d'après les Pères de l'Église* (1962), 9–10.

[69] For the details, see Suzanne Poque, introduction to Augustine's *Sermons sur la Pâque* (116, 1966), 21–26 and 59–64.

[70] In his *Sermo* 215, Augustine says "*credimus*" in one phrase where he is speaking to the group of *competentes* (i.e., the candidates for baptism); but in no. 1, "*singuli hodie reddidistis*"; and in *Sermo* 56, no. 7, he says: "*Mementote quod in symbolo reddidistis: Credo . . .*" (ed. Poque, 63). However, see Chapter Ten below.

[71] Cf. my *Méditation sur l'Église*, 2nd ed. (1953), 27, n. 37.

[72] *In symbolum apostolorum*, 23.

ator of this universe.... We rightly adore also the one who has taught us all these things, Jesus Christ.... And in the third place we adore the prophetic Spirit."[73] St. Irenaeus too, in that doctrinal précis which he entitled "Demonstration of the Apostolic Preaching", says: "We have received baptism for the remission of sins in the name of God the Father and in the name of Jesus Christ the incarnate Son of God, who died and rose again, and in the Holy Spirit of God."[74] These are, as Irenaeus also tells us,[75] "the three principal articles of our baptism", "the three chapters of our seal"; this is "the methodical teaching of our faith, the basis of the edifice and the foundation of our salvation". All heretics deviate from it because "either they scorn the Father or they refuse to accept the Son by speaking against the economy of his Incarnation or else they deny the Holy Spirit by rejecting prophecy." The same tripartite division appears again in two doctrinal resumés found in the great work of the Bishop of Lyons, *Adversus haereses*,[76] and also in the writings of Tertullian, for instance in the second chapter of his *Adversus Praxean*[77] or the thirteenth chapter of his *De praescriptione haereticorum*: "There is only one God,

---

[73] I *Apol.*, chap. 13, nos. 1–3 (trans. Pautigny, 23–25). Cf. chap. 61, nos. 10–13 (131). Cf. Clement of Rome, Cor 58:2 (ed. Hemmer, 118).

[74] Chap. 3 (ed. Froidevaux, SC, 62 [1959]), 32.

[75] Op. cit., chaps. 6 and 100 (39–42 and 170).

[76] *Adversus haereses*, bk. 1, chap. 10, no. 1: "*Ecclesia ... accepit fidem, quae est in unum Deum Patrem..., et in unum Christum Jesum Filium Dei..., et in Spiritum sanctum*" (PG, 7:550 A–B; Harvey, 1:90–91). Bk. 4, chap. 33, no. 7 (1077 A–B; Harvey 2:261–62). Cf. Henri Holstein, "Formules de symbole dans saint Irénée", RSR 34 (1947): 457–59.

[77] Cf. Moingt, 1:84–86.

A TRINITARIAN CREED

who brought forth all things out of nothing, by his Word. . . . The Word was called his Son. . . . He lived under the name Jesus Christ, proclaimed the new law . . . and sent the power of the Holy Spirit to take his place."[78] We are also familiar with the famous formula of St. Cyprian in his treatise on the Lord's Prayer, where he speaks of the Christian people "gathered by the unity of the Father, the Son and the Holy Spirit".[79] Let us recall, too, among others, the testimony of Firmicus Maternus,[80] of St. John Chrysostom,[81] of St. Jerome[82] and of St. Augustine.[83]

The baptismal rite by triple immersion, still in use today in the Orthodox Church, gives striking emphasis to this belief in the Trinity. It is described in the *Apostolic Tradition* of St. Hippolytus;[84] and one may agree with Jungmann that it was in use long before the third century, because it is found later in very diverse regions, accompanied by the tripartite Creed.[85] St. Ambrose's *Explanatio symboli* clearly alludes to it: "See then, you believe in the

---

[78] Chap. 13, nos. 2–5 (SC, 46:106).

[79] *De oratione dominica*, chap. 23: "*Sacrificium Deo majus est pax nostra . . . et de unitate Patris et Filii et Spiritus sancti plebs adunata.*" Cf. F. J. Badcock, "Le Credo primitif d'Afrique", in *Revue bénédictine* 45 (1953): 3–5.

[80] *Consultationes Zacchaei et Apollinii*, bk. 1, chap. 1 (ed. G. Morin, 49).

[81] *Deuxième Catéchèse baptismale*, no. 26 (ed. A. Wenger, SC, 50:148). Cf. Gregory of Nazianzen, *Discours* 40, chap. 41 (PG, 36:417 A).

[82] Cf. Badcock, 5.

[83] *Sermo* 215, nos. 3 and 8 (PL, 38:1073 and 1076), etc.

[84] No. 20 (ed. Botte, SC, 11:50–51).

[85] On the triple interrogation joined to the triple immersion, see J. M. Hanssens, "La Concélébration des catéchumènes dans l'acte du baptême", in *Gregorianum* 27 (1946): 417–43. In Jerome's time this rite was held to be of apostolic origin.

Father; you also believe in the Son; and in the third place, what? And also in the Holy Spirit. The sacraments which you are going to receive, you will receive in this Trinity."[86] The *Instructio ad competentes* by Nicetas of Remesiana is still more explicit.[87] The catechetical homilies of Theodore of Mopsuestia show us that in Syria the same rite was linked to the same profession of faith: faith in the Father, "the author of all things"; faith in the *Monogenes*, the "Firstborn"; faith in the Spirit, "the sanctifier and giver of life".

> Three times you plunge [into the water] . . . , once in the name of the Father, once in the name of the Son and once again in the name of the Holy Spirit. . . . You make your descent into the water only once, but you plunge into it three times, according to the Pontiff's word; and after that, only once do you emerge; thus you may understand that baptism is one, and one also is the grace imparted therein by the Father, the Son and the Holy Spirit, who are absolutely inseparable from one another because their nature is one.[88]

The same thing took place in the West during the following centuries. The trinitarian formula can be found not only in the Gelasian sacramentary but also, somewhat lengthened, in the Gregorian sacramentary. In both cases it consists of a threefold interrogation that the bishop addresses to the catechumen while baptizing

---

[86] No. 5 (ed. Botte, SC, 25 *bis*:52). Cf. *De sacramentis*, tract. 2, chap. 7, no. 20 (ibid., 84–86). In his *De Elia et jejunio*, chap. 22, no. 83 (ed. C. Schenkl, CSEL, 32:463), Ambrose sees a figure of this triple immersion in the triple sprinkling of the altar with water done by Elijah's order before the sacrifice on Carmel (1 Kings 18:30–39).

[87] Bk. 6, *Sermo* 2, no. 20 (ed. Gamber, 137).

[88] 2nd *Homily*, nos. 6–9; 14th *Homily*, no. 20 (trans. Tonneau [1949], 443–45).

him.[89] Several pseudo-Augustinian sermons remark that such is the *ordo baptismi* "because the whole law of our faith consists in the Trinity".[90] St. Caesarius of Arles, who never ceases to demand that the faithful know by heart the creed they received at baptism just as they know the Our Father,[91] shows the capital importance he attaches to having them all be well aware of its trinitarian character: "As you well know, my very dear brothers, the faith of all Christians consists in the Trinity; and it is for this reason that we are repeating to you for a third time the text of the Creed, so that the very number of repetitions may be for you a sign of the Trinity."[92]

Now, the text of the creed commented on by Caesarius was already at that date, as we have said—except for a few editorial details—the text of our present Creed. So it is indeed our Creed which, divided superficially into twelve articles, is really ternary in structure.

Like Caesarius of Arles, the *Missale gallicanum vetus* calls for a triple profession of faith from the candidate for baptism "*ut ipse numerus repetitionis in signo conveniat Trinitatis*".[93] We find the same triple repetition of the word *Credo* in the creed of Cyprian of Toulouse, a contemporary of Caesarius.[94] In Spain, the *Liber mozarabicus ordinum*, setting forth the rite of baptism for children, has the priest put three questions, which sum up the entire creed, to the sponsor: "*Credit ille in Deum*

---

[89] See the two formulas in Badcock, *The History of the Creeds*, 117–18.

[90] *Sermo* 239, no. 1; *Sermo* 242, no. 2 (PL, 39:2187, 2190, 2192).

[91] *Sermons*, passim; especially *Sermo* 16, no. 2 and *Sermo* 130, no. 5 (CCL, 103:78 and 538).

[92] *Sermo* 9 (CCL, 103:47).

[93] Ed. Mohlberg (1958), 14. Cf. Jungmann, *Tradition liturgique et problèmes actuels de pastorale* (1963), 50.

[94] Vacandard, 367: "This is, it would seem, one of the characteristics of the Gallican creed."

Patrem. . . ?—Et in Jesum Christum. . . ?—Et in Spiritum sanctum. . . ?" Each time the godfather replies: *"Credit"*. Then baptism is administered in the name of the Trinity.[95]

From these texts and these practices, many other examples of which might be adduced, it is clear that the Christian faith that is summed up in the creed is identical to "belief in the Trinity" or "the faith of the Trinity"; *"Triadikè pistis"*, as the Egyptian anaphora of St. Basil says; *"trina fides"*, as the poet Arator puts it;[96] *"Trinitatis fides"*, says the letter written about 386 by Paula, Eustochium and Marcella to St. Jerome.[97] This was one of Origen's expressions in the translation by Rufinus;[98] it is also that of Nicetas of Remesiana.[99] St. Patrick's *Confessio*, so personal in its mode of expression, speaks in the same way.[100] So too St. Gregory the Great in his *Moralia in Job*:[101] "Let them [the baptized] persevere in the Catholic faith of the Holy Trinity"; such is the liturgical wish that the Gelasian sacramentary formulates.[102] St. Bede the Venerable, at the beginning

---

[95] J.-Ch. Didier, "Une Adaptation de la liturgie baptismale au baptême des enfants dans l'Église ancienne", in *Mélanges de science religieuse* 22 (1956): 85–86. This was already found in Africa in Augustine's time: 82–85.

[96] *De Actibus apostolorum*, bk. 1, verses 114 and 857.

[97] Jerome, *Epistle* 46, chap. 3 (PL, 22:485).

[98] *In Exod.*, Homily 9, no. 3: *"Funis enim triplex non rumpitur, quae est Trinitatis fides"* (ed. Baehrens, 239).

[99] Bk. 5, *Sermo* 3, no. 19 (ed. Gamber, 118).

[100] Chap. 6 (PL, 53:804 A). Faustus ("Eusebius"), *Sermons* 5 and 33: *"confessio Trinitatis"* (PL, Suppl., 3:560, 629). Magnes of Sens, *Libellus de mysterio baptismatis* (PL, 102:981 D).

[101] Bk. 23, chap. 10, nos. 18–20 (PL, 76:683–84).

[102] *Gelasianum*, 3, 50: *"In sanctae Trinitatis fide catholica perseverent"* (ed. Wilson, 2nd ed., 264). Cf. Alcuin, *De Fide Trinitatis*.

of the eighth century, similarly encapsulates the essence of the Creed in this short summary: "to confess faith in the Holy Trinity for the remission of sins".[103] The pseudo-Boniface says: "Such is the word of faith which we preach; we must believe in the Father almighty and in Jesus Christ, his only Son, our Lord, and in the Holy Spirit—who are one God almighty in unity and in trinity."[104]

"Because I believe in the living God and in his Christ whose Spirit has imprinted me with his seal, I have learned to fear nothing, not even death." Such is the declaration by which Nicetas of Remesiana closes his explanation of the creed, exhorting all the faithful to make it their own when they are prey to the persecutions or temptations of various sorts which will not fail, in due time, to assail them.[105]

So it is indeed in line with all these testimonies which go back to the earliest antiquity that Abbé Monchanin could affirm: "If I am a Christian, it is because of the Holy Trinity." This was also his inspiration in saying, soon after his arrival in India: "My life has no other meaning than praising and contemplating this unique and total mystery." When he and his companion founded the little ashram on the banks of the Kaveri, he wrote: "The adoration of the Trinity is our sole purpose."[106] There are various forms of vocations; the foundation of Christian faith and life remains unchanged.

However, to keep strictly to our subject, let me con-

---

[103] *In Tobiam* (PL, 91:930 C).
[104] *Sermo* 6, no. 1 (PL, 89:855 B).
[105] *De symbolo*, no. 14 (PL, 52:874 A).
[106] Cf. H. de Lubac, *Images de l'abbé Monchanin* (Paris: Aubier, 1967), 19–21 and 101; cf. 75 and 92.

clude by saying that the mention of the three divine Persons in the Apostles' Creed indicates something more than "three major points in Christian teaching".[107] For these three points belong to a different order than the rest—or rather, these three points include the rest entirely. Whatever the form in which it has been made, the profession of faith in the Father, Son and Holy Spirit has always constituted not only the principal part but the essential framework of our Creed.[108] "In the Trinity consists the faith of all Christians."[109]

Finally, if it is true that this Creed thus contains a summary of "the whole body of dogma" and brings out its basic unity, one can also say that the Creed itself is summed up in the "striking formula of the Sign of the Cross: 'In the name of the Father and of the Son and of the Holy Spirit' ".[110] A sign which unites in a remarkable way the christological expression of the faith with its trinitarian expression. A sign which the liturgy so rightly designates as "the sign of faith". A sign which should not be lightly used, but which the Christian should always trace upon himself with the greatest respect.

[107] Jungmann, 140.
[108] A. Vacant in "Apôtres, Symbole des", *Dictionnaire de théologie catholique*, vol. 1, col. 1676; col. 1674: "Le Cadre et le noyau".
[109] *Expositio vel traditio symboli*: "*Sicut optime novit caritas vestra, carissimi, fides omnium christianorum in Trinitate consistit*" (PL, 72:349 C).
[110] Émile Delaye, S.J., *Qu'est-ce qu'un catholique?* (Paris: Éd. Spes, 1948), 18. On the history of the Sign of the Cross, see A. Boudinhon, *Revue du clergé français* 72 (1912); 20–38; H. Leclercq, *Dictionnaire d'archéologie chrétienne et de liturgie* 3 (1914), cols. 3139–44. Cf. D. Bonhoeffer, November 21, 1943: "I felt, very naturally, as it were, an assistance from God to make the Sign of the Cross at morning prayer and at night prayer, as Luther ordains": *Résistance et soumission*, Labor et Fides (Geneva, 1963), 70.

But we should also note that this ternary structure of the Creed which so forcefully expresses our faith in the Trinity does not do so at the expense of the divine unity. The triple proclamation of the Father, the Son and the Holy Spirit is made under the sign of this unity, which is stated at the beginning: *Credo in Deum*, or, as the Creed of Nicaea-Constantinople puts it, *Credo in unum Deum*.[111] "See that there is a distinction between the Persons, but that this entire mystery of the Trinity is one":[112] so spoke St. Ambrose when explaining baptism. And, arguing subtly from "name", in the singular, he says: "Do not be surprised that we are baptized in a single name, i.e., '*in the name* of the Father and of the Son and of the Holy Spirit', for we can only speak in the singular when there is only one substance, a single divinity, a single majesty."[113] From the Father, the Son and the Holy Spirit there come to us therefore a single grace, a single peace and a single administration of Providence.[114]

Christian faith does not have three objects but only one. We believe in a single God; this does not signify merely that we exclude all the pagan gods (although this exclusion has its importance today, and always will, because false gods keep being reborn in the heart of man, and the ancient and remote forms of paganism are not the

---

[111] Although the word "God" here refers especially to the Father, as being the *"fons divinitatis"*.

[112] *De sacramentis*, bk. 6, chap. 2, no. 8: "*Vides distinctionem personarum esse, sed connexum omne mysterium Trinitatis*" (ed. Botte, SC, 25 bis:140).

[113] Ibid., bk. 2, chap. 7, no. 22 (86). Nicetas follows this closely in bk. 5, *Sermo* 1, no. 19 (ed. Gamber, 106).

[114] Nicetas, bk. 3, *Sermo* 1, no. 25 (ed. Gamber, 48).

only ones). It also signifies that we recognize the inner unity of the one God, *Deus unicus et unus*. This inner unity is not only the unity "of the divine nature", considered as it were independently of the three Persons, as one might be tempted to explain it. That would be to conceive a sort of impersonal divinity and then to remain defenseless before a contrary tendency to tritheism as soon as one reintroduced the consideration of the three Persons. To avoid both of these dangers, which in fact are always latent, some would like to suppress or at least to restrict the use of the word "nature", while others suggest that we give up the word "person". It is well known that, while taking great care not to encourage unitarianism, Karl Barth freely replaces "person" by "mode of being" or "form of existence", expressions he sees as equivalent to *subsistentia*. "Paternity", he tells us, for instance, "is an eternal mode of being belonging to the divine essence".[115] For this he invokes the authority of Calvin, who translated the Greek word "hypostasis" as "subsistence", but without rejecting the word "person".[116] No doubt there would be more drawbacks than advantages in systematically deviating from the established language. We know, of course, that our words are never adequate; but here, as Karl Rahner

[115] *Dogmatics*, vol. 1, 1, 57 ss., 83, 89, etc.; cf. vol. 4, 1, 216. *Credo* (French trans.), 23, 38, 40.

[116] *Institution chrétienne*, bk. 1, chap. 13, no. 2: "And since the Latin doctors have chosen to express the same idea by the word 'Person', it would be unfortunate, indeed, far too obstinate, to plead that . . ." (*Corpus Reformatorum* 31 [Brunvigae, 1865], col. 147). Ibid., no. 5: "When this is admitted without any attempt to deceive, we should not bother about the words used" (col. 152). And in the 1541 edition: "I am not so rude or extreme as to wish to stir up a great battle over mere words."

remarks, better ones are not to be found. One must only take great care to maintain at all times "the inner unity of the unicity and the Trinity of God".[117] We must not lose sight of the fact that the divine unity is the unity of God himself, the unity of the living God, of a God so eminently personal that one should call him—stammering with awe—tripersonal. *Plena et adunata Trinitas.*[118] *Trina unitas et adunata trinitas.*[119] When at the close of the eucharistic celebration the priest blesses the assembly saying, "May the all-powerful God bless you . . .", he is not by this first part of the benediction formula imploring the intervention of a "divine", but impersonal, "nature"; rather, he is calling on a God who is personal, tripersonal, one in three Persons, Father, Son and Holy Spirit. These three names, which come next, are not those of three independent subjects; they are placed in apposition to the unique subject of the whole formula: to "God".

---

[117] *Ecrits théologiques* 8 (trans. R. Givord): 138–39. See the balanced remarks by G. Philips, *Ephemerides theologicae lovanienses* 45 (1969): 103–11. The Orthodox theologians might rather complain that Latin theology has de-emphasized the reality of the Persons by defining them by their relations, somewhat veiled and shadowed by their common nature. See Timothy Ware, *L'Orthodoxie*, French trans. Charité de Saint Servais (Paris: Desclée de Brouwer, 1968), 292–93.

[118] St. Cyprian, *Epist.* 73, chap. 18 (ed. Hartel, CSEL, 3:2, 791).

[119] Quodvultdeus, *De accedentibus ad gratiam*, no. 8 (PL, Suppl., 3:267). Faustus of Riez, *De Spiritu sancto*, bk. 1, chap. 1: "*In hac symboli perfectione et unitas evidenter aperitur et trinitas, dum ter repetita confessio Patri et Filio et Spiritui sancto unum credulitatis reddit obsequium*" (CSEL, 21:102). Cf. Irenaeus, *Demonstratio*, chap. 100 (*in fine*): "Glory to the all holy Trinity and to the one Divinity, Father, Son and Holy Spirit, the universal Providence, in all ages. Amen" (ed. Froidevaux, SC, 62:170).

CHAPTER THREE

THE ECONOMIC TRINITY

There has always been an awareness in the Church that the creed, however brief and in whatever state it might be, contains the totality of the faith. This was so even at the time of the christological formulas. As for the earliest trinitarian formulas, they grew, not by the addition of new articles placed at the end of the first three, but by the explanation or development of each of these. This was the case for the *forma antiquissima*, the ancestor of the Roman Creed, which, as we mentioned, goes back to the middle of the second century. We can ascertain this from the fact that, having been transmitted from Rome to Egypt very early on, it was maintained there without any change for a long time. Each of the three articles is itself composed of three parts, which gives us, if you wish, a total of nine articles. There may have been a symbolic intention behind this arrangement, or perhaps there was a desire, after the event, to justify it by appealing to the mystical significance of the numbers. This detail is of little importance to us. But the text is significant: "I believe in God, the Father almighty—and in Jesus Christ, his only Son our Lord—and in the Holy Spirit, the holy Church, the resurrection of the flesh."[1]

---

[1] H. Lietzmann, *Histoire de l'Église ancienne* 2 (French trans., Paris: Payot, 1937): 109. Cf. Kattenbusch, in J. de Ghellinck, *Patristique et moyen âge* 3, *Les Recherches sur les origines du symbole des apôtres* (1964): 143.

This God in whom the Christian thus declares that he believes, this God who is all his faith and in whose name he has come to ask the Church for baptism, is not merely some remote, inaccessible divinity whose reality compels the recognition of man's intellect; he is not merely that divinity that man glimpses as best he can through the created universe—and often mistakes, just as much in the loftiest flights of his thinking as in his grossest mythologies, for the universe itself—and about whom he attempts to say something in his halting language; that mute divinity of whom, at best, we must say that man conceives of him only from the outside and without finding any way of communicating with him. God has so to speak laid bare his own inner life by unveiling his designs to us. "Having spoken in times past through the prophets, in these last days he has spoken to us through his Son."[2] He himself has spoken about himself. He has revealed himself to men, Father, Son and Spirit; the one God, the living God. Men, if they do not refuse to believe him, and if they consent to allow themselves to be penetrated by it, will never cease to be filled with wonder before this partially revealed mystery.

> A divinity without a superior degree that elevates or an inferior degree that lowers; equal in all respects, the same in every way. . . . This is the infinite connaturality of three infinitudes. Each one is wholly God, considered in himself, the Son as well as the Father, the Spirit as well as the Son, each preserving his own personal character: God, the Three considered together. Each one is God because of their consubstantiality; the Three are God by reason of their monarchy. . . . No sooner have I begun to think of their Unity than their Trinity bathes me in its

[2] Heb 1:1–2.

splendor. No sooner have I begun to think of their Trinity than their Unity again takes hold of me. When one of the Three presents himself to me I think that this is all, so filled is my eye, so completely does the rest escape me; for in my mind, too limited to understand even a single one of the Three, there remains no place to give to the other Two. And when I join all Three in a single concept I see a single flame without being able to divide or to analyze the unified light.[3]

Obviously, it is not under this form that the revelation of God in Jesus Christ took place. When God told man about himself, he did not leave man to his own devices. The mystery of the Trinity was not made known to us as a sublime theory, a celestial theorem, with no connection with what we are and what we must become. God, the Creator of our world, has chosen to intervene in our history. It is by acting in our favor, by calling us to himself, by bringing about our salvation, that he has made himself known to us. Our faith in him, which is a response to his call, cannot be separated from the knowledge that he has given us of his activity in our midst.[4] "As the snow and the rain come down from heaven and do not return there until they have watered the land and made it fertile and fruitful, so too the Word which issues from my mouth will not return to me without having fulfilled its mission."[5] The structure of

[3] St. Gregory of Nazianzen, *Discours* 40, chap. 41 (PG, 36:417 B C).
[4] Vatican II, dogmatic constitution *Dei verbum*, chap. 1. See *Vatican II, La Révélation divine*, edited by B. D. Dupuy, 1 (Paris: Éd. du Cerf, 1968): 172–96. Not to widen the topic unduly, we leave aside here what refers to the revelation which, in revealing himself to us, God makes of us to ourselves.
[5] Is 55:10–11.

the Creed reflects the Word of God at work in the world, transforming the history of mankind into salvation history; it tells us of that all-powerful Word accomplishing the work for which it was sent.[6]

Even for Israel, the inconceivable marvel did not consist in some internal characteristic of the divinity which Israel alone would have knowledge of. It consisted in the fact that the absolutely free and sovereign Being had decided to communicate with men, to give them access to the realm of his holiness. This grace was at the same time an unheard-of exigency, "delivering the creature from his proper place in the land of slavery and bringing him into a 'land' which is God's".[7] Such is the revelation that finds its accomplishment and apogee in Christ: "God", says St. Peter in the home of the centurion Cornelius, "has sent his Word to the children of Israel. . . . You know what has taken place in all of Judea."[8] Jesus himself, in reply to the messengers sent by John the Baptist, tells them to relate to their master "what you have heard and seen".[9] If every act of revelation is in the last analysis a revelation of the Trinity, the entire revelation of the Trinity is a revelation through action, and all this action is directly concerned with man.

This can be expressed by using the word with which the Fathers of the Church commonly summed up this revealing act: "economy" (οἰκονομία). We need not go into detail here concerning the meanings that this word can have. "Economy" (*dispensatio*) means administration;

[6] Msgr. Cahal Daly, *We Believe* (Ardagh, 1969), 8.

[7] Hans Urs von Balthasar, *Herrlichkeit*, vol. 3, 2: 164.

[8] Acts, 10:36–43. Cf. H. Schlier, *Essais sur le Nouveau Testament* (trans. Liefooghe, Paris: Éd. du Cerf, 1968), 50–51.

[9] Mt 11:4.

and from this meaning there flows first of all that of design, then that of disposition.[10] In the language of the Fathers—if we leave aside Tatian and Tertullian, who use it to designate the inner organization of the divinity[11]—it refers to all of God's work, in all its phases and under all its aspects: creation, providence, history, the works of nature and those of grace.[12] It is the accomplishment of God's design on earth; it is the mystery of man's salvation[13] taking place within creation and unfolding through time; *dispensatio temporalis*,[14] which is condensed entirely in the *dispensatio carnis*,[15] i.e., in the

---

[10] G. L. Prestige, *Dieu dans la pensée patristique* (French trans., Paris: Aubier, 1955), 69–77 and 99–108. R. A. Markus, "Trinitarian Theology and the Economy", in *The Journal of Theological Studies* (1958), 89–102. J. P. Jossua, *Le Salut, incarnation ou mystère pascal* (Paris: Éd. du Cerf, 1968), 51–54 and 72. Adhémar d'Alès, *Le Mot* οἰκονομία *dans la langue théologique de saint Irénée*, Revue des études grecques (1919).

[11] Tertullian, *Adversus Praxean*, chap. 2. He distinguishes in God the *substantiae unitas* and the *oeconomiae sacramentum quae unitatem in trinitatem disponit* (CCL, 2:1161; see chapters 3, 9, 13, 23, 30; 1161, 1168, 1175, 1192, 1204). We are simplifying here a bit what he says. Cf. J. Moingt, *Théologie trinitaire de Tertullien*, 3:891–932; René Braun, 158–67. J. Daniélou, *Recherches de science religieuse* (1969), 104–5.

[12] In its biblical and patristic sense, the word goes beyond the meaning of "salvation history". Cf. André Scrima, in *Mythe et foi* (Paris: Aubier, 1966), 311. André Feuillet, *Le Prologue du quatrième Évangile* (Paris: Desclée de Brouwer, 1968), 43, where the author distinguishes, following St. Paul, a double mediation by Christ: "cosmic" and "soteriological". This overemphasis on history is, in Protestantism, a characteristic of the Calvinistic tendency.

[13] "Sacramentum salutis humanae": St. Hilary, *De Trinitate*, bk. 2, no. 1 (PL, 10:50 C).

[14] Augustine, *De vera religione*, 7:13; 55:110 (Bibl. aug., 8, 42 and 184). Basil, *On the Holy Spirit*, chap. 15, no. 34: "The Economy of God our Savior regarding man" (SC, 17 *bis*:364).

[15] Origen, *In Jesu Nave*, hom. 3, no. 2 (Baehrens, 302). Eusebius,

90 THE CHRISTIAN FAITH

redemptive and divinizing Incarnation,[16] or, as Gregory of Nyssa says, in "the divine mystery of the 'economy' according to man", so as to expand to "the 'economy' of the Church". "The entire mystery", says St. Cyril of Alexandria,[17] "is the kenosis [of the Lord] and his abasement in the carnal economy. . . . He took on the form of a slave, οἰκονομικῶς because of us."[18] St. Paul had said the same thing previously when he spoke of the "economy of the fullness of time", which was to bring about God's "beneficent design" in the world.[19]

From the fourth century onward, the Fathers habitually distinguished the two parts that make up all sacred science (what we today call "theology") by using the two contrasting words: "economy" and "theology".[20] Like them we shall maintain that it is through the

---

Démonstration évangélique, bk. 3, preface (Heikel, 94). Pseudo-Chrysostom (PG, 55:692). Jerome, *In die Paschae* (Morin, Anecd. Maredsolana, vol. 3, 2: 416). Maximus the Confessor, *Ambiguorum liber* (PG, 91:1385 D). Cf. Eph 1:9.

[16] Irenaeus, *Adversus haereses*, bk. 4, chap. 33, no. 7 (PG, 7:1077 A). Severus of Antioch, *hom.* 90: "In addition to theology, there is also the Economy, a marvel beyond our comprehension. . . ; for Isaiah adds, 'See, this live coal has touched your lips; it will take away your iniquities and wipe out your sins' (6:7). It is clear that this live coal symbolizes the Emmanuel" (*Patrologie orientale* 23:148). St. Gregory the Great (PL, 75:874 A), etc.

[17] *Vie de Moïse* (Daniélou, SC, 1 ter [1968]: 207–8).

[18] PG, 69:396 B; 301 D, etc; 70:240 B.

[19] Eph 1:9–10.

[20] There are innumerable examples. Clement of Alexandria used a synonym, distinguishing between "theology" and "prophecy" (4th *stromate*, chap. 1; Stählin, 2:248). One should, therefore, moderate the statement by Mr. Olivier Clement: "Pre-Nicean thinking . . . was not aware of the distinction between 'theology' and the 'economy' ", while agreeing with the author that "it did sense all the immanence of

"economy", and only through it, that we have access to "theology". Even more, all of "theology" remains marked for us with the seal of the "economy". "We believe in one God... who sent his Son,... who sent the Holy Spirit."[21] It is in this sense that we can agree with the formula used by a contemporary theologian, Gerhard Ebeling, who writes: "The doctrine about God and the doctrine about salvation are identical."[22] This too was what the language of Scholasticism wished to express by saying that the (internal) "processions" of the Persons of the Trinity are known to us exclusively through their (external) "missions"; or again, in the words of St. Thomas Aquinas, that we glimpse the "*occultum divinitatis*" only through the "*mysterium humanitatis Christi*", in whom the entire "economy" resides—and is transcended.[23]

For this distinction does not create a separation—quite the contrary. In no way does it mean that nothing concerning the internal "processions", nothing concerning "theology", properly speaking, is accessible to us. In no way does it mean that the doctrine about God must be reduced to the doctrine about salvation, for in that case the latter would risk being purely illusory doctrine. "If the Incarnation", says Cyril of Jerusalem, "were pure imagination, then salvation too would be pure imagi-

---

the Trinity in history and in the universe": "Berdiaeff et la tradition orthodoxe", in *Contacts* 20 (1968): 191.

[21] Tertullian, *De praescriptione*, chap. 13 (SC, 46:106); *Adv. Praxean*, chap. 2 (CCL, 2:1160). Cf. Moingt, 1:68.

[22] *Wort und Glaube*, 490; quoted by René Marlé, *Recherches de science religieuse* 50 (1962): 21.

[23] Cf. Yves Congar, *Situation et tâches présentes de la théologie* (Éd. du Cerf, 1967), 10: "God reveals the 'in-himself' side of his mystery

nation."²⁴ St. Athanasius described the being of the Trinity solely in terms of its external activity, but this was the structure of God's immanent life which the great defender of the "consubstantial" thereby wished to reach,²⁵ although always in a human manner. St. Ambrose explained that the Word of God, whose profound majesty is secret, incomprehensible and unspeakable, became recognizable for us through his humanity—but he certainly thought that in this abasement *pro captu nostro* we do indeed recognize him.²⁶ In other words, neither the Fathers of the Church nor any other authorized witness of our Christian faith have ever thought that our knowledge of the Trinity was condemned to remain purely "functional". For it is indeed true, and it is essential to say, that "God, in his supernatural revelation, teaches us nothing that does not concern our salvation",²⁷ that the whole gospel is *evangelium salutis*,²⁸ that the proclamation of the gospel is *salutis praeconium*;²⁹ but precisely, the salvation of man is God himself.

"The expression of the faith", we are told, "must respect the mystery of the faith and avoid making any

---

in the 'for-us' aspect of the union of grace and the Incarnation."

²⁴ *Quatrième Catéchèse*, chap. 9 (PG, 33:468 A).

²⁵ Cf. Joseph Wolinski, *Mission et procession du Saint-Esprit chez saint Athanase à la lumière d'Origène et de la tradition alexandrine* (unpublished thesis, Paris Theological Faculty, 1968).

²⁶ *De fide ad Gratianum*, bk. 5, chap. 7, 99 (PL, 16:668). Cf. Augustine, *De Trinitate*, bk. 4, chap. 20, no. 28 (PL, 42:907).

²⁷ Pierre Grelot, *Sens chrétien de l'Ancien Testament* (Tournai: Desclée, 1962), 425. Cf. the *Benedictus*: "*ad dandam scientiam salutis plebi ejus, in remissionem peccatorum eorum*" (Lk 1:77).

²⁸ Acts 13:26. Eph 1:13.

²⁹ Cf. our commentary on the constitution *Dei verbum*, chap. 1; vol. 1, especially 165–71.

ontological affirmations."[30] There, at least if one wishes to interpret it strictly, we have a statement which in its second part depends more on the anti-intellectual and anti-objectivistic currents in contemporary thought[31] than on a reflection upon the Christian faith as made known to us by the primitive writings.[32] This thesis has found support in Bultmann's philosophy, which proposes an "existential" interpretation of the biblical texts. Bultmann seems to begin by setting up a kind of radical (and entirely fictitious) opposition between the idea of a revelation accomplished "outside of ourselves" and which would not affect us at all and that of a revelation which, in order to affect us, would tell us nothing and could tell us nothing beyond the actuality of our existence. Revelation, he declares, "brings us absolutely nothing if we expect it to make known to us some teaching which man cannot attain to by himself,

---

[30] *Le Christianisme au XXe siècle*, June 16, 1966.

[31] According to R. Bultmann, the formula "Christ is God" is false whenever one understands by the word "God" a greatness that can be objectified, whether it be in the Arian or the Nicean sense, in the orthodox or liberal one; the expression is correct if by "God" one understands the event of God's action. *Glauben und Verstehen* 2:246–61. Henri Bouillard sums up this position in *Le Problème de la démythologisation selon Bultmann*, in *Logique de la foi* (Paris: Aubier, 1964), 139. But how can one speak of "God's action" without objectifying to some degree the word "God"? And if one does not admit that our intelligence includes a power of self-criticism, one will perpetually waver between an untenable objectifying thought and an equally untenable agnosticism.

[32] For instance, as Thomas F. Torrance observes, the presence of the Spirit who had come upon the Apostles was already for them "an ontological reality", in *L'Esprit Saint et l'Église* (Paris: Fayard, 1969), 40.

mysteries which must remain sacrosanct once they are communicated to us; but it brings us everything if we expect it to enlighten man about himself and to help him understand himself."[33] Given that sort of dichotomy (at least if one seeks to adhere to it systematically), it seems to us that, while trying to avoid an imaginary Charybdis (or one imagined by some "extrinsicists" who do not know what they are talking about), one would inevitably fall into a Scylla in which all the reality of revelation would be engulfed. Indeed, one would reduce Christianity "to a transcendental condition of man's understanding of himself, whether it be a question of thought, life, understanding or action". But to reduce it to this would be "to annihilate it".[34]

Bultmann's undertaking, wrote Karl Barth in his famous address *The Humanity of God*, simply brings us back to

> the anthropocentric myth. . . . It is certain that existentialism demonstrates once again the particular truth taught by the ancient theological schools when it repeats that we cannot in any way speak of God without speaking of man. Provided that it does not at the same time bring us back to the old error according to which one could speak of man without first, and very concretely, making reference to the living God![35]

---

[33] *La Notion de révélation dans le Nouveau Testament*, article quoted and criticized by R. Schnackenburg in *La Verité qui libère* (French trans., Paris-Tours: Mame, 1966), 22–23.

[34] Hans Urs von Balthasar, *L'Amour seul est digne de foi* (trans. R. Givord, Paris: Aubier, 1966), 61.

[35] *L'Humanité de Dieu* (Geneva: Labor et Fides, 1956), 40; cf. 37. See also Louis Bouyer, *Le Rite et l'homme* (Paris: Éd. du Cerf, 1962), 298–302.

THE ECONOMIC TRINITY

Without wishing to subscribe in any way to this "old error", but in a concern for exegetical reserve, Mr. Oscar Cullmann nevertheless usually adopts a rather restrictive position. "The New Testament", he has written, "cannot and does not propose to give us information about the being of God considered apart from the act by which he reveals himself; all research into 'being' in the philosophical sense is totally foreign to it." Thus formulated, the remark is acceptable; but it could also be turned around; one could say with just as much reason that the New Testament does not claim to speak to us of an act considered without any relationship with the one who performs it, since by that act the latter "reveals himself". It is also true that

> the early Christian writings speak only of the God who reveals himself, of God as turned toward the world, in other words, of the history which unfolds from the "beginning" of John 1:1, up to the "all in all" of 1 Corinthians 15:28, i.e., from the instant at which the Word began to issue forth from God as his creative Word, to the moment when the Son to whom the Father has subjected all things will submit himself to the Father after everything else has been subjected to him.[36]

But this assertion bears within itself at least a part of its own corrective, since none of this "history" would be what it is if it did not unfold between the two extremes which encompass and explain it. Indeed, Mr. Oscar Cullmann himself states this very well in a more recent book: "If the Bible, from beginning to end, speaks of the action rather than of the being of God, Father, Son and Holy Spirit, it is still God's being which is manifested in

---

[36] Oscar Cullmann, *Christologie du Nouveau Testament* (Paris: Delachaux et Niestlé, 1958), 286.

that action, and insofar as it is action." When the author adds that this being of God "can and must be the object of dogmatic reflection, but not of exegetical analysis",[37] this is merely a question of semantics or of determining the limits between two disciplines; the word *exegesis* being taken here in a narrow sense, in conformity with modern usage, to designate only the first phase of textual analysis.

The history of Christian thought shows us, at all events, that the second phase, that of dogmatic reflection, has followed hard upon the first. This had to be, not only as a pragmatic necessity but as a logical one as well. The ontological theandric character of the Incarnation had to be explained and defended so that the paschal soteriology might be understood and preserved. The Fathers of the Church in fact had a clear perception that "the mystery of the death and Resurrection of the Savior is unintelligible without the mystery of his personality."[38] An analogous process followed with regard to the "Spirit of adoption", the one in whom alone we can say that "Jesus is the Lord."[39] One can, no doubt, consider that the later developments of the doctrine sometimes lacked due sobriety; one can expose in these developments an intellectualism as shallow as it was unrestrained; one can likewise discern the influence of certain systems of thought which were not essential to the expression of the faith and which sometimes were even harmful not only to its simplicity but to its very purity. Still, this does not prevent the transition from the first phase to the second from constituting in itself a legitimate procedure,

[37] Id., *Le Salut dans l'histoire* (ibid., 1966), 11.
[38] J. P. Jossua, *Le Salut, incarnation ou mystère pascal* (coll. *Cogitatio fidei* 28, Paris: Éd. du Cerf, 1968), 8–9 and 386.
[39] Rom 8:15; 1 Cor 12:3.

indeed, an indispensable one. "Theology" already exists potentially in the "economy"; it is in a way required by it.[40]

So there is an essential difference, nay, an unbridgeable gap, between the idea of an "economic" revelation and the idea of a purely functional one. Those who wish to reduce the former to the latter sometimes appeal to a passage from Luther where they say they can hear an authentic echo of the New Testament affirmations:

> Christ has two natures: what does that have to do with me? If he bears this name of Christ, magnificent and consoling as it is, it is because of the ministry and the task he took upon himself; that is what gives him that name. That he is by nature both man and God, this is something for himself. But that he consecrated his ministry and poured out his love to become my Savior and my Redeemer, that is where I find my consolation and my good. . . . To believe in Christ does not mean that Christ is a person who is both God and man, for that is of no help to anybody. It means that this person is Christ; that for our sake he came forth from the Father and descended into the world. . . . It is from this office that he derives his name.[41]

Without taking into account the paradoxical character

---

[40] Cf. Yves Congar, in *Mélanges M. D. Chenu* (1967), 156–57. Pierre Grelot, *Que penser de l'interprétation existentiale?* in *Ephemerides theologicae lovanienses* 43 (1967): 436. Cf. Paul Tillich, *Systematic Theology* 1:157: "The doctrine of revelation is based on a trinitarian interpretation of the divine life and of its manifestation to itself." (Quoted by G. Tavard, *Initiation à Paul Tillich* [Paris: Éd. du Centurion, 1968], 96.) On the oneness of the "economic" Trinity and the "immanent" Trinity (i.e., the Trinity in itself), see further Karl Rahner, *Écrits théologiques* 8:129–36 and 98–103, and also chap. 5 of *Mysterium salutis* 2 (1967).

[41] Erlang. Ausg. 35:207–8.

of so many of Luther's statements, and without trying, either, to understand the polemical edge of this eloquent passage, Ritschl[42] and Harnack[43] in the last century quoted it in an attempt to justify their Christianity without dogmas. Others have imitated them since. Before their time, Ludwig Feuerbach had also drawn his inspiration from it in a wrong sense; carrying to the extreme "the anthropocentric virtualities of Luther's *pro me, pro nobis*",[44] he had concluded that Luther's Christology, freed from all theology, was no more than a "religious anthropology", and he had sought to find in this the path that leads to an absolute anthropocentricity, denying any other divinity but that of man.[45] Still, on this point as on many others, Luther also offers us the opposite point of view. Take, for instance, his sermon for Christmas in 1521:

> We must learn to know Christ well and the relationship that exists between his two natures, the divine nature and the human nature, for on this point many people are in error.... As regards Christ's words, the capital question is to discern which of them belong to his divine nature and which to his human nature.[46]

[42] *Die christliche Lehre von der Rechtfertigung und Versöhnung* 3 (3rd ed.): 374, note.

[43] *Dogmengeschichte* 3 (3rd ed.): 564, in the epigraph of the last book. Also *Lehrbuch der Dogmengeschichte* 3 (1897): 773.

[44] Henri Arvon, *Feuerbach, sa vie, son oeuvre* (Paris: P.U.F, 1964), 39–40. Karl Barth took up again the *pro me* of Luther but with a totally different stress: *Dogmatics* (trans. Fernand Ryser, Geneva: Labor et Fides), vol. 4, 1 (1967): 135–36.

[45] *Principes de la philosophie de l'avenir*: "Protestantism no longer concerns itself ... with what God is in himself but only with what he is with regard to man...; it is no longer theology—essentially, it is only Christology, i.e., religious anthropology." (Trans. Louis Althusser, 1960, 128.)

[46] *Oeuvres*, French trans., 10 (Geneva: Labor et Fides, 1967): 303.

He also says in his *Great Catechism*: "I believe that Jesus Christ, the true Son of God, has become my Lord", etc.[47] On the other hand, it is certain that he never gave up his faith in the fundamental Christian dogmas.

Dietrich Bonhoeffer was, therefore, not entirely wrong when he stated that "for Luther it is the person who gives meaning to the work", and that "there is no access to the work except through the person".[48] For Bonhoeffer, it was Melanchthon, not Luther, who reduced the person of Jesus Christ to his work, i.e., dogmatic Christology to soteriology, according to his famous formula: "To know Christ is to know his benefits, not to consider his natures and the modalities of his Incarnation." In fact, however, it seems very difficult to oppose Luther on this point to his disciple, Melanchthon. The formula given by the disciple is a faithful echo of the first passage we quoted from the master, and neither of them necessarily requires an exclusive meaning. While attributing the entire Creed to trust in the forgiveness of sins, which sums up all of Christ's benefits, Melanchthon, like Luther, professed his belief in each of the other articles of traditional dogma.[49] On occasion both of them freely express themselves in a paradoxical, antithetical way which one should not always take literally. Still, their language does indicate a tendency. Neither Luther nor Melanchthon—nor Calvin either, for that matter—"pauses to analyze

---

[47] Second part, art. 2, no. 27.

[48] *Wer ist und wer war Jesus Christus?* (Hamburg, 1962), 25 and 39. Quoted by René Marlé, *Dietrich Bonhoeffer témoin de Jésus-Christ parmi ses frères* (Casterman, 1967), 77–78.

[49] "*Fides est virtus apprehendens et applicans promissiones et quietans corda. . . . Cum autem dicimus de assensu promissionis, complectimur omnium articulorum notitiam et in symbolo ceteri articuli referuntur ad hunc: credo remissionem peccatorum.*" *Loci praecipui theologi*, ad editionem Lipsiensem, anno 1559 (Berlin, 1856), 63. See below, Chapter Nine.

the *being* of the eternal Son of God made man, i.e., to describe the hypostatic union; rather, they proceed directly to the explanation of his redemptive work"; their entire perspective remains soteriological.[50] With Luther most particularly, his customary language manifests a thought which is "less concerned about knowing Christ's inner mystery than about hearing his promises and the sovereign call of his voice"[51]—and even, we must admit, "a certain scorn for all intellectual dogmatic statements, which he considers as only a side issue in true religious life".[52] There was present in this, at the very least, a certain tendency which history has revealed to be dangerous.

Luther was, no doubt, imbued even to the marrow of his bones with his Catholic atavism, with the doctrines concerning Christ and the Trinity; his imagination and his sensibility naturally played within this framework; his religious experience, it seemed to him, found in these doctrines its normal intellectual, spontaneous and solely legitimate expression. For him, the words *pro me* thus referred, as has been said, "to God's objective intervention in Christ, that saving act, independent of man, by which man is delivered from himself"; while among some of his successors, "concentration on the meaning which the gospel assumes for me, here and now, in-

---

[50] Alexandre Ganoczy, *Le Jeune Calvin, genèse et évolution de sa vocation réformatrice* (Wiesbaden, 1966), 141–42, speaking of Luther's *Little Catechism* and the first edition of Calvin's *Institution*.

[51] René Marlé, *Bultmann et la foi chrétienne* (coll. *Foi vivante*, Paris: Aubier, 1967), 134.

[52] Yves de Montcheuil, *Leçons sur le Christ* (Paris: Éd. de l'Épi, 1949), 53. Cf. Henri Bouillard, *Logique de la foi*, 138–46; Yves Congar, *La Christologie de Luther*, in *Das Konzil von Chalkedon*, published by A. Grillmeier and H. Bacht, vol. 3 (Würzburg, 1954).

dependently of past historical events, leads to an egocentricity in which the meaning of *pro me* is entirely drawn away from its objective pole to its subjective pole". It follows that then "the gospel disappears in favor of man's existentialized self-understanding; the very reality of God is reduced to what he signifies for me, in the needs and contingencies of my own life"—and no divine action comes to deliver me from this prison. Obviously, there are many sorts of influences under which, here or there, such a reversal takes place. We may, however, observe that this consequence is logical enough: if one begins with an experience in which the person of Christ tends to disappear behind his gifts, if the Incarnation is looked upon as a simple prelude to the redemption, it is quite natural to find oneself being carried away to a more and more subjective theology.[53]

How then can we fail to recognize, despite the misuse, a certain legitimacy in the assertions of Ritschl and Harnack, of Bultmann today, and, before their time, of Hegel, when they cite Luther as their reference? For the great Reformer, Hegel tells us, what is required of man is his feelings, his faith, to such an extent that the principle of subjectivity, of reference to the self, is not only recognized but is declared to be the only important thing.[54] One can in fact find in Luther two more or less

---

[53] Here we summarize T. F. Torrance, "Cheap and Costly Grace", in *The Baptist Quarterly* 22 (1968): 291–96.

[54] *Histoire de la philosophie* (Berlin, 1844; WW, 15:230 ss.). It has been remarked that Hegel "does not speak of a trinitarian God but of belief in the Trinity. The passages that explicitly deal with the Trinity always appear to be explanations of the believing awareness of the Christian community": P. Henrici, according to Splett, *Archives de philosophie* (1968), 50. See also C. Fabro, *La Dissolution du Christ dans le rationalisme* (*La Table ronde* [Nov. 1968], 49–50).

reconcilable concepts of faith; but the emphasis in the first text we quoted from his writings does not deceive us about what is most personal, most deeply rooted in his thinking: "That lively sentiment which he called faith breaks out in it with such strong naiveté that it immediately transcends all the logical consequences he draws, and which his successors had to spend three centuries to develop slowly."[55]

Who could fail to see at the same time, when this aspect of Luther's thinking comes to a point of exclusive domination, what a contrast exists between it and the Catholic concept by which Luther lived and which has left so many traces in his works? For Catholicism, the dogmatic affirmation, without constituting by itself alone the act of faith, is essential in order to nourish and orient the latter. It always maintains the primacy of objective being over personal meanings and appropriations. Such an attitude is not aimed at satisfying intellectual curiosity, which would transform the Christian into a detached spectator of the object of his faith: in religious matters such curiosity "is always out of place and sometimes dangerous" because it is contrary to the submissive disposition which must be that of the believer, and it destroys or at least weakens the spontaneous movement of his faith. But maintaining this primacy of being is something "necessary for religious living itself. One must know who Christ is in himself if one wishes to understand his function".[56] The doctrinal character of faith is not opposed to its existential character: the latter

---

[55] Pierre Rousselot, *Études sur la foi et le dogmatisme* (unpublished course of lectures in Latin; Paris Theological Faculty, 1909–1910).
[56] Yves de Montcheuil, loc. cit.

always presupposes the former to avoid becoming an illusory dream or an anthropocentric withdrawal.[57] Thus, today we see Christians belonging to certain sects that have issued from the Reformation, who are disturbed by the destructive subjectivism they can see at work and who, aware of the source from which this springs, deplore what they think was an overreaction against the "Roman error" and call for a "turning backward" on this very important point. "Everything depends on what Jesus Christ, the Son of God, was. The significance of his acts, in his life and in his death, depends on the nature of his personal being. It was *he* who died for us; *he* who redeemed us by *his own* offering in life and in death."[58] The Christians who speak in this fashion have thus come back precisely to what Fr. Pierre Rousselot wrote sixty years ago:

> *Christ has two natures; what is that to me?*—But the substantial reparation of humanity lies in that very fact. But this joining of the divine and the human touches and heals what is most profound and most inalienable in me, my very nature. *Christ has two natures; what is that to me?* But every living intelligence is directly, personally, profoundly involved in this central fact of the history of being, which brings divinization to creatures. *At the moment that affects the depths of being itself, it affects the depths of my own being.*[59]

Now, through the dogma concerning Christ we are

[57] Cf. the similar and complementary thoughts of L. Malevez, in *Pour une théologie de la foi* (Paris-Bruges: Desclée de Brouwer, 1969), especially the two chapters "Foi existentielle et foi doctrinale" and "Jésus de l'histoire, fondement de la foi".
[58] T. F. Torrance, art. cit., 297.
[59] Rousselot, loc. cit.

immediately led to the dogma of the Trinity; "Trinitarian doctrine in itself can be justified in biblical terms only as the background for the doctrine of the Incarnation"— but that background is "indispensable".[60] This is, precisely, let us repeat, what revelation teaches us, as we find it recorded in the pages of Scripture and faithfully summed up in our Creed.[61] True, "the New Testament, while presupposing the pre-existing divine being and the divine person of Christ, does not consider them in terms of their origin and nature but in terms of the reparation they accomplish in salvation history."[62] It is no less true that through this manifestation we distinctly perceive the unique relationship between Jesus and God, the relationship between his person, the Father and the Spirit. So then, if one admits the distinction between the disciplines, as Mr. Cullmann proposes we should, one should specify, in the very spirit of the latter, that exegesis or, if one prefers, biblical theology, "cannot be self-sufficient but needs to be completed by dogmatic

[60] Hans Urs von Balthasar, *La Gloire et la croix* 1 (1965): 368. Cf. Bernard Lonergan, S.J., *De Deo trino*, 1, pars dogmatica (Rome: Gregorian University, 1964), where he establishes the objective equivalence of dogmatic truth and the revealed data.

[61] Cf. André Feuillet, *Le Prologue du quatrième Évangile*, 117; "Just as in the Book of Wisdom the revelation of Wisdom's nature is connected with the revelation of its action in history; 'What Wisdom is and how she came to be, I will now make known, without hiding any of the secrets from you; . . . I will set out knowledge of her, plainly, not swerving from the truth' (Wis 6:22). In the same way in the fourth Gospel our understanding of the Logos' saving intervention depends on our understanding of the mystery of his origin and his nature, hence of the very mystery of God."

[62] O. Cullmann, in *Choisir* (Geneva, August 1960) 21; and, speaking of Melanchthon, *Christologie du Nouveau Testament*, 285. On this idea of the history of salvation, cf. *La Révélation divine* (1968), 184–95.

reflection which must clarify the implications of the biblical data. This has been the object of the great councils",[63] which have themselves been prepared from the earliest times.

> Even though it be a light inaccessible to reason, the divine Trinity is the unique hypothesis which permits us to throw light in a phenomenologically correct manner, and without doing violence to the data given us, on the phenomenon of Christ as he makes himself constantly present in the Bible, in the Church and in history. Everywhere in Scripture . . . the absolute image of God is necessarily cosignified in the image of the economy of salvation which emerges. To suppose that Paul, for instance, had in view *only* a Trinity dependent upon the economy shows no less theological poverty than would dogmatics that offhandedly enter into the categories of the inner life of the Trinity without keeping in touch, as regards form and content, with the event of the Trinity manifested by the economy of salvation.[64]

In the Epistle to the Ephesians, St. Paul speaks of the "mystery of the benevolent will" of God toward men, and of the "economy of this mystery",[65] i.e., of the design hidden in God from all eternity, and of its fulfillment in the course of time, which is now revealed in Jesus Christ. When the Fathers of the Church in their turn speak of "the mystery of the economy" or, as

[63] Jean Daniélou, *Recherches de science religieuse* 55 (1967): 124–26.

[64] Hans Urs von Balthasar, *L'Amour seul est digne de foi* (trans. Robert Givord, coll. *Foi vivante*, Paris: Aubier, 1966), 111–12. Cf. *La Foi du Christ*: Total faith "goes beyond the Lutheran viewpoint of pure confidence and obviously goes much farther than 'holding as true' the dogmatic truths, a simple caricature of the Catholic concept." (Ibid., 1968, 14 ss.)

[65] Eph 1:9–10 and 3:8–11.

Clement of Alexandria calls it, "the economy of God", the "salvific economy",[66] they join into a single expression the two successive parts that made up Paul's idea.[67] Whereas, in this expression, "mystery" means more especially the totality of the divine plan and its ultimate end, "economy", according to the profane meaning of the word (i.e., organization, inner arrangement or administration), rather designates the totality of the means chosen by God for the execution of his plan, namely, the series of *magnalia Dei*, of deeds accomplished in view of man's salvation. For the Fathers, as for St. Paul, these deeds culminate in the "economy" par excellence,[68] in the unique fact of the Incarnation which Paul himself calls "the mystery of Christ".[69] For him as well as for the Fathers, this mystery of the economy introduces us into the mystery of theology.[70] The

[66] *Stromata*, bk. 2, chap. 2, 4; chap. 6, 29; bk. 3, chap. 5, 20. *Paedag.*, 8, 1, chap. 6, 25, 3, etc.

[67] Hippolytus, *Adversus haereses* (three times). Pseudo-Chrysostom (PG, 55:673 and 744). Jerome, *In die Paschae* (ed. G. Morin, *Anecdota Maredsolana* 3:2 and 416). Hesychius, *In Leviticum* (PG, 93:806 D). Gregory the Great, *Moralia in Job*, bk. 30, no. 21; *In evangelia*, hom. 25, no. 3: "Dispensationis ejus mysterium" (PL, 76:535 C and 1191 D). Cf. Alois Grillmeier, *Du "symbolisme" à la Somme théologique* (trans. H. Bourboulon), in *Église et tradition* (X. Mappus, Le Puy, 1963), 117.

[68] Origen, *In Ps.* 2, 8 (PG, 12:1108 C). Maximus, *In epist. quartam Dionysii* (PG, 4:532 B). Cf. *Const. apost.*, bk. 8, chap. 33, no. 4 (ed. Funk, 1:538); Gregory of Nyssa, *In Cant.* hom. 8 (PG, 44:948 C).

[69] Eph 3:2–5. Cf. Louis Bouyer, *Le Rite et l'homme* (Paris: Éd. du Cerf, 1962), 194–208.

[70] Cf. Thomas F. Torrance, "The Implication of Oikonomia for Knowledge and Speech of God in Early Christian Theology", in *Oikonomia, Heilsgeschichte als Thema der Theologie* (Hamburg, 1967), 223–38. (A book published in honor of Oscar Cullmann.)

"economic" aspect of this *"theologia"* naturally leads them to inquire into the "theological" depths of the "oikonomia". Knowledge of God's works cannot fail to throw some indirect light on God himself, a light which eliminates many unworthy or insufficient ideas rather than providing us with positive enlightenment.

> The mystery of the Trinity is the expression at one and the same time of the proximity and of the remoteness of God with regard to his creatures. For the Trinity is revealed to us only to the extent in which it makes possible our elevation and our redemption through the work of salvation. This Trinity of salvation presupposes a Trinity in and of itself, dwelling in light inaccessible, whose names, derived from this work of salvation, tell us nothing about the Trinity itself. So, it is in the mystery where God draws closest to us that we best perceive how infinitely far above us he is.[71]

When Christian reflection has succeeded in drawing from the the "mystery of the economy" the implications concerning "theology",[72] we can begin to study to a slight extent the Trinity "in itself"; and, proceeding according to a logical plan, we can do this even before coming to consider the work of human salvation. This process was begun, as we mentioned above, in the celebrated *Theological Discourses* of St. Gregory of Nazianzen and in the other Cappadocian Fathers.[73] We also find it to some extent in the work of St. Augustine. In 390, in

---

[71] Erik Przywara, *Philosophie de la religion catholique*, 2nd part, *in fine* (in German, Munich-Berlin, 1927; 65–66).

[72] Cf. A. Grillmeier, "De l'Oikonomia à la Theologia", in *Église et tradition* (Lyons-Paris: X. Mappus, 1963), 113–20.

[73] It was given added impetus at this time by the struggle against Arianism.

his *De moribus Ecclesiae*, Augustine still adhered entirely to the primacy of the "economic" point of view: he showed, in the Church, the Spirit leading to the Son, by whom the Father himself is known.[74] But in 393, in the *De fide et symbolo*, we find the order reversed: "To faith in the eternal realities we also add the temporal mission of our Lord, which he deigned to take upon himself for our sake and to fulfill for our salvation."[75] Again, in 396, in the *De agone christiano*:

> Faith . . . includes eternal realities which carnal man cannot understand and also temporal realities, past and future, which eternal Providence has accomplished and will accomplish for man's salvation. . . . Thus, believing in the immutable Trinity, let us also believe in its temporal action for the salvation of the human race.[76]

However, even though we adopt this logical and descending order, contrary to the ascending order of discovery, it should never make us forget that our knowledge of the Trinity always remains tied to our knowledge of its action, and that, from this action itself, the total and

---

[74] Bk. 1, chap. 17, no. 31: "This is the work of God's simple, pure charity. . . . Inspired by the Holy Spirit, she brings men to the Son, i.e., to the Wisdom of God by whom the Father himself is known." (Trans. B. Roland-Gosselin, Bibl. aug., 1:185.)

[75] Chap. 4, no. 6: "*Addimus itaque fidei rerum aeternarum etiam temporalem dispensationem Domini nostri, quam gerere nobis et ministrare pro nostra salute dignatus est.*" (J. Rivière, Bibl. aug., 9:32.) Augustine also says "*humana dispensatio*" (chap. 9, no. 16; 46).

[76] Chap. 13, no. 15, and chap. 17, no. 19: "*Credentes ergo incommutabilem Trinitatem, credamus etiam dispensationem temporalem pro salute generis humani.*" (Roland-Gosselin; 1:400–402 and 404.) "*Dispensatio temporalis*" translates οἰκονομία; cf. *De vera religione*, no. 19 (J. Pegon, 8, 50).

THE ECONOMIC TRINITY

final form will never be defined. The revelation of the economy of the mystery always leaves unsolved "the mystery of the economy".[77] *O altitudo!*

This is something which even the most intrepid theologians, those at least whom Catholic tradition recognizes as fully its own, have never forgotten. Continually, "the Greek Fathers connect the relationships between the Divine Persons with their relationships with creatures."[78] Their language is extremely cautious; one can say the same of Tertullian[79] and even of Justin. "The Creator of the universe", says the latter, "has no name because he was not engendered. . . . Father, God, Creator, Lord and Master are not names but titles suggested by his benefactions and his deeds."[80] The school to which St. Gregory of Nazianzen belonged is also the one which did battle to defend the unfathomable mystery of the divinity against the satisfied rationalism of the Anomeans, those men, says Theodoret, who made "a technology out of theology".[81] Gregory of Nazianzen himself declares that "no prophet ever penetrated the Divine Substance, as Scripture testifies; none of them either beheld or explained God's nature".[82] And his friend, Gregory

---

[77] Pseudo-Chrysostom (PG, 55:744); Hesychius (PG, 93:806 D); Gregory the Great (PL, 76:535 C).

[78] Théodore de Régnon, *Études sur le dogme de la Trinité* 3 (Paris, 1898): 70.

[79] Cf. Joseph Moingt, loc. cit.

[80] *Seconde Apologie*, chap. 6, nos. 1–2 (L. Pautigny, Paris: Picard, 1904), 160–61.

[81] Theodoret of Cyr, *Résumé des fables hérétiques*, bk. 4, chap. 3 (PG, 83:420 B).

[82] *Discours* 28, chap. 19 (PG, 36:52 B). *Discours* 31 (136–38, 160, 164).

of Nyssa, commenting on the Apostle's words about "the name which is above every name"[83] says: "The only thing appropriate to him is to believe that he is above every name, for the fact that he transcends every flight of thought and that he is beyond being comprehended under any name constitutes the proof of his greatness, a greatness that man cannot express".[84] Drawing the conclusion implied in this, John Chrysostom prescribes for every Christian the only conceivable attitude, which is one of submissive adoration. "Would you, a man, take part in scrutinizing God? You would outrage him if you curiously sought to grasp his essence. . . . The indiscretion which scrutinizes him draws down his indignation."[85] St. Hilary shows an equal reserve.[86] As for St. Augustine, in many passages he criticizes those who imagine that they can understand God.

> Better to recognize your ignorance than to presume to know. . . . To attain God through one's mind, in some slight degree, is a great blessing; but to comprehend him is impossible.[87] If you have understood, then it is not God![88] It is good for you to falter in praising God, for when you praise him without being able to explain what you would wish, your thought expands within you, and

[83] Phil 2:8.
[84] *Contra Eunomium*, bk. 12 (PG, 45:1108 B C); bk. 1 (365–68); many other passages. Cf. the works of Elie Moutsoulas, especially *Grégoire de Nysse interprète de la sainte Écriture* (in Greek, Athens, 1968). Basil, *Epist.* 234, no. 2 (PG, 32:869 B C). John Damascene, *De fide orthodoxa*, bk. 4.
[85] *Sur l'incompréhensibilité de Dieu* (SC, 28); especially hom. 2: 124, 126, 140.
[86] *De Trinitate*, bk. 11, chap. 47 (PL, 10:430–31).
[87] *Sermo* 117, no. 5 (PL 38:663–64).
[88] *Sermons* 52 and 53 (PL, 38:360, 370).

this enlargement makes you more capable of receiving the one you praise. . . .[89] God is ineffable; if, not being able to express what he is, you are still bound not to be silent, what remains for you to do except to rejoice in your heart that you can find no words?[90]

Nor should we accord too much importance to the reversal of procedure which we noticed in Augustine's works; this merely affects a certain order of catechetical exposition, not Augustine's fundamental attitude or the movement of his faith; and his great treatise *De Trinitate* itself explores the inner relationships of the divine Trinity only after an exploration of the human soul, as revelation alone allowed him to undertake. If we now question St. Bernard we shall find him as severe as the Cappadocians or St. John Chrysostom in condemning the audacity shown by man when he assumes the role of a "scrutator", of an *effractor Majestatis*; with the Book of Proverbs he predicts that such a man will be "crushed by glory". No doubt, he explains, it is possible for man to approach the Divinity, but he must do it *quasi admirans, non quasi scrutans*, and this presupposes that the initiative comes from God; the only thing proper for man, at any time, is to examine diligently the mystery of the divine will so as to obey it in all things.[91] Finally, we know that

---

[89] *In ps.* 145, no. 4. "*Expedit tibi deficere laudando Deum. . . . Cum enim laudas Deum et non explicas quod vis, extenditur in interiora cogitatio tua; ipsa extensio capaciorem te facit ejus quem laudas.*" (CCL, 40:2108.)

[90] *In ps.* 32, 2, *Sermo* 1, no. 8: "*Ineffabilis est, quem fari non potes; et si eum fari non potes et tacere non debes, quid restat nisi ut jubiles, ut gaudeat cor sine verbis, et immensa latitudo gaudiorum metas non habeat syllabarum?*" (CCL, 38:254.)

[91] *De consideratione*, bk. 5, no. 6; *In Cantica, Sermo* 62, chaps. 3 and 4, nos. 4, 5 and 6 (*Opera*, ed. Jean Leclercq, vol. 3 [Rome, 1963]:

St. Thomas Aquinas shows the link which unites the "processions" and the "missions", and we are also aware of the index of rigidly restrictive analogy to which he assigns all his investigations, apparently so sure of themselves, concerning the being of God.[92] In short, if the "economy" really opens to us the way leading to "theology", the latter always maintains in the last analysis—it should have maintained in all cases—the finest of the meanings it has in the Christian language: that of praise and silent adoration in the recognition of the unfathomable mystery.[93]

On the other hand, the very terms in which revelation is given to us, and the faith of the first generation of Christians which these terms express, suggest a certain "homogeneity" in the supraconceptual order "between God's being and his manifestations", or, as the Greek Fathers also put it, between the θεὸς πρός ἑαυτόν and the θεὸς πρός ἡμᾶς, the "God for himself" and the "God for us":

> No doubt . . . God remains a mystery; and the Apostle Paul speaks of the "profound depths of God". . . . But God reveals himself as a hidden God. He makes himself known in his mystery. . . . This permanent dialectic between the revealed God and the hidden God comes out

---

471; vol. 2 [1958]: 157–59). We find the same attitude in a number of medieval spiritual writers; H. de Lubac, *Exégèse médiévale* 3 (Paris: Aubier, 1961): 301–17; 2:638 where a beautiful passage from Bérengaud is quoted.

[92] Cf. *Prima*, 9, 13, a. 10, ad 5: "*Ipsam naturam Dei, prout in se est, neque Catholicus neque paganus cognoscit.*"

[93] See below, Chapter Seven. Cf. the *Profession de foi de Paul VI*, alluding to a text from the fourth Lateran Council, on "the inner life of the thrice-holy God, infinitely beyond all that we can conceive of by human understanding".

strongly in the Incarnation. . . . God is himself totally present in his Word. In his Word, God makes himself known as the holy and merciful God. He makes himself known as what he really is.[94]

This is precisely what Newman, following the whole of Catholic tradition, said in 1841: "Christianity is a supernatural history, almost a pageant; it tells us what its Author is by telling us what he has done."[95] Hans Urs von Balthasar repeats the same thing to us today:

> Beyond existence and essence the constitution of being becomes clearer; it appears to us only in "not holding onto itself", in going out of itself to take flesh in concrete finiteness. This permits finite creatures to receive and to understand him as he is in himself, as the one who does not seek to preserve himself. Thus are they initiated by him into the love that gives without ceasing. . . . Thanks to the sign of God who abases himself in becoming incarnate and empties himself in death and the absence of God, one can throw some light on why God, as the Creator of the world, has already gone out of himself and has descended below himself; it is because it corresponded to his own being, to his absolute essence, to reveal himself, in his sovereign and unfathomable liberty, as the measureless love which is . . . the height and depth, the length and breadth of Being itself.[96]

---

[94] Roger Mehl, *La Théologie protestante* (Paris: P.U.F., 1966), 10–11 and 62. For Mr. Mehl, this "homogeneity" is a postulate which is "undoubtedly much more stressed in Protestant than in Catholic theology".

[95] "The Tamworth Reading Room" (1841), in *Discussions and Arguments on Various Subjects*, 296; quoted by C. S. Dessain, *John Henry Newman* (London, 1966), 24.

[96] *L'Amour seul est digne de foi* (trans. R. Givord, coll. *Foi vivante*, Paris: Aubier, 1966), 183–86. Cf. Torrance, loc. cit.: "To think and

So, without ceasing to cry out in adoration with St. Paul, *"O altitudo"*, the Christian's faith dwells in St. John's affirmation: *"Deus caritas."*

The "economy", the unfolding of divine action in favor of man, comes about, one might say, in three phases. Hence three successive series of operations which are different in nature, and each of which is attributed by our Creed to one of the three Persons—even though it has always been understood that never does any one of them act separately from the other two. So, the works of creation belong to the Father, the works of redemption to the Son, the works of sanctification to the Holy Spirit. This is what Origen explains in the first book of his *Peri archôn*.[97] All through tradition we see this same schema used as the framework for elementary catechetical teaching as well as for more extensive works, such as the great treatise of Rupert of Deutz, *De Trinitate et operibus ejus*, in the twelfth century.[98] Each of the three series thus distinguished can be more or less fully detailed, but from the beginning they cover together the entire range of history, from creation to the final consummation. From the beginning, the framework is laid down. Before being adopted by the Apostles' Creed, it was used in the primitive preaching, such as we find it in Acts; the entire divine plan of salvation, as explained by the first witnesses of Christ, unfolds in "three historical stages which

---

speak κατ'οἰκονομίαν is to think and speak *truly* of God, that is, in accordance with his own nature as revealed in his acts and words."

[97] *Peri archôn*, bk. 1, chap. 3, nos. 5–7 (PG, 11:150–54; Koetschau, 36–60). Cf. St. Athanasius, *On the Incarnation and against the Arians*, chap. 8: "The Word became flesh so that we might receive the Spirit." (PG, 26:996 C.)

[98] PL, 167; cf. *De glorificatione Trinitatis et processione sancti Spiritus*, bk. 1, chap. 4 (PL, 169:17 B).

readily correspond to the three Persons".[99] This is the same framework Luther used, and there is no innovation whatever to be seen in the fact that "the trinitarian division adopted by" the leader of the Reformation in his *Little Catechism* makes the Church "only a consequence of the Holy Spirit".[100] For this is, in the Creed, a framework laid down once and for all, which can be neither transformed nor transcended. It measures and encloses the faith. The creed of the Christian faith, which explains the mystery of the "economy", is necessarily and strictly trinitarian.

Historians have generally recognized the inner logic of this process in the formation of the first two of the three parts making up the Creed. They properly observed how the texts grew by successive additions—more so in the case of the second part, since the christological formula had first been developed in its own right. But the third part of the Creed, the one that begins by mentioning the Holy Spirit, caused them more hesitation. Several writers saw in it nothing but the adding on of various *credenda*. This was Kattenbusch's view not long ago; for him, the Holy Spirit himself simply designated, in the most ancient formulas, one of the benefits in which Christians were said to share.[101] More recently, J. N. D. Kelly, in a study which is otherwise quite remarkable, seeks to show how the mention of the Holy Spirit changed in character belatedly in order to copy those of the Father and the Son, from the period

---

[99] Pierre Benoit, *Les origines du symbole des apôtres dans le Nouveau Testament*, loc. cit., 45.

[100] Cf. Émile G. Léonard, *Histoire générale du protestantisme* 1 (Paris: P.U.F., 1961): 109.

[101] Cf. Jules Lebreton, *Histoire du dogme de la Trinité*, 4th ed., 2:170–71.

when, the metaphysical doctrine about the Trinity having been elaborated, they wanted to find it already preformed in the creed of the faith.[102]

These opinions have been received favorably by one of the best experts of the Creed's history, Dom Bernard Capelle.[103] They are rather attractive on the surface. When we read, for instance, certain sermons by St. Caesarius of Arles, we might be tempted to agree with them. Caesarius, in fact, commenting on the article about the Holy Spirit, says that it was formulated with the purpose of excluding the heresies which refused to recognize in the Holy Spirit the fullness of the divinity.

> Credo in Spiritum sanctum. Ad excludenda haereticorum omnium calamitosa commenta, eodem verbo credulitatis, quo in principio sui symbolum Patrem honoravit et Filium, in conclusione textus sui nunc honorat Spiritum sanctum, cum ait: "Credo in Spiritum sanctum." Ne inferioris ergo fortasse contumeliam pateretur, jure eum sibi aequaliter vindicare et deitatis ostendit plenitudinem, et Patris ac Filii dignitatem. . . .[104]

But it would be imprudent to seek in these words of a popular preacher any chronological indication.[105]

---

[102] *Early Christian Creeds* (Oxford, 1950), 152–53.

[103] In *Bulletin de théologie ancienne et médiévale* 6 (1951): 292 (no. 988).

[104] *Sermo* 9 (CCL, 103:49–50): "I believe in the Holy Spirit. To eliminate the unfortunate commentaries of all the heretics, the Creed makes use of the same word of faith that, at the beginning, it used to honor the Father and the Son; now, in concluding, it honors the Holy Spirit in the same way by saying, 'I believe in the Holy Spirit'. So that he may not have to undergo the affront of being treated as an inferior partner, the Holy Spirit rightly claims for himself, in full equality, both the fullness of the Divinity and the dignity of the Father and the Son."

[105] We find a similar perspective, concerning the entire Creed, in

THE ECONOMIC TRINITY

Caesarius reordered history in his own fashion for the instruction of his hearers, not by retarding the date of the formula, but rather by antedating the heresies to which it was supposedly opposed at the outset; this is an anachronism similar to the one by which he explained the entire composition of the Creed.[106] The explanations given by Kattenbusch and Kelly are contradicted by the fact that, before any development, the Church used baptismal formulas which were quite strictly trinitarian, as we saw in the preceding chapter. It is true that the Holy Spirit was not considered at first "in himself"; it is equally true that his divinity was not declared by the Doctors in so many words, in a theoretical and distinct manner, save at a rather late period; this was due to scruples about language, something we find admitted very frankly by St. Cyril of Jerusalem. In one of his Catecheses he says:

> Let us say nothing about the Holy Spirit except what is found in the Scriptures. If something is not found there, let us not delve into it with curiosity. It was the Holy Spirit himself who spoke in the Scriptures. Now he said what he wished about himself and what we might be able to understand. So, let us say what he said, and as for what he did not say, let us not be audacious enough to say it.[107]

The same declarations can be found under the pen of

Paul Tillich, who thinks that the Church adopted it as a "protective formulation" against heresies, at a time when it was "a question of life or death" for the Christian faith. That would be to retard or to falsify the *dogmatic* faith of the Church. Cf. *Systematic theology* 1:30. Cf. Tavard, 148.

[106] See above, Chapter One, note 49.
[107] Translation by Théodore de Régnon, *Catéchèse*, 16, chap. 2.

St. Basil in his two treatises on the Holy Spirit.[108] These passages show both the reserve observed out of respect for Scripture and the genuine belief in the divine personality of the Spirit, the inspirer of the Scriptures. This divine personality was then recognized *in actu*, without any hesitation, by the living faith which was manifested in liturgical prayer and of which our Creed is precisely one of the main expressions.[109]

But even those who today recognize the rigorous parallelism between the mention of the Holy Spirit and the two preceding mentions of the Father and the Son do not always think that the various articles which follow are organically connected with the Holy Spirit, as enumerating the works proper to the third Person. In the eyes of a number of authors, the third part of the Creed is of a different type from the first two. Its structure, if we can even use that word, is considered to be much more loose.

For H. Lietzmann, for instance, if some of the Creed's formulas give to the Spirit a qualifier such as "Paraclete, Sanctifier, inspirer of the prophets" in order to establish a better symmetry with the articles concerning the Father

---

[108] Cf. Bernard Pruche, O.P., Sources chrétiennes, 17. See also Gregory of Nazianzen, *Eloge de Basile*, chap. 69, nos. 3–4 (ed. A. Boulenger, 207). Gregory of Nyssa, *Contra Eunomium* (PG, 45:468, 476 B C, etc.). Nicetas of Remesiana, *De Spiritus sancti potentia*, no. 2 (PL, 52:853).

[109] This, we repeat, does not mean that a long elaboration was not necessary in order to arrive at the conceptual precisions of trinitarian theology. "Christians were perfectly aware of their trinitarian faith, even though they did not argue about theological propositions concerning it." J. Moingt, 1:65; on Tertullian, 66: "The ample space given to the Holy Spirit in his works shows that his faith in the latter was in no way deficient."

THE ECONOMIC TRINITY

and the Son, the other additions, which are more important, mention various beliefs considered fundamental enough to be inserted into the profession of faith; but there is no intention to indicate any direct or special relationship between them and the third Person of the Trinity.[110] Fr. Joseph de Ghellinck also thinks they simply added here and there, as an appendix to the Creed, after the mention of the Holy Spirit, "a list of other benefits conferred by the Savior" because "great importance was attached to these [points]". Fr. de Ghellinck does admit that this was done "in imitation of the other two articles" which are also laden with "additions"; but here no connection exists between the works and the Person, as was the case in the other two sections.[111] Fr. Jules Lebreton could discern better a certain link between the Holy Spirit and the various things mentioned after him: the Church, the forgiveness of sins, the resurrection of the body . . . , but, in his opinion, the connection was a merely extrinsic one. All these things were linked, in the profession of faith, to the "prophetic Spirit" but only "in memory of the prophecies"; they were mentioned in this place not so much as works of the Spirit but as mysteries foretold by him in the ancient Scriptures.[112]

The main defect in this theory is that it seeks to be exclusive. There is some truth in it, as we can see in this

---

[110] Cf. J. de Ghellinck, 173–74. Still, Lietzmann (2:121–22) comes close to the explanation which we are defending.

[111] J. de Ghellinck, 229.

[112] In A. Fliche and V. Martin, *Histoire de l'Église*, 1:370, n. 4. Cf. his *Histoire du dogme de la Trinité*, 4th ed., 2:170–71, where he refutes Kattenbusch but limits himself to excluding a purely Economic interpretation of the Spirit.

trinitarian text by St. Justin on baptism: It is given, says Justin, "in the name of God the Father and Master of the universe, . . . and in the name of Jesus Christ, who was crucified under Pontius Pilate, . . . and in the name of the Holy Spirit, who through the prophets predicted the whole history of Jesus."[113] St. Irenaeus uses nearly the same language in a passage of *Adversus haereses*,[114] and toward the end of his *Demonstratio* he says of the heretics that they "do not acknowledge the Holy Spirit, which is to say they scorn the prophecies".[115] Origen, too, speaks of Christians who agree in recognizing the essential truths "about the one God . . . , and about Jesus Christ . . . , and also about the Holy Spirit, namely, that it is he who was at first in the patriarchs and prophets and who then was given to the Apostles".[116] To the Holy Spirit, Rufinus explicitly attributes only the inspiration of the Scriptures, the Old and New Testaments.[117] We may note, too, that in the Nicean-Constantinople Creed, the article on the Holy Spirit, before mentioning the Church, ends with the words "who spoke through the prophets". It should however be noted that the prophecy attributed to the Holy Spirit, when it is spelled out, concerns the "history of Jesus" rather than the subjects enumerated at the end of the Creed. But we further believe that in reality the con-

---

[113] I *Apol.*, chap. 61, nos. 10–13 (Pautigny, 130).

[114] Bk. 1, chap. 10, no. 1: "et in Spiritum sanctum, qui per prophetas praedicavit dispositiones Dei" (PG, 7:550 A).

[115] *Demonstratio*, chap. 100 (ed. Froidevaux, SC, 62:170). See above, PL, 9:7–8.

[116] *In Matt. comm. series*, chap. 33 (E. Klostermann, 61).

[117] *Expositio symboli*, chaps. 34–36 (CCL, 20:170–71).

nection between these subjects and the Holy Spirit is more intimate and more specific. For these subjects deal with the works proper to the Holy Spirit—or rather, let us say, with his own proper work, since, whatever their number, they form a whole[118]—just as in the two preceding parts, we had the enumeration of the works proper to the Father and to the Son.

Let us observe, in reading through the *Refutation of the Pseudo-Gnosis*,[119] that great treatise by St. Irenaeus which is more commonly called his *Adversus haereses*, and which we have already quoted under that title several times, the role that the author attributes to the Holy Spirit in the totality of the divine "economy". For Irenaeus, the Spirit is, without doubt, the one who inspired the prophets and guided the ancient Fathers in the ways of justice; but he is also the one who, "at the end of time, was poured forth in a new manner on our humanity in order to renew man over all the face of the earth in God's sight".[120] He is the one who sanctifies, who gives life, who resuscitates the body, who makes man immortal. It is communion with him that transforms our whole being by making it like to God.[121] We should recall as well the significant expression in the treatise of St. Hippolytus *Against Noet*, where he speaks

[118] See below, Chapter Six.

[119] For the word *gnosis*, which comes from St. Paul, had at that time an orthodox meaning. Cf. Louis Bouyer, "Gnosis, le sens orthodoxe de l'expression jusqu'aux Pères alexandrins", in *The Journal of Theological Studies* (Oct. 1953), 188–203.

[120] *Demonstratio*, chap. 6 (ed. Froidevaux, SC, 62:40).

[121] *Adversus haereses*, bk. 4, chap. 33, no. 7 (PG, 7:1077 A B); bk. 5, chap. 8, no. 1 (1141–42); chap. 9, no. 1 (1144 B C); chap. 12, no. 2 (1152–53).

of "the third economy, which is the grace of the Holy Spirit";[122] and that other passage in Tertullian on the sanctifying Spirit, whose role is to sanctify those who believe in the three Persons.[123] Or, closer to the beginning, we might even refer to the Gospel of St. John where the Holy Spirit is the Spirit of Jesus, the one whom Jesus will send, or whom the Father will send in his name, in order to take his place when he himself has returned to the Father; the one who not only will lead Jesus' disciples to complete truth but who, abiding with them and in them, will dispense to them all the good things that Jesus has won for them: "All that he shares with you will be taken from what is mine."[124] Thus the Spirit is in truth the first of the gifts which come to us from the redemption accomplished by Christ; in other words, it is indeed in the "economy" that he is revealed to us. He is, says Irenaeus, the gift that was given to the Church when the Apostles received their mission, "so that we might receive through him the image and seal of the Father and of the Son". He is the Gift par excellence— *Altissimi Donum Dei*—whom the believers receive from the Church in baptism, and all the mysteries of baptism and of the Christian life are summed up in this *donatio Spiritus*.[125] But this is a personal gift; and if all the gifts

---

[122] Chap. 14.

[123] *Adversus Praxean*, chap. 2, no. 1: "*Spiritum sanctum Paracletum, sanctificatorem fidei eorum qui credunt in Patrem et Filium et Spiritum sanctum.*" (CCL, 2:1100).

[124] Jn 14:16–17; 14:26; 16:7–14.

[125] *Adversus haereses*, bk. 3, chap. 17, nos. 2–3; chap. 24, no. 1; bk. 4, chap. 33, no. 7; bk. 5, chap. 20, no. 1 (PG, 7:930, 966, 1077 A, 1177 B). On the Spirit, the Gift of God, see St. Augustine, *De fide et symbolo*, chap. 9, no. 19 (Bibl. aug., 9:56–60). See below, Chapter Six.

which are enumerated afterward are summed up in him, it is because they all flow from him. We should also reread the Acts of the Apostles. From the first pages we hear the promise that Jesus made to his disciples before his Ascension; they will soon be baptized in the Holy Spirit, whose power will come upon them—and the entire book, which relates the first expansion of the Church, celebrates at the same time the action of the Holy Spirit, in particular with respect to the admission of all categories of persons into the one Christian community in view of the forgiveness of sins.[126] This is so true that the book of Acts has been called both "the book of the Church" and "the Gospel of the Spirit". Thus it was entirely natural, and indeed in some way necessary, to place under the aegis of the Spirit, in the third and last part of the Creed, the group of truths relating to man's salvation and to the means of his salvation, namely, the effects of the redemptive work accomplished in his time by Jesus Christ.

There is nothing here, in principle, either artificial or belated. All this is entirely "according to the spirit of the primitive Church". "All these affirmations about the means of salvation simply amplify the first such statement, which deals with the Holy Spirit." He "takes possession of individuals through the forgiveness of their sins and brings about his final effect by the resurrection of the body."[127] If the list of these effects or works of the Holy Spirit, as we recite them today, was

---

[126] Acts 1:5 and 8; 2:38; 10:44–45; 15:8; 19:6, etc.

[127] Josef A. Jungmann, 145 and 148. Cf. William Durand, *Rationale*, bk. 4, chap. 25, nos. 24–25: "*Ille enim docet, ille sanctificat, ille vivificat, ille peccata remittit, per hunc resurrectionem in gloria, per hunc consequimur vitam aeternam*", etc.

not established without some hesitations, these hesitations are not, for all that, an indication of a period when the faith was still seeking expression in purely empirical fashion. Far from being a certain number of points added to the Holy Spirit without any inner necessity, these points would rather have been subtracted from it in order to give the Creed better balance by dividing the roles of the three Persons more equally.

Here, for instance, is what we read in St. Irenaeus:

> The Church . . . , spread throughout the universe even to the ends of the world, received from the Apostles and their disciples this faith in only one God, the Father almighty, "who made the heavens, the earth, the seas and all that they contain" (Ps 145:6)—and in one Jesus Christ, the Son of God, incarnate for our salvation—and in the Holy Spirit, who announced through the prophets the "dispositions" ["economies"] of God, and the coming of Christ, his birth from the Virgin, his Passion, his Resurrection from the dead, his Ascension in his body into heaven, and his return from heaven in the glory of the Father to recapitulate all things (Eph 1:10) and the resurrection of the bodies of all the human race.[128]

Whether it was, in St. Irenaeus' mind, because the Spirit had predicted them through the prophets, or per-

---

[128] *Adversus haereses*, bk. 1, chap. 10, no. 1: "*Ecclesia . . . per universum orbem usque ad fines terrae seminata, et ab apostolis et a discipulis eorum accepit eam fidem, quae est in unum Deum, Patrem omnipotentem, 'qui fecit coelum et terram et mare et omnia quae in eis sunt'—et in unum Jesum Christum Filium Dei, incarnatum pro nostra salute—et in Spiritum sanctum, qui per prophetas praedicavit dispositiones Dei et adventum, et eam quae ex virgine generationem, et passionem, et resurrectionem a mortuis, et in carne in caelos ascensionem dilecti Jesu Christi Domini nostri, et de caelis in gloria Patris adventum ejus, ad recapitulanda universa et ressuscitandam omnem carnem humani generis*" (PG, 7:550 A B).

THE ECONOMIC TRINITY

haps also because he himself was their author,[129] the Saint in this passage has placed the redemptive acts after the mention of the Spirit and not after that of the Son, of whom he simply says that "he became incarnate for our salvation". We shall have to inquire farther on where this form of composition came from. Irenaeus himself does not always follow it. It will quickly be abandoned, in the places where it had once prevailed, and replaced by an arrangement similar to the one we now know. This transformation, which seems to have been completed by the time of Tertullian, was probably Roman in origin; and it seems to be explained by a desire to combat the Adoptionist heresy by bringing out more forcefully the personal power of Jesus Christ in his redemptive acts.[130] The order thus adopted is, furthermore, more natural. It is the order which controls, for instance, the *De Trinitate et operibus ejus*, by Rupert of Deutz, who sets forth at full length the *opus tripartitum Trinitatis*.[131] This same arrangement is found in the sixteenth-century Roman Catechism:

> As our ancestors observed . . . , the Creed seems to have been divided into three parts precisely so that the first might deal with the first Divine Person and the admirable

[129] The first of these two explanations is that of J. Lebreton, *Histoire du dogme de la Trinité*, 3rd ed., 2:156, which here seems better established. It would seem that both explanations can refer to this other passage, bk. 4, chap. 33, no. 7: "*In Spiritu Dei, qui praestat agnitionem veritatis, qui dispositiones Patris et Filii exposuit, secundum quas aderat generi humano, quemadmodum vult Pater.*" (1077 A B.)

[130] Cf. J. Lebreton, 161–62.

[131] Prologue (PL, 167:198–200): "*Est autem tripartitum Trinitatis opus, a conditione mundi usque ad finem ejus.*" Cf. *In Genesim*, bk. 2, chap. 1 (167, 247 A D). *De divinis officiis*, bk. 7, chap. 10 (170, 189 D).

work of creation; the second with the second Divine Person and the mystery of man's redemption; and the third with the third Divine Person, the source of our sanctification.[132]

God is one, and none of the three Divine Persons can be conceived, in himself or in his operations, as separate from the other two. On this general principle, all Christian tradition is unanimous. "The first Christians taught that each of the three Persons formally took part in all the external operations of the Divinity."[133] The Fathers, of both East and West, were as positive on this point as Latin Scholasticism would be later on. Thus St. Irenaeus says on the one hand that "the Spirit prepares man for the Son of God, that the Son leads him to the Father, that the Father then gives him eternal life", but he also specifies on the other hand, in the same chapter, that in all these various phases it is always the one God who is manifesting himself, "the Spirit at work, the Son fulfilling his ministry, the Father approving", all this so that man may be "rendered perfect in view of his salvation".[134] In another passage Irenaeus attributes to each of the three Persons, from a certain particular angle, the universal activity of the Divinity: *"Super omnia quidem Pater, et ipse est caput Christi; per omnia autem Verbum, et ipse est caput Ecclesiae; in omnibus autem nobis Spiritus, et ipse est aqua viva quam praestat Dominus in se recte credentibus et diligentibus."*[135]

---

[132] First part, chap. 1, no. 3.

[133] Théodore de Régnon, *Études sur le dogme de la Trinité* 3:82. That is true even for what concerns the work of Christ.

[134] *Adversus haereses*, bk. 4, chap. 20, nos. 5 and 6 (SC, 100:638 and 644).

[135] Op. cit., bk. 5, chap. 18, no. 2 (PG, 7:1173 A). Note that the Spirit is at the same time immanent to the faithful, as the Gift of the

THE ECONOMIC TRINITY

More specific yet, on this point, are other witnesses to the patristic tradition. Thus St. Cyril of Jerusalem, explaining to his catechumens that "the economy of our salvation, which comes to us from the Father, Son and Holy Spirit, is indivisible and common" because "the Father, through the Son and with the Holy Spirit, gives all things; the gifts do not come, therefore, some from the Father, others from the Son and still others from the Holy Spirit; for the salvation is in fact one, the power is one, the faith is one."[136] St. Chromatius of Aquilea: "The Father does nothing without the Son, nothing without the Holy Spirit; for the work of the Father is that of the Son, and the work of the Son is that of the Spirit. It is one and the same grace that comes to us from the Trinity. We are saved now by the Trinity because it is by the Trinity that we were made from the beginning."[137] With perhaps more subtlety, St. Ambrose affirms the common operation of the Trinity in a formula which implicitly distinguishes the three Persons, thanks to the use of three different prepositions: *"Omnis creatura, et ex voluntate, et per operationem, et in virtute est Trinitatis"*.[138] Everything comes *from* the Father, *through* the Son, *in* the Spirit. It is through the Son that the Father created the

---

Lord, and transcendent in himself, as are the Father and the Son. Cf. Origen, *In Cantica*, bk. 3: *"Idem namque ipse qui ibi Trinitas propter distinctionem personarum, hic unus Deus intelligitur pro unitate substantiae."* (Baehrens, 214.)

[136] *Dix-septième Catéchèse*, chap. 5, *Dix-huitième Catéchèse*, chap. 29: "The true life is that which the Father, by means of the Son, in the Holy Spirit, causes to spring forth with heavenly gifts for all." (PG, 33:976 A, 1049 B.) Gregory of Nazianzen: "The creating Spirit does all that God does." (PG, 36:168 A.) Gregory of Nyssa, *Non tres dii* (PG, 45:125 C).

[137] Homily 18 (ed. J. Lemarié, *Revue bénédictine* 73 (1963): 196.

[138] *De Spiritu sancto*, bk. 2, chap. 9 (CSEL, 79:125; PL, 16:764).

world and brought about salvation; and if one can say with St. Paul that Christians are *"in Christo"*, this is because he is talking about the Risen Christ who has become "lifegiving Spirit",[139] and because, reciprocally, the Spirit is a "communicaton of Christ".[140] Rufinus of Aquilea, when explaining the Creed, says approximately the same thing about the moment of the Incarnation: "See then the Trinity cooperating with itself. . . . It is the Trinity which is hidden everywhere and appears everywhere; distinct by the names and the Persons but inseparable by the substance of the deity."[141] And St. Augustine, who has at times been unjustly accused of a unitary tendency, in fact finds a "trinitarian economy" everywhere, in creation itself, in the physical world as well as the spiritual.[142] "Many things are said about the Son because the Son assumed human nature; but it is the

---

[139] François Szabó, S.J., *Le Christ créateur chez saint Ambroise* (*Studia Ephemeridis* "Augustinianum" 2, Rome, 1968); especially 103–13, where he explains the passage in Ephesians 2:10: "Created in Christ Jesus".

[140] Irenaeus, *Adversus haereses*, bk. 3, chap. 24, no. 1 (PG, 7:966 B).

[141] *In symbolum apostolorum*, chap. 8 (on Lk 1:35): *"Vide ergo cooperantem sibi invicem trinitatem. . . . Haec est Trinitas ubique latens, ubique apparens, vocabulis personisque discreta, inseparabilis substantia deitatis."* (CCL, 20:145–61.)

[142] Thus, at the end of his *De vera religione*, in his *De Genesi contra Manichaeos*, or in *De Genesi ad litteram*, etc. "The theme of 'trinitarian creation' will never disappear from Augustine's work but will grow more and more precise until the *De Trinitate*": Olivier du Roy, *L'Intelligence de la foi en la Trinité selon saint Augustin, genèse de sa théologie trinitaire jusqu'en 391* (*Études augustiniennes*, Paris, 1966), 421. For Augustine, the work of creation prefigures the mystery of the redemption; this is why he explained (the former) to the neophytes in a series of paschal sermons. Cf. C. Lambot, in *Mélanges* offered to Miss Christine Mohrmann (Utrecht-Antwerp, 1963), 213–21.

entire Trinity which contributed to the Incarnation of the Son, for the works of the Trinity are inseparable."[143]

In the twelfth century, Rupert of Deutz set forth with clarity the two sides of traditional thinking: he explained how "the operation proper to each of the Persons" does not prevent "the inseparable operation of the entire Trinity".

> Man's regeneration as a whole, while the work of the entire Trinity, is nonetheless the operation proper to the Holy Spirit. For the Holy Trinity, as Leo the Great says, shared in the work concerning man: the Father created him, the Son redeemed him, the Holy Spirit sanctified him, inflaming him with his fire. And yet, if the Father created man, it was in union with the Son and the Spirit. The Son redeemed him in union with the Father and the Spirit; and finally the Spirit regenerates and enlightens him in union with the Father and the Son.[144]

If there is inevitably something rather artificial in these kinds of explanations and allocations,[145] they at least follow the plan of the Creed and furthermore are accompanied by complementary formulas which balance

---

[143] *Sermo Guelferb.*, 1, no. 7: "*De Filio multa sunt dicta, quia Filius suscepit hominem. . . . Sed carnem Filii tota Trinitas fecit: inseparabilia enim sunt opera Trinitatis.*" (Morin, 446.) This reminds one of the verse in Romance 8 of St. John of the Cross: "The Three have accomplished their work, but it was done in the One." (*Oeuvres*, ed. by Fr. Lucien-Marie [1967], 953.)

[144] *De divinis officiis*, bk. 7, chap. 10 (PL, 170:189 D). Cf. *De glorificatione Trinitatis*, bk. 1, chap. 16: "*Tantum in effectum operis distantia agnoscenda est processionis utriusque, scilicet Filii et Spiritus sancti. . . . A sanctificatione vero naturae rationalis (quod opus per Spiritum sanctum fit), nondum Pater et Filius requievit, nondum cessavit.*" (PL, 169:28–29.)

[145] Cf. Hans Urs von Balthasar, *La Gloire et la croix* 1:557.

them. The Scholastic doctrine of "attribution" or appropriation is only a particular application of the general principle which governs this balance and which Rupert laid down for us.[146] The principle has at times been wrongly interpreted, in more recent centuries, as though all the divine activity *ad extra* was caused by the single divine nature, to the exclusion as it were of the Persons. At least it was explained that way in matters relating to the "natural" sphere or in the order of "creation". This, however, is not the true meaning. The principle simply maintains that, since God is one, none of the three Persons is to be conceived of, whether *ad intra* or *ad extra*, as separated from the other two. St. Thomas Aquinas explains this with reference to creation: "To create", he says, "is proper to God according to his being, which is his essence, and this is common to the three Persons; consequently [creation] is not the work proper to one of the Three, but the common work of the entire Trinity. . . . God the Father creates through his Word, who is the Son, and through his love, which is the Holy Spirit; the processions of the Persons are therefore the reasons for the production of creatures, insofar as they include God's essential attributes, which are his knowledge and will." And a little farther on: "As the divine nature, while being common to all three Persons,

---

[146] We can find another expression of it in a spiritual writer of the seventeenth century, the Capuchin François d'Argentan, *Conférences théologiques et spirituelles sur les grandeurs de Dieu* (4th ed. [1750], 182), 10th conference, art. 3: "The work of creation is attributed principally to the Father. . . . The great work of redemption is attributed particularly to the Son. . . . Finally, it is to the Holy Spirit that the work of the justification and even the glorification of souls is attributed."

is nevertheless proper to them according to a certain order, insofar as the Son receives it from the Father and the Holy Spirit from both of them, so it is with regard to the creative power: although common to the three Persons, it is nevertheless proper to each one according to a certain order."[147]

We have already stated this at the end of the previous chapter. It is not a "God-nature" that acts, but a tri-personal God whose nature is one. In any event, whatever may be the exact manner in which the works of the three Persons may be allocated among them, it is certain that from the beginning it was the revelation of the Trinity in its works and by its works that gave to our Creed the essence of its structure. The three primordial articles are the mother-cells of all the subsequent developments. It is to them that all the theological speculation we have yet evolved must be referred; and to them all future speculation in the Church must return.[148]

---

[147] *Summa theologica*, Prima pars, q. 45, art. 6, c. and ad 2; (*Opera*, ed. Fretté et Maré, vol. 1, Paris: Éd. Vivès, 1871), 304. The editors' "conclusio" stresses the essentialistic tendency of this doctrine. "*Creare commune est toti Trinitati, at personis divinis, nonnisi ut essentialia attributa includunt, scientiam sc. et voluntatem, convenire potest.*" As regards the Fathers, one might consult: Gervais Aeby, *Les Missions divines de saint Justin à Origène* (Paradosis, 12; Fribourg, 1958); Jean Louis Maier, *Les Missions divines selon saint Augustin* (Paradosis, 16; Fribourg, 1960).

[148] See Chapter Seven below.

CHAPTER FOUR

BELIEF AND FAITH

From three primary articles, three mother-cells, our Creed has been formed. They constitute its entire structure. But this acknowledgment still does not provide us with its essence.

We must now turn our attention to a grammatical detail, a detail repeated three times, which throws into bold relief these three primary articles and distinguishes them from all others, to the point of establishing between them and the others, at least at first glance and in appearance, a kind of abyss. It is the little preposition "in", repeated three times: "I believe in God . . . in Jesus Christ . . . in the Holy Spirit." So too in the Latin version of the Nicean Creed (325): *"Credimus in unum Deum Patrem omnipotentem. . . . Et in unum Dominum Jesum Christum. . . . Et in Spiritum sanctum."*[1] So too in the African creed used in the Church at Hippo, such as we can reconstruct it from one of St. Augustine's sermons: *"Credo in Deum Patrem omnipotentem. . . . Credo in filium ejus Jesum Christum Dominum nostrum. . . . Credo in Spiritum sanctum."*[2]

---

[1] Giuseppe Luigi Dossetti, *Il Simbolo di Nicea e di Constantinopoli*, edizione critica (Herder, 1967). So too in the translation of the Creed of Constantinople (381). See also St. Hilary, *De synodis*, chaps. 29, 34 and 38 (PL, 10:502–10).

[2] *Sermo* 215 (S. Poque, Saint Augustine, *Sermons sur la Pâque*, SC, 116 [1966]: 63). Cf. Irenaeus, *Adversus haereses*, bk. 1, chap. 10, no. 1: *"Hanc fidem, quae est in Deum Patrem . . . et in . . . Jesum Christum*

As nearly always happens, this distinctive form may have developed gradually, may have taken a considerable while before being definitively fixed; and we come across various exceptions, some even rather late in date (of which more will be said in Chapter Six). Still, in the Latin Church, this form characterizes the great majority of the ancient formulas of the creed, as well as that which was finally adopted as our present text. St. Ambrose's *Explanatio symboli*, which is so direct, connects it closely with the triple mention of the Divine Persons.

"Well, then, you believe in the Father; you also believe in the Son; and in the third place? And in the Holy Spirit. All the sacraments you receive you will receive in this Trinity."[3]

Examples of this kind could be multiplied.[4] True, in some of the texts the preposition "in" is followed, not by the accusative, but by the ablative case. We find several examples of this in Rufinus of Aquilea: "*Credo in Deo Patre . . . , et in Christo Jesu . . . , et in Spiritu sancto.*"[5] In the Latin Vulgate version of the Bible, the ablative is the case usually employed for formulas such as "*credere in*

. . . *et in Spiritum sanctum* (PG, 7:550 A). Pseudo-Fulgentius (eighth-ninth century) (PL, Suppl., 3:1371–76). Pseudo-Augustine (ninth century; PL, Suppl., 2:1361–63).

[3] No. 5: "*Ergo vide: Credis in Patrem, credis et in Filium. Et quid tertio? Et in Spiritum sanctum. Quaecumque accipis sacramenta, in hac Trinitate accipies.*" Ambrose adds: "*Nemo te fallat! Vides ergo unius operationis, unius sanctificationis, unius majestatis esse venerabilem Trinitatem.*" (Botte, SC, 25 bis:52).

[4] Cf. Pseudo-Maximus of Turin, *homilia* 83 (PL, 57:433–36). Other identical formulas in the work of Badcock already cited, 2nd ed., 24, 33, 63–64, 69, 72, 97–102, 158–60, 199–200. See also J. E. L. Oulten, in *The Journal of Theological Studies* 39 (1938): 239ff.

[5] *Comm. in symbolum apostolorum* (CCL, 20:135, 137, 141, 169).

nomine Filii Dei" or *"in Deo sperare"*.[6] But this shift from the accusative to the ablative, rather frequent during the first centuries of our era,[7] does not in any way modify the meaning. What matters here is the word "in". It is in fact the significance of this "in" that Rufinus' commentary is very particular to bring out.

"Just as one says that he believes in God the Father (*in Deo Patre*) by using the preposition 'in', so too one is reminded that he believes also in Christ (*in Christo*) his Son, and so also in the Holy Spirit (*in Spiritu sancto*)."[8]

It would even seem that this ablative following "in" underlines all the better the contrast between it and the simple accusatives which follow the mention of the Holy Spirit. In the very formulation of the Creed, the change from one case to the other appears to have been common. Thus, St. Hilary of Poitiers, in the same paragraph where he affirms that God the Father and God the Son are *"unum de fide nostra"*, i.e., "inseparable in our faith", "forming a single object for our faith", reminds us that the Christian believes *"in Deum Patrem"* and that he hopes *"in Christo Dei Filio"*.[9] Other examples are even more characteristic. In the three baptismal interrogations spoken of in the ἀποστολικὴ παράδεις (*Apostolic Tradition*) of St. Hippolytus, the Latin translation of the second interrogation reads: *"Credis in Christum Jesum. . . ?"* and

---

[6] Thus Ps 55: *"In Deo speravi, non timebo quid faciat mihi homo."*

[7] Christine Mohrmann, in *Mélanges Joseph de Ghellinck* (1951), 1:278. See also Victrice de Rouen, *Liber de lande sanctorum* (vv. 390–400): *"et in Spiritu sancto"* (Badcock, 97).

[8] Op. cit., chap. 33: *"Sicut dictum est in Deo Patre credi, adjecta praepositione in, ita et in Christo Filio ejus, ita et in Spiritu sancto memoratur."* (CCL, 20:169.)

[9] *De Trinitate*, bk. 1, chap. 17 (PL, 10:37 B C).

of the third: "*Credis in Spiritu sancto?*".[10] Again, in his *Explanation of the Creed*, Nicetas of Remesiana speaks of the man who "*credit in Christo*" but says, a few lines farther on, "*Credis ergo in Deum Patrem*, then, "*Credens ergo in Deum Patrem, statim te confiteberis credere et in Filium ejus Jesum Christum. . . .*" "*Credis et in Spiritum sanctum.*"[11] So, both the ablative and the accusative were used in turn in precisely the same context to refer to the same Person. Evidently, this rather commonplace change of case reveals no special intention. Consequently, the important thing is not the case, accusative or ablative, even though the former is in itself more expressive; the important thing is the preposition "in". It is a transcription of the Greek εἰς, and we transcribe it similarly in both French and English: "I believe *in* God, *in* Jesus Christ. . . ." In French, it has become the custom to say next: "Je crois *au* Saint Esprit", but this is a grammatical inaccuracy which is undoubtedly due to a simple concern for euphony,[12] and which has most fortunately disappeared in the new translation of the Creed of the Mass.

After the mention in this form of each of the three Persons, all that is enumerated in the Creed consists either of appositives ("Almighty", "Creator", etc.) or of direct objects of the verb "believe". Thus we say, for

[10] B. Botte, SC, 11 *bis* (1968): 86. Cf. Pierre Nautin, 11. So too in the creed discovered by Mr. Bratke in 1895 in a seventh-century manuscript, and which is supposed to reproduce a Gallican creed earlier than the year 400: "*Credo in Deum Patrem . . . et in Jesum Christum. . . . Credo in Spiritu sancto.*" (P. Battifol, *Dict. de théologie catholique*, vol. 1, col. 1662.)

[11] *Instructio ad competentes*, bk. 5, *Sermo* 3, nos. 1, 2, 3, 5, 17 (Gamber, 115–18).

[12] "*En le Saint-Esprit*" is not very harmonious in French; but it might be put: "*en l'Esprit-Saint*".

example, "*Credo . . . Ecclesiam*", i.e., not "I believe in the Church", but simply, "I believe that the Church exists"; and so too, "I believe that there exists a communion of saints, a forgiveness of sins", etc., and I believe that these realities whose existence I affirm are the fruits of the Holy Spirit *in whom* I believe. This was explained by Alexander of Halès, among others, in his *Summa theologica*: "After the mention of the Holy Spirit", he says, "there follow four general effects".[13] Erasmus repeated this: "It is in conformity with the nature of things that the holy Church should be attributed or connected (*annectitur*) to the Holy Spirit", because "all holiness comes from him"; as for the articles which follow, they simply amplify what refers to the Church: the resurrection of the body, for instance, is the transition from the militant status to the triumphant one; it is for the Church her "final consummation".[14] In reality, all the final articles of the Creed are a series of appositions to the Holy Spirit, considered in the effects he produces.

The author of a sermon attributed to St. Augustine, speaking to those who have come to be instructed in the faith in view of receiving baptism, tells them: "Believe in the Holy Spirit, believe the holy Church."[15] His intention is clear. One can recognize this again, for instance, in the sermon on the "handing on of the Creed"

[13] After "*in Spiritum sanctum*", "*ponuntur autem effectus generales quatuor*" (4:1135).

[14] *Explicatio in Symbolum Apostolorum*: "*Et congruenter Ecclesia sancta sancto Spiritui annectitur*" (25–26). "*Didicisti Spiritum omnia sanctificantem; nunc accipe Ecclesiam ab illo sanctificatam.*" ([Lugduni Batavorum, 1541], 151.)

[15] "*Credite in Spiritum sanctum, credite sanctam Ecclesiam*": *Sermo* 244 (PL, 39:2195). See also Nicetas of Remesiana, *De symbolo*, chaps. 7 and 10 (PL, 52:870 A and 871 A).

wrongly attributed to St. Maximus of Turin. After the triple formula: *"Credis in Deum"*, when the preacher comes to the article about the Church, he stresses the contrast by using a different turn of phrase: *"Vere sancta est Ecclesia* confitenda."[16] As if the simple omission of the "in" did not seem enough to him, he brings in a different verb, the same verb found in our so-called Athanasian Creed, for the article on baptism: *"Confiteor unum baptisma"*.

Both Rufinus of Aquilea and Faustus of Riez, in their commentaries, had already strongly stressed this difference in grammatical construction.[17] The entire Latin tradition did the same, from the fifth to the twentieth century, as we shall see farther on. Now, these are not "the ingenious explanations given by preachers and commentators" who are trying, after the event, to justify an anomaly which they do not understand, and who seek to take advantage of the occasion to differentiate the article which refers to the Holy Spirit from those that follow it. This is the assumption made by J. N. D. Kelly in his learned work *Early Christian Creeds*.[18] But this assump-

---

[16] PL, 57:433–36 and 437 A.

[17] Rufinus, *Expositio Symboli*, no. 34 (CCL, 20:169–70). Fr. A. Jungmann writes, 149: "Rufinus himself, when discussing the differences between his own formula of faith, the one employed at Aquilea, and the one which he considered to be the Roman Creed, points out these grammatical differences but does not consider them important." We think that there is some confusion here. Rufinus does not attach much importance to the differences he points out between the Creed used in Rome and the one used in Aquilea, but, on the contrary, he deems very important, within each of these creeds, the difference between the articles preceded by *in* and those which are not.

[18] Oxford, 1950, 152–53. Cf. above, Chapter Three.

tion itself presupposes the hypothesis that the Holy Spirit and the subsequent articles originally belonged to a rather incongruous collection of things to be believed. Rev. Fr. Jungmann also thinks that "the ancient Fathers of the Church did not attach any special significance to this particular usage".[19] But if this is so, one might wonder how such a usage came to be established. In reality, we believe there is good reason to make here a distinction which has a more general application, one which the facts oblige us to make: the distinction between lived faith and reflective faith.

The historian can note in certain texts a theology "which is expressed there with all desirable coherence, even if it does not belong to the discursive order and does not conform to the parameters of a formal and pre-existing definition".[20] Thus, "the primacy of the interpersonal relationship and the irreducible character of the events" which constituted the divine and human history of Christ were "primary facts in the Christian consciousness long before theory could elaborate speculative categories of person, event and history".[21] In the question under consideration here, the first Christian generations did not need to wait for the results of a long metaphysical elaboration in order to unite in their faith the Holy Spirit with the Father and the Son or to distinguish God from everything that is not God. This distinction regarding objects naturally led to a distinction in their attitudes, and the latter in turn demanded the creation of a spon-

[19] Op. cit., 149.
[20] Archimandrite Andrew Scrima, ecumenical colloquy of Heverlee, Pentecost, 1966. (*Le Saint-Esprit et l'Église*, Paris: Fayard, 1969.)
[21] Paul Toinet, *Existence chrétienne et philosophie* (Paris: Aubier, 1965), 268.

taneous expression in a difference of language within the creed of faith itself. Erasmus thus seems to us to have shown a more sagacious spirit of observation than do some more recent historians when he discerned in St. Cyprian (whose language is, however, a bit fluid)[22] a definite intention, even if this intention had not yet been reflected upon, even if it had not yet been objectified in theoretical considerations. "Cyprian", observes the great humanist, "recites the Creed in this way, showing that the preposition accompanies only the mention of the Father, the Son and the Holy Spirit, and nothing else".[23]

In St. Augustine's writings, on the contrary, the reflection has already become systematized. Miss Christine Mohrmann judges that in his works "theological speculation is at the root of his linguistic differentiation".[24] While not rejecting this statement, we should prefer to modify it slightly and say that with Augustine a certain theological speculation—which is not moreover without precedent—seeks to account as best it can for the linguistic differentiation which attracted his attention. The result of such an effort is far from being entirely subjective. It is less a specifically Augustinian theory than an objective analysis that Augustine makes of the believing Christian consciousness as it had existed long before his time. And without doubt, the truth which Augustine thus succeeds in bringing to light has other bases besides a simple grammatical fact. This latter was not strictly necessary,

---

[22] Cf. Christine Mohrmann, 279.

[23] "*Ostendens enim soli Patri, Filio et Spiritui addi praepositionem, caeteris nequaquam, ita recitat*", *Expositio in symbolum apostolorum*, 36. See St. Cyprian, *Epist.* 58, no. 7 (Hartel, CSEL, 3, 2: 674).

[24] *Mélanges Joseph de Ghellinck*, 29.

BELIEF AND FAITH

and it should be taken as a sign, not as a proof. There can be no question about this. But Augustine's analysis, even though itself incomplete, is nonetheless enlightening.

When in the *Enchiridion* he comes to the article of the Creed which mentions the Holy Spirit, Augustine explains after the fashion of Rufinus and of the pseudo-Maximus: "We add that we also believe in the Holy Spirit, in order to complete that Trinity in which God consists; then the Church is called to mind. . . ."[25] But he does not stop there. Several times in his preaching he remarks that with reference to God we use the word *credere* in three different ways: *credere Deum—credere Deo—credere in Deum*. Here we have three acts which are linked to each other and follow a necessary progression. Only the third, which presupposes and incorporates the first two, characterizes true faith. It alone makes one a Christian. Commenting on the words addressed by Jesus to the Jews around him, "The work of God is that you should believe in him whom he has sent" (Jn 6:29), Augustine specifies:

> that you should believe in him (*in eum*); not that you should believe things about him (*ei*). But if you believe in him, that is because you believe what you have heard about him; whereas whoever believes things about him does not by that fact believe in him; for the demons too believe truths about him but still do not believe in him.[26]

And in another place: "To believe in God is certainly

---

[25] *Enchiridion*, chap. 15, no. 56: "*Adjungimus sic credere nos et in Spiritum sanctum, ut illa Trinitas compleatur, quae Deus est; deinde sancta commemoratur Ecclesia.*" (Bibl. aug., 9:202.) Cf. *De fide et symbolo*, vol. 10, no. 21 (9:64).

[26] *In Joannem*, tract. 29, no. 6: "*Ut credatis in eum, non, ut credatis ei. Sed si creditis in eum, creditis ei; non autem continuo qui credit ei,*

more than to believe things about God."²⁷

This threefold distinction made by Augustine was constantly repeated during the Latin Middle Ages. Yves of Chartres explains it at length in a sermon on the Apostles' Creed. If, he says, the first two expressions are necessary for salvation, they are still not sufficient, because only our faith *in* God, in the triune God, expresses our divine filiation through adoption and grace.²⁸ Sometimes even an increased subtlety enters in here to complicate Augustine's explanation. Thus, in the twelfth century, the author of a collection of "Questions and Decisions on the Epistle to the Romans", unwilling to let any nuance escape, introduces a fourth term by distinguishing between *credere in Deo*, which is trusting faith (*fides fiduciae*), and *credere in Deum*, which means a tending toward God through faith combined with love.²⁹ In the thirteenth century, the great Scholastics, Albert the Great and Thomas Aquinas, limit themselves to the triple distinction but proceed to exploit it methodically.³⁰ Dionysius the Carthusian, in the fifteenth century, summed up all his predecessors by saying that the very infidels can believe that God exists (*Deum esse*);

---

credit in eum. Nam daemones credebant ei, et non credebant in eum." (CCL, 36:387.)

²⁷ *In ps.* 77, no. 8: "*Hoc est etiam credere in Deum, quod utique plus est quam credere Deo.*" (CCL, 39:1073.) See below, Chapter Nine.

²⁸ *Sermo* 23 (PL, 162:604–6).

²⁹ "*Aliud est credere Deum esse, quae est fides cognitionis; aliud est credere Deo, quae dicitur fides consensus; aliud credere in Deo, quae dicitur fides fiduciae; aliud credere in Deum, quod est per fidem et dilectionem in Deum tendere.*" Pseudo-Hugues of St. Victor (PL, 183:668 B C). St. Bernard, *De diversis sermo* 45, no. 5 (PL, 183:668 B C).

³⁰ See below, Chapter Nine. So too in the fourteenth century, Durand of Mende, *Rationale*, bk. 4, chap. 25, no. 15.

they may even believe things about God (*credere Deo*), and yet not have true faith, or at least complete faith, because they do not believe in God (*in Deum*); and he explained the reason for this essential difference in the following words: "*Insuper, quia voluntas intellectum et alias vires movet in finem, secundum hoc ponitur credere in Deum actus fidei*", i.e., "Because the will moves the intellect and the other powers of the soul toward its end, it should be said that the act of faith consists in believing *in* God."[31]

The same doctrinal basis on which St. Augustine's analyses were built can be found in St. Irenaeus, although with a different emphasis. In fact, in a spirit of generous openness to the "evangelical preparations" found throughout history, Irenaeus had stressed no less firmly than Augustine the unique and personal character of the movement of faith which brings man to God. "In the New Testament", we read in the fourth book of his *Adversus haereses*, "the faith which brings men toward God, (*ea, quae est ad Deum, fides hominum*) has been increased, receiving in addition the Son of God by whom man becomes a participant in God."[32]

This characteristic of a faith which can be called personal was also expressed in antiquity in a more general manner, even without always bringing in the word "faith". Becoming a Christian did not mean, as we sometimes say today, "adhering to transcendental values". Converting did not mean merely giving up erroneous beliefs in order to embrace the true teaching offered by

[31] *Opera omnia*, 17:341–42: "*Primus motus mentis in Deum est per fidem quae est omnis boni origo.*" Cf. K. Krog-Tonning, *Der Letzte Scholastiker, eine Apologie* (1904), 140.

[32] *Adversus haereses*, bk. 4, chap. 28 (PG, 7:1061–62).

the Church; it meant, essentially, renouncing Satan in order to adhere to Christ, or, as St. Justin put it, turning from idols in order to consecrate oneself through Christ to the unbegotten God.[33] It meant, as Hermas said in his vivid language, apostatizing from the angel of evil in order to follow the angel of justice and to live for God.[34]

If we consider the French vocabulary, we at once perceive an apparent anomaly. Corresponding to the one verb "believe" (*croire*), there are two nouns: *faith* (*foi*) and *belief* (*croyance*). These terms, as Msgr. Maurice Nédoncelle rightly observes, as well as the related word *trust* (*confiance*), involve us in "deep confusion".[35] We shall not attempt here to make an exhaustive analysis of the matter. Let us simply point out a few facts which should dissuade us from using the two words "faith" and "belief" indiscriminately. "Belief" comes from *credentia*, a word which "is found from one end to the other in the domain of romance languages".[36] It occurs in profane as well as in religious usage. Further, even in its religious sense, it is used as often in the plural as in the singular: "our beliefs" is an ordinary expression. On the other hand, any opinion which is not based on intrinsic reasons or on direct observation can be called a belief regardless, not only of its nature, but also of the degree of certitude or probability with which it is held. Thus, I believe that far from here there exists a certain city

---

[33] I *Apol.*, chap. 49, no. 5 (ed. L. Pautigny, 100).

[34] *Pastor*, sixth precept, chap. 2, no. 9 (ed. Robert Joly, SC, 53:194).

[35] *Croyance, confiance et foi en philosophie*, in *Conscience et Logos* (Paris: Éd. de l'Épi, 1961), 177.

[36] A. Meillet, in *Mémoires de la société de linguistique*, 22:218. (A. Ernout et A. Meillet, *Dictionnaire étymologique de la langue latine* [Paris: Klincksieck, 1951], 265.)

named Tokyo; my belief is sufficiently sure, even though I have never been there; but since the testimony of others on which beliefs usually rest is not always so firmly guaranteed as this one, a given belief may be held with firm conviction whereas a different one (and this is most frequently the case) may be a more or less hesitant opinion, mixed with numerous subjective factors. Even when I do not need to have recourse to the testimony of others, there are many things which I do not come to know with certainty about which I also form, out of practical necessity and with the uncertain means at my disposal, a series of opinions which are also only beliefs. We can then say, for instance, with Mr. Jean Rostand, "This is what I believe, because one cannot help believing a number of things, even though the most reasonable position might be to suspend judgment about them."[37] Expressing himself like that, Mr. Jean Rostand clearly could not have said, "This is my faith". Such is the inevitable ambiguity hidden in the expression "What I believe".

In its fullest meaning, faith presents an ensemble of characteristics that distinguish it from simple belief. Of all modes of knowing, it is in itself, paradoxically, the firmest and most assured, even though it always remains free and threatened. Whereas a belief, whatever it be, can only possess a greater or lesser degree of firmness, faith which as such is firm is always capable of having very diverse degrees of depth.[38] For it is not only a mode of knowing. It is something completely different from a simple conviction. It is an essentially personal act which,

---

[37] *Ce que je crois* (Paris: Grasset, 1953), 13.
[38] Cf. 2 Cor 10:15.

if rightly understood, involves the depths of one's being. It gives a definite orientation to one's entire being. Hence it has been said that faith is a "total synthesis".[39] In addition, if faith, like many other beliefs, is based on testimony, this testimony is of a unique kind; it is God's testimony; it does not remain, like human testimony, entirely extrinsic to the mind that receives it. For God is not exterior to the being he has created; if in one sense he is indeed the "wholly Other", by that very fact he is not "purely other". He is, said Abbé Monchanin, "wholly other than the other". His transcendence brings about an intimate presence.[40] "The transcendent source of spirits, he is their immanent link; he is the Power to whom *alone* man can and must give absolute obedience, unlimited sacrifice of self; he is the Power who urges us to what is good *as such*."[41] As Paul Tillich also says, speaking of the faith of the prophets, he is "the creative substratum of all things, always present in all, ever creating and destroying, always felt closer to us than we are to ourselves, while still remaining inaccessible".[42] The voice resounds both outside and inside of the one he calls to believe, and it is in this sense that one can say that the experience of God, which is a sacred experience, since it is the experience of the sacrosanct, is not a simple

[39] M. Nédoncelle, *Conscience et Logos*, 181: "My faith is my total synthesis."

[40] One might recall St. Augustine's famous exclamation: *"Deus, interior intimo meo et superior summo meo."*

[41] George Tyrrell, *Revelation as Experience*, lecture (unpublished) dated March 26, 1909. (The text was kindly given to the author by Mrs. A. David.)

[42] Quoted by Georges Tavard, *Initiation à Paul Tillich* (Paris: Centurion, 1968), 55.

experience of otherness. On the other hand, if one can speak of beliefs in the plural, it is clear that one cannot speak of faith except in the singular. Finally, faith is essentially a response: the response, which cannot be divided, to the Word of God who reveals and who, in revealing, reveals himself. By an ordinary belief, we believe something about a man; by faith, we believe something about God, as St. Augustine has just explained to us; but also, and more deeply, more totally, by an act of an entirely different nature, we believe *in* God. Our faith is our response to his call.[43] Even if we consider it under its noetic aspect, it is an act not only of knowledge but of recognition.[44] *Fecisti nos ad te, Deus—credimus in te*. "God, you have made us for yourself; we believe in you." We give you our faith.

Now we can come to realize this: the antinomy that we observed in our French vocabulary is only apparent. If to the two nouns, belief and faith, there corresponds only one verb, two very different forms of that verb (*croire*) correspond to the two nouns respectively, depending on the manner in which their attribute is connected with them.

When I believe *in* God, when I give him my faith, when in answer to his initiative I turn myself over to him from the bottom of my being, there is established between him and me a bond of reciprocity of such a kind that the same word, faith, can be applied to each of the two partners: "The faith of the two parties", writes

[43] Cf. M. D. Chenu, "Foi et religion", in *Études philosophiques* (July–September 1966).
[44] Pierre Teilhard de Chardin, *Esquisse d'une dialectique de l'esprit*, Oeuvres 7 (Paris: Éd. du Seuil, 1964): 155.

St. John of the Cross with a certain audacity, speaking of the relationship of the believing soul with God.[45] For what we have here indeed is "the encounter of two persons offering themselves to each other in a fullness of presence, a total engagement".[46] In fact, "in its primitive and natural sense, the word *faith* suggests the idea of 'loyal fidelity' "[47] and calls to mind the reciprocal gift of spouses.[48] This is the analogy used by Scripture in inviting us to think of the encounter between man and God,[49] although the word "faith" most often suggests as well that which can be said only of man: submission, total confidence, expectation of God's help, reliance on the pledges he has given us of his love and fidelity; in a word: Amen to God.

If, by all the characteristics which have been pointed out, faith is distinguished from simple belief, it does not for all that exclude the latter. Quite the contrary. It requires it and cannot do without it. When we distinguish the two terms under consideration, even when we con-

---

[45] *The Living Flame*, strophe 1, no. 4: "The faith of the two parties is confirmed when the soul's faith in God is confirmed." Cf. Louis Cognet, *Histoire de la spiritualité moderne* (Paris: Aubier, 1967), 142.

[46] Paul-Marie de la Croix, O.C.D., *L'Évangile de Jean et son témoignage spirituel* (1959), 299.

[47] F. Mallet (= M. Blondel), "La Foi et la science", in *Revue du clergé français* (August 1, 1906), 3.

[48] Cf. Cyril of Jerusalem, *Cinquième Catéchèse*, chap. 1: "God is called faithful (πιστός). . . . See the dignity to which thou art elevated, since thou art called by the same name as God himself." (PG, 33:505 A.) Gregory of Nazianzen, *Discours* 40, chap. 8: Baptism is "a pact concluded with God for a new life." (PG, 36:368 B.)

[49] Cf. Augustine, *In ps.* 32, 2, *Sermo* 1, no. 9: "*Fidelis homo est credens promittenti Deo; fidelis Deus est exhibens quod promisit homini.*" (CCL, 38:254.)

trast them, the better to discern their respective traits, we are not excluding or condemning either of the two. The intimate union, in a single act, of what we designate as belief and as faith is essential to Christianity and indissoluble. As enlightening as the distinction between the two concepts is, the dissociation of the two things would be fatal. Faith makes the beliefs which it includes share in its own characteristics; and, on the other hand, to pretend to exalt faith by eliminating beliefs would in reality be to destroy it. To progress "from beliefs to faith" may be a fine program if one means by this that it is not enough to entertain "beliefs", to adhere to "truths", in order to be a Christian, that it is still necessary to enliven one's beliefs and to integrate them in an act which involves one's whole being. But if one wished to imply that we must abandon our beliefs in order to find faith, to replace them by a faith with no definite object, this would be a delusion.

It has been written, very rightly, that "the danger for a Christian would consist in forgetting the unity of the faith while stressing the variety of his beliefs".[50] This may not be the peril most to be feared today for restless spirits; but it is undoubtedly a tendency of many Christians at all times, people who see little more in their religion than a series of things they must believe, accompanied by a series of precepts and interdictions. It is the role of Christian education to help them reach a better understanding, most essentially by showing them the unity of beliefs in the faith. Let us recall here what was said in the previous chapter. The Trinity reveals itself to

---

[50] Jean Lacroix, *Histoire et mystère*, 124. Cf. *Vatican II, la révélation divine* 1 (1968): 290–91.

us in its works: creation, redemption, sanctification; and it is through its works, in which we believe, and only through those works, that our faith can attain the Trinity itself. So all Christian tradition, clearly shown from the earliest days, joins together in a single act the *credo in* and the *credo quod*. It is in response to God's gift of himself to us in his works that we in return give ourselves to him. If it is not to remain purely formal and empty, our faith, in order to exist, must therefore be nourished by belief, which it presupposes, integrates and encloses. "The obedience of faith", as St. Paul says, necessarily includes an act of intellectual adherence to a series of beliefs, or, to speak more objectively, a belief in a series of revealed acts, which we come to know through the apostolic preaching; these are the very acts which in the Creed accompany the mention of each of the three Persons. Our faith itself, in fact, is adherence to this Word of God which, in order to be uttered and to make itself heard by us, to reach us in our earthly condition, is fragmented in becoming objectified; and it is only in this way that we can come into contact with it in its oneness. Then, turning away from all conditions, faith "radically renounces all limitation in the field of its adherence".[51]

Faith and belief; faith and religion; these two pairs of notions are closely linked. Whoever dissociates one of them is by that very fact dissociating the other.[52] Just as faith does not exclude simple belief, neither is it opposed

---

[51] Hans Urs von Balthasar, *La Foi du Christ* (coll. *Foi vivante*, Paris: Aubier, 1968), 105.

[52] Just as religion cannot live without beliefs, neither can beliefs survive without religion. Both beliefs and religion are necessary for the life of faith.

to religion in the sense that it would tend to destroy it. It integrates it, rather; it purifies and gives it all its meaning. To oppose religion in the name of faith, with some semblance of reason, we would have to begin by giving religion a narrow and pejorative definition; this definition would be arbitrary and tendentious, would contradict the constant usage of Christian tradition from the beginning and would not be justified either by the most current etymological explanation. Religion establishes a link between man and the Divinity.[53] This link is not necessarily to be conceived as being (falsely) founded on man's initiative, the illusory result of his ambition, nor as being by nature incompatible with faith. Religion also establishes a link between believers; that is eminently true in the case of Christianity, which gathers its faithful into a Church, which unites them mystically in the Body of Christ and which seeks to gather all men into a truly "catholic" unity. The "Christian religion", which is empirically one religion among others, is for the Christian the religion par excellence, the perfection of religion. In

[53] The two Greek words closest to *religio* in the Christian language are θρησκεία and εὐσέβεια (or θεοσέβεια); the one translates rather the idea of an objective cult and the other the sentiment of piety and adoration. Cf. Acts 17:23 and 26:5; the Pastoral Epistles and 2 Peter. In Titus 1:1, "the truth according to piety" is "religious truth". In 1 Timothy 3:9 and 3:16, "mystery of faith" and "mystery of piety" are about equivalent. Cf. Cyril of Jerusalem, *Cinquième Catéchèse*, chap. 12: τῆς εὐσεβείας γνῶσιν (PG, 33:524 A); Gregory of Nyssa, *Vie de Moïse*, nos. 14 and 15 (Daniélou, SC, 1 *ter*:114–15); no. 166 (212–13): τῆς κατ' εὐσέβειαν ἀρετῆς = of the virtue of religion. John Chrysostom, *Sur l'Incompréhensibilité*, 2: τὰ τῆς εὐσεβείας δόγματα (SC, 28:116). On the word "piety", see Yves Congar: *Au milieu des orages* (Paris: Éd. du Cerf, 1969), 68.

this traditional way of speaking, there is no concession to either superstition or idolatry.[54]

Neither the great humanists nor the great reformers constitute exceptions to this universal rule. Neither Luther, Calvin nor Zwingli perceived between the two words, "faith" and "religion", the kind of contradiction which today appears to be of capital importance to some of their disciples. Calvin, especially, seems to have had a particular liking for the word "religion". He associates it with the word "piety":[55] "We shall not say that God is known where there is neither religion nor piety." He often contrasts religion, "true religion", "pure religion", "right religion", which is also "true piety", with superstition; this latter, instead of remaining within the limits set by God, "amasses a superfluity of useless and vain things"; it perverts religion, or at least causes it to degenerate by mingling "errors and falsehoods" with it. In religion, on the contrary, one finds "a heavenly wisdom",[56] which consists in remaining "suspended on God's lips alone". Calvin himself declared that he wished to "restore religion"; when he arrived in Geneva, he rejoiced to see "religion established" there. He won-

---

[54] *Apologie d'Appollonius* before his judges (Greek Acts): "If I have become θεοσεβής, it was in order not to adore the idols any more." Cf. Fr. Calmette on certain passages of the Vedas that he recently discovered: "We have already drawn considerable fruit from them for the progress of religion."

[55] Cf. Augustine, *De civitate Dei*, bk. 10, chap. 1, no. 3: "*Pietas proprie Dei cultus intelligi solet, quam Graeci* εὐσέβειαν *vocant*", etc.

[56] Compare Lactantius: *Divinae Institutiones*, bk. 4, no. 4: "*Non potest nec religio a sapientia separari, nec sapientia a religione secerni.*" (Ed. S. Brandt, CSEL, 19:282.) Calvin himself referred to Lactantius: "We have to conclude with Lactantius that there is no religion unless it is joined with the truth." (Loc. cit., col. 56.)

dered at the fact that there is a "seed of religion planted in all by the secret inspiration of God", and that even men who have fallen into degradation "always retain some seed of religion". Moreover, he also spoke objectively of the "Jewish religion" as well as the Christian religion. He was indignant to see someone like Lucretius howling like a dog "to do away with all religion"; but he knew, of course, that this is an impossible undertaking, for "it is easier to suppress all natural affection than to do without religion". Finally, as he saw it, "religion is proper to the children of God".[57]

If in our own century a man like Karl Barth began by attacking "religion" bitterly in the name of faith, this was in a particular sense, with a polemical purpose corresponding to a certain precise situation.[58] He was aiming above all at nineteenth-century liberal Protestantism and its wholly humanized "religion", submerged in contemporary "culture". This was a perverted religion, which had become a purely anthropological phenomenon; a "disguised" religion, he further called it, a "camouflage borrowed by human pride" to renew in its own way the adventure of the Titans; it was the production of the *homo religiosus incurvatus in se*; "a Christianity domesticated" by men who had forgotten both the divine transcendence and the scandal of the Cross.[59] This had been prepared for a long time in the bosom of Protestantism, even before the *Aufklärung*, by a certain

---

[57] *Institution chrétienne* (Corpus Reformatorum, vol. 31, Brunswick, 1865), 43–66, 77–87, 106, 141.

[58] Cf. Henri Bouillard, *Karl Barth*, vol. 1: *Genèse et évolution de la théologie dialectique* (Paris: Aubier, 1957), 53–60, 137–56, 203, etc.

[59] *Dogmatics* (Fr. trans., Fernand Ryser, Geneva: Labor et Fides), vol. 4, 1 (1966): 162; 2:113–14, 137, 298.

school of theology whose original mistake was "to scorn Christ"; this modern "religion" had "given in to the devil". The consequence was the dissolution of Christianity in our century. Barth wanted to react against this. He battled at the same time against the "Kantian rationalism" which reduced the whole of revelation to the "actualization of moral reason", and against the opposite but similar doctrine inherited from Schleiermacher which, he said, "wanted to find the alpha and the omega of theology in religion considered as a human sentiment".[60] What he attacked directly was the outcome of these two doctrines, which he summed up in the names of Hegel, Strauss and Feuerbach, as well as of Ritschl and Troeltsch. He saw that this kind of "religion" was becoming "a Christianity without Christ", condemned to rapid extinction.[61] To this exaltation of an

---

[60] He may have been unfair toward Schleiermacher, whose "feeling of dependence" seems to have been quite contrary to the pretentions of the Titans.

[61] *Dogmatics*, vol. 1,2 (Fr. trans., Fernand Ryser, 1954): 81, 113, 134–35, 139. In *Römerbrief*, Barth had already maintained his thesis violently. Fifteen years later, he again insisted in his *Credo*: "It can be affirmed, with precise and accurate proofs as support, that the great theological and ecclesiastical catastrophe which is now taking place in German Protestantism, would never have happened if the three words *Filium ejus unicum* in the exact sense of the Nicene doctrine on the Trinity, had not in fact disappeared as far as the German church was concerned, over two centuries ago, buried under a cluttered mass of mollifying interpretations. In other countries they would do well to consider this catastrophe as a warning." (Trans. P. and J. Jundt, "*Je Sers*" [Paris, 1936], 67.) May all our Catholic theologians today listen to this warning. In more recent times, Barth more than once begged them not to fall, in their turn, into the errors which are scattered throughout the history of Protestant theology over the last two centuries.

anonymous and indefinite word, wholly interior and hidden, he therefore contrasted, in all its grandeur and integrity, obedience to the Word of God, which is objective, explicit and clearly determined. He reestablished the principle of dogmatism. In this way, one might say, he "preserved the religious substance of Protestantism during a turbulent period". As the future was soon to show, it was at least in part, "thanks to this dialectic theology that German Protestantism was able to resist the German mysticism" that sprang up in the 1930s, the new phase of that "mysticism of immanence" in endlessly renewed forms.[62]

Barth's answer was unilateral.[63] "Sound and necessary" in principle, it was not preserved from all excess. However, even in the first volume of his monumental *Dogmatics* (1932), Barth admitted, using the word in a wider sense or at first in a more neutral one, that if religion "should dialectically be destroyed in its covetousness", it should "also be justified in its accomplishment through grace":[64]

> To affirm that religion is "assumed" by revelation does not mean that it is purely and simply denied. . . . Revelation has the power to make religion true. . . . There is even more, for how could we affirm that it has this power if it had not already manifested it in reality? In other words, there exists a true religion, just as there exist

[62] Hasso Jaeger, *Mystique protestante et anglicane*, in *La Mystique et les mystiques*, by André Ravier (Paris: DDB, 1965), 349–53. Cf. H. E. Weber, *Glaube und Mystik* (1927), 54.

[63] Jaeger, loc. cit. Jean Zumstein, *Revue de théologie et de philosophie* (1968), 389–92.

[64] André Dumas, *La parole dans la tradition protestante*, in *Lumière et vie* 88 (1968): 39.

justified sinners. And, on condition that we hold firmly to this analogy. . . , we can declare without any hesitation: *the Christian religion is the true religion*.[65]

That was already to establish balance, by recognizing that religion, which is natural for man created by God and made for God, but which, along with him, had been drawn into sin, could be purified and Christianized. Even earlier, in 1922, in a review of *Römerbrief*, Rudolf Bultmann had written, not without reason: "This book seeks to demonstrate the independence and the absolute character of religion."[66] With time it became even more apparent that it is impossible to lock Barth's thought into an antithesis inspired by passing circumstances. Barth himself said that he did not wish to persist "in the attitude of rupture" which he had at first adopted. Later still he explained that his reaction against the "religion" of liberalism "was critical and polemical in character"; he admitted that such a reversal "was not the final word of truth", and that in his manner of advocating it he had "been only partly right".[67]

---

[65] *Dogmatics*, vol. 1, 2: 115; cf. 133. Emphasis ours.

[66] "No doubt, Barth does not speak of religion in this sense. . . , but let us not indulge in quarrels over words." Quoted by James M. Robinson, *Le Kérygme de l'Église et le Jésus de l'histoire* (trans. Étienne de Peyer, Geneva: Labor et Fides, 1961), 23, n. 3.

[67] *L'Humanité de Dieu* (1956), 7, 8, and 14. One should note the similarity between Barth's expressions and some formulas in present use in Catholicism, for instance the following from Louis Bouyer's *Le Rite et l'homme*, 28: The Incarnation leads us, not to "the disappearance of the naturally sacred, but to its transformation". Every Catholic can also agree with Mr. Gabriel Widmer when he denounces an "idolatry" or an "ideolatry" found in a theology which fails to recognize "the essential reality" while pretending to make God emerge from some kind of feeling, imagination or faith; so too a

BELIEF AND FAITH

In a context which differed from that of Barth's youth, but still alluding to the history and the internal situation of the Protestant churches, Dietrich Bonhoeffer resumed Barth's antithesis, adding new inflections. Still, aware of the ambiguity of words, he was usually careful to put the word "religion" (and its derivatives: "religious", "religiosity") within quotation marks. Despite this precaution, his thinking has been misrepresented. The least one can say is that he has become "the involuntary ancestor of a trend which has not always inherited his spiritual depth".[68] Max Thurian rightly calls attention to this fact: no more than Barth did Bonhoeffer advocate "a Christianity without religion, i.e., without liturgy, without mystery, without prayer; an intellectual and moral Christianity, a life lived according to a gospel stripped of all contemplation, the existence of any generosity toward God";[69] or, quite simply, as with so many others, a vague "faith in the future", a political utopia. Just the opposite. All that is needed to be convinced of this is to read what Bonhoeffer wrote, not only in his

---

philosophy which seeks in some way to derive being from reason, experience or intuition would be a pure "ideology". *Théologie et philosophie; Revue de théologie et de philosophie* (1968), 375. One cannot fail to note also the kinship of these remarks with the criticism of "ideosophie" made by Mr. Jacques Maritain in *Le Paysan de la Garonne*.

[68] André Manaranche, *Y a-t-il une éthique sociale chrétienne?* (Paris: Éd. du Seuil, 1969), 30.

[69] Max Thurian, *La Foi en crise* (Taize, 1968), 76. Cf. René Marlé, *Dietrich Bonhoeffer* (1967). On "religion" as understood by Barth and Bonhoeffer, see Gustave Thils, *Christianisme sans religion?* (Castermann, 1968), 14-20 and 28-36. By the same author, *Désacralisation et sécularité*, in *Au service de la Parole de Dieu* (Duculot, Gembloux, 1968), 395-405.

earlier books, but also in his notes and letters from captivity.

Of course, we can well see that fear of immanentism sometimes deviates into a refusal of all interiority, and this makes some unjust with respect to Catholic spirituality, favors a certain aridity of soul and can create an obstacle to the deepening of faith. On the other hand, Catholic doctrine is less absolute about the corruption of nature, and consequently its judgment of non-Christian religions is less negative; Catholic theology, better balanced as a rule because of its knowledge of and respect for a long tradition, is wary of overly radical antitheses, even when seeking to reestablish a neglected truth to its full worth; and its language makes less frequent use of dialectics and paradox.[70] Finally, of course, there are differing ecclesiologies, and we do not wish in any way to minimize these differences. But on the main point in question here, the thinking does converge. Those today,

---

[70] Cf. Paul Ricoeur, *Tâches de la communauté ecclésiale dans le monde moderne*: "I do not think that faith can exist without a continuing restating and correction of the religious vehicle. From the beginning, the faith of Israel was a struggle against religion, in and for religion. The battle for Yahweh's name against the idols of Baal . . . proceeded through institutions which were at once the obstacle to and the vehicle for preaching. . . . Without the worship of the Church, the death of religion is no longer just a platitude, irreligion then would become non-faith—the non-faith of man delivered over to the comfort and nonsense of his modernity." In *La Théologie du renouveau*, Congress held at Toronto, 1967 (Montreal-Paris, 1968), 2:58. Or Paul Tillich, in *L'Être nouveau* (trans. J. M. Saint, 1969), 38: "It is the spiritual power of religion which permits the religious man to consider without fear the vanity of religion." And in *Le Christianisme et les religions*, he speaks of the offensive directed by the prophets and the theologians who criticize "religion in the interest of religion" (trans. F. Chapey [Paris: Aubier, 1968], 167).

on the contrary, who, by borrowing words from Barth and Bonhoeffer, revive the antithesis between religion and faith, do so either in extreme confusion or with a completely different meaning and a completely different spirit. In reality, they are moving in a direction opposite to what Barth and Bonhoeffer had wanted. It is a real inversion.[71] Whereas Barth in particular protested against "any relaxation as regards the objectivity of faith"; whereas he opposed the secularization of mystery and sought to reawaken faith in a personal and transcendent God as well as in the revelation of Jesus Christ in consciences bewitched by immanentism,[72] we see today disguised under these same words a growing criticism of religion which endorses all the negations of the "theoreticians of suspicion"; we see once more taking place, in the name of faith, said to be "adult"(!), the "passage from transcendence to immanence", or, in plain language, from Christian faith to atheism.[73]

[71] *Mutatis mutandis*, and with far different consequences, the history of theology offers us other examples of these inversions of meaning; thus the very word theology has ended up by being considered as the opposite of "mysticism", although it previously designated nearly the same thing as this latter word; so too the expression *corpus mysticum*, which first was applied to the Eucharist and now refers to the Church. (Cf. H. de Lubac, *Corpus mysticum*, 2nd ed. Paris: Aubier, 1949.)

[72] *Dogmatics*, vol. 1, 2, 2 (1954): 84–85, etc. Bouillard, 232. Such contrasts in words, as Fr. Georges Cottier, O.P., sagely remarks, "are of importance only insofar as one does not lose sight of the precise definition that the authors give of them". *L'Athéisme religieux*, in *Nova et vetera* (1968), 38.

[73] This was noted by Mr. Roger Garaudy: "Christianity without religion is the same as going from transcendence to immanence." Cf. *Peut-on être communiste aujourd'hui?* (Paris: Grasset, 1968); cf. Postface to J. Girardi, *Marxisme et christianisme* (Desclée, 1968), 314.

Without wishing always to arrive at so radical a negation, and even seeking to avoid it, but anxious for a more absolute transcendence, a certain purism of the faith, which at first may seem to be the result of a lofty spiritual necessity, follows the path that leads to it. Refusing to "have" anything, to possess any "security", emptying the faith of any "religious" element which is judged to be "too human", too interested, too earthly and too impure, this is at best nothing but an intellectual fiction. A faith which little by little comes to the point of excluding any external sign, feast, cult or social institution, any reference to history, any belief that can be objectively formulated, even any sentiments, no longer corresponds to the faith of the average Christian or of the churchman or of the saint. In the past twenty centuries, no faithful follower of Jesus Christ has ever entertained such an attitude of mind; none has even been inclined toward it. Remote from the teaching of Scripture as well as from living tradition, this attitude presupposes a double misconception: of human nature and of the universal character of Christianity, which is to be "preached to every creature". When it is deprived not only of all support but of the elements that nourish it, faith dies of asphyxiation.[74] God himself fades from its horizon.

---

[74] "By wanting to affirm only the divine transcendence and the unfathomable liberty of the Spirit", observes Mr. Jean Louis Leuba very correctly, "how can we avoid ending up by confusing God and nothingness? If God has given himself to us . . . then we must be able to receive him." *A la découverte de l'espace oecuménique* (Neuchâtel: Delachaux et Niestlé, 1967), 231, n. 1; and 212: "The Church could not give up formulating her faith without her witness becoming obscure and ambiguous."

Jesus Christ, if one still thinks of him, is only a distant originator. All that remains is an ideology without any consistency which is called "openness to the future" or some other equally meaningless name. Simple honesty would require one to recognize that at this point he is talking about something other than Christian faith.

What remains true is that for an exact phenomenology it would not be enough to distinguish various religions, including Christianity, as diverse species of a same genus. Nor would it be enough to distinguish, from a dogmatic point of view, true religion from false religions. Like many other words in the religious vocabulary, in fact, the very word religion is very analogical. It is not hard to see why the politico-religious world in which the first Christian churches were born and grew, felt disconcerted, displeased, because it could not apply the usual categories to them. Now, what distinguishes the Christian religion from every other religious concept and from every other religious organism, even before a detailed inventory of its beliefs or of its other elements, is precisely the fact that it is based on faith.[75] This is as true of the great Asiatic religions as it is of the ancient cults found in the Mediterranean basin.[76] "Faith", as Fr. Chenu says so

[75] One might say, then, in other words—close to those used by Barth—that Christianity is not first of all a religion; it is "something else first of all"; it is "God's saving action"; but it "has exercised an influence over religion by helping it to purify itself, by being instrumental in freeing it from its obscurities". Hence the practical problem is "not to purify Christianity from its religious component", which would be to de-humanize and dis-incarnate it, but "to purify this religious component itself": Jean Daniélou, *L'Oraison, problème politique* (Paris: Fayard, 1965), 102.

[76] If Buddhism, too, seems to stand quite apart, this is because of

aptly, "introduces something radically new into the sphere of religion".[77] This whole sphere is transformed by it. But we shall say nevertheless that the act of faith is an essentially religious act. It is the fundamental religious act, the one which establishes true religion, which effectively establishes man in his true relationship with God. In that act, the tendency of natural religion, which is always inefficacious and usually perverted, finds the principle which redirects it and completes it by transforming it. We see no valid reason why we should not continue to say with St. Ambrose that there is nothing more religious than confessing one's faith and exhorting others to embrace it;[78] or again, why we should not pray to God as St. Hilary does at the conclusion of his great work on the Trinity, which he had originally entitled "On Faith": "*Conserva, oro, hanc fidei meae incontamina-*

---

very different characteristics. Nothing is more foreign to it than faith in the Judeo-Christian sense. Islam understands the concept of faith in the sense of submission, not in the sense of *credo in*, of a response to God who reveals himself and offers us entry into his own life.

[77] Loc. cit. For faith supposes "an event, and then we are no longer in the area of nature but in that of history. . . . God is neither conceived of nor invoked because of his usefulness; love is gratuitous". Still, these oppositions, at least in their expression, may be too radical. There is in fact nature and nature. And we take nothing away from history or the gratuitous nature of divine love, nor do we bring in God for the sake of some "usefulness", when we acknowledge with St. Augustine and St. Thomas Aquinas that God has made man for himself and that he has placed within man the desire to find him.

[78] Ambrose, *De fide ad Gratianum*, bk. 1, chap. 4: "*Mallem quidem cohortandi ad fidem subire officium, quam de fide disceptandi; in altero enim religiosa confessio est, in altero incauta praesumptio.*" (O. Faller, CSEL, 78:6.) Cf. Cyprian, *De lapsis*, chap. 1: "*Religiosa vox Christum locuta est, in quem se semel credidisse locuta est.*" (Hartel, CSEL, 3, 1: 237–38).

tam religionem."⁷⁹ So we shall not depreciate religion in the vain hope of exalting the faith which brings it to perfection.

All words can be disputed. But for us systematically to set aside those recommended by a long history would involve real drawbacks. If one lets oneself fall into the habit of thinking in antitheses, one runs the risk of losing or of falsifying the very part of truth which one had hoped to safeguard. Furthermore, the very word "faith" is no more impervious than the word "religion" to distortions of its meaning, whether it be by a philosophical secularization like that of Karl Jaspers or by a degradation to the commonplace or by the undue sacralization of the object to which one applies it. But we shall keep to the meaning given to it in Scripture, and more precisely in the New Testament, which is also the meaning given in the Creed of faith. In this sense, it is faith which makes one a Christian.⁸⁰ The word is so characteristic that there is no need at all to add to it any kind of complementary expression. Christians are "those who believe"; that by itself is how the Acts of the Apostles designates them: πιστοί, πιστεύσαντες.⁸¹ For

---

⁷⁹ Hilary, *De Trinitate*, bk. 12, chap. 57 (PL, 10:471 A). Cf. chap. 55: "*Magna enim erga res tuas religio est*" (469 A). Cf. Augustine, *In Joannem*, tract. 97, no. 4 (PL, 35:1879).

⁸⁰ Cf. Jean Duplacy, *La Foi dans le Nouveau Testament* (*Sacra pagina* 2 [1959]: 431). The author remarks that recent New Testament studies "have been guided much more by a concern to specify the role of faith than by that of determining its exact nature".

⁸¹ *Acts* 2:44; 4:32; 5:14; 10:45. Cf. 6:7. Cf. Ambrose, *De sacramentis*, bk. 1, chap. 1, no. 1: "*Romae fideles dicuntur qui baptizati sunt.*" (Botte, SC, 25 *bis*:60.) Hippolytus, passim (cf. Marcel Richard, *Dict. de spiritualité*, fasc. 45, col. 555).

St. Paul, faith is all of Christianity; "believer" is the synonym for "Christian" and for "saint".[82] The verb πιστεύω and the noun πίστις are both frequently found in the New Testament writings.[83] Now it is clear that πίστις, in Latin *fides*, can be translated only by "faith", not by "belief".

A number of historians have noted the duality of meanings which we have been considering and have taken this into consideration in their analyses of the Apostles' Creed. They call attention to the fact that when the verb *credere* is followed by the preposition *in*, it refers to persons, whereas followed by a simple indicative, it refers to objects. This is what we find in Fr. Joseph de Ghellinck, following Oulton and von Dobschütz.[84] And again in the etymological dictionary of the Latin language by Ernout and Meillet,[85] which points out the form which it designates "in the language of the Church" by the words *credere in aliquem*. But this does not go far enough, or perhaps it is poorly expressed. The difference goes deeper than this.

Certainly, it is clear that one cannot believe *in* a thing; one cannot give one's faith to an object. Such an assertion would make no sense. But neither can one or, more exactly, should one do so to just any person whomsoever. St. Paschasius Radbert explained this extremely well in the ninth century, repeating what others had said before him,[86] and in words which are perfectly applicable today:

[82] 2 Cor 6:15; Col 1:1; Eph 1:1; 2 Th 1:10; 1 Tim 4:1 and 6.
[83] See Chapter Eight below. The Old Testament has only the verbal form.
[84] *Patristique et moyen âge* 3 (1946): 199–200.
[85] 1952. P. 119, s.v. *Credo*.
[86] Thus "Eusebius", *Sermo* 10, *De symbolo* 2: "*Credere et Paulo et*

BELIEF AND FAITH

No one can rightly say, I believe in my neighbor or in an angel or in any creature whatever. Everywhere in the divine Scriptures you will find the right to this confession reserved to God alone. . . . We can indeed say, I believe that man, just as we say, I believe God; but we do not believe in that man or in any other. For they are not in themselves truth or goodness or light or life; they only share in these. That is why when the Lord wishes in the Gospel to show that he is consubstantial with the Father, he says, "You believe in God; believe also in me" (Jn 14:1). For if he were not God, it would not be necessary to believe in him.[87]

Only that Being which is at once personal and transcendent, only the One who is the Absolute, and the absolutely personal, the source and locus of all spirits,[88] is worthy to receive the homage of our faith. So, we do not believe generally *in aliquem, in someone*, any person whatever, but *in solum Deum*, in God alone. Here again is confirmed the great law which governs all our knowledge of God and all our relationships with him: God is unique in all respects; he cannot be included in any genus. To believe, in the full sense of the word as we have defined it from our consideration of the Creed, i.e., to believe absolutely, unconditionally, definitively, in a way that irrevocably involves the very depths of our

---

Petro jure debemus; in Petrum vero ac in Paulum credere, id est, in servos conferre honorem Domini non debemus." (PL, Suppl., 3:583.) See St. Augustine (168, below).

[87] *De fide, spe et caritate*, bk. 1, chap. 6, no. 1 (PL, 120:1402–3).

[88] The One who is, as Paul Tillich says, the Ultimate and Unconditional One; but who is also a concrete being, not a simple principle. Tillich admits, on the other hand, that we must search for "unity between the personal and the Unconditional, or again, between the ethical and the religious". *The Protestant Era*, 216. (Tavard, 179–80.)

being, to believe with that kind of faith is not possible unless we believe in that personal, unique Being whom we call God. Such a faith could not be given to a man without sacrilege, idolatry and enslavement.[89] Man has no right to abdicate his dignity in this way. Fr. Teilhard de Chardin observed one day while pondering the words of the Apocalypse: "I fell at his feet as though dead":

> It is an inter-human dignity, when the "mighty one" is *another* man. It is noble to look straight into the eyes of any other man—but it is absurd in the case of the greater Being. In that case dignity and self-respect consist in *giving oneself*. . . . When a powerful man meets a weak one, his reaction may be to destroy that other. God's reaction is to create something higher.[90]

Newman had said something similar in response to a criticism coming from certain Anglicans. We might translate here what he calls "absolute obedience" as "obedience of faith". "Pope or Queen, whoever asks of me an absolute obedience goes beyond his rights. I vow absolute obedience to no one."[91] We all know where

---

[89] Cf. Hans Urs von Balthasar, *La Gloire et la croix* (trans. R. Givord), 1 (1965): 162: "We are not talking about any sort of love, like the love between two human beings which, if pushed to the absolute degree, could only become something diabolical (because then one finite being would give itself infinitely to another finite being, thereby surrendering its own eternal salvation)."

[90] Manuscript note from his 1940 retreat, October 26, at Peking.

[91] *Anglican Difficulties* 2:243. Although Paul Tillich is joining together some very disparate things, one might agree when he says, loc. cit., 214: "Political or religious traditions, conventions and authorities . . . possess no final authority."

disregard for such a principle has led those who vowed an unconditional allegiance to their *führer* or to their party.[92]

In statements such as these by Teilhard and Newman, it would be wrong to see a reaction specific to modern man, to modern Christians. Nor should we see this in the words of Paul Tillich, who deplored that "all sorts of questionable ideas and methods have been imposed on individuals and groups in the name of some unconditional truth" and who denounced "the destructive consequences of this demonic absolutism"; or who explained in a similar way that even holy things "become diabolical the moment they are given the unconditional and absolute character of the Sacred One himself".[93] These reactions have been specific to the Christian in all ages. The testimony of Paschasius Radbert has shown this to us already; but there are many other examples of it besides. Such, toward the end of the eleventh century, was the case of Gilbert Crespin, in his *Disputatio Judaei et Christiani*. When one Jew objected: "Never could I believe in Christ, even if I believe Christ, for I believe in no one but God", Gilbert Crespin replied: "If Jesus Christ were only a man, then surely the prophet would be inviting us to idolatry when he invites us to believe in

---

[92] Cf. Stefan George, "Cadet's Hymn to His Führer" (1900). Cf. H. I. Marrou, *Théologie de l'histoire* (Paris: Éd. du Seuil, 1968), 152.

[93] *Théologie de la culture* (trans. J. P. Gabus and J. M. Saint, 1968), 116 and 211. When we quote and adopt as our own these formulas by Tillich, we do not underwrite the applications he makes of them elsewhere, when he seems to reject the ultimate character of the God of Christian revelation or to see the same sort of relative truth in all religious symbols. Cf. *Dynamics of Faith* (New York, 1957).

him."⁹⁴ This apologist for the Christian faith was only handing on the teaching of all the Christian centuries, based on the attitude of all the authentic messengers of divine revelation, other than Jesus himself. St. Augustine had stated it very well in texts precisely where he commented on the Creed: "Very often", he wrote, "we must believe a man, but we must not believe in him."⁹⁵ And again, with greater emphasis and precision: "Speaking of the Apostles of Jesus Christ, we can say: we believe Paul, but not: we believe in Paul; or: we believe Peter, but not: we believe in Peter."⁹⁶ That was precisely what Newman had in mind. And it is what Venantius Fortunatus declared in a concise formula in his explanation of the Creed: "In, *ubi praepositio ponitur, ibi divinitas adprobatur*"—"Where we use the preposition *in*, we recognize the Divinity."⁹⁷ Faustus of Riez said it too

---

⁹⁴ "*Judaeus: Christum credo prophetam . . . et Christo credam. . . , sed in Christum neque credo neque credam, quia non nisi in Deum et unum. . . . Christianus: Si homo tantum esset, profecto idolatriam . . . propheta suaderet, qui in hominem credi oportere nos admonet.*" (Ed. Blumenkranz, 33 and 42.)

⁹⁵ *In ps.* 77, no. 8: "*Et homini cuilibet plerumque credendum est, quamvis in eum non sit credendum.*" (CCL, 39:1073.) *De ordine*, bk. 2, chap. 54: "*Varroni quis non credat?*"

⁹⁶ *In Joannem*, tract. 29, no. 6: "*De apostolis ipsius (Christi) possumus dicere: credimus Paulo, sed non: credimus in Paulum; credimus Petro, sed non: credimus in Petrum.*" (CCL, 36:287.) Peter speaks to us in the name of Christ; through Peter, whose testimony we believe, it is in Christ whom we believe; he speaks to us in the name of Christ, not in his own name, and it is Christ who asks of us, as he first asked of him, an "absolute obedience".

⁹⁷ *Carmina*, bk. 2, chap. 1, *Expositio symboli*, no. 36 (MGH, AA, 4:257). No. 35: "*Credo in Spiritum sanctum. In hujus commemoratione mysterium Trinitatis impletur. . . .*" (Ibid.)

BELIEF AND FAITH

in a similar context, when he invited his reader to note "the privilege" of this little word.[98] So did Rufinus of Aquilea, when he wrote in his commentary: "By the effect of this syllable, the Creator is distinguished from all his creatures, and what is divine is separated from what is human."[99]

After many others, this was repeated by the Venetian Fantius Duodolo, the author of a cathechism, *Compendium catholicae fidei*, which aims at nothing but reflecting the common teaching:

> Credo in Spiritum sanctum. Et per hunc (articulum) debemus credere in Spiritum sanctum, qui est tertia persona Trinitatis, quoniam sicut in primo et secundo articulo demonstratum est quod debemus credere in Patrem et Filium, ita debemus credere in Spiritum sanctum. . . .
>
> Sanctam Ecclesiam . . . : Et per hunc debemus credere Ecclesiam catholicam esse veram Dei Ecclesiam. . . .[100]

We find substantially the same thing taught by Ven. Marie of the Incarnation to her young Ursuline Sisters at Tours in the seventeenth century, when she commented on the first words of the Creed.[101] And today the Calvinist Karl Barth speaks in witness to the most Catholic tradition when he tells us that Christian faith is "a *credere in* . . . , according to the formula of the Apostles' Creed which it is impossible to neglect; it has God himself for

---

[98] *De Spiritu sancto*, loc. cit.

[99] *Commentarius in symbolum apostolorum*, no. 34: "*Hac itaque Propositionis syllaba, creator a creaturis secernitur, et divina separantur ab humanis*" (PL, 21:373 B; CCL, 20:170); and no. 37: "*Tenet deinde traditio fidei: sanctam Ecclesiam*" (171).

[100] Ed. A. Desguine (1964), 59.

[101] *Explication des mystères de la foi*, 3rd ed. (1708), 9.

its object, the God of the gospel, Father, Son and Holy Spirit";[102] it is "an event which takes place *in the encounter* between the believer and the One in whom he believes".[103] Finally, this is what the Second Vatican Council, without the least innovation, ratified by its authority in the first chapter of the constitution *Dei verbum*.[104] It was, then, because of a false scruple that in the English edition of the little work by Canon Jean Mouroux, *Je crois en Toi*, the title was shortened to read simply *I Believe*, so great, in certain theological circles in the middle of this century, was the fear of a personalistic attitude, suspected of undermining the intellectualism of belief and the objectivism of the truth.[105]

We shall see this still more farther on.

In short, to limit ourselves to the history of the creed of our faith, we may conclude that it was not by chance but in virtue of a deep logic in the Christian faith itself that, from the earliest centuries, even before the doctors began to explain and to justify it in their learned commentaries, "more and more the *credere in* became the habitual expression used to designate the Christian act of faith".[106]

---

[102] *Introduction à la théologie évangelique* (trans. Fernand Ryser, Geneva, 1962), 83.

[103] Ibid., 79. The locus of this encounter is the Church.

[104] Chap. 1, no. 6, on faith. Cf. our commentary in the collective volume by Éditions du Cerf, 1968, 241–62.

[105] The Italian translation is more accurate: "*Io credo in te*" (Brescia, 1950).

[106] Christine Mohrmann, loc. cit., 278. See below, Chapter Eight.

CHAPTER FIVE

THE BELIEVING CHURCH

With regard to the contrasting formulas we have been considering, one essential point must be stressed: the one which deals with the Church. We have already alluded to this. The Roman Catechism, faithful to a long tradition, explains the matter with all desirable clarity:

> It is necessary to believe that there exists a Church which is one, holy and catholic. As regards the three Persons of the Trinity, Father, Son and Holy Spirit, we believe in them in such a way as to place our faith in them. But now, changing our mode of expression, we declare that we believe the holy Church and not in the holy Church. Thus, just by this difference in language, God, who is the Author of all things, is distinguished from all his creatures; and when we receive all the precious blessings which he has conferred on his Church, we attribute them to his divine goodness.[1]

The very word *Church* can be understood according to two possible etymologies. It is either the *convocatio* or *evocatio* or else the *congregatio* of the faithful, i.e., the

---

[1] *Pars prima*, art. 9, no. 23 (Lyons ed. [1741], 111; Latin text): "*Ut hac etiam diversa loquendi ratione Deus omnium effector a creatis rebus distinguatur, praeclaraque omnia quae in Ecclesiam collata sunt, beneficia divinae bonitati accepta referamus.*" On the Church as the object of faith, see Yves de Montcheuil, *Aspects de l'Église*, Unam Sanctam 18 (Paris: Éd. du Cerf, 1949), 16–18.

Church can be considered either as calling all men to herself in order to gather them together in view of their salvation or as being this very gathering of those who have become "believers", the faithful.[2] The first of these two meanings predominated during the early centuries of Christianity.[3] It was the one employed by St. Cyril of Jerusalem, for instance, in his *Catecheses*.[4] St. Augustine even appeals to it with a certain insistency, but more because it was a useful means of distinguishing between the Church of Christ (the *convocatio*) and the Jewish Synagogue (*congregatio*) than because of any essential difference between the two words themselves.[5] But the second word is also found more than once in the writings of the Fathers: in the *Explanatio symboli* of Nicetas of Remesiana,[6] for instance, or in the *Treatise on the Mysteries* by St. Hilary of Poitiers.[7] St. Thomas Aquinas prefers to use this word, saying, *"Ecclesia est idem quod congregatio."*[8] So, it is not surprising to find a similar definition in the Roman Catechism, whose authors were

---

[2] Cf. *Méditation sur l'Église*, 2nd ed. (Paris: Aubier, 1953), 87–89.

[3] Erik Peterson, *Le Mystère des Juifs et des Gentils dans l'Église* (Paris: Desclée de Brouwer, 1932), 16–17 and 70.

[4] *Dix-huitième Catéchèse*, chap. 24: "The Church is called by a very correct name δία τὸ πάντας ἐκκαλεῖσται καὶ ὁμοῦ συνάγειν" (PG, 33:1043–44). Cf. Rom 1:7; 1 Cor 1:2.

[5] *In ps.* 81, no. 1 (CCL, 39:1135–36).

[6] Bk. 5, *Sermo* 3, no. 23 (Gamber, 119).

[7] Bk. 1, preface: *"nostra congregatio"*. Cf. *Commentarius Fortunati in symbolum Athanasianum* (fifth century): "*Ecclesia dicitur congregatio christianorum sive conventus populorum*" (PL, Suppl., 3:726–27).

[8] *Opusc.* 7, chap. 12. Cf. Yves Congar, *Esquisses du mystère de l'Église*, 61ff. Also Cajetan, *In Tertiam*, q. 8, art. 3. Cf. Paul VI, homily at Pentecost, 1964 (*Documentation catholique* 61 [1964], col. 696).

all staunch Thomists.⁹ For the Reformed churches also, "*ecclesia* is first of all the *congregatio fidelium*",¹⁰ as we read in the Augsburg Confession; and this similarity of language, pointed out by Karl Barth,¹¹ shows that there is no total and across-the-board opposition between the Protestant and the Catholic ecclesiologies in the post-Tridentine period.

If we make use of two other words which are very nearly equivalent to *convocatio* and *congregatio*, and which are also part of the traditional Christian vocabulary, we may also think of the Church as either the place or "house" which gathers and shelters the believing people or as this people itself which is gathered together, or in the process of being gathered together, in this house. The two meanings are correlative and complementary, and one may begin by explaining the one or the other, or one may stress one or the other, depending on the point of view one has in mind. Unlike many modern treatises, the conciliar constitution *Lumen Gentium* insists, although not exclusively, on the idea of the Church as the People of God.¹² But as far as our explanation of the Creed is concerned, such a difference does not matter. For from whatever angle we consider her, it is clear that the Church is not the object of our faith in the same way as God is. She cannot be such an object, in the same sense;

---

⁹ "*Congregatio fidelium qui se ad lucem veritatis et Dei notitiam per fidem vocati sunt.*"

¹⁰ Jean Bosc, *La Constitution* "Lumen Gentium", in *Vatican II, Points de vue de théologiens protestants* (Paris: Éd. du Cerf, 1967), 22.

¹¹ *Dogmatics*, (trans. Fernand Ryser, Geneva, Labor et Fides), vol. 4, t. 1, 3 (1967): 10 and 48.

¹² Cf. *Paradoxe et mystère de l'Église* (Paris: Aubier, 1967), 75–88: "*Le Peuple de Dieu*".

and between the two meanings there is not only a nuance but an abyss. "I do not believe in the Church because she is not God".[13] There, in a word, is the abyss created. And this is what tradition keeps telling us under many different forms.

The Church is not God; she is "his footstool"; "she remains at the Lord's feet and washes them with her tears".[14] We frequently find similar declarations all through the centuries on the lips of those who comment on the Creed. "The Church is holy and catholic because her faith in God is right. So, we have not invited you to believe in the Church as we must believe in God; but understand well what we have told you and tell you again: you who are now within the holy, catholic Church, believe in God."[15] The insistent preciseness of such language does not proceed, as we can well see, from some subtle theology; nor is it the product of a more or less esoteric, overly refined school of thought. The Fathers of the Church explained it to the common throng of catechumens.[16] Rufinus of Aquilea handed it

---

[13] Bruno de Wurtzbourg, *In symbolum apostolorum*: "*Credo sanctam Ecclesiam, sed non in illam credo, quia non Deus, sed convocatio vel congregatio christianorum et domus Dei est.*" (PL, 142:561 C.)

[14] Origen, *In Matthaeum series*, chap. 8 (ed. Klostermann, 11, 13).

[15] Pseudo-Maximus of Turin, *tractatus 2, de baptismo*: "*Propterea sancta et catholica est (Ecclesia), quia recte credit in Deum. Non ergo diximus ut in Ecclesiam, quasi in Deum, crederetis; sed intelligite nos dicere et dixisse ut, in Ecclesia sancta et catholica conversantes, in Deum crederetis.*" (PL, 57:776 B C.) Cf. St. Ildefonsus of Toledo (or Julian of Valencia?), *De cognitione baptismi*, chap. 37 (PL, 96:127 D). This passage is used with some variants by Durand of Mende, *Rationale*, bk. 4, chap. 25, nos. 25–26.

[16] Pseudo-Augustine, *Sermo de mysterio baptismatis* (PL, 40:1210); another sermon by an imitator of St. Augustine (PL, Suppl., 2:1362–63).

THE BELIEVING CHURCH

on in a work destined for common use, something we today would call pastoral or catechetical, composed "for the little ones in Christ and for beginners".[17] St. Augustine restated the distinction in some of his brief expositions of the faith.[18] Like Rufinus and Augustine, Alcuin too saw here an elementary truth which he taught to little children. He puts to them the question: "Do you believe in the holy Church?" because he wants to teach them to reply: "No; I believe that the holy Church exists, or rather, I believe that the Church is holy; but I do not believe in her because she is not God but only the *convocation* or *congregation*, the gathering of Christians."[19] The same precision can be found in the humblest medieval catechetical works.[20] John of Fécamp's (eleventh-century) *Confession of Faith* explains this with particular insistence:

I believe in the Holy Spirit just as I believe in the Father and in the Son because the Holy Spirit is God, like the

---

[17] *Expositio symboli*, chap. 1: "*ad parvulorum in Christo et incipientium auditum*" (ed. Manlius Simonetti, CCL, 20 [1961]: 133). Cf. chap. 34 and 37 (169–72).

[18] *De fide et symbolo*, chap. 10, no. 21: "*Credimus et sanctam Ecclesiam.*" Enchiridion, chap. 15, no. 56: "*Adjungimus sic credere nos et in Spiritum sanctum, ut illa Trinitas compleatur, quae Deus est; deinde sancta commemoratur Ecclesia.*" (Bibl. aug., 9:64 and 202.) Magnes of Sens, *Libellus de mysterio baptismatis* (PL, 018:982 B C). Cf. Venantius Fortunatus, *Carmina*, 11, 1; Eligius of Noyon, *De rectitudine catholicae conversationis* (Badcock, 99–100).

[19] *Disputatio puerorum*, chap. 11: "*Esse etenim sanctam Ecclesiam, sed in illam non credo, quia non Deus, sed convocatio seu congregatio christianorum est.*" (PL, 101:1137 D; cf. 1142 A.)

[20] "*In Spiritum sanctum credimus, quia Deus est sicut Pater et Filius; sanctam Ecclesiam catholicam, subauditur: credo esse.*" (*Revue bénédictine* [1907], 198.)

Father and the Son. We must not believe in anyone but God. . . . I believe the holy Church, apostolic, universal and orthodox, which has taught us this sound doctrine. I do not believe in her as I believe in God, but I confess that she is in God, and God is in her, not as though she herself contained God, but rather insofar as she is herself contained by God.[21]

To neglect so fundamental a distinction was not only to use incorrect language. It was, as people realized, to enter upon a dangerous path.

> As the doctrine of the Fathers which is spread throughout the universe confirms, we must believe *in* the Trinity alone; so, remove that syllable from before the name of the Church. . . . Whoever believes in the Church believes in man. . . . Away with that blasphemous conviction.

It was Faustus of Riez who spoke in this manner, consistent with the principles he had laid down.[22] One could hardly be more emphatic. Ten centuries later a famous theologian echoed his words with equal emphasis: Cardinal John de Torquemada, the uncle of the Grand Inquisitor of Spain. Torquemada cites his authorities: "Pope St. Leo",[23] Anselm, Alexander of Halès, Albert the Great, Thomas Aquinas. He could have cited many more. It was a point he took much to heart. As Pope Eugenius IV's theologian at the Council of Basel, he had witnessed there, with indignation, the excesses to which the wrong use of a formula can lead.

---

[21] *Confessio fidei*, pars 3, chaps. 22 and 26 (PL, 101:1069 C, 1072 B): "*Non in illam credo, tamquam in Deum, sed eam in Deo, et Deum in ea esse confiteor; non quasi ipsa contineat Deum, sed potius ipsa contineatur a Deo.*"

[22] *De Spiritu sancto*, bk. 1, chap. 2 (ed. A. G. Engelbrecht, CSEL, 21 [1881]: 104–5).

[23] This was very probably Rufinus.

THE BELIEVING CHURCH

For there are some who understand this in a perverted sense. We ourselves witnessed this at Basel, during the universal Council. The members of that assembly deliberated so much about the authority of the Church that, at the words *"et in unam sanctam Ecclesiam"*, they bent their knees and venerated this article with signs of deepest humility, just as the Christian people usually do at the words *"et homo factus est."*[24]

No doubt these are extreme examples. The insistence and the dramatic language of Faustus of Riez are explained by his desire to refute the "pneumatomactic" error of the Macedonians, which was a menace in his time, by contrasting the divinity of the Holy Spirit with the humanness of the Church.[25] As for Cardinal Torquemada, who received from Eugenius IV the title of *Defensor fidei*, we know that in his time he was the great champion of the papacy—not always a very moderate and enlightened one[26]—against the conciliaristic theories then in vogue. The "Basel crowd" were, he thought, wild, idiotic, demented, lying, blaspheming, impious, arrogant and haughty men; they were *"semen diaboli"*.[27] Never at a loss for images, he further compared them to frogs with their bodies stuck in the mud, with

[24] *Summa de Ecclesia*, bk. 1, chap. 20 (1448; Venice ed., 1561, fol. 232); and chap. 9: "*In quo ostenditur quod Ecclesia sancta sit*": "*Credo sanctam Ecclesiam.*" The book was printed at Cologne in 1480. Cf. N. López Martinez, *El Cardenal Torquemada y la unidad de la Iglesia*, in *Burgense* 1 (1960): 45–71; the same author is preparing a critical edition of the *Summa de Ecclesia* (*Bulletin de théologie ancienne et médiévale* 10, no. 1184).

[25] *De Spiritu sancto*, bk. 1, chaps. 1 and 2 (CSEL, 21:102–5); *De ratione fidei* 4 (458–59).

[26] He defended the divine institution of the cardinals, to the detriment of the bishops.

[27] Discourse of 1441, Mansi, vol. 31, col. 70, 74, 99, 102–4, 112.

only their heads emerging to fill the air with their croakings.[28] The essential observation made by Faustus of Riez and Torquemada nonetheless is that made by all. Erasmus, less than a century after the Council of Basel, made the same remark in his reply to the censures that the Sorbonne had just published against his book of *Colloquies*. In the colloquy entitled *Inquisitio de fide* (March 1524), which is a commmentary on the Creed, Erasmus had recalled the difference existing between the two wordings: *credo Ecclesiam* and *credo in Deum*.[29] The Parisian theologians, very shortsighted traditionalists, had been disturbed by this. Three censures had been drawn up,[30] accusing him of temerity for having dared to suppress the preposition *in* in the article of the Creed dealing with the Church. Was it not in fact true, they demanded, that in their liturgy "many churches sing *in sanctam Ecclesiam*"? As clever as he was erudite, Erasmus defended himself at first by observing that he had not condemned the formula preferred by his censors; he did

---

[28] Loc. cit., col. 102. One must regret such exaggerations. It is true that in the fourth century the gentle Gregory of Nazianzen, disillusioned with the councils of his day, those "gangs of Christ-sellers", denounced the "viciousness", the "fury", the "rage", the "petty quarreling" of those "intriguers" gathered together, who, he continued, "crow like roosters", "fly in your face like wasps", "sharpen their teeth, as cruel as those of wild boars". But these compliments were given in verse. (Poem "on his life"; Gregory of Nazianzen, *Poèmes et lettres*, Lyons-Paris: Vitte, 1941.)

[29] *Opera omnia* (Leyden ed., t. 1, vol. 731 D F). Cf. C. R. Thompson, *Inquisitio de fide, A Colloquy by Desiderius Erasmus Roterdamus* (Yale University Press, 1950).

[30] Dated May 16, 1526, but they were not published until 1531. The story is told by Mr. Jean-Pierre Massaut in *Érasme, la Sorbonne et la nature de l'Église*, in *Colloquium Erasmianum* (Mons: Centre Universitaire de l'État, 1968), 89–116.

THE BELIEVING CHURCH

not attach any great importance to this verbal distinction, taken in itself; furthermore, he had not launched any special investigation to find out what this or that particular church was then singing; but what is sung here or there is not necessarily correct for that reason. Then he went on to the argument from tradition: it is not temerity, he concluded, to speak according to the formal teaching of Cyprian, Augustine, Leo, Thomas Aquinas, Jean Gerson and innumerable others, nor, finally, to speak according to the usage that the Catholic Church has adopted in her official profession of faith and which she has constantly preserved even to this day.[31]

Calvin adopted the traditional idea in his turn when he wrote in his *Institution chrétienne*: "We bear witness that we believe in God, since our heart confides in him as being true and our trust is placed in him, something which cannot be said of the Church."[32] Karl Barth, referring to Calvin as well as to the Roman Catechism, wrote:

> The Creed says: *credo ecclesiam*, not *in ecclesiam*. One cannot believe *in* the Church—the holy Church—as one believes in God, the Father, Son and Holy Spirit. According to this third article, one can believe only in God, in the Holy Spirit, and it is by knowing and confessing his

---

[31] D. Erasmi, *Declarationes ad Censuras Colloquiorum* (*Opera*, Leyden ed., vol. 9, col. 946). This was the "fourth error" denounced in the Colloquy *Inquisitio de fide*.

[32] *Institution chrétienne*, bk. 4, chap. 1; "As for the fact that several bring in the word 'in', there is no probable reason for it"; Augustine and others "teach that this expression would be improper if one added this preposition 'in'; and they confirm their opinion by a reason which bears considerable weight." (Ed. of the *Corpus Reformatorum*, vol. 3, col. 563.)

work that one can believe that the holy Church exists, can believe that forgiveness of sins is granted by the Holy Spirit to man; or, as the first article declares, believe that heaven and earth were created by God the Father. The holiness of the Church, however truly it may exist and may be known by faith, is not the holiness of the Holy Spirit; it is the holiness that the Holy Spirit created and bestows on her. The Holy Spirit separates the Church and sets her apart; he distinguishes her. He gives her a specific being and a particular law. The Church is holy because she remains a part of the created world, in which it is not possible to believe as one believes in God.[33]

Fr. Karl Rahner justifies the Creed's way of expressing this by a consideration which, without going into the question too deeply, comes back to the same argument.

The personal and reciprocal confidence implied by *credere in Deum* cannot be referred to the Church. Although it is true that the Church can and must be "personified", that she is more than the mere numerical sum of individual Christians, that she is not only an . . . ideological construction nor a mere "moral unity", it is likewise true that she is not a person as such; this means that, insofar as we must distinguish her from real individual persons, she cannot in herself be responsible for herself or decide things for herself; nor is she eternal.[34]

Perhaps today there exist even several other reasons, more directly relevant to present-day circumstances, for maintaining or reviving, if not always in exactly the same manner of speaking used by so many authoritative witnesses, at least the essence of the explanations they

[33] *Dogmatics*, (trans. Fernand Ryser) vol. 4, t. 1, 3: 48.
[34] *La piété ecclésiale*, in *Écrits théologiques*, French trans. (DDB), 6 (1967): 180.

THE BELIEVING CHURCH 181

themselves gave for it. These were the reasons which inspired Paul VI in his opening and closing discourses at the second session of the Council in 1963, when he referred to the mosaic in St. Paul's Outside the Walls, which shows Pope Honorius III kissing the feet of Christ, and when he announced his intention of making a pilgrimage to Jerusalem to venerate the holy places. This was a gesture of faith par excellence, which showed the Church of Christ in her fullest sense as totally submissive to Christ.[35] These same reasons led him to choose as the title of his first encyclical these two words which refer to Christ: *"Ecclesiam suam"*. The same reasons, again, prompted the Fathers of Vatican II to begin the doctrinal constitution on the Church by the words: *"Lumen gentium cum sit Christus"* and, on the other hand, to change a number of practices in order to bring out more forcibly that priests and bishops are the "servants of the Word", the "ministers of Christ" and the "dispensers of the mysteries of God".[36] The entire Church always wants to refer humbly to her Lord. She does not wish in any way, even by simple passing preterition, to make herself equal to God or to substitute herself for him.[37]

---

[35] Cf. "Paul VI, pèlerin de Jérusalem", in *Paradoxe et mystère de l'Église* (Paris: Aubier, 1967).

[36] 1 Cor 4:1, etc. Acts 6:4 and 8:25.

[37] Hence, to speak only of the most external signs, the disappearance of certain phrases which up to recent times were quite customary in certain circles, e.g., "for the honor and glory of the holy Church", which usurped the place of the only fully acceptable expression: "for the greater glory of God". However we must not give in to a spirit of quibbling. Once we have received from tradition the teachings which do away with all misunderstandings, we can without doing any harm, in our everyday language, especially when we refer to those whose mission it is to enlighten us and guide us, give to the Church

By doing this the Church puts aside more firmly than ever something which can in fact be called her "permanent temptation", that of self-idolatry. It was certainly very exaggerated, and even a bit ridiculous, to speak in this connection of "the tragic situation confronting the Roman Church", as though the Church must inevitably succumb to it.[38] Still, it may be that such a peril did in the past threaten some of those who held authority in her ranks, not, of course, in the doctrine they taught, but in certain attitudes they assumed. Today it is more likely at the "grass roots", as they say, of certain communities, that a similar and more serious malady might attack the Catholic consciousness. For example, when the liturgical assembly tends to become nothing more than a horizontal dialogue, when adoration, sacred praise, the acknowledgment of sin and supplication for grace lose their force;[39] when the attention of the theoreticians (we shall not call them theologians!) is totally concentrated on "the act by which the community realizes itself"; in short, when a certain exaltation of the human takes precedence over the life of faith. Then one would have a

---

who is our mother a sign of our filial confidence by saying that we believe in her. Such language is undoubtedly less strictly dogmatic (at least insofar as it is incomplete), but there is nothing hyperbolic about it, for we know how faithful she is to our one Lord.

[38] Cf. Paul Tillich, *Perspective d'une analyse religieuse de la culture*, in *Théologie de la culture* (trans. J. P. Gabus and J. M. Saint; coll. "*L'Expérience intérieure*", 1968), 90.

[39] Or again, when the preaching of the word of God tends to be supplanted by the exposition of personal theories; when the hearing of that word tends to be replaced by exegetical or political discussion; when the celebration of the mystery in a joyful yet "holy sobriety" tends to be replaced by unrestrained liberty which "degenerates into a lively game" (R. Guardini).

situation rather closely resembling the one that Torquemada revealed to us at the Council of Basel or that which Paul Tillich denounced. If such a deformation can hardly occur in liturgical assemblies where the sense of the universal Church is maintained and sharpened, one cannot say as much of certain small groups which are formed on the fringes of the official gatherings and whose members have already lost more or less completely their sense of the great community which the eucharistic mystery always gathers completely together in principle. It was with good reason that Dietrich Bonhoeffer some forty years ago warned Christian youth in Germany against such a peril. His admonitions have lost none of their timeliness today, and his voice deserves to be heard far beyond the frontiers of his country and his own church.

> If we ask where it is that faith creates an "experience of the Church" of the purest type, it will certainly not be in communities made up of similar members, romantically bound together, but rather there where individuals are linked to each other by nothing other than their ecclesial community, where Jew and Greek, the pietist and the liberal rub shoulders and still confess the same faith, praying for one another. . . . What our times lack is not experiences but *faith*. Now faith alone gives rise to an authentic experience of the Church. So, we think it important to introduce people into God's community through faith rather than to encourage this community to develop experiences which, as such, are of no use at all, but which, wherever faith is found in the *sanctorum communio*, will come about by themselves.[40]

---

[40] *Sanctorum communio*, republication (Munich, 1954), 211–12 (trans. René Marlé, 47). Cf. *Gemeinsames Leben*, 9th ed. (Munich, 1958), 21: "A community life under the auspices of the Word will

Finally, it is worth remarking here the perfect convergence between the attitudes suggested by the Creed's language, so eloquent in its conciseness, as we have analyzed it in this and in the previous chapter, and the definition of faith, correlative to the one of revelation, given in the first chapter of the constitution *Dei verbum*, promulgated in 1965. The latter, in fact, invites us without any doubt to restore to a position of primacy, if this be necessary, the unique and total character of our faith commitment to the God who reveals himself to us in Jesus Christ. It is to this God, Father, Son and Holy Spirit, that man must "abandon himself freely and entirely", by giving willing assent to all that has been revealed to him.[41] This perfect, fundamental concurrence between the oldest expression of our faith and the most recent conciliar constitution brings out very well the eminently traditional character of Vatican II.[42] It would be hard to find a better sign of the continuity of our faith.

We believe in God, then, and we profess that the Church is from God and for God. *"Ipse in Deum credit, qui in Deum sanctam Ecclesiam confitetur."*[43] But, once we have thus recognized that the Church (like any other object of faith which is not God himself) does not

---

remain healthy only where . . . it is understood as an element of the one, holy and universal Church. . . . Any principle of selection and any consequent separation that are not conditioned by complete objectivity . . . are of the greatest danger for a Christian community. On this path of spiritual selectivity, psychological factors always creep in . . . and lead to the sectarian spirit." (Ibid., 98.)

[41] *Vatican II, la révélation divine* (Paris: Éd. du Cerf, 1968), 1:241–62.

[42] The same should be said of Paul VI's *Profession of Faith*: "We believe in the Church."

[43] Peter Chrysologus, *Sermo* 57 (PL, 52:360 B).

merit the preposition that would seem to put her on an equal footing with God, it is important to recognize the privileged place she does occupy, nonetheless, in the economy of the Christian faith.

We are speaking of faith. We say, "I believe in God." But where does this faith reside in all its fullness? Where is that profession perfectly fulfilled? Obviously not in me, in my individual being. Nor is it in any of my brothers; and it would be an odious pharisaism to demand it of any of them in the name of the idea I have so easily conceived of it. So, who is this "I" who can always say with humble yet total assurance, "I believe in God; I believe in Jesus Christ"? What is this being which in the ardor of her faith, without faltering, without illusion or reservation, adheres to Christ as the bride clings to her spouse? What is this being, if not precisely that spouse which the Word of God chose, to whom he came to join himself by becoming incarnate in mortal flesh and whom he "purchased with his own blood"?[44] This "I" which believes in Jesus Christ can be only the Church of Jesus Christ. Not, indeed, some hypostasis dreamed up by us somewhere above ourselves in an imaginary heaven, but this very community of believers, created by the power of the Word, animated by the Spirit of Christ and in which each of us shares far more than he contributes to it.[45] In her alone is found this fullness and this

[44] Perhaps one should bring in a corrective here, by comparing the Church rather to the Messianic "betrothed", whose union with Christ will be perfect only at the consummation; thus the perfection of her faith should then be called the perfection of its tendency and aim, the certain, straight direction of its course, rather than the perfection of acquired fullness. See below, Chapter Nine.

[45] Regarding the personality of the Church, see Hans Urs von Balthasar, *Sponsa Verbi* (1961), 148–203: "Wer ist die Kirche?", and

constant perfection of faith received from God, as a prayer in the Mozarabic liturgy so admirably states.[46] Our Creed is not the expression of the faith of isolated believers.[47] St. Thomas Aquinas had noted this: "The confession of our faith is made in the Creed, as being made in the name of the whole Church, which is united to God by faith."[48]

Once again, let us listen to Karl Barth expressing in his turn the truth that complements the one he reminded us of just a short while ago. Without trying in the least to minimize the opposition between his ecclesiology and that of the Roman Church, we can note once again on this specific point a convergence which is not without its significance.

> [One might say] *cum grano salis*, that as regards Jesus Christ we do not have, first of all, believers and then a Church formed by them. First of all we have the Church; and then, through her and in her, the believers. God is certainly not bound to the Church any more than he was to the Synagogue. But those who receive revelation are so bound; they are what they are because a Church exists, because they are in that Church and because they do not exist without the Church or apart from her. By "Church" we must understand not only the inner and

---

La Gloire et la croix 1 (trans. Robert Givord, Paris: Aubier, 1965): 215 and 295–96. Cf. Karl Rahner, quoted above, 180.

[46] "*Da Ecclesiae tuae catholicae et sanctae fidei plenitudinem, quam illi dedisti semper perfecte tenere.*" *Liber mozarabicus sacramentorum* (ed. M. Ferotin, 1912, col. 637).

[47] "All private Christianity is illegitimate": Karl Barth, *Dogmatics*, 4, 1: 770. See Chapter Ten below.

[48] *Summa theologica*, Secunda secundae, q. 1, art. 9, ad 3: "*Confessio fidei traditur in symbolo, quasi ex persona totius Ecclesiae, quae per fidem unitur.*"

THE BELIEVING CHURCH

visible gathering of those whom God has called in Jesus Christ to be his own but also the external and visible gathering of those who, in time, have heard and confessed what they heard.[49]

Te per orbem terrarum sancta confitetur Ecclesia. It is the Church that believes.[50] It is she who confesses the Trinity, she who offers praise and thanksgiving; it is she who hopes and awaits the return of her Lord,[51] she who bears witness to him by her unfailing faith which bears fruit throughout the world.[52] It is she who, advancing in faith, prays and works, seeking in all things to fulfill the divine will.[53] It is she whom the Spirit of Christ gathers into one and unifies; she whom he enlightens and guides throughout her long earthly pilgrimage.[54] It is she who, while awaiting the face-to-face vision, faithful amidst

---

[49] *Kirchliche Dogmatik*, 1, 2: 230–31. We have borrowed the translation by Mr. Jean-Louis Leuba, in *A la découverte de l'espace oecuménique* (Neuchâtel: Delachaux et Niestlé, 1967), 89–90 ("Le Probléme de l'Église chez Karl Barth"). By the same author: *Credo* (Fr. trans., P. and J. Jundt, *"Je Sers"*, Paris, 1936), 179.

[50] Ambrose, *In Lucam*, bk. 6, chap. 38: *"Ecclesiam quae credidit"* (ed. G. Tissot, SC, 45:242). Quodvultdeus, *De accedentibus ad gratiam*, no. 8 (PL, Suppl., 3:268).

[51] Gregory, *In Cantica*, proemium, no. 10: *"Sancta Ecclesia, diu praestolans adventum Domini, diu sitiens fontem vitae"* (PL, 79:478 A); *Moralia in Job*, bk. 4, no. 46 (75, 660 B); bk. 35, no. 25 (76, 762 C).

[52] Irenaeus, *Adversus haereses*, bk. 3, chap. 12, no. 7; chap. 24, no. 1 (ed. F. Sagnard, SC, 34:228 and 398); Augustine, *Sermo* 214, no. 11 (PL, 38:1071), etc.

[53] Vatican II, constitution *Lumen Gentium*, nos. 17 and 65: *"Orat et laborat Ecclesia. . . . Continuo progrediens in fide, spe et caritate, ac divinam voluntatem in omnibus quaerens et obsequens."*

[54] Isaac of the Star, *Epistola de anima*: *"Spiritus igitur regit, consolatur, erudit et perducit Ecclesiam ad Christum, quam Ipse simul sine macula et ruga offerret regnum Deo et Patri"* (PL, 194:1889 A), etc.

trials and darkness, resisting all scandal, jealously preserves the deposit entrusted to her.[55] For every one of us, the Church is the archeytpe of the perfect "yes". *Ne respicias peccata mea sed fidem Ecclesiae tuae....*

> What in us is impure and fallible is, there, in the innermost heart [of the Church], pure and infallible. Our obedience in faith, when confronted with the absolute Norm, takes flesh in our relationships with the Church (as Spouse of the Lord and our Mother); we share, as her members, in her perfect obedience as servant.[56]

It was the reflection of this faith, so intrepid, full and perfect in its submission to the Lord, that Fr. Teilhard de Chardin noticed on the countenance of the Church when for the first time he visited Rome, her visible center. Unlike so many travellers, even Christian travellers, he had, in a single stroke, penetrated to the essence. This Roman Church seemed to him unshakeable, in her "paradoxical and humble assurance that she represented the earthly extremity of an arch that extended between earthly man and that which is beyond man". He felt in her the "security that arises from a faith that nothing can disturb"; and this experience communicated to him not

---

[55] Irenaeus, *Adversus haereses*, bk. 1, chap. 10, no. 2: "*Hanc praedicationem cum acceperit, et hanc fidem, quemadmodum praediximus, Ecclesia, et quidem in universum mundum disseminata, diligenter custodit.*" (PG, 7:551 A.) Ambroise Autpert, *Sermo in Purificatione*, chap. 5 "*Haec est enim Ecclesia catholica, quae fidem uni Domino tanquam legitimo viro conservat, et congregationem multorum in fide multiplicat.*" Hugues de Rouen, *Contra haereticos*, bk. 3, chaps. 8 and 9 (PL, 192:1296 B, 1297 D).

[56] Hans Urs von Balthasar, *L'Amour seul est digne de foi* (Fr. trans., R. Givord, *"Foi vivante"*, Paris: Aubier, 1966), 151. Cf. Dom Odon Casel, *Le Mystère de l'Église* (Mame, 1965), 262–70.

only a sentiment of deep admiration but also a renewed confidence in his own faith. Through the Church and in the Church the link which, through her and in her, had already bound him to the "personal Center of the Universe" grew firmer than ever.[57]

Prior to any distinction between the Church teaching and the Church taught, there exists, therefore, the *believing Church*: *Ipsa credit mater Ecclesia*.[58] By its two dogmatic constitutions, the recent Council placed renewed emphasis on this traditional truth. Thus the Christian's faith is, and can only be, a sharing in this common faith of the Church. It is through the mediation of the Church, and within the Church, that the Christian can say in all truth: "I believe in God." If he turned aside to follow some solitary way in his faith, how could he continue to believe in this God who revealed himself in Christ so that we might live in communion with those who impart his message to us, and through them, with him?[59] The Church is not God; but she is "the house of God".[60] She is "the Church of the living God",[61] the

---

[57] See the passages quoted in our *L'Eternel Féminin, étude sur un texte du Père Teilhard de Chardin* (Paris: Aubier, 1968), 317–19.

[58] Gilbert de Hoyland, *In Cantica*, Sermo 21, no. 5 (PL, 184:113 A). Cf. Augustine, *De duabus animabus*, chap. 15, no. 24: "*Trina unitas, quam catholic Ecclesia colit*" (Bibl. aug., 17:114).

[59] Cf. 1 Jn 1:2–3.

[60] Isaiah 60:13: "*Domum majestatis suae glorificabo*." Augustine, *Confessions*, bk. 12, chap. 15, no. 19 (Bibl. aug., 14:370). Pseudo-Augustine, *Sermo* 242, no. 4: "*Quia Ecclesia non est Deus, sed domus Dei est.*" (PL, 39:2193.) Gregory, *In evangelia*, hom. 38, no. 11: "*Nos . . . qui jam fidem in Ecclesia habemus*" (PL, 76:1289 B). Fulgentius of Ruspe, *Contra Fabianum*, fragm. 35 (PL, 65:826–27); cf. Origen, *In Mattheum*, series c, 46 (ed. Klostermann [1933], 94), etc.

[61] 1 Tim 3:15; cf. Eph 2:20–22.

dwelling place where "the Lord's majesty" resides,[62] the city which he built, the school where he teaches,[63] the temple where he is adored.[64] She is the treasure house, the rich cellar where the Apostles have deposited the truth, that life-giving beverage which is Christ.[65] If the sinner whose faith has become "unformed", mutilated, even "dead", can still continue to recite the Creed without lying, it is insofar as he still remains within this household of believers where the Spirit of truth resides; it is insofar as he is never excluded from this heritage; insofar as he borrows, so to speak, the voice of the entire Church.[66] Developed in the thirteenth century by the great Scholastics, this particular doctrine is closely connected with the general principle which we are considering in this chapter; and we might say as much of the doctrine about "implicit faith" set forth by St. Thomas with respect to the baptism of infants.[67] "We must

---

[62] Rupert of Deutz, *In Isaiam*, chap. 22: "*Domus majestatis Domini, sancta catholicae fidei Ecclesia est.*" (PL, 167:1346 A.)

[63] Augustine, *Sermo* Guelferb., 32, no. 4 (Morin, 566).

[64] Augustine, *Enchiridion*, chap. 15, no. 56 (Bibl. aug., 9:202 and 204). Other references in A. M. La Bonnardière, *Revue des études augustiniennes* 13 (1967): 40–41. Origen, *In Joannem*, 13, 13, 83–85: "The Church is above all an adoring community", says the Orthodox theologian Georges Florovsky (quoted by T. Wale, 356).

[65] St. Irenaeus, *Adversus haereses*, bk. 3, chap. 4, no. 1 (SC, 34 [1952]: 114).

[66] St. Thomas, *Summa theologica*, Secunda secundae, q. 1, art. 9, ad 3. *In 3 Sent.*, dist. 25, q. 1, art. 2, ad 4: "*Nihilominus habens fidem informen, dicens symbolum, non secat, quia hoc dicit in persona Ecclesiae.*" *Summa* of Alexander of Halès, tertia pars, inq. 2, tract. 2, q. 1, tit. 1, chap. 2, *De expositione articulorum symboli apostolorum* (ed. Quaracchi, 4:1124). William Durand, *Rationale*, bk. 4, chap. 25, nos. 15–16 (Lyons ed. [1672], 135).

[67] *In 4 Sent.*, dist. 6, q. 2, art. 2, sol. 3. Cf. *Tertia*, q. 68, art. 9; q. 69, art. 8; q. 71, art. 1, ad 3.

admit", writes a Presbyterian theologian, "that one of the unquestionable advantages of this doctrine is the element of permanence which it gives to faith by making the believer share in the collective faith of the Church."[68] The adult, and even the righteous, can recite this same Creed without presumption only on the same condition, in the same ecclesial perspective. More or less explicitly, all authentic faith is bound up with the faith of the Church, with that perfect, chaste, integral and indefectible faith,[69] the first expression of which was Simon Peter's "confession" on the road to Caesarea Philippi: "O blessed confession, not dictated by either flesh or blood, but which the heavenly Father has revealed. It was that faith which founded the Church on earth!"[70]

"Christianity was born, not when a man called Jesus was born, but when one of his disciples, in an irresistible impulse, said to him: You are the Christ!" In this passage from Paul Tillich we can disregard a certain assumed indifference toward the person of Jesus.[71] The idea in itself is correct. One might only add that this confession of Peter's marked not only the birth of

[68] T. F. Torrance, *Les Réformateurs et la fin des temps*, in *Cahiers théologiques* 35 (Neuchâtel-Paris, 1955). One must admit this, says the author, "while profoundly disapproving the Roman doctrine of *fides implicita*".

[69] Cyprian, *Epist.* 73, chap. 11: "*Et ipsa Ecclesia incorrupta, et casta, et pudica est*" (G. Hartel, CSEL, 3, 2 [1871]: 786). Epiphanius Latinus, *Interpretatio evangeliorum*, chap. 47: "*Ecce aperta et manifesta Trinitas, quam pura conscientia tenet sancta catholica et apostolica Ecclesia.*" (PL, Suppl., 3:921.) Cf. Vatican II, constitution *Lumen Gentium*, no. 64 (with the references).

[70] "*O beata confessio, quam non caro et sanguis, sed Pater caelestis revelat! Haec in terris fundat Ecclesiam!*" St. Thomas, *Catena super Matthaei evangelium*, ad Urbanum IV epistola dedicatoria.

[71] *Systematic Theology* 1:224 (quoted in G. Tavard, *Introduction à Paul Tillich* [1968], 87).

"Christianity"—a rather vague term—but of the Church of Christ.

In his great masterpiece, the *City of God*, St. Augustine succeeded in expressing admirably the two aspects of the truth which we are trying to grasp in this chapter. "We, therefore," he writes, "who are Christians and are called by that name do not believe in Peter but in the One in whom Peter believed; and thus we are 'built up' by the words of Peter in proclaiming Christ."[72] So too at the very end of his preaching on John's Gospel, in the process of comparing the two great Apostles: Peter, he remarks, received his name (*Petrus*) from "rock" (*petra*) and not vice versa (*"non enim a Petro petra, sed Petrus a petra"*)—just as the Christian receives his name from Christ, and not vice versa. Peter is not, therefore, the foundation of the building; there can be no other foundation than Christ Jesus; but it is in Peter, because of his faith, that the Church has recieved the keys of the kingdom of heaven; and it is because of his apostolic primacy (*"propter apostolatus sui primatum"*) that Peter bears in himself the figure of the entire Church.[73] It was his act of faith that made him the "first Apostle".

Consequently, my faith is not, properly speaking, and cannot be "faith in the Church". Not in any of her members, not in the representatives of her authority any more than in the others does the Church require that of

---

[72] "*Nos ergo qui sumus vocamurque christiani, non in Petrum credimus, sed in quem credidit Petrus, Petri de Christo aedificati sermonibus.*" *De civitate Dei*, bk. 8, chap. 54, no. 1 (Bibl. aug., 36:686–88). Cf. above, Chapter Four, 140ff.

[73] *Tractatus in Joannem*, 124, no. 5 (CCL, 36:684–85). Cf. *Sermo* Lambot 3, De amore Petri: "*Videmus in Petro commendatam petram. . . . Iste discipulus a petra Petrus, quomodo a Christo christianus. Quare ista volui praeloqui? Ut commendarem vobis in Petro Ecclesiam cognoscendam. Aedificavit enim Christus Ecclesiam non super hominem, sed super Petri*

THE BELIEVING CHURCH

me. It is God who, in giving himself to men, subjects them to himself in return—"God, to whom, exclusively, the act of faith can be addressed". Just as the act of faith demanded long ago by the God of the Covenant was not demanded by the prophets for themselves, so too the total abandonment in faith which can be owed and given only to God is not claimed in the New Testament by the Church or by her representatives. In spite of the authority imparted to them, and which proceeds directly from Christ, the testimony of the Apostles and their successors has only an "indicative" character. As has been said about John the Baptist pointing out Christ, it is not on their finger that we are asked to fix our attention, but on the One to whom their finger points."[74]

> In a very real sense every human word is already transcended by the event which it announces, even if the ecclesial dimension remains indispensable in the world of human experience.... The word proclaimed by the Church is by its nature a transient phenomenon, a pure reference to the fact which makes itself visible and present in that word and which rises with its own evidence above and beyond the Church's word.

The faith which preaching calls for, therefore, "is not adherence to the word that preaches, but to the Word of God incarnate, crucified and risen again; this fulfills and goes beyond the mysterious passage in Deuteronomy: 'The word is very close to you, on your lips and in your hearts.' "[75]

---

confessionem." (PL, Suppl., 2:756.)

[74] Or again, as Origen says, John the Baptist was the *voice*, and he should have been listened to, but only so as to be brought to the *Word* whom he pointed out. *Commentaire sur saint Jean*, 2:193–94. (C. Blanc, SC, 120 [1966]: 339.)

[75] Deut 30:14; Rom 10:8. Hans Urs von Balthasar, *La Foi du Christ*

But if my faith is not faith in the Church, this is because in reality it is nothing but the very faith of that Church, which I have received from her and in which I share in proportion to my capacity. "Carrying forward and upholding my personal faith, there is the faith of the Church. . . . It is the Church first of all, as a community, which believes in her Lord; and with her and in her I am moved to say personally: I believe."[76]

For the sake of clarity we may at this point distinguish two phases, as it were.

In a first step, since I am not one of the original Apostles of Christ, I heard, in one way or another, the preaching of the Good News, which was announced in our times by the Church, the heiress of the Apostles. I heard and I believed. Then through her Magisterium, the Church handed on to me with authority the word of salvation which she had received from her Master; she handed on to me the body of truths in which that word was expressed, and she gave it to me with as much clarity as she herself possesses at this time. Through her, therefore, I learned that a God exists who is one in three Persons, and all the rest of revealed doctrine. The for-

---

("*Foi vivante*", Paris: Aubier, 1968), 98–104. *La Gloire et la croix* 1 (1965): 177. Cf. Louis Bouyer, *La Spiritualité orthodoxe et la spiritualité protestante et anglicane* (Paris: Aubier, 1965), 290: In modern Catholicism, "has not the personal character of faith . . . too often given place to a piety where social and external factors counted for too much?"

[76] Roger Schutz and Max Thurian, *La Parole vivante au Concile* (Les Presses de Taizé, 1966), 43. Epiphanius Latinus (fifth or sixth century?), *Interpretatio evangeliorum*, chap. 28: "*Fides apostoli quae est supra petram Christi fundata, semper invicta et inconcussa permanet. . . . Ergo, dilectissimi, usque in finem in beati Petri confessione permaneamus.*" (PL, Suppl., 3:869–70.)

mulations in which she specified the object of her faith have become those of my own faith. In this first phase—which is not necessarily chronological but which will last as long as my earthly pilgrimage lasts—the Church was for me simply the one who proclaimed and the mistress of saving truth. In her regard I was only a hearer, as it were, then a disciple; or, if one prefers, after I had acknowledged her credentials, I became subject, as it were, to her Magisterium, through which it was to God himself that I realized I was submitting myself. My relationship with her in this perspective was still an external one. She said to me on the day of my baptism, in the words of Cyril of Jerusalem: "Embrace and preserve the faith which has been given to you by the Church."[77]

But this was only a beginning. "By her preaching, the Church invites men to be bound to her faith; first *through* her, then *in* her and *with* her."[78] So there comes a second phase—contained in the first like a seed, and which the first demands—a phase which, without ever eliminating the former, deepens and interiorizes my relationship with the Church, in proportion as the Church's faith penetrates me more deeply and becomes more interiorly mine. "The Pauline formula *fides ex auditu* describes only our access to the faith; the confession in baptism is still only the entry into the living covenant relationship with God."[79] But in baptism, the Church of Christ has infused her life into me, a life which is the life of Christ. By her I have entered that mysterious organism that St. Paul called the "body of Christ", animated by his Spirit; I became one of his members. The body as a whole is the entire Church, united to her Head as the members of a

[77] *Cinquième Catéchèse baptismale*, chap. 12 (PG, 33:520 B).
[78] Hans Urs von Balthasar, *La Gloire et la croix* 1:499.
[79] Id., 185 and 189.

body are to the head and as the bride is to her spouse. The People of God to which I now belong is not like the people of earthly cities; its visible organization is entirely at the service of a "communion" in which each one can share in the good of all—in that good which is Christ. Then I too, no longer solely through the intermediary of a Church to which I am joined by a merely external link of teaching and authority, but in her, through her mediation and thanks to the same Spirit which assists her from without and inspires me from within, I adhere to Christ.

St. Augustine, the Doctor of the Church and the Doctor of the "Master within", said it all in a few words: "*Ille Petri magister Christus in doctrina, quae ad vitam ducit aeternam, ipse est magister noster*"; "Christ, who was (and is) Peter's master by teaching him the doctrine which leads to eternal life, is himself also our master."[80] In the last century this process of interiorization of the faith in each member of the Church was described at length by Moehler, the great Catholic theologian from Tubingen.

> In St. Cyprian's time, the Catholic believed this or that Christian dogma not only *because* it had been believed earlier in the time of St. Irenaeus or because in his day the Church professed it; *this external faith is only a starting point*; but because in him truth bore witness to itself by the power of the Holy Spirit. But since it is the same

---

[80] *De civitate Dei*, loc. cit. (Bibl. aug., 36:688). The Church's experience becomes my experience: "What evolves in this way is an immense spiritual experience. . . . For the Catholic there is no personal experience of the Spirit achieved within an isolated individuality, but an experience inserted into that of the Church and guaranteed by the latter": Jean Mouroux, *Je crois en Toi* (1965 ed., "Foi vivante", chap. 4).

Spirit who animated the Church at the time of these great Christians, and which continues to animate her now, the Spirit must manifest himself to the believer of today in the same manner as to his forefathers. It is because of this testimony which the Spirit bears to himself *in us* that we believe what all the Christian centuries believed. Faith, then, is not a blind submission to authority, as heretics have claimed ever since the second century. It compels our recognition as having its own authority in itself. Its harmony with the faith of all centuries is a necessary consequence of the essence of Christianity. The same cause always produces the same effect: all the faithful have *one and the same* consciousness, the same faith, because one and the same power is at the origin of this faith.[81]

Nothing less adequately expresses the truth than the extrinsicist doctrines which maintain in the Church only a unity resulting from constraint—unless it be a unity resulting from indifference, having no other link than a visible transmission and a visible authority.[82] They transform the obedience of faith into a faith which is mere obedience. Totally oblivious of the Spirit of Christ, they suffocate Christian liberty; then, rejected sooner or later as an intolerable yoke, they soon give way to spiritual anarchy. But of course the movement toward interiorization described by Moehler is not, and never has been, something achieved by all. It depends less on

---

[81] *L'Unité dans l'Église*, part 1, chap. 2, no. 13 (*"Unam Sanctam"* 2 [Paris: Éd du Cerf, 1938]: 39–40; trans. A. de Lilienfeld).

[82] This is what Maurice Blondel showed in his brave battle against extrinsicism. See in particular his *Histoire et dogme* (1904) and his articles in *La Semaine sociale de Bordeaux* (under the pseudonym of Testis, in *Annales de philosophie chrétienne*, 1910–1911). See below, Chapter Seven, 230.

profound doctrinal study than on the inner depth of one's Christian life. Far from relaxing, it tightens the bond between the faithful and the Church; it is what makes martyrs. Only by a complete misinterpretation could one see in it a kind of individualistic withdrawal into oneself or a claim to private judgment. Quite the contrary; faith's interior quality is deepened and developed only within the ecclesial communion. It is within this communion that we adore the Father, the Creator of the universe, and the Son and the Spirit.[83] For the Church is "a people gathered together in the unity of the Father, Son and Holy Spirit".[84]

To express fully the interior character of this link binding the believer to the Church, the image of the house into which he is introduced, or that of a temple in which he worships, would be too feeble. The only fitting image here is that of motherhood, which has been recognized since the earliest Christian times.[85] Faustus of Riez himself, at the same time as he protested against those who spoke of believing in the Church as though she were the author of our salvation, saluted her as "the mother of our regeneration".[86] The Church is a mother who "gives birth according to the faith" or "to the

[83] Cf. Erasmus, *Explicatio in symbolum* (Lugduni Batavorum, 1541), 170: "*Venimus ad sanctam Ecclesiam, in qua adoramus Patrem omnium conditorem.*"

[84] Vatican II, constitution *Lumen Gentium*, no. 4.

[85] Cf. H. de Lubac, *Paradoxe et mystère de l'Église* (Paris: Aubier, 1967), 84–86, 104–6. Aloïs Müller, *Ecclesia-Maria* (Fribourg: Paradosis, 5, 1951).

[86] *De Spiritu sancto*, bk. 1, chap. 2: "Credimus Ecclesiam, quasi regenerationis matrem; non in Ecclesiam, quasi in salutis auctorem." (Engelbrecht, CSEL, 21:104.) See other passages in Fr. Th. Camelot, O.P., *Le Sens de l'Église chez les Pères latins*, Nouvelle revue théologique (1961), 367–81.

faith", who nourishes her children with her life-giving faith.[87] The metaphor survived through the centuries, and the sixteenth-century Reformers did not reject it. In 1518, Luther advised believers to confide their doubts to the Church, "like a child who entrusts himself to his mother's breast".[88] In 1538, Bucer at Strasbourg taught the motherhood of the Church. Calvin received this doctrine from him and repeated it in his *Institution chrétienne*—to the astonishment of his admirers and historians, unaccustomed to such "Catholic ideas" and fearing an "ecclesiolatry" which would risk becoming a "Quaternity".[89]

> You can see how necessary it is for us to believe the Church, since in order for us to be regenerated unto immortal life, she must conceive us as a mother conceives her children; and if we are to be preserved, she must maintain and nourish us in her bosom. For she is the mother of us all, to whom our Lord has entrusted all the treasures of his grace, so that she may be the guardian thereof and may dispense them through her ministry.[90]

In the last edition of the *Institution*, Calvin expanded this same doctrine even more, in similar terms:

---

[87] Irenaeus, *Adversus haereses*, bk. 3, preface and chap. 24, no. 1 (PG, 7:843 and 966). Augustine, *Sermo* 213, no. 7 (PL, 38:1063–64). Epiphanius Latinus (PL, Suppl., 3:878–79). Rupert, *In Cantica* (PL, 168:941 A), etc.

[88] Quoted by Émile G. Léonard, *Histoire générale du protestantisme* 1 (1961): 50.

[89] Alexandre Ganoczy, *Calvin théologien de l'Église et du ministère* (Paris: Éd. du Cerf, 1964), 193–96. Cf. Émile Doumergue, *Jean Calvin* 5 (Lausanne, 1917): 32. E. G. Léonard, 1:306.

[90] *Institution*, 1541 ed., bk. 4, chap. 3: the translation is by Calvin himself from the second Latin edition, 1539. (*Opera selecta*, 4:568; cf. *Corpus Reformatorum*, vol. 29, col. 539.)

But since I now intend to speak of the visible Church, let us learn from her one title of "mother" how useful, indeed necessary, it is for us to know her. For there is no entering into everlasting life unless we are conceived in the womb of this mother, unless she brings us forth, unless she nourishes us at her breast, and finally unless she holds us and keeps us under her guidance and control until we are finally freed from this mortal body and become like unto the angels. For our weakness does not allow us to withdraw from her school until we have been her disciples throughout the entire course of our life. It should also be noted that outside of her one cannot hope for the remission of sins or for any salvation.[91]

As a faithful disciple of Calvin, Philippe du Plessis-Mornay in his monumental *Traité de l'Église* (1600) made use once again of the traditional metaphor, so expressive of the basic truth on this point. "God", he says on the first page, "has willed that the Church be honored and recognized as a Mother by all those whose Father he has deigned to become."[92]

Still, one should understand—and Calvin, following St. Augustine, invites us to do so—that if the Church is our mother she is "not so in the same way as Eve"; she is not the mother "of a people whose birth would be a tearing away and the principle of numberless oppositions" but the mother "of a people which is born by being brought together into a single body of God's children who had been scattered".[93] Unlike earthly mothers, she gives life to her children by receiving them into her

---

[91] 1559 ed., translation of 1560, bk. 4, chap. 1 (*Corpus Reformatorum*, vol. 32, col. 568).

[92] *Traité de l'Église*, 1.

[93] Louis Bouyer, *Le Sens de la vie monastique* (Desclée, 1950), 160.

womb where she nourishes, educates and liberates them; she brings them up to the adult stage of Christian manhood by keeping them there.[94] She is the "mother of unity".[95]

So, let us say with Augustine, in whom we hear the voice of Irenaeus and many others: "See the womb of the mother Church; see how she groans and is in travail to bring you to birth and make you reach the light of faith."[96]

---

[94] Augustine, *Sermo* May 94, no. 1 (Morin, 334). Quodvultdeus, *De accedentibus ad gratiam*, 2, 12 (PL, Suppl., 3:285), etc. Cf. Yves Congar, *Au milieu des orages* (1969), 115–20: "Église, mon foyer maternel."

[95] Augustine, *Sermo* 192, no. 2 (PL, 38:1013). Bernard, *In Cant.*, s. 68, no. 4.

[96] S. 216, no. 7: "*Ecce uterus matris Ecclesiae, ecce ut te pariat atque in lucem fidei producat, laborat in gemitu suo.*" (PL, 38:1080.) No. 8: "*Pater Deus est, mater Ecclesia*" (1081), etc. Irenaeus, *Adversus haereses*, bk. 5, chap. 20, no. 2, which Moehler quoted in his *L'Unité dans l'Église* (trans. already cited, 47). Gregory of Nyssa, *Vie de Moïse*, 12 (SC, 1 ter:113).

CHAPTER SIX

THE BELIEVER IN THE CHURCH

All that we have considered in the previous chapter is obviously not explicitly contained in the simple words: *"Credo in sanctam Ecclesiam."* Yet all of it is already found, in germ so to speak (*quasi in nuce*), in an ancient form of the baptismal creed used in a number of churches, particularly those of Syria, Egypt and Africa. The catechumen was questioned three times by the bishop (or deacon), as we saw before. What interests us here is that after the first two interrogations: *"Credis in Deum. . . ? in Jesum Christum. . . ?"*, the bishop finally asked: *"Credis in Spiritum sanctum in sancta Ecclesia?"* Now these last three words, "in the holy Church", i.e., "within the holy Church", apparently referred not only to the candidate's faith in the Holy Spirit[1] but also to his faith in God the Father and in his Son Jesus Christ. Be that as it may, these words did not constitute an extra article of faith, as though they were the last in a list, rather they formed the conclusion or, to be more exact, the summing up of the whole. They marked the end of the triple *"credis?"*, the triple interrogation by the bishop and also, thereby, of the triple *"credo"*, the triple profession of faith by the catechumen. For the three baptismal interrogations formed an indissoluble unity, like all our trinitarian formulas, which all profess the one God. One may

[1] J. A. Jungmann seems to recognize this, op. cit., 148.

further observe, as Dom Bernard Botte does, that if the final mention of the holy Church had referred only to the Holy Spirit, we would have had a formula such as: "Do you believe in the Holy Spirit *who is*, who resides, in the holy Church?"[2]

A passage from Tertullian, in his *Treatise on Baptism*, seems to echo this arrangement.

> If every word of God is supported by three witnesses, how much more his gift! In virtue of the baptismal blessing, we have as witnesses of the faith the very ones who are the guarantors of our salvation. This triad of divine names also suffices to establish our hope. Since the witness of our faith as well as the promise of our salvation are guaranteed by the three Persons, the mention of the Church is necessarily joined thereto. For where the Three are, Father, Son and Holy Spirit, there too is the Church, which is the body of the Three.[3]

St. Irenaeus had already said much the same thing: "The communication of Christ, which is the Holy Spirit", is found in the Church.[4] St. Hippolytus' ἀποστολικὴ αραδοσις (*Apostolic Tradition*), in its original ver-

---

[2] Dom B. Botte, *Note sur le symbole baptismal de saint Hippolyte*, in *Mélanges Joseph de Ghellinck* (1951), 1:189–200. P. Nautin: "I believe in the Holy Spirit in the holy Church for the resurrection of the body", *Étude sur l'histoire et la théologie du Symbole*, "*Unam Sanctam*" 17 (Paris: Éd. du Cerf, 1947). This latter work is well worth reading; it is short but extremely provocative.

[3] *De baptismo*, chap. 61, no. 2 (trans. F. Refoulé and M. Crouzy, SC, 75): "*Necessario adicitur ecclesiae mentio, quoniam ubi tres, id est pater et filius et spiritus sanctus, ibi ecclesia quae trium corpus est.*" Cf. *De Pudicitia*, chap. 21, no. 16.

[4] *Adversus haereses*, bk. 3, chap. 24, no. 1 (PG, 7:966 B): "*Ubi enim Ecclesia, ibi et Spiritus Dei, et ubi Spiritus Dei, illic Ecclesia et omnis gratia.*" Cf. P. Nautin, 45. See below, n. 62.

sion as restored by Dom Botte in conformity with the Sahidic text and supported by the Arabian and Ethiopian texts, uses similar language: "Do you believe in the Spirit, holy, good, life-giving and purifying everything, in (=inside) the holy Church?"[5] In this same context of the liturgical ceremonies accompanying baptism, the bishop ends an invocation by saying: "To you be glory, Father and Son with the Holy Spirit, in the holy Church, now and forever and ever."[6] The essence of the formula is again given by Hippolytus in the prayer of episcopal consecration, in the epiclesis of the prayer of offering, and he recommends that this be repeated "in every blessing".[7] After reproducing a tripartite formula of faith, Origen declares that all this "has been handed down in the churches".[8] Much later, in one of his *Catechetical Homilies*, Theodore of Mopsuestia concluded his explanation of the baptismal creed by these words: "I believe, and I am baptized in the name of the Father and of the Son and of the Holy Spirit, in one, holy and catholic Church."[9]

---

[5] Chap. 21, *De la tradition de saint Baptême*: "*Et credis in sanctum, bonum et vivificantem spiritum purificantem universa in sancta Ecclesia?*" (Botte, SC, 11 *bis*:86.)

[6] "*Tibi gloria, patri et filio cum spiritu sancto, in sancta ecclesia . . .*" (88). The privilege extends even to the church building itself, the gathering place of Christians; cf. chap. 35: "*Solliciti sint (fideles) ire ad ecclesiam ubi floret spiritus*" (118).

[7] Chap. 3 (47; see n. 2); chap. 4 (53); chap. 6 (55).

[8] *In Matt. comm. series* 33 (ed. Klostermann, 61).

[9] *Dixième Homélie Catéchétique*, no. 19 (ed. Tonneau, 275). Cf. the liturgical papyrus from Der-Balysch (second century): "I believe in God the Sovereign Father of the universe, and in his only Son our Lord Jesus Christ, and in the Holy Spirit, and (I believe) the resurrection of the body—within the holy catholic Church."

In short, the same idea emerges from all these various texts: "The entire process of salvation unfolds in the bosom of the Church",[10] because it is within the Church (*in*, ἐν) that Christ is confessed[11] and the Trinity is found.

With or without this final mention of the Church as the place where one believes, adores, gives glory to and finds the living God, the womb in which one receives life, for quite some time a number of the creeds did not contain any other article after the one that mentions the Holy Spirit. Here again, as we know, the Creed promulgated in 315 by the Council of Nicaea comes to our attention. Whereas it dwells at length on the divine attributes of Jesus Christ, in combatting the Arian heresy, and includes the famous word "consubstantial", it terminates rather abruptly with the mere words: "and in the Holy Spirit".[12] Pope St. Leo quotes it the same way in one of his letters to the Emperor Leo.[13] However, when the text of our Apostles' Creed did include the clause referring to the Church, later developments came about in two different ways, depending on the locality. The more or less numerous items that came to be added to the third part, i.e., to the Holy Spirit, were inserted either before or after that phrase.

The first of these practices we find, for instance, in

---

[10] J. A. Jungmann, 148. Cf. St. Cyprian, *Epist.* 73, chap. 1: "*Statuentes unum baptisma esse quod sit in Ecclesia constitutum*" (G. Hartel, CSEL, 3, 2 [1871]: 779).

[11] St. Peter Chrysologus, *Expositio fidei* (PL, Suppl., 3, 171–72).

[12] Giuseppe Luigi Dossetti, *Il Simbolo di Nicea e di Costantinopoli*, critical edition (Herder, 1967), 236. Cf. Ortez de Urbina, *El Simbolo Niceno* (Madrid, 1947).

[13] *Epist.* 165, chap. 3 (PL, 54:1159 B).

several of the explanations of the Apostles' Creed included among the sermons of St. Augustine and which are the work of his disciple St. Quodvultdeus. The Church is dealt with right at the end, after the section concerning the final article, i.e., the one about eternal life. And the orator gives us the reason for this: "It is by the holy Catholic Church that the conclusion of this 'sacrament' comes to an end,[14] because if anyone is separated from her he is a stranger among her sons", etc.[15] In this first case we find no difficulty, no ambiguity. Just as before, the Church here is less a particular article of faith than the place in which they are all professed, the place in which one finds not only their expression but the reality which they express.[16] The schema of the briefer and more ancient formulas remains unchanged.

But in the second case,[17] a difficulty may arise, as

[14] This word has a complex meaning here, difficult to render. It refers to the mysterious and sacred character of the whole creed of faith, considered as a baptismal, and hence sacramental, creed. See below, Chapter Ten.

[15] *"Propterea hujus conclusio sacramenti per sanctam Ecclesiam terminatur, quoniam si quis."*

[16] We find the same thing in an Armenian formula of uncertain date, cited by Dom Morin, loc. cit., 227–28: "We believe in the forgiveness of sins in the Holy Church."

[17] One can even find an intermediary case, as in the (unofficial) creed of St. Jerome (fifth century): *"Credo remissionem peccatorum in sancta Ecclesia catholica, sanctorum communionem, carnis resurrectionem ad vitam aeternam."* The authenticity of this creed has been questioned. See. G. Morin, *Un Symbole inédit attribué à Saint Jérôme*, Revue bénédictine 21 (1904): 3 ss. J. de Aldama, *El Simbolo Toledano* I (Rome, 1934): 87 and 148. This is apparently wrong. According to Badcock, 72–77, Jerome simply reproduced, with some personal additions, the creed used in his native country, Stridon in Pannonia. This would explain its similarity to that of Nicetas of Remesiana.

history has well demonstrated. For now the mention of the Church is followed by another article, or by a series of other articles. Thus it no longer serves as the conclusion of the Creed. It tends to become just one article among others. This is undoubtedly why in certain localities the ablative form, *"in sancta Ecclesia"*, whose meaning was no longer apparent, was changed to read *"in sanctam Ecclesiam"*.[18] And by a natural phenomenon of grammatical attraction, the articles which followed—the forgiveness of sins, the resurrection of the body and life everlasting—were also sometimes introduced by the same preposition "in", followed by the accusative. This gave rise to some perplexity on the part of a number of commentators, who were convinced on the other hand that this manner of speaking should be reserved for the three Persons of the Trinity.

In the Creed as Rufinus of Aquilea read it, there was no problem. In fact, after the article *"et in Spiritu sancto"*, there immediately followed, without any preposition: *"sanctam Ecclesiam, remissionem peccatorum, hujus carnis*

---

[18] Such, as we know, was the wording used in the Nicene-Constantinopole version (381) in its Latin translation: "... *et in Spiritum sanctum...*, *in unam catholicam et apostolicam Ecclesiam* ..." (Dossetti, 250; Alberigo, 20). The Greeks, who do not officially recognize our Apostles' Creed, have found less need than the Latins to establish a differentiation in their professions of faith. All their theology, faithful on this point to the earliest explanations of the faith, was more explicitly trinitarian than that of the Latins. In his work on the *Paraclete* (trans. C. Andronikof [Paris: Aubier, 1946], 88), Serge Boulgakof remarks that they expressed the divinity of the Holy Spirit "in a periphrastic way" ("who is adored and glorified together with the Father and the Son")—which our Creed expresses by using the word "in".

resurrectionem".[19] Still, as though remembering a time or a place where the Creed had ended by: *"in sancta Ecclesia"*, Rufinus found an ingenious way of explaining both forms in a single stroke:

> Finally, we come to the tradition of our belief: *"sanctam Ecclesiam"*.
>
> We have already explained above why it does not say here, as previously, *"in sanctam Ecclesiam"* but *"sanctam Ecclesiam"*. Those who have learned up to this point to believe in one God under the mystery of the Trinity must therefore also believe this: that there exists one holy Church, in which there is one faith and one baptism, in which belief is professed in one God the Father, in one Lord Jesus Christ his Son and in one Holy Spirit.[20]

But the situation was entirely different for St. Ambrose, who was confronted with an unvarying series of *"in's"*. Noting that the creed which he was trying to explain to his catechumens used the same terms when it referred to faith in God as when it referred to belief in the other things mentioned, the Bishop wanted to prevent the faithful from being misled by this similarity of language into mistaking the one for the other. So he works around this difficulty as best he can:

---

[19] So too, there was no difficulty for Nicetas, who, after the three "in's" added: *"Post confessionem beatae Trinitatis, jam profiteris credere sanctam Ecclesiam (catholicam)."* (Bk. 5, s. 3, no. 23; Gamber, 119.)

[20] *"Venit deinde traditio fidei; sanctam Ecclesiam. Causam jam superius diximus, cur non dixerit etiam hic: 'in sanctam Ecclesiam' sed 'sanctam Ecclesiam'. Hi igitur qui supra in uno Deo credere edocti sunt sub mysterio Trinitatis, credere etiam hoc debent: unam esse Ecclesiam sanctam, in qua est una fides et unum baptisma, in qua unus Deus creditur Pater et unus Dominus Jesus Christus Filius ejus et unus Spiritus sanctus"* (no. 13).

Pay close attention to the unique manner in which we believe in the Author of all things, lest you begin to say: "But the text also says '*in* the Church', and '*in* the forgiveness of sins', and '*in* the resurrection'!" What then? The grounds seem to be similar. . . . But what is the reason for this? The reason is that whoever believes in the Author also believes in the Author's work.[21]

This explanation seems very close to a default. At least it is not a differentiation in the formula that leads St. Ambrose to seek artificially some subtle distinction between faith (in God) and simple belief. Quite the contrary, this distinction seems to him absolutely essential, and he strives to preserve it even when the formulas provide him with no grounds for his explanations.

This same type of perplexity reappears more than once later on. We notice it even in St. Thomas Aquinas and later still in William Durand of Mende. But like Ambrose, neither of them allowed himself to deviate from the traditional interpretation, so strongly did they hold to its principle. St. Thomas gave his explanation on two occasions, first when commenting on the third book of the *Sentences*, then in the *Summa theologica*. In the former work, he compares the opinion of "Leo Papa", who forbids the use of "in" before "the Church", and that of St. Anselm, who, he thinks, tolerates it.[22] But in this

---

[21] *Explanatio symboli*, no. 6: "*Sane, accipe rationem, quemadmodum credimus in auctorem, ne forte dicas: Sed habet et 'in Ecclesiam', sed habet et 'in remissionem peccatorus', sed habet et 'in resurrectionem'. Quid ergo? Par causa est. . . . Quae ratio est? Quia, qui credit in auctorem, credit et in opus auctoris . . .*" (*Opera*, ed. O. Faller, 7:8–9).

[22] "Leo Papa" as we have said above, is no doubt Rufinus. As for Anselm, in his *Monologium*, chap. 76, he does speak of "*credere in illam*", but this feminine pronoun refers to the "*summa essentia*",

case, he remarks, Anselm wants us to understand that "I believe in the Holy Spirit producing the unity of the Church"; in other words, through this created effect which is the Church, I aim at the uncreated truth, which is the efficient cause thereof.[23] In the *Summa*, St. Thomas himself adopts, in case further explanation be needed, the one given by Ambrose, which he likewise attributes to Anselm; but he also indicates his preference for the simple, current formula which does not demand any special justification.

> If one says: "in the holy Church", one should understand these words in the sense that our faith refers to the Holy Spirit who sanctifies the Church, so that these words mean: "I believe in the Holy Spirit, sanctifying the Church." It is preferable, however, to follow the more common practice, which does not put the preposition *in* here and says simply "the Catholic Church".[24]

In this last passage one can observe both the involved subtleties to which the commentators sometimes felt obliged to turn in order to salvage an aberrant formula

---

namely, God. (*Opera omnia*, ed. Fr. L. Schmitt, 1 [Edinburgh, 1940]: 83–84). Was it to this text that St. Thomas was referring? It seems hardly likely.

[23] *In 3 Sent.*, dist. 25, q. 1, art. 2, ad 5: "*Leo papa dicit quod non debet ibi addi haec praepositio in, ut dicatur: 'et in unam sanctam . . .' sed debet dici: 'et unam sanctam . . .' Anselmus vero dicit, quod potest dici: 'in unam', in quantum in isto effectu intelligitur veritas increata, scilicet ut sit sensus: In unam sanctam, id est, in Spiritum sanctum unientem Ecclesiam.*"

[24] *Summa theologica*, Secunda secundae, q. 1, art. 9, ad 5: "*Si dicatur, in sanctam Ecclesiam, est intelligendum secundum quod fides nostra refertur ad Spiritum sanctum, qui sanctificat Ecclesiam, ut sit sensus: Credo in Spiritum sanctum sanctificantem Ecclesiam. Sed melius est, et secundum communiorem usum, ut non ponatur 'in' sed simpliciter dicatur: 'Ecclesiam catholicam' sicut etiam Leo papa dicit.*"

which might threaten the transcendence of faith in God alone and also the fact that this formula, in St. Thomas' day, was indeed aberrant, not in common and justified use. At bottom, St. Thomas agreed with the objector who based his argument on the doctrine of St. Augustine and declared: "In *inconvenienter dicitur*."[25]

St. Albert the Great, for his part, holds to the simple and common formula, *"sanctam Ecclesiam catholicam"*, which is the only one with which he seems to be familiar. He indicates nonetheless, as do all the other writers, the link between this article about the Church and the previous article on the Holy Spirit.

> Considering that the Holy Spirit is given and sent to sanctify creatures and that this holiness, which can be lacking in individuals, is never lacking in the Church, he says:[26] *"sanctam Ecclesiam"*. And because every article is based on divine and eternal truth, not on any created truth . . . , this article must be understood as designating the work proper to the Holy Spirit. The latter is no longer considered in himself alone, as he was in the previous article, but now I believe in him according to his own characteristic work, which consists in sanctifying the Church by the sacraments, the virtues and the gifts.[27]

By the Scholastic precisions found in these last words, this text shows its date. One can also recognize in it the influence of the twelve-part division of articles by the

[25] Cardinal Torquemada repeats the two explanations given by St. Thomas in his *Summa de Ecclesia*, bk. 1, chap. 20 (1448; ed. of Venice, 1561, fol. 23).

[26] Albert places this article in the mouth of the Apostle St. James the Less. See above, Chapter One, 40f.

[27] *De sacrificio missae*, bk. 2, chap. 9, art. 9 (*Opera*, ed. Borgnet, 38:64–65).

distinction he makes between the Holy Spirit believed first of all "in himself" and then only in "his proper work". But as far as essentials go, Albert the Great, like Thomas Aquinas, remains faithful to the explanation which flows directly from the trinitarian structure of the Creed.

William Durand of Mende knew the reading *"in Ecclesiam"*, which had once proved embarrassing for St. Ambrose and more recently for St. Thomas. But he understood very well, on the other hand, the unique and privileged meaning of the wording *"credo in Deum"*. No doubt because of the liturgical point of view which he adopts, he succeeds in rediscovering beneath this derived form, although still imperfectly, the original expression *"in Ecclesia"* and its true signification. In those places, he explains, where people today sometimes sing "in the holy Church", one should understand: "By the faith which I possess by living (dwelling) within the holy and universal Church, I profess the communion of saints, the forgiveness of sins, etc."[28]

A sermon by the Cistercian Hélinand de Froidmont, a century earlier than William Durand's *Rationale*, commented on both formulas then in use. Hélinand realized that there was no reason to choose between them but that both of them expressed a true meaning; thus he in actual fact went back to the old meaning of the form with *in*: *"in Ecclesia"*, along with the classical form: *"Ecclesiam"*. This was in a sermon on the dedication of churches:

Here is how one should understand this: Do you believe

[28] *Rationale divinorum officiorum*, bk. 4, chap. 25, nos. 15–16 and nos. 24–31: *"Per fidem quam habeo existens in sancta et universa Ecclesia, assequor sanctorum communionem, remissionem peccatorum."*

that there exists a Church which is one, spread throughout the entire world, hoping through faith and in love, bound to God by an eternal and inseparable union? Do you believe that no one can be saved except by remaining faithfully in the unity of the body of this Church?[29]

We note that in these final words Hélinand de Froidmont returns to the original meaning of the celebrated dictum: "Outside the Church, there is no salvation" (*"extra Ecclesiam, nulla salus"*), a saying which did not apply, as people have too often imagined in order to criticize it, to the case of those innumerable people not reached by Christian revelation but rather to the promoters of schism, revolt and betrayal. It applied to those Christians who voluntarily "shattered the concord of the holy body of the Church", who abandoned "the source of truth and the domicile of the faith" and thus "made themselves strangers to the hope of life".[30] However harsh the words used in their regard, the thought, therefore, was very different. This was how Origen understood the matter when he warned the one who was preparing to become a deserter that "if anyone takes it upon himself to leave the house, he brings about his own death".[31] So too St. Cyprian, making use of the biblical image of the unfaithful spouse: "Whoever separates himself from the Church in order to go unite himself with an

---

[29] *Sermo* 27: *"Sic est intelligendum: Credis unam esse Ecclesiam per totum mundum diffusam, per fidem in dilectione sperantem, aeterno et inseparabili connubio Deo conjunctam? . . . Credis neminem posse salvari nisi in unitate corporis Ecclesiae fideliter permanentem?"* (PL, 212:707 C D).

[30] Lactantius, *Div. Instit.* bk. 4, chap. 30 (CSEL [1890] 394–96).

[31] *In Jesu Nave*, hom. 3, no. 5: *"Nemo semet ipsum decipiat: extra hanc domum, id est extra Ecclesiam, nemo salvatur; si quis foras exierit, mortis suae ipse fit reus."* (W. A. Baehrens, *Opera* 7 [Leipzig, 1921]: 307.)

adulterous party separates himself from the promises made to the Church . . . ; he will no longer be anything but a stranger, a profane person, an enemy."[32] Lactantius too shows himself doubly severe toward those who lead astray along with themselves a part of the people who are "*simplex et incauta*".[33] Later, Calvin understood the saying in the same way, when he declared in his *Institution chrétienne* that "whoever separates himself from the Church renounces God and Christ"; if he pretends to remain a Christian as far as he is concerned, he is in reality only "a deserter and a turncoat".[34] It is again in this true sense that Dietrich Bonhoeffer adopts the saying as his own;[35] and so does Karl Barth, rightly quoting Calvin as his authority:

> If a Christian withdraws from the communion of the Church, he denies by that fact that he himself is a *sanctus*, a believer who knows the truth. All private Christianity is illegitimate. . . . The situation of such a man would be worse than that of the one who, not having as yet acceded to the faith and to the knowledge of the truth, is "outside

---

[32] *De catholicae Ecclesiae unitate*, chap. 6: "*Quisquis ab Ecclesia segregatus adulterae jungitur, a promissis Ecclesiae separatur. . . . Alienus est, profanus est, hostis est. . . .*" (Hartel, 1:214.)

[33] Loc. cit. The "sixth error" denounced by the Parisian faculty in Erasmus' work was this proposition: "*Extra Ecclesiam non est ulla peccatorum remissio*", which shows that Erasmus knew and understood the Fathers better than the Sorbonne theologians did.

[34] Bk. 4, chap. 1, no. 10. This role of the Church appeared so important to Calvin that, in the explanation of the Creed itself after the three sections devoted "respectively to the work of the Father, of the Son and of the Holy Spirit", he added a fourth on the Church. Cf. Alexandre Ganoczy, loc. cit., 141. See above, Chapter Five, n. 89.

[35] *Gemmelte Schriften* 2:238; in René Marlé: *Dietrich Bonhoeffer* (Castermann, 1967), 65.

the Church", is not yet a "saint" and may never be one. Such a "deserter and turncoat" runs the risk of gambling and losing his salvation, his share in the reconciliation of the world with God. He might even commit, in some way, the "sin against the Holy Spirit". For the Holy Spirit leads him directly into the community, not apart from it into a private community with Christ. This is why "no crime is more detestable than to violate by our disloyalty the sacred marriage which the only Son of God deigned to contract with us" (and not "with me").[36]

If in the closing formula *"in Ecclesia"* the Church often seemed to be ascribed to the Trinity and consequently, as regards the believer, to his entire faith as a whole, in the formula *"Ecclesiam"*, *"sanctam Ecclesiam"* forming an integral part of the series of articles to be believed, she was ascribed more particularly to the Holy Spirit. She was designated, as St. Albert reminded us, as his "proper effect", his "proper work". *Credo in Spiritum sanctum— sanctam Ecclesiam*: "It was no doubt on purpose that the two words *sanctum* and *sanctam* were placed one after the other, to indicate the source of the Church's holiness."[37] One might call attention here to the analogy existing with other texts, in which it is by an allusion to the Spirit that the Church is described as "spiritual". Indeed, says St. Cyril of Jerusalem, "the Holy Spirit is the sanctifier of the Church".[38] And Nassaï (d. 502), in his seventeenth homily, states: "We also profess one single, catholic and apostolic Church, sanctified by the Holy

[36] *Dogmatics*, vol. 4, t. 1 (Fr. trans., Fernand Ryser [Geneva: Labor et Fides, 1967], 51).

[37] J. A. Jungmann, *La Liturgie des premiers siècles* (Paris: Éd. du Cerf, 1962), 146. P. Nautin, 61.

[38] *Seizième Catéchèse*, chap. 14 (PG, 33:937 B), etc.

Spirit."[39] The source of all holiness, the Spirit is also the principle of unity, and in that respect too the Church which is one, the gathering together of all the faithful of Christ, *"congregatio sanctorum"*, is ascribed to the Holy Spirit.[40] "We must believe", says Ruysbroeck, "that the Holy Spirit is love which is poured out and which has filled heaven and earth with all good things. Thanks to this love the holy Church is one and universal all over the world."[41]

As the first named effect of the Holy Spirit, the Church in this perspective too might be said to play an inclusive role, in the sense that she is the effect which determines and includes all the others; that is why we spoke above of the "proper work" (in the singular) of the Holy Spirit. He himself is the great Gift we received in baptism, the Gift above all others. That is how St. Paul[42] speaks of him; and the liturgy sings:

Altissimi donum Dei.[43]

"God has given the Holy Spirit", says St. Peter in Acts, "to those who obey him."[44] "He is", declares Irenaeus, "the communication of Christ"; he is "the Gift

---

[39] In Adalbert Hamman, *L'Initiation chrétienne* (1963), 219.

[40] In St. Basil's liturgy, *koinōnia* is celebrated as the specific gift of the Spirit. Cf. 2 Cor 13:13; 1 Jn 1:3 and 1:6–7. *De controversia paschali*: "Si credis unitatem Ecclesiae?" (PL, 87:974). St. Thomas, *In 3 Sent.*, dist. 25, q. 1, art. 2, ad 5 (see above, n. 23).

[41] *La Foi chrétienne* (*Oeuvres*, ed. of the Benedictines of St. Paul of Oosterhout, 5 [1930]: 246).

[42] Rom 5:5: "Per Spiritum sanctum, qui datus est nobis."

[43] Hymn *Veni Creator Spiritus*.

[44] Acts 5:32. In the beginning the Spirit seemed to be "a charismatic reality, experienced by the communion of the faithful"; the problem of his place and role in the structure of the Trinity had not yet

which through the Son the Father grants unto men" and who "perfects everything belonging to man. Once imbued with the power of the Spirit, man will no longer be carnal but spiritual, thanks to this communion of the Spirit."[45] "It is by the Spirit", says Basil, "that our readmission into paradise, our rising to the kingdom of heaven, our return to filial adoption take place"; and again, using the same word employed by Irenaeus, "He is the cause that makes perfect".[46]

In the text of our Creed this global operation of the Spirit ended up by being divided into four effects. The first of these is the "communion of saints". This too is a synthetic formula which is not simply a synonym for the Church but which includes all the benefits found in her. The original formula is a Greek one and comes from Asia Minor. It would seem that its primary meaning is the communication or sharing in the "sacraments", understanding by that word all the sacred goods by which one obtains the *teleiōsis*, the completion, the final perfection; the most important of these goods being the Eucharist.[47] St. Augustine in particular frequently refers to it.[48]

---

arisen. Cf. Serge Boulgakof, *Le Paraclet* (trans. C. Andronikof, Paris: Aubier, 1946), 7–10; see also Chapter Three above.

[45] *Adversus haereses*, bk. 3, chap. 24, no. 1 (PG, 7:966 B; see above, Chapter Four, n. 106); bk. 5, chap. 9, no. 2 (1144–45); he "purifies man and lifts him up to the life of God" (ibid.). Cf. Bishop Cahal Daly, *We Believe*, 16: "The articles of faith listed here are not things we believe *in addition* to believing in the Holy Ghost. They are all part of our belief in the Holy Ghost."

[46] *Sur le Saint-Esprit* (B. Pruche, SC, 17 *bis*:327: chap. 15, no. 36), etc.

[47] Badcock, 243–72; "*Communio sanctorum*". Stephen Benko, *The Meaning of Sanctorum Communio* (London, 1964).

[48] *Sermo* 214, no. 11; *De catech. rudibus*, chap. 8, no. 12. *C. epist. Parm.*, 2, 8; *Retract.*, bk. 2, chap. 17, etc.

THE BELIEVER IN THE CHURCH   219

Through it there is brought about the "communion of saints", in other words, the union of the faithful among themselves. This derivative meaning appeared quite early, so much so that some have thought it to be the original one.[49] It frequently prevailed later on, and it is the one which we usually retain today. Yet even during the Middle Ages, in Abelard,[50] in Yves of Chartres,[51] the first meaning remains in use alongside the secondary ones, and this is the one retained by the Roman Catechism.[52] In his commentary on the Creed, Calvin like many others joins the two meanings together in a way by saying that the *"communio sanctorum"* consists in the mutual sharing of all in all the salvific goods within the Church.[53]

Next comes the "forgiveness of sins". This is essentially the effect produced by baptism, and it is in this way that the Christian becomes a "new man".[54] This is to such an extent the work of the Holy Spirit that a liturgical collect in the Gelasian sacramentary says: "We beseech thee, Lord, may the Holy Spirit prepare our souls for (or by) the divine sacraments, for *he himself is the remission of sins.*"[55] In the oldest texts of the Creed this "forgiveness

---

[49] Cf. G. Morin, *Sanctorum communio*, in *Revue d'histoire et de littérature religieuses* 9 (1904): 209–35, speaking of Nicetas.

[50] *Expositio symboli* (PL, 178:629–30).

[51] *Sermo* 23 (PL, 162:606).

[52] First part, chap. 9.

[53] *Institutio* of 1536, chap. 4, *De fide* (Basel, 1536, 148–49). Cf. Augustine, *C. Cres.*, bk. 3, chap. 36, no. 40: "*Illa . . . sacramenta communicet cum eis*"; "*cum quibus tamen in communione divinorum sacramentorum manebat.*" (Bibl. aug., 31:348.)

[54] Thus the *Epistle of Barnabas*, 6:11; 8:3; 11:1; 16:8 (Hemmer, 2nd ed., Paris: Picard, 1926), ph. 50–51, 58–59, 68–70, 90–91.

[55] "*Mentes nostras, quaesumus, Domine, Sanctus Spiritus divinis praeparet sacramentis, quia ipse est omnium remissio peccatorum.*" Secret for

of sins" is the only thing that appears after "the holy Church"; sometimes it precedes the "communion of saints";[56] or else, as in the *Treatise on the Creed* inserted into the sacramentary of Florence, we read "*sanctorum communio in remissionem peccatorum*".[57] The resurrection of the body, which is mentioned afterward, is the fruit of this renovation of man liberated from sin by baptism and fed by the Eucharist. "Such is", says Rufinus, "the last word (of the Creed), which in its brevity concludes and sums up all perfection."[58] In the Creed used at Hippo in St. Augustine's time, this was still the end of the Creed, so that the Bishop could say in one of his sermons, "This is the end (of the Creed). But the resurrection of the body will be an end without an end."[59] The mention of "life everlasting" is nothing but an explanatory addition which we find after the end of the fourth century,[60] and in which is expressed the eternal glory promised to our risen bodies.[61]

If, in its final form, this conclusion of the Creed seems at first to be made up of a series of juxtaposed items, a

---

Pentecost (*Liber sacramentorum Romanae Ecclesiae*, ed. H. A. Wilson [Oxford], 1894, 122; ed. L. C. Mohlberg [Rome, 1960], 100). Same wording in the *Sacramentarium leonianum* (ed. Ch. L. Feltoe [Cambridge, 1896], 27) and in the *Sacramentarium Veronense* (ed. Mohlberg [Rome, 1956], 29).

[56] So we read in the *Creed* of Jerome; in the Bangor Antiphonary.

[57] Caspari, *Alte und neue Quellen*, 301.

[58] S. Guelferb., 1, no. 10: "*Post haec, carnis resurrectionem. Iste jam finis est, sed finis sine fine erit resurrectio carnis*" (Morin, 449). Cf. *De fide et symbolo*, nos. 23–24. Rufinus, *Expositio Symboli*, chap. 46: "*Inveniri inter eos qui resurgunt in vitam aeternam*" (CCL, 20:182).

[59] *Expositio Symboli*, chap. 39 (CCL, 20:175).

[60] It is found in the *Creed* of Jerome.

[61] J. A. Jungmann, *La Liturgie des premiers siècles*, 147.

simple analysis thus enables us to see the connection between them. It is the work of the Spirit which unfolds within the Church and is concluded in God.

In the Church, and through her, the life of the Holy Spirit, which is also a life of holiness and of union, springs forth into life eternal. "Such is", concludes St. Irenaeus, "the task which God has confided to the Church; he has placed in her the universal operation of the Spirit."[62]

This idea gave rise to another series of texts in which the mention of the Church is introduced by the preposition *per*. To some extent this third manner of speaking synthesizes the other two. It was customary in the Church of Africa at the beginning of the third century. After the triple interrogation cited above concerning faith in the Trinity, St. Cyprian has preserved for us the content of a fourth interrogation which the candidate for baptism still had to answer. "Do you believe in eternal life and the forgiveness of sins through the holy Church ('*per sanctam Ecclesiam*')?"[63] And when Tertullian said that the Church is "the body of the Three", speaking in

---

[62] *Adversus haereses*, bk. 3, chap. 24, no. 1: "*Quam (fidem) perceptam ab Ecclesia custodimus. . . . Et in ea disposita est communicatio Christi, id est Spiritus sanctus, arrha incorruptelae, et confirmatio fidei nostrae, et scala ascensionis in Deum. In Ecclesia enim, inquit, posuit Deus apostolos, prophetas, doctores, et universam reliquam operationem Spiritus.*" (PG, 7:966 A.) Cf. Pierre Nautin, 26–27 and 67–68; see, on 40–41, the parallel between this ending of the third part and that of the second.

[63] *Epist.*, 70, chap. 2: "*Sed et ipsa interrogatio quae fit in baptismo testis est veritatis. Nam cum dicimus: Credis in vitam aeternam et remissionem peccatorum per sanctam Ecclesiam, intelligimus remissionem peccatorum non nisi in Ecclesia dari.*" (Ed. G. Hartel, CSEL, 3, 2 [1871]: 768.) Cf. *Epist.*, 69, chap. 7 (756): "*Ipsi (Novatiani) confitentur remissionem peccatorum non dari nisi per sanctam Ecclesiam posse.*" Pseudo-Fulgentius,

conformity with his idea that the body is essentially the instrument of the soul, he meant that the Church is "the instrument of the Divinity; through her we receive the graces of God; through her we enter into communion with the Trinity".[64] A sermon by St. Augustine "on the giving back of the creed", which enables us to reconstitute the creed in use in the Church at Hippo, attests to the continuance in the fifth century of this African use of *per* to indicate instrumentality.

> You can see, my beloved brothers, even in the very words of the sacred creed, how, at the end of all the articles which refer to the sacrament of faith, there is added a sort of supplement expressed as, "through the holy Church". The forgiveness of sins, the resurrection of the body, life everlasting—it is in fact through the one, true, holy and catholic Church that you obtain them.[65]

This is why Tertullian, when discussing baptism and the profession of faith, after having said, as we saw above, that "the triad of the divine names suffices to found our hope", nonetheless immediately declares: "It is necessary to add the mention of the Church."[66] And even when commenting on the other form, the more

---

Sermo de symbolo (eighth–ninth century): "*Accipiemus itaque vitam aeternam per sanctam Ecclesiam . . .*" (PL, Suppl., 3:1376).

[64] F. Refoulé, in Tertullian's *De baptismo*, loc. cit., 75. Cf. *De anima*, chap. 40, 3.

[65] *Sermo* 215, no. 9: "*Videtis certe, carissimi, etiam in ipsis sancti symboli verbis, quomodo conclusioni omnium regularum, quae ad sacramentum fidei pertinent, quasi supplementum quoddam additum, ut diceretur, 'per sanctam Ecclesiam'.*" (PL, 38:1076.) Cf. S. Poque, *Saint Augustine, Sermons sur la Pâque* (SC, 116), 63.

[66] *De baptismo*, chap. 6: "*necessario adicitur Ecclesiae mentio*" (Refoulé and Drouzy, 74).

classical one used by Rufinus of Aquilea and by us today, which says *"sanctam Ecclesiam"*, the pseudo-Maximus of Turin declares: "We must confess the Church which is truly holy, *by which* sanctification is given to mortals."[67] This *per* certainly indicates this transmission of the holiness of the Spirit to man through the reality which is the Church and by that very fact the twofold holiness of the Church considered as the instrument of the sanctifying Spirit in regard to men and as made up of members who have been sanctified.[68]

Now let us consider again for the last time the ancient clause *"in sancta Ecclesia"*. It leads us to complete, while confirming them, the reflections which brought the previous chapter to a close.

> The word of God is not frozen in a dead letter; it has never ceased to resound; but no one can hear it in solitude: it is within the community of believers that it remains a living word. The speech which transmits the witness of the faith gathers together into one body all those who accept it.

We still have not exhausted the meaning of this fundamental truth. If it is truly within the Church that the Christian's faith is born, developed and deepened, and if this faith is truly an intimate sharing in the faith of the Church herself, who can fail to see the consequences? The Church's faith is a living faith which blossoms forth into hope and charity. It is the faith which the Bride never ceases to give to her Spouse. Thus, the Christian's entire spiritual life, rooted in faith, is a sharing in the life

---

[67] *Homelia* 83 (PL, 57:437 A).
[68] On this twofold aspect of the Church's holiness, see G. Martelet, *Sainteté de l'Église et vie religieuse* ("*Prière et vie*" ed., Toulouse, 1964), chaps. 1 and 2.

of the Church. It is such from its initial seed all the way to its final blossoming. The Christian soul, as Origen said and as the Latin tradition has constantly reaffirmed since his time, in an expression which is difficult to translate, is essentially an *"anima ecclesiastica"*.[69] The most intimate relationships with Jesus Christ are the very ones that belong to the Church.[70] It is in the most profound depths of his interior life that a Christian is most fully a Catholic; it is in this interiority that he comes to share in the universal concern which belongs to the one whose mission it is to gather all things together into Christ. With this in mind we can understand better the significance of the teaching of the Creed, as it has been commented on for instance by St. Augustine in his *Enchiridion* or in his *Treatise on the Creed*.

> The proper order in the profession of our faith required that the Trinity precede the Church, just as the dweller precedes his house, God precedes his temple, the founder precedes his city. Here the Church must be understood in her totality; not only that portion of her which journeys upon earth praising the name of the Lord "from the rising of the sun to its setting" (Ps 112:3) and which once its old slavery is ended will sing a new song (Rev 5:9); but also that part which is in heaven, which was always united to God ever since the day of her creation and which will never experience the misfortune of a fall.[71]

---

[69] Cf. H. de Lubac, *Méditation sur l'Église*, 1st ed. (Paris: Aubier, 1953), 181; *Histoire et Esprit* (ibid., 1950), 61–64.

[70] Cf. St. Bernard, *In Cantica*, Sermo 12, no. 11: The Church is a spouse, and each one of us shares in this privilege. Cf. *Méditation sur l'Église*, 313. Louis Bouyer, *Le Sens de la vie monastique* (1950), 116–17.

[71] *Enchiridion*, chap. 15, no. 56: *"Rectus itaque confessionis ordo poscebat, ut Trinitati subjungeretur Ecclesia, tanquam habitatori domus sua, et Deo templum suum, et conditori civitas sua. Quae tota hic accipienda est."* (Jean Rivière, Bibl. aug., 9:202.)

Honor, love and make known the holy Church, our mother, as the Jerusalem on high, the holy City of God; throughout the entire universe it is she who bears fruit and grows in this faith which you have received, she, the Church of the living God, the pillar and ground of truth.[72]

What is true of the Christian's faith and of all his life is equally true of the theologian's work, which is of value only if it is carried on in faith. Thus it is situated entirely "within the Church"; and even in its most specialized research it must always aim, in the final analysis, at better "defining the faith of the Church". "If this condition is not observed, we are no longer in the presence of a theology but of a religious philosophy in which the Church is only indirectly and secondarily interested"[73] and which can soon become for its author and for those who follow him an occasion of aberration. On the other hand, the true theologian finds in his belonging to the Church the principle of sovereign liberty, beyond all literalism, all opportunism and all slavish conformity, because the closer he draws to the heart of the Church the more he finds the Spirit.

Whether it be in the area of theological speculation or in any other form of Christian activity, the Spirit which is in the Church and which is the Spirit of Christ, far from paralyzing the Christian in his adherence to the Church, always raises him along with her, in the obscurity of a purer faith, up to the very mystery of God.[74] In the end, the entire program of this life in the

[72] *Tractatus S. Augustini episcopi de Symbolo* (*Sermo* 214) (ed. P. Verbreken, *Revue bénédictine* 72 [1962]), 20–21.
[73] Roger Mehl, *La Théologie protestante* (P.U.F., 1966), 33.
[74] Cf. St. Peter Chrysologus, *Sermo* 57: "*Ipse in Deum credit, qui in Deum sanctam Ecclesiam confitetur.*" (PL, 52:360 C.)

Church, which is life in the Spirit, is summed up in a line we have quoted before, the exclamation, four times repeated, from the *Apostolic Tradition*, which is itself an echo of the Epistle to the Ephesians: "Glory to the Father and to the Son and to the Holy Spirit in the holy Church!"[75] Glory to God in the Church and in Christ Jesus![76]

---

[75] In Pierre Nautin, 17–20. Cf. Cyril of Jerusalem: *Dix-huitième Catéchèse*, chap. 26: *"Prius quidam cecinerat Psalmista, 'In ecclesia benedicite Deum Dominum ex fontibus Israël'* (Ps 67:27)." (PG, 33:1045–56 A B.)

[76] Eph 3:21. Cf. Augustine, *Sermo* 216 de tempore, chap. 4: *"In Ecclesia, in fide, benedicitis Dominum."* (PL, 38:1079.)

Chapter Seven

The Unity of the Faith

We have just examined, at least in its essentials, the structure of the Apostles' Creed. In this chapter and in the two which follow, there remains nothing more for us to do than to draw some conclusions from what has been said.

The first consequence, which will be the subject of the present chapter, is the *unity of our faith*. Whether one views it in the life of the believers or whether one studies its contents in themselves—in other words, whether one observes its subject or its object—the Christian faith always appears to be profoundly *one*. No doubt it has been lived, all throughout the ages or at any given time, by very different people who were far from living it with the same intensity. No doubt, too, one can and should distinguish in it (if only through its "twelve articles") a certain multiplicity of objects. But it is nonetheless radically one; and despite all factual diversities and all necessary distinctions, its unity remains indivisible.

Believers are more or less numerous. Their faith, which is always imperfect, varies from one to the other in many ways. Each individual does not actualize exactly the same potentialities. There are varying theologies and diverse spiritualities; from one country to another and from one century to another there are many differences in emphasis. Still, wherever genuine Christians may be found, in each one of them the faith remains substantially the same. This should not be understood merely in the sense that they agree in the profession of common beliefs. Their faith is one; and it is this faith, in the unique singularity of its principle, which unites them. This is what St. Hilary of Poitiers explained: "All are one", he said, "by the faith, by the reality of a single faith; how then could we refuse to admit a real unity among them if they are united by the unique reality of this faith?"[1]

This unique reality, as we have seen, is the faith of the Church, of the whole Church, in which each of the believers shares according to his own measure—which can often be weak. It is the one faith of Peter which lives on and spreads throughout the body of the Church, ever since its birth on the road to Caesarea.[2] In this great body, and in each of the faithful, it is the same life. This is what the ancient writers designated by *"fides ecclesiastica"*.

"Ecclesiastical faith": in the specialized language employed by theology in recent centuries, these words usually suggest something quite different. To put an end to the claims and counterclaims which threatened to wreck the cohesion of the Christian community, one

---

[1] *De Trinitate*, bk. 8, chap. 7: *"Quorum anima et cor unum erat, quaero utrum per fidem Dei unum erat. Utique per fidem. . . . Si ergo per fidem, id est, per unius fidei naturam unum omnes erant, quomodo non naturalem in his intelligis unitatem, qui per naturam unius fidei unum sunt?"* (PL, 10:241 B.) In these expressions, *"per unius fidei naturam"* and *"naturalem unitatem"*, we translate *"natura, naturalis"* by "reality, real". Cf. bk. 8, chaps. 13 and 15: *"naturaliter"* = "really" (10:246 A and 248 A). This is what Hilary also calls the *"totum atque absolutum fidei evangelicae sacramentum"*: bk. 11, chaps. 2 and 3 (cols. 399–400).

[2] By this Peter has become *"felix Ecclesiae fundamentum"*: Hilary, In Matt., 16 (PL, 9:1010 A).

theological school thought of distinguishing "divine faith", which imposes its object on us directly in the name of revelation, from "ecclesiastical faith". The latter was to consist in the interior assent given to certain declarations made by the Magisterium concerning, not points of doctrine, but simple questions of fact, declarations considered indispensable in order to safeguard divine faith and the unity of the Church. On this subject, one recalls the all-too-famous "de facto" and "de jure" quarrel raised by the condemnation of the four propositions in Jansenius' book. His adherents admitted that these propositions might be worthy of condemnation in one sense but denied that they could actually be found in the book itself. Thus, according to the theologians in question, this was a matter of a sort of supplementary kind of faith, faith of a lower degree, based on ecclesiastical authority and not, as in the primary meaning of the term, the very faith of the Church herself, which is, precisely, "divine faith".

It is this primary meaning which it is important to reestablish. By doing so we shall not only set aside a notion based on weak doctrinal foundations, devised mainly because of opportunistic considerations and which in fact stirred up more controversy than it settled; it is one more of those dead branches of which it is most profitable for the tree of theology to be relieved. At the same time we shall be reacting against the whole "extrinsicist" mentality, which sought to insure the perfect unity of the faith at too cheap a price. Not sufficiently respectful of the Christian's dignity, not sufficiently concerned about the Holy Spirit's action in souls, this mentality aroused many protests among

Catholic thinkers during the last century, especially on the part of Maurice Blondel,[3] before being repudiated more decidedly than ever by the recent Council. By a sort of violent paradox, it produced a type of theology which dug a double moat between the faith of two groups of people within the Church; worse yet, it almost seemed to reserve faith properly so called, but understood in a degraded and humiliating sense, to the flock of the "simple faithful". The unanimity of the Church was bound to suffer from all this.

The theory assumed two forms, differing in origin, but in modern times frequently associated or even merged in the writings of the same theoreticians.

On the one hand the distinction was made between the *"majores"* and the *"minores"*; the former were the intellectuals, those who knew, those whose faith was scientifically enlightened, based on reasons that were objectively reliable and doctrinally elaborated; the latter, the common men, were to believe too, but as "minors",

---

[3] See especially Maurice Blondel, *La Semaine sociale de Bordeaux*, in *Annales de philosophie chrétienne*, 1910–1911, under the pseudonym of "Testis". Recently Fr. Louis Bouyer has shown how the same extrinsicism also characterized yesterday's "integralism" and today's "progressivism": *La Décomposition du catholicisme*, (Paris: Aubier, 1968), chap. 2. This word "extrinsicism" had been coined by Blondel in his *Histoire et dogme* (first article in *la Quinzaine*, January 1904): "To indicate clearly that I am dealing with pure entities, and also to bring out the new aspects of old questions whose recent conflicts have led to a sharpening of the terms used, I shall make use of barbarous neologisms, which will at least serve to hold one's attention and to bring out the exclusive character of each of the theses. *Extrinsicism* and *historicism* are, for the problem now confronting the Christian consciousness, two solutions that are incomplete, each in its own way." (*Les Premiers écrits de Maurice Blondel* [Paris: P.U.F., 1956], 154.)

on the authority of and according to the explanations given them by these "majors". The distinction was not new. It started with the pseudo-Dionysius. According to his hierarchical doctrine, the divine light came down from the superior to the inferior angels, and from these to men. Following this descending movement, St. Thomas Aquinas thought that it belonged to superior men, to those who enjoyed a fuller understanding of divine things, to communicate this to the others. Only, to attentuate what might be offensive in such an explanation, St. Thomas did not merely say that the *"minores"* did not give their adherence in reality to the thoughts of the *"majores"*, but to the same divine doctrine which was communicated to them through these *"majores"*; he further specified that this dependence of certain men on certain others in questions of faith referred only to the *"materialiter credenda"*, not to the *"ratio formalis"* or to the substance of faith itself, so that from this second point of view, and as regards their adherence to the "primary truth", the faith of the *"minores"*, or *"simplices"*, could be more perfect even than that of the *"majores"*.[4] However, the distinction became less acceptable in proportion as St. Thomas' doctrine on the substance of faith became blurred, leaving in view only the series of "articles" or "statements", i.e., in proportion as the unique object of faith lost its personal character and was fragmented into multiple objects of belief. However, at the same time, this distinction drew new strength, or, if one prefers, found a new basis in more recent theories about "natural faith" or "scientific

---

[4] *Summa theologica*, Secunda secundae, q. 2, art. 6, c. and ad 2; q. 5, art. 4. Cf. Dionysius, *The Heavenly Hierarchies*, chap. 2, 2; 7, 3; 12, 2.

faith". Having reached, thanks to their elaborate studies and without the need for any supernatural enlightenment, a rational certitude concerning divine revelation, the *"majores"* seemed to be intellectually much more like learned men than like believers; and the gap grew wider still between their caste and the mass of the faithful. All this contained a principle of pride and subtle perversion, as contrary to the divine constitution of the Church as to the spirit of the gospel; no doubt this was not clearly perceived by those who promoted this point of view, but it still produced some very pernicious effects. One can easily understand why a Jules Lebreton, who on the contrary liked to bring out all the true intellectuality and profound correctness that can be found in the spontaneous faith of simple souls, in its least "scientifically elaborated" expression, criticized the distinction between the *"majores"* and the *"minores"*.[5] One can also understand that a Pierre Rousselot, that vigorous adversary of "natural faith", should also have opposed this distinction.[6]

Another form of this extrinsicist theory we are considering consisted in understanding, if not in an exaggerated way, at least in an oversimplified and ill-founded way, the traditional distinction between the "Church teaching" and the "Church taught". Vatican II sought to discourage this error by recalling on several occasions a fundamental point of doctrine essential to Christianity: every type of classification must be rejected if it tends to

---

[5] See for instance *L'Encyclique Pascendi et la théologie moderniste* (Paris: Beauchesne, 1908), 56.

[6] *Les Yeux de la foi*, Recherches de science religieuse 1 (1910): 241–59 and 444–75. *Remarques sur l'histoire de la notion de foi naturelle*, same review, 4 (1913): 1–36.

divide the body of Christians into *radically* different categories; all situational differences in Christ's Church are of secondary importance; they do not define various levels of Christian being but simply determine certain functions, certain particular ministries within the one body. All men are called to become part of this body; in virtue of this body all the members are endowed with the same fundamental dignity and are destined for the same end. This is something that the Fathers of the early centuries, faithfully maintaining the spirit of the gospel, so strongly and so frequently affirmed against the "gnostic" claims. It is something that the Catholic faith will always maintain against the tendencies toward esoterism and the elitist spirit, which subsist in all ages. It is something which the constitution *Lumen Gentium*, in particular, brought out by dealing with the Church in general and with the People of God before embarking on the chapters about the episcopate and the laity;[7] something which the constitution *Dei verbum* stressed by declaring that divine revelation was a treasure entrusted to the guardianship of the entire Church, before specifying the role of the Magisterium in this guardianship.[8]

There are no *"majores"* who are exempt from believing as much and in the same sense as the most humble of those called *"minores"*. So too, before they can teach

[7] See Msgr. G. Philips, *L'Église et son mystère au deuxième concile du Vatican* (Desclée, 1 [1967]: 136–50; 2 [1968]: 299–300 and 304). Cf. my *Méditation sur l'Église*, chap. 4 (new edition in coll. *"Foi vivante"* [Paris: Aubier, 1968], 104–8).

[8] Cf. *Vatican II, la Révélation divine*, "Unam Sanctam" (Paris: Éd. du Cerf, 1968), 242–44. Today one can note sometimes an opposite exaggeration, due to the abuse of the expression "People of God" understood in a wrong way, as pointed out by Fr. Yves Congar in *Au milieu des orages*, 86.

authoritatively in accordance with the duties of their position, the bishops and the popes must believe, humbly and personally, just like any of the faithful.[9] Clearly, we shall find among Christians many differences in their manner of believing; but whatever their varying degrees of intelligence or of conceptual grasp of the faith, whatever the involuntary errors regarding the faith's contents or the blindness concerning some of its demands found among certain believers, they are all one in proportion as they participate in a single faith, which is the faith of the Church. All of them have received the same basic instruction, the unique Christian initiation.

Need we insist that this takes nothing away from the authority of those who have received the mission to govern and to teach and who would fail in their primary duty if they did not courageously exercise this sacred mission as a service they owe to all. Nor does this take anything away from the task—assuredly a very different one—of theologians. A very different task, but one which requires courage, even as it demands fidelity. More than once in the course of history certain ones among them, swept along by the march of events, have been tempted to arrogate to themselves a spurious superiority in the Church, to set themselves up, in the name of their "science", as a sort of parallel or even superior power; to forget that if their "science" no longer serves the faith of all, they no longer have the right to the title of Catholic theologians, and that they must scrutinize Christian tradition, to be formed at its school, before proceeding to construct their own theories. More than once we have seen them tempted to

---

[9] *Paradoxe et mystère de l'Église* (Paris: Aubier, 1967), 172–79.

disregard their condition as believers and to seek "in their own current ideas all the enlightenment needed for life",[10] as though their competence, elevating them to doctrinal authority, dispensed them from showing themselves docile to the only authentic Magisterium as well as from opening themselves up to the inspirations of the Spirit.[11] When they gave in to this tendency, their critical spirit sometimes blinded them, or their theology became nothing more than a form of gnosticism. It has also happened that they determined to impose themselves on everyone else as being of the *"majores"* and mistook themselves for the "stewards of the mysteries of God".[12] This has led to the attitude rightly criticized by Fr. Yves Congar under the name of "the magisterium of the experts": this claim to "the supremacy of a critical judgment that owes more to humanism than to ecclesiastical reality".[13] Then, according to circumstances, we have seen such men bring indiscreet pressure to bear on the

---

[10] Maurice Blondel, *Lettre inédite sur l'obéissance*, in *Revue d'ascétique et de mystique* (1957), 317.

[11] It is well known how insistently St. Augustine demanded that the theologian be, not a pure scholar, but a "spiritual man". Thus, in *De fide et symbolo*, chap. 1, no. 1: *"Quibus (haereticis) restitit et resistit divina misericordia per spirituales viros, qui catholicam fidem non tantum in illis verbis (symboli) accipere et credere, sed etiam Domino revelante intelligere atque cognoscere meruerunt"*; also chap. 4, no. 7: *"Spiritualibus animis patere confido . . ."*; chap. 9, no. 18: *"Multis libris disseruerunt docti et spirituales viri"* (Bibl. aug., 9:20, 34, 52), etc. Cf. C. Kannengiesser, *Science de la révélation et progrès spirituel* (Enarratio in Ps 118), in *Recherches augustiniennes* 2:359–81. Augustine knows that there can be *"magna magnorum deliramenta doctorum"*, and he prefers to give his trust to *"magna magnorum sacramenta sanctorum"*. (*Sermo* 242, chap. 6. PL, 38:1137); cf. *De utilitate credendi*, no. 27, etc.

[12] 1 Cor 4:1.

[13] *Vraie et fausse réforme dans l'Église* (Paris: Éd. du Cerf, 1950), 520.

decisions of the Magisterium in order to have their theses canonized or turn into agitators in order to arouse public opinion against the Magisterium. That this sort of temptation still exists at the present time is something anyone can easily see for himself. But every time it meets with some measure of success, the unity of the faith lived in the Church suffers a blow.[14]

The object of this faith, its objective contents, is nonetheless one. *Objectum fidei est quid incomplexum*.[15] Here, plurality is secondary; it is the fruit of analysis, and this analysis must not result in disassociating the elements it has distinguished in the whole. What we have here, therefore, is not a mere external unity resulting from the fact that the same Magisterium proposes to the believer an indivisible list of truths. The demand thus expressed is not at all arbitrary; it does not proceed solely or principally from a concern for discipline or social cohesion. No doubt, constituted authority must be on the watch to maintain this cohesion of the Christian community, and this obliges it to discourage individualism in matters of faith just as in matters of worship or morality, even while it permits or encourages all kinds of diversity in expression. But the objective unity of our faith has

---

[14] Cf. Umberto Betti, *Le Magistère au service de la Parole de Dieu*: the Magisterium "never ceases being the authority willed by Christ and the qualified expert on the Word of God; as such it should be the object of a religious veneration, and not of an intolerant resignation which always ends up by becoming offensive". In *Au service de la Parole de Dieu* (Gembloux: Duclot, 1968), 260.

[15] Dionysius the Carthusian, summing up the common doctrine: *Summa fidei orthodoxae*, bk. 3, art. 2, no. 1 (*Opera omnia* 16 [1899]: 337). Cf. Baudoin de Ford, *De sacramento altaris*: "*Cum sit in hac fidei confessione multa verborum diversitas, una est tamen fidei pietas et individua confessionis unitas.*" (J. Morson, SC, 93:148.)

THE UNITY OF THE FAITH

deeper roots. In the first place, it is imperative for all, for those who exercise the Magisterium as well as for those who receive its teaching. The Church herself, we must repeat, the Church in her totality, believes. As a single body she is judged by one Word. Her indispensable mediation does not make of her an intermediary between God and the believer. In her and through her, God gives himself immediately to the one who believes in him.

Nor does it suffice to say that the object of faith derives its unity from divine revelation, meaning merely that all the truths it contains are believed "en masse" on the formal authority of God; "these truths really make up an internal unity, they hold together; they refer to one another."[16] Each one is an aspect of a global and unique truth, one which shares in some manner in the very unity of the one God in three Persons, of the God who reveals himself in his works, manifesting to man his unique plan of salvation, from the creation of the world up to the entry of this created world into eternal life. So, let us now complete the passage whose first words we quoted a moment ago; in Scholastic terminology, in abstract language that can be questioned, it gives us the basis of the Christian idea of faith: "The object of faith is something simple (uncomplex), namely, that which is one, i.e., God."[17]

Newman said the same thing in other, more subtle terms in his famous University sermon of February 2, 1843: "Creeds and dogmas live in the one idea which they are designed to express, and the human mind can-

[16] Karl Rahner, "Écriture et tradition", in *L'Homme devant Dieu* (coll. *"Théologie"*, Paris: Aubier, 1964), 3:220.

[17] "*Objectum fidei est quid incomplexum, videlicet, res de qua fides habetur, scilicet, Deus.*"

not reflect upon it, except piecemeal, cannot use it in its oneness and entireness, nor without resolving it into a series of aspects and relations. . . . And thus the Catholic dogmas are, after all, but symbols of a Divine fact, which, far from being compassed by those very propositions, would not be exhausted, nor fathomed, by a thousand."[18]

Considered in its substance, the act of faith, then, cannot be anything but a global, indivisible act embracing this one "object", or rather this "Subject" par excellence who offers himself to the free embrace of the one whom he has created in his own image. In other words, in this act which involves his total being, the believer replies with an undivided response to the God who reveals himself to him by manifesting to him his plan of salvation. We are always speaking of course of the model believer, the ideal, perfect believer, in whom the act of faith is fully achieved through an entire correspondence with the perfect faith of the Church, realizing full well that in each one of us, this act is always deficient, and that even in the best of us, faith always needs to be educated, nourished, sustained. But however imperfectly it begins to live in the depths of one's heart, this is indeed that "obedience of faith" spoken of by St. Paul in his Epistle to the Romans.[19] All are called to this. This is something very different from that "faith of obedience" to which we have already alluded.[20] The latter, placing the individual in a position of purely external submission to

[18] John Henry Newman, "The Theory of Developments in Religious Doctrine", Oxford University Sermon 15, in *Sermons and Discourses* (1839–57), ed. Charles Frederick Harrold.

[19] Rom 1:5; 16:26. Cf. Rom 4:18; Gal 3:6–8; 2 Cor 10:6, etc.

[20] See above, Chapter Five.

authority, delivers him over, through his fault, to a tyranny from which he can escape only by insubordination or which he can tolerate cheerfully only through indifference. Then, as Fenelon says, "the practice of faith only amounts to not daring to contradict the incomprehensible mysteries, a vague submission to which costs nothing".[21] Whoever is satisfied with this is caught up in a sterile, parrot-like discourse. He "does not meddle with dogmas", as he sometimes likes to say, but he does not live by them either. He may be a perfect conformist, but he does not know what it means to be a Christian. Obedience of faith, on the contrary, is interior; *obedistis ex corde*, says the Apostle.[22] It takes interest in its object; it binds the believer to this object, which is God himself, "the Father of our Lord Jesus Christ". Thus it fully deserves to be called a theological virtue.[23]

On the other hand, because it adheres from the start to the primary and final unity of its object, this obedience of faith, wherever it exists, remains substantially the same. It can be found in the most varied situations, notwithstanding all the changes in perspective and differences in conceptual development. Whatever their level of culture, whatever their role in the drama of history, all true believers thus share, objectively, the same faith. The same Spirit who never varies, enlightens and unites them

[21] *Mandement pour le Jubilé de l'année sainte 1701*. The case is quite different for the believer, who, aware of his individual limitations, puts his trust in the Church, and consequently in her authority, in order to resolve the practical or doctrinal problems which are over his head.

[22] Rom 6:17: "*Gratias autem Deo, quod fuistis servi peccati, obedistis autem ex corde in eam formam doctrinae, in quam traditi estis.*"

[23] The expression was used again by Vatican II in the constitution *Dei verbum*, chap. 1, and in the decree *Ad gentes*.

all. And this unity does not extend only to the Christian era; in spite of an undeniable difference, it constitutes the most fundamental aspect of that unity existing between the Old and the New Testaments, which all Christian tradition proclaims—with the help in times past, it is true, of certain historical illusions—at which the great Doctors marvelled and which tradition never ceased to contemplate.[24]

This objective unity of the faith, then, is not only one of *dogma*; it is at the same time one of *mystery*.

Dogma and mystery; the two notions play an essential role in clarifying the object of our faith. Still, they remain quite distinct from each other. The notion of dogma is closely connected with that of authority. The Greek word δόγμα was a juridical term. Megasthenes, quoted by Strabo, says that "for the philosophers of India, it is not a 'dogma' (δόγμα; in Latin, *decretum*) that puts an end to his days".[25] Everywhere in the New Testament the word means "decree, ordinance emanating from an unquestioned authority: like the edict of Caesar Augustus (Lk 2:1) or the prescriptions of the Mosaic Thora (Eph 2:15; Col 2:14), commandments

---

[24] Cf. H. de Lubac, *L'Écriture dans la Tradition* (Paris: Aubier, 1966). St. Leo(?), *De Machabeis* 2: "*Tunc enim erat fides occulta, modo manifesta, nam eadem credebant, eademque sperabant omnes sancti et justi.*" (PL, Suppl., 3:337.) Certain amateur Scholastics who liked to speculate on the "futuribles" went even farther, to the point of trying to prove the unity of the Christian faith and that faith which, they claimed, would have existed in a sinless world. Cf. Jean de Paris, *In 1 Sent.*, dist. 1: "*Si homo non cecidisset, nec deberet cadere in posterum, adhuc eamdem fidem habuisset quam modo, et eamdem theologiam, etsi non in codice scriptam, saltem in mente expressam.*" (Ed. J. P. Muller [1961], 6.)

[25] Strabo, *Geography*, bk. 15, chap. 1 ([Paris: Firmin-Didot, 1833], 611).

THE UNITY OF THE FAITH

coming from on high".[26] The practical decisions handed down by the Council of Jerusalem are *dogmata* (Acts 16:4). In the Acts of the martyr Apollonius (second century), we find an allusion to a "dogma of Commodus" and to a "dogma" of the Senate, which can be understood as either an imperial decree and a Senatus-consultus or simply the will manifested by authorities. "The will of the Senate is that there should be no more Christians", says the judge to Apollonius, who proudly replies, "The will (δόγμα) of God cannot be thwarted by a human will."[27] Little by little in Christian language the word's meaning was restricted "to the rules which are addressed first of all to reason, to the truths which demand an intellectual assent. This development, already observable in the Alexandrian writers, was completed by the beginning of the fifth century." The Council of Chalcedon in 451 contrasts the "right dogmas" (ὀρθῶν δογμάτων) concerning Christ to the "wrong opinions" (κακοδοζοντων, *prava dogmata*);[28] and for Vincent of Lerins the *caelestis philosophiae dogmata* are unchangeable religious truths because they were revealed. After falling into almost complete disuse during the Middle Ages—St. Thomas does not use it at all in his theological works—the word then came into increasing favor again and took on new life as it were.[29] It became customary to

---

[26] Léonce de Grandmaison, *Le Dogme chrétien* (Paris: Beauchesne, 1928), 277.

[27] Cf. E. Griffe, *Les Persécutions contre les chrétiens aux premier et deuxième siècles* (Paris: Letouzey et Ané, 1967), 80–87.

[28] Denzinger-Schönmetzer, *Enchiridion symbolorum* (Herder, 1963), 300:107.

[29] L. de Grandmaison, 277–78. Cf. Yves Congar, *La Foi et la théologie* (Desclée, 1962), 54–55.

speak of Christian dogmas, giving them the collective name "Dogma", in the singular. It meant the ensemble of Christian truth insofar as it is accepted by faith on God's authority,[30] transmitted to us by the authority of the Church. As St. Augustine frequently repeated, in opposing the Manichean gnostic claims which had seduced him for a while, belief is everywhere and inevitable in the area of social relationships; but in religious matters, the last teachers who should be followed are those who imagine themselves to have been initiated into some higher sphere and who promise us immediate access to knowledge, to rational certitude. Catholicism was right in holding authoritatively that those who come to religion are required above all to believe.[31]

From this point of view, there is no discrimination to be made, as if the believer were free to choose among the dogmas and to reject those which, rightly or wrongly, seem to him less important. "The character of dogma . . . is the same whatever may be the relative importance of the truth in question",[32] and every truth is equally obligatory.

However, if we considered only the dogmatic or

---

[30] Cf. St. Thomas, *Summa theologica*, Secunda secundae, q. 5, art. 3, where he distinguishes faith from opinion and from heresy. Cf. Gabriel Widmer, *L'Actualité de Karl Barth*, in *Choisir* (Geneva, February 1969), 16: the Word of God "can be thought only dogmatically and can be expressed only in dogmatic language".

[31] Augustine, *Confessions*, bk. 6, chap. 5, no. 7 (PL, 32:722): *De utilitate credendi*, chap. 13, nos. 28–29; chap. 14, no. 32 (J. Pegon, Bibl. aug., 8:276–79 and 284–87); *De fide rerum quae non videntur* (ibid., 310–41), etc.

[32] Jean Daniélou, *La Profession de foi de Paul VI*, in *Études* (November 1968), 602.

authoritarian character of Christian truth, we should form only a superficial and finally odious notion of it—the very notion that became current at certain periods when the faith grew weak. It was a Catholic author, more of a canonist, it is true, than a theologian, who wrote in the first quarter of the nineteenth century: "God had the right to reveal truths superior to human intelligence and to demand that man should believe them fully; and this is precisely what God did in order to exercise his sovereign dominion, to restrain human pride and to put our faith to the test."[33] One could hardly imagine a worse caricature. And the author added, as if to carry his misinterpretation to the extreme: "Thus, there are mysteries." The supposed unintelligibility of the mystery thus in his view completed the authoritarianism of the dogma.[34] The Christian reality is something quite different. The notion of mystery which is complementary to that of dogma and cannot be separated from it without being distorted invites us to look beyond the authority which our faith recognizes to the object itself which is proposed to us. Moreover, just as one can legitimately enumerate dogmas, one can also enumerate mysteries—and these are in both cases the same truths. But if the "Dogmas" find their unity, as we have said, in their origin, the "Mysteries" find their unity interiorly, through their substance. They offer

[33] Canon Muzzarelli, *Du péché originel* (trans. from the Italian, Séguin aîné, Avignon, 1826), 3.

[34] Among the numerous authors who have reacted against such ideas, we might mention Gaston Salet, S.J.: *Brèves réflexions sur le Credo* (Paris: Lethielleux, 1965) and *Le Christ notre Vie*, 3rd ed. (Casterman, 1958), 127–36: "Le Mystère dans la vie chrétienne."

themselves not only for our adherence but also for our meditation, as a total reality.[35] It is, as St. Irenaeus said, "the total body of the work of the Son of God"—*integrum corpus operis Filii Dei*;[36] or, in St. Paul's more concise way of putting it, "the Mystery of Christ".[37] In its complete and unbreakable unity it can be neither increased nor diminished.[38] In Christ and through him, it is the mystery of God revealing himself and offering himself to man in order to draw him to himself. It is that great "divine Deed", of which the various dogmas are only "a sort of projection"[39]—*semel locutus est, et plura audita sunt* (a single Word was pronounced, and we heard many)—and far from being entirely encompassed by this set of projections, this great Deed "would neither be exhausted nor plumbed to its depths by thousands more of them".[40] In terms already familiar to us, this is the

---

[35] Cf. Newman, *Sermons and Discourses*, Sermon 15, no. 22: "All religious men have, each according to his own capacity, an idea or vision of the blessed Trinity in unity, of the incarnate Word and of his presence, not as a collection of qualities, attributes and actions, nor as the object of a certain number of propositions, but as a unique, individual object, independent of all qualifications." Loc. cit.

[36] *Démonstration de la foi évangélique*, chap. 1. Cf. *Adversus haereses*, bk. 1, chap. 9, no. 4 (PG, 7:584).

[37] Eph 3:4.

[38] St. Leo, *In nativitate Domini Sermo* 4, chap. 6: "*Magnum praesidium est fides integra, fides vera, in qua nec augeri ab ullo quidquam, nec minui potest: qui nisi una est, fides non est.*" (PL, 54:207.)

[39] We can see better now why every dogma, whatever be its relative importance, demands absolute adherence: "If all dogmas are only one in the reality of Christ, to neglect even one of them means clouding over one aspect of Christ's reality. To reject even one of them is like tearing a piece of flesh away from Christ's body." Charles Gobert, S.J., *La Foi au Christ* (Toulouse, 1965), 56.

[40] Newman, Sermon 15, nos. 16 and 23 (loc. cit.).

mystery of the "economy", and, through it, in a manner which always remains inseparable from it, it is the mystery of "theology".[41]

Here then we are brought back to the text of our Creed. At first the Church placed it on our lips, and, like so many generations of Christians before us, we received it from her in its entirety, without choosing between the articles according to our personal evaluations, which are so often deceptive. We trusted Christ's messenger. Already in this first sense, the Creed is one for us. But it is one in a more intrinsic sense, which it is part of our Christian vocation to try to attain. From end to end it expresses this unique mystery which, as Bérulle said, tends "to enclose everything, Creator and creature, in an admirable circle of unity".[42] The Creed presents itself, "not as a line, but as a circle":

> The propositions it sets forth one after the other are linked to one another; and the last brings all the intermediary ones back inside the first: by his creative action, followed up by Jesus in the redemption and by the Holy Spirit in the work of sanctification, the Father gathers back into his bosom those whom Jesus his incarnate Son and in the Holy Spirit he wills to make his sons for eternal life.[43]

Unlike a straight line, which can always be prolonged, a circle, if it is truly a circle, is always something com-

---

[41] Christian dogmas "are the unfolding of the one mystery", for "they tell us only one thing: that God has communicated himself to us through Jesus Christ, in his Spirit, as he is in himself . . .": Karl Rahner, *Écrits théologiques* (French trans., Paris: Desclée de Brouwer), 8:102–3.
[42] Quoted by Gaston Salet, *Le Christ notre vie*, 136.
[43] Cardinal G. M. Garrone.

plete. The enclosed space it determines is something definitive. It is a totality. Nothing can be added to it without breaking it, without denaturing its shape. The Creed is like that. This impossibility of breaking its circle "is not a sign of limitation but of fullness.... One truly progresses in faith and in the understanding of the Creed only by deepening and clarification, not by addition."[44]

Just as no further secret Divinity exists beyond the Trinity, no fourth Person in God, and just as we do not have to await in the future of the world a new Christ or a third "testament",[45] so too and for the same reason, there is nothing to be added to our Creed. It leaves no new mystery outside itself to be discovered.[46] But this definitive character is in no way equivalent to an order for the believing mind to stop. The total truth which the Creed encloses in its circle is in the highest degree a living and life-giving truth. It is an indefinitely fruitful truth; and even as it is one, both in itself and in the act of the subject who embraces it, it is also the principle of two-fold progress: on the one hand, its objective implications lend themselves to endless clarification, and, on the other hand, it can be more and more deeply studied by the interior gaze of the believer. Development of dogma and deepening of the mystery, such are the two paths into which the entire Church is drawn by the formula of the Creed; such is the double movement of the Spirit which

---

[44] Ibid.

[45] Every Christian must agree with Calvin's words against those who "Christo non contenti, nituntur altius penetrare": *Opera selecta* 1 (1926): 88.

[46] Cf. Rufinus, *Expositio symboli*, chap. 33: "*In sancti Spiritus commemoratione adimpletur mysterium Trinitatis.*" (CCL, 20:169.)

has often been defined *per modum unius*, in approximate fashion, in speaking of the "understanding of faith".[47]

In Jesus Christ everything is accomplished. In him, divine revelation, like the redemption, is definitively acquired. The Spirit who lives in the Church and animates her as her soul[48] is the Spirit of the Son,[49] the Spirit of the Lord,[50] the Spirit of Jesus,[51] the Spirit of Jesus Christ,[52] the Spirit of Christ.[53] He gives us understanding of his Word; he makes it fruitful within us, as he sanctifies us through the effect of his sacrifice. In this twofold sense he continues his task: he brings it to completion. But just as the sanctifying role of the Spirit must not make us misunderstand the absolute objective sufficiency and the unique and definitive character of the redemption accomplished on Calvary, neither should his role as enlightener make us imagine that there can ever be a continuation of divine revelation in the world, as though the revelation given to us in Jesus Christ were only a stage; as though it were not, like the redemption, ἐφ' ἅπαξ; as though it did not possess the same unique and definitive character.[54] The *"plenitudo temporis"* spoken of by St. Paul is also the *"tempus plenitudinis"*, as St.

---

[47] I have tried to discern some of the meanings of this expression in *Corpus mysticum*, 2nd ed. (1949), 252–67.

[48] This is obviously only an analogy.

[49] Gal 4:6.

[50] 2 Cor 3:17.

[51] Acts 16:7.

[52] Phil 1:19.

[53] Rom 8:9.

[54] We find it hard to understand the reasoning of Gabriel Moran, F.S.C., in *Vivante Révélation, étude de théologie* (Fr. trans., Paul Martin [Paris: Ligel, 1967], 77). He finds it strange that Catholic authors hesitate to say that revelation is continuing to take place in the world, when they affirm without any hesitation that sanctification is going

Thomas Aquinas remarks.[55] The Spirit of Christ enables us to penetrate into the depths of Christ, but he will never lead us beyond him.[56] He neither speaks nor acts "of himself", no more than Christ spoke or acted of himself; he is sent by Christ as Christ was sent by the Father; the Apostles received him when Jesus breathed on them and said: "Receive the Holy Spirit";[57] "The goodness of God poured him out abundantly upon us through Jesus Christ our Savior".[58] He is, as Tertullian said, *"Christi vicarius"*, the *"Domini vicarius"*, *"vicaria vis"* sent by Christ.[59] Thus he glorifies Christ in all his action, just as Christ glorified his Father before men.[60]

---

on continuously. The parallel is faulty. What corresponds with revelation is the redemption, and what is said here of the one must be said also of the other. We agree with Msgr. B. C. Butler that the author "proves convincingly that Christ, in his human nature, was the first to benefit from the fullness of Revelation, in his communion with his heavenly Father"; but we would also add with him that "the disciples, in their own communion with Christ, were made sharers in that Revelation": *Écriture et Tradition*, in *Au service de la Parole de Dieu* (Gembloux, 1968), 234, n. 2. Cf. St. Irenaeus, *Adversus haereses*, bk. 3, chap. 1, no. 1 (PG, 7:844 A B).

[55] *Summa theologica*, Secunda secundae, q. 1, art. 7, ad 4. Cf. Roger Mehl, *La Condition du philosophe chrétien* (Neuchâtel: Delachaux et Niestlé, 1947), 22: "Dogmatics . . . is the interpretation, or preferably the understanding, of a revelation given totally right from the start."

[56] Cyril of Jerusalem, *Catéchèses* 16, chaps. 3–4; 17, chaps. 19, 30, 31 (PG, 33:920–24, 989–92; 1002–5). Nicetas, bk. 5, *Sermo* 3, no. 36 (Gamber, 122); etc. Cf. Barth, *Credo* (French trans.), 167.

[57] Jn 2:22.

[58] Titus 3:6.

[59] *De praescriptione*, chap. 13, no. 5 (CCL, 1:198); chap. 28 (209); *De virginibus velandis*, chap. 1 (2, 1209).

[60] Jn 16:5, 7, 14. Note that if the Orthodox Christians do not admit that the Spirit proceeds from the Son within the Trinity, "they do admit completely the mission of the Spirit, sent to the world by the

He does this, not by adding something to his message, but by inspiring and guiding within the Church this double movement of the spirit along the two paths we have indicated, that of the development of dogma and that of the deepening of the mystery.

The *development of dogma* is an objective phenomenon which has unfolded down through the centuries. But it really does not lead us any farther than the Creed itself. All it ever does is to clarify it. Contrary to what the expression might suggest, it does not involve either any true growth or continued progress. It is much less a linear unfolding than a perpetual reaction to surrounding circumstances, as history endlessly changes them, in view of maintaining, protecting and making the faith relevant. Without sharing Rudolf Bultmann's restrictive views, one can admire with him "this continual vitality which, thanks to the force of its original thrust, enables faith to dominate ever new historical situations by embracing them".[61] To a process of analysis and of increasing precision, the main driving force behind which is the elimination of error or protection against error,[62] there is joined another process which is rather one of selection, transformation, purification, "co-aptation", assimilation, symbiosis. In fact, the tools forged by human culture for

---

Son, and that he is in truth 'the Spirit of the Son' ". Timothy Ware, 291. The Spirit, said Photius, proceeds eternally from the Father alone, and he has received from the Son a temporal mission. On this point see the reflections of Thomas F. Torrance, *Spiritus creator*, in *Verbum Caro* 89 (1969): 73–84. Cf. Serge Boulgakof, *Le Paraclet* (Fr. trans., C. Andronikof [Paris: Aubier, 1946], especially 143 and 177–78).

[61] *L'Interprétation du Nouveau Testament* (trans. O. Laffoucrière, Paris: Aubier, 1955), 28.

[62] Cf. Rufinus, *Expositio symboli*, chap. 3 (136).

its own use must always undergo certain indispensable but singular, paradoxical, unpredictable modifications if they are to be applied to the data of revelation.[63] The new wine causes the old wineskins to burst. The water must be changed into wine.[64] This is an activity impossible to avoid and one which constantly renews the perspectives of theology. But all this activity is always pursued *within the circle*. No matter how the results to which it leads may multiply or replace each other, they add nothing substantial to the "fullness of the apostolic times" reflected in the Creed.[65] Even the "new dogmas" which emerge from time to time do not, properly speaking, constitute new articles of faith, or rather, to avoid all ambiguity, let us say, using a formula less open to question, that they are not "revealed articles". Whoever would oppose in principle this increase in the number of propositions in which our faith is expressed would mis-

---

[63] William of Saint Thierry, *Aenigma fidei*: "*Hujusmodi enim cum sint communis rationis instrumenta circa res communes, cum in causa fidei assumuntur, nonnisi scandala sunt, si non rationi fidei fideliter coaptentur.*" (PL, 180:409 D.) Cf. P. Hadot, *Stoïcisme et monarchianisme au IVe siècle*, in *Recherches de théologie ancienne et médiévale* 18 (1951): 187: "Heresy . . . is a refusal to think; it consists in pouring the data of revelation into the mold of a ready-made philosophy. In the last analysis it seeks to elude the Christian paradox . . . to reduce it to an easily assimilated system."

[64] Cf. St. Thomas, *In Boetium de Trinitate*, q. 2, art. 3. See below, Chapter Eight.

[65] Cf. L. de Grandmaison, *Le Dogme chrétien*, 264: "Although it may be more amply formulated and more sharply defined in details, our knowledge of dogma will never surpass nor even equal the direct, living, infused knowledge that the first disciples, the 'ministers of the word', had of it." Henri Holstein, *La Tradition dans l'Église* (1960), 225. J. P. Jossua, *Immutabilité, progrès ou structurations multiples des doctrines chrétiennes?* in *Revue des sciences philosophiques et théologiques* 52 (1968): 173–200.

THE UNITY OF THE FAITH

understand their role as well as the laws of human intelligence and the contingencies of history and the nature of the faith itself; for—and we must always come back to this—if these propositions are multiplied, this is not done to introduce a larger number of things but always in order to express a single one of them.[66] Even today we can repeat in all truth what St. Ambrose said to his catechumens: "This is what the Creed teaches. Should we, in the audacity of our thinking, exceed the limits of the Apostles' faith? Would we enjoy in our faith guarantees surpassing theirs?"[67] We can always maintain with Rufinus that "the tower of the faith" erected by the twelve Apostles, was complete from that time on.[68]

Still, even if we understood it in this way, and as necessary as it may appear, this movement of the mind by which dogma is developed very often provokes a sort of profound regret even among its most resolute promoters. They accept it, but reluctantly. Listen to St. Hilary's complaint: "They are forcing us", he moans

> to do illicit things. We have to climb inaccessible peaks and speak of ineffable topics when it should be enough to carry out in a simple view of faith what is prescribed, namely, to adore the Father, venerate the Son with him and fill ourselves with the Holy Spirit. Instead, we find ourselves obliged to apply our humble words to the most

---

[66] Cf. Newman, *Textes newmaniens*, no. 21 (Paris: Desclée de Brouwer, 1955), 342.

[67] *Explanatio symboli*, no. 3: "*Hoc habet scriptura divina (= symbolum). Numquid supra apostolorum fines progredi audaci mente debemus? Numquid nos sumus apostolis cautiores?*" (Botte, SC, 25 *bis*:48). Cf. H. de Lubac, *Le Problème du développement du dogme*, in *Recherches de science religieuse* 35 (1948): 130–60.

[68] *Expositio symboli*, chap. 2 (135).

indescribable realities. The mistake of others leads us to commit the same mistake of exposing to the hazards of human language mysteries which should have been restricted to the religion of our soul.[69]

What Hilary is experiencing here—for this is not some cool reflection but a deeply felt emotion[70]—and what so many others have felt along with him, is that the effort of our intellect when we apply it to the divine object of revelation runs the risk of becoming a profanation the more complicated and amplified it grows. "Happy", continues Hilary, "are they whose consciousness retains in its perfection the faith of the Apostles, who are as yet unaware of the written professions! . . . But it has become necessary to introduce the custom of giving explanations and to having people subscribe to them."[71] Since the beginning, the movement has been inevitable, each generation carrying it forward in turn. As Newman remarked with a sort of awe, "the explanations grow in our hands, in spite of the efforts we make to restrain them".[72] If the movement proceeded by itself, it would in fact not fail to result, in practice, in an ever more

---

[69] *De Trinitate*, bk. 1, chap. 2: "*Compellimur . . . illicita agere, ardua scandere, ineffabilia eloqui, inconcussa praesumere. Et cum sola fide expleri quae praecepta sunt oporteret, adorare videlicet Patrem, et venerari Filium, sancto Spiritu abundare, cogimur sermonis nostri humilitatem ad ea quae sunt inenerrabilia extendere, et in vitium vitio coarctamur alieno, ut quae contineri religione mentium oportuissent, nunc in periculum humani eloquii proferantur.*" (PL, 10:51 A B.) Trans. Th. de Régnon, in *Études trinitaires* 1 (1892): 126, abridged and retouched.

[70] For this first book of the *De Trinitate* "is a sort of autobiography": Charles Kannengiesser, art. "Hilary", in *Dictionnaire de spiritualité*, fasc. 45 (1968), cols. 476–81.

[71] *Liber de synodis*, chap. 63; cf. chap. 92 (PL, 10:523 B; 546 A), etc.

[72] Loc. cit., 339 (no. 17).

THE UNITY OF THE FAITH

weighty and exteriorizing complexity. As Calvin once said, the elements involved in revealed truth would eventually become too "fine spun",[73] or as Cardinal Charles Journet put it, if one gave oneself up solely to "the discourse of theological reasoning", one would find oneself swept away in "a process of differentiation" which "could only throw one off center, and make one wither and go astray".[74]

But this movement is constantly accompanied in the Church, more or less powerfully depending on the times, by a contrary movement which affords it more balance. Unlike the former, this other movement is in itself independent of the course of history; it does not consist in a continual process; it does not presuppose a particularly advanced state of concepts in order to take place; for if it is natural "that the interior notion of divine Truth should express itself in an explicit form, thanks to the activity of reflective faculties, a precise formulation is nevertheless not essential to its authenticity and perfection".[75] This compensatory movement is that of *deepening the mystery*. Its results are not cumulative, even though it may have unlimited fecundity in later generations. It always brings us back to the center and tends to recreate or to rediscover unity in the simplicity of contemplative vision. It is the passage from the laborious and multiple word to the unified recollection of silence. It is, across the "silvery waves" or the "silvery spray" of

---

[73] *Institution chrétienne*, 1541 ed.

[74] *Introduction à la théologie* (Desclée de Brouwer, 1947), 113. He is talking about a process "which would fail to keep coming back, in order to be nourished by them, to its original implications, to its root idea" (ibid.).

[75] Newman, loc. cit., no. 11, 334.

the fountain, access to the "crystalline fountain" itself.[76] The mind was seeking in some way to penetrate faith; it was exploring the dimensions of it, defining its contours, examining its presuppositions, bringing to light its consequences; now it is faith that penetrates the soul; and the more it penetrates, the more simplified it grows, until it becomes inexpressible.[77] In this sense too one can say with St. Ambrose, "The sign of God is in the simplicity of faith."[78]

There is no laziness in this, nor any mitigation, no tendency toward abstraction, no agnosticism. For such a silence is not a starting point on which one would settle down indefinitely. Such simplicity does not eliminate any of the attainments of the word; it unifies them by interiorizing them. It is not rejection; it is, on the contrary, integration. It is achieved, not within, but beyond the expansion of concepts—even if, in a single bound, it has risen above that zone[79]—and is itself maintained

---

[76] St. John of the Cross, *Spiritual Canticle*, 11th strophe. The "silvery spray" is the propositions of faith; their hidden substance is the fountain itself.

[77] Jules Lebreton, S.J., *Dogme et critique*, in *Revue pratique d'apologétique* 4:204. This does not prevent the words of the Creed from remaining the norm.

[78] *De fide ad Gratianum*, bk. 1, chap. 5, no. 42 (PL, 16:537 A). Cf. 1 Cor 4:20. *De mysterio SS. Trinitatis* (fifth century): "*Invisibilis et inenarrabilis, non verborum circuitu, sed fidei virtute cognoscitur. Crede, ut cognoscas; noli loqui ut credas; virtutem enim fidei tacens plus quam loquens capit. Verba disputant: nam fides plus sentit, quam disputari queat.*" (PL, Suppl., 3:713.) The author is a disciple of Faustus of Riez. *Diadoque de Photicé, Cent chapitres*, chap. 22: "The depths of faith cannot be plumbed by indiscreet reasoning." (Éd. des Places, SC, 5 *ter*:96.)

[79] So too, "the thought of the mystic, in its apparent nudity, contains more true reality than all the speculations of the metaphysicians." Victor Delbos, quoted by Maurice Blondel, in *Qu'est-ce*

and grows continually deeper only through an activity which has no limits: "In the face of mystery, it is impossible to entertain the illusion that one understands God and that one can come to a standstill; it is impossible to yield to the temptation to reduce God to the human level. And this is the great benefit, the great light of dogma's mystery."[80]

> I surround the Word
> With a frontier of silence;
> May everyone who loves Thee
> Praise thy secret Being.[81]

Whatever is understood through knowledge is delimited by the understanding of the one who knows. So, if you have understood, it is not God. If you are able to understand, it is because you mistook something else for God. If you almost understood, it is again because you allowed your own thoughts to deceive you.[82]

---

que la mystique? Cahiers de la Nouvelle Journée, 3:58.

[80] G. Salet, *Brèves réflexions sur le Credo* (Paris: Lethielleux, 1965), 17. The parallel movement of the will was expressed by Marie de l'Incarnation in these words (*Lettres de conscience*, 8): "Once the mind has been purified of all things and no longer dwells on the gifts, it springs into God by a certain transport which does not allow it to stop at anything less than the Object for which it was created; and it is in this that perfect nudity consists." (Jamet, 1:363.)

[81] St. Ephrem, *Hymnes sur le Paradis*, Hymn 4, no. 11 (R. Lavenant and Fr. Graffin, SC, 137:68; cf. no. 9, 67).

[82] Augustine, *De civitate Dei*, bk. 12, chap. 18: "Quidquid scientia comprehenditur, scientis comprehensione finitur." (PL, 41:368.) *Sermo* 52, no. 16: "Si comprehendisti, non est Deus. Si comprehendere potuisti, aliud pro Deo comprehendisti. Si quasi comprehendere, potuisti, cogitatione tua te decepisti." (PL, 38:360.) Cf. *Sermo* 53, no. 12: "Si finisti, non est Deus" (PL, 38:370); *Sermo* 117, no. 5 (663).

So the deepening of mystery ends in a "negative theology". Or rather, it does not end but continues in it. It is always a movement. It is continual passage from light to shadows and from word to silence, from a more luminous light and a more intelligible word to thicker darkness, to a denser silence. *Verbo crescente, verba deficiunt*. Darkness and silence, at each stage, are qualified by the light and the word from which they issue. So they are not emptiness but fullness. They do not constitute a turning back, for they are engendered by fidelity to the light and to the word; hence they bear within themselves, becoming ever more alive in proportion as the spirit of the believer penetrates them, the affirmation of the unfading Light and of the perfect Word.[83] To this movement of faith, the Spirit always gives an impetus to go farther still. In this abandonment, the believer finds at once his torment and his joy.

For we are still talking about the believer. The expression "negative theology", which custom does not permit us to avoid entirely, is an ambiguous one.[84] The negative theology with which we are dealing here is not that of the philosopher—even though the two possess common characteristics.[85] Nor will we say it is the same

[83] Cf. Gregory of Nyssa, *Vie de Moïse*, nos. 162–63: "Then it was in light, now it is in darkness that God appears. . . . Religious knowledge is at first a light for those who receive it. . . , but the more the mind, in its forward progress, manages . . . to understand what understanding of reality actually is, and draws closer to contemplation, the more it sees that divine nature is invisible. . . ." (Trans. J. Daniélou: SC, 1 *ter* [1968]: 211–13.)

[84] It would be preferable to use the traditional Greek term: apophatic theology.

[85] Of both of these one might say with Étienne Gilson, commenting on St. Thomas: "It is not affirmative theology with something subtracted, for if one affirmed nothing about God, what could

as that of the mystic, for there is a mysticism which draws its inspiration elsewhere than from the Christian mystery.[86] Now, it is precisely into *this* mystery that the believer sinks. It is before *this* mystery that his weakness falters, and it is through *this* mystery that the glory of God dazzles him; it is in the contemplation of this mystery that darkness hems him in and that the silence of praise deepens within him. Mystery, not primarily of the Divinity in itself, of the "God above God" of whom one of our contemporaries speaks, using a phrase which can be understood in various ways,[87] but of the divine action among us, of the Trinity in its operations: the "mystery of the economy", the "mystery of Christ". St. Paul was not considering any other mystery when he cried out, "Oh, the depth of the riches, of the wisdom and of the knowledge of God! How inscrutable are his judgments and how unsearchable his ways. For who has ever

---

one deny in order to transcend him? It is, on the contrary, a going beyond what we know about God in order to situate him beyond all that we can say of him. . . . There is nothing more positive than this negative method." *Introduction à la philosophie chrétienne* (Paris: Vrin, 1960), 75 and 77. With even greater reason should it be distinguished from a so-called negative theology which is actually "a-theology" or even "a-theism". We have given explanations of this matter in *Athéisme et sens de l'homme*, "*Foi vivante*" (Paris: Éd. du Cerf, 1968), especially 79–89. With regard to Dionysius, see René Roques, *Symbolisme et théologie négative chez le Pseudo-Denys*, in *Bulletin de l'Association Guillaume Budé* (1957), 97–112.

[86] Cf. our introduction to André Ravier's *La Mystique et les mystiques* (Paris: Desclée de Brouwer, 1965).

[87] We do not understand it exactly as Paul Tillich does; for him this superior God is a sort of common denominator of the Absolute which every religion views in its own way. Each of them becomes an idolatry as soon as it becomes attached to its own particular view. Cf. *Dynamique de la foi* (trans. F. Chapey, Casterman, 1968), 45, 61–62, 75, 93, 110–11.

known the mind of the Lord? . . . To him be glory forever!"[88] And neither was St. Leo the Great speaking of any other mystery when he said: "No one draws nearer to the truth than the man who realizes that in divine things, even if he has advanced very far, he always must still seek; for whoever presumes to think that he has reached the goal toward which he was going has not found what he was looking for but has grown weak in his pursuit."[89] And again, in that ringing language to which no translation can do justice, "Let human infirmity, then, succumb to the glory of God, and in trying to explain the works of his mercy, let it recognize itself as always unequal to the task!"[90]

Each of these two movements—systolic and dyastolic—which we have just briefly tried to distinguish and describe, needs the other. Within the Church the two of them combine in syntheses of various kinds. They react

---

[88] Rom 11:33–36.

[89] *Sermo* 9 on the Nativity of the Lord, chap. 1: "*Nemo enim ad cognitionem veritatis magis propinquat, quam qui intelligit in rebus divinis, etiamsi multum proficiat, semper sibi superesse quod quaerat. Nam qui se ad id in quod tendit pervenisse praesumit, non quaesita reperit, sed in inquisitione defecit.*" (PL, 54:226.)

[90] *Sermo* 11 on the Passion of the Lord, chap. 1: "*Succumbat ergo humana infirmitas gloriae Dei, et in explicandis operibus misericordiae ejus imparem se semper inveniat.*" (PL, 54:549–50.) For St. Paul, the knowledge of divine revelation "culminates in the silent amazement provoked by its object which transcends this knowledge"; it "introduces 'into all the fullness of God' the one . . . whose knowledge, if one can so speak, is annihilated by this experience" and thus finds its fulfillment. See Heinrich Schlier, *La Connaissance de Dieu chez saint Paul*, in *Le Message de Jésus et l'interprétation moderne* (Paris: Éd. du Cerf, 1969), 229.

on each other.[91] Both of them correspond to needs of the human condition. Both are the fruits of the same Spirit of God. Each in its own way and in all the forms of their combined action, they constitute the test and insure the final victory of faith.

---

[91] For there is a "close relationship" between "lived spiritual experience and dogmatic formulas": G. Dejaifve, S.J., *Diversité dogmatique et unité de la Révélation*, in *Nouvelle revue théologique* (1967), 22.

CHAPTER EIGHT

CHRISTIAN SOLECISMS

If we wish to grasp in all its force the privileged expression of our Creed, the one which emphasizes its three parts, suggesting at three different times the essential impetus of the faith and thus distinguishing the originality of Christianity, it will be useful for us to consider it in the history of early Christian language. When we do this, it will appear to us as the most significant—and most fortunate—of "solecisms".

"What we call a solecism is simply an instance of words that are not connected with each other after the manner, taken to be a rule, in which our ancestors expressed themselves, not without a certain authority." This definition is St. Augustine's.[1] The remarkable thing is that he gives it in his *De doctrina christiana*, a work in which he outlines the rules of Christian language. Augustine believes, in fact, that this *"auctoritas aliqua"* of those who went before us, the ordinary rule of good syntax, which determines the "coaptation" of the various members of the sentence to each other, should in certain cases be disregarded. It must sometimes yield to a superior authority. This superior authority is that of divine revelation itself, unknown to "our ancestors"; because of the new modes of thinking which revelation intro-

---

[1] Bk. 2, chap. 13, no. 19: *"Soloecismus qui dicitur, nihil est aliud quam cum verba non ea lege sibi coaptantur, qua coaptaverunt qui priores nobis non sine auctoritate aliqua locuti sunt."* (J. Martin, CCL, 32:45.)

duces, a different manner of speaking may be necessary.[2] St. Jerome, an expert in this field, implied the same thing as St. Augustine when he observed that the Apostle Paul, writing to the Corinthians, had committed solecisms at the very moment when, professing his disdain for the prestige of words or of human wisdom, he boldly claimed a superior wisdom.[3] How could Paul ever have been able adequately to make known the "majesty of the divine meaning" if all the while he had been concerned about respecting Greek forms of discourse?[4]

Certainly, more simply and more generally, the Christian writers of the early centuries were dependent not so much on the hebraisms derived from the Jewish Bible as on the verbal and syntactical practices of their milieu and their times. In Latin as in Greek, these were no longer entirely the practices of the classical period. With greater reason, since it wished to address everybody, Christian preaching had to adopt the phraseology and vocabulary of everyday speech, what we call the nonliterary "Koine".[5]

---

[2] Ibid.: "*Quid est ergo integritas locutionis, nisi alienae consuetudinis conservatio loquentium veterum auctoritate firmatae?*"

[3] *In Eph.*, 3 (after quoting 1 Cor 2): "*Iste igitur qui solecismos in verbis facit, qui non potest hyperbaton reddere sententiamque concludere, audacter sibi vindicat sapientiam.*" (PL, 26:509 C.)

[4] *Epist.* 120, chap. 11, no. 4: "*Divinorum sensuum majestatem digno non poterat graeci eloquii explicare sermone.*" (CSEL, 55:507.) Cf. *Epist.* 121, chap. 10, no. 2: "*Profundos enim et reconditos sensus lingua non explicat et, cum ipse sentiat, quod loquatur, in alienas aures puro non potest transferre sermone.*" (56:41.) *In Ps.* 90:7 (CCL, 78:130–31).

[5] Koine was, at the beginning of the Christian era, the "common and current language used in the eastern part of the Roman empire and also by a great number of Orientals who had come to live in the West": Christine Mohrmann, *Études sur le latin des chrétiens* (Rome), 1 (1958): 142.

The New Testament writings are not drawn up in flawless language. Origen remarked on this with respect to St. Paul, whose sentences, he did not hesitate to say, are often poorly composed.[6] He readily granted to Celsus that the first Apostles of Christ lacked culture—which, he concluded, forced one to seek elsewhere the reason for their extraordinary power of persuasion.[7] In the Latin world, Minucius Felix argued in the same way.[8] It was also in a late and popular language that the first, very literal translations of the Sacred Books made their appearance; and we know what an obstacle this presented to the conversion of certain men whose high culture was essentially literary. According to the testimony of Arnobius[9] and Lactantius,[10] this constituted the major obstacle. St. Gregory of Nyssa, writing to the pagan teacher of rhetoric, Libanios, admitted with much elegant urbanity that frequenting the Bible seemed like "deserting Hellenism for a barbaric tongue".[11] St. Jerome and St. Augustine make more personal admissions. The *"sermo*

---

[6] *In Rom*, 7:18: "*Saepe de incompositis elucutionibus apostoli defectibusque earum commonuimus, quod et in praesenti loco nihilominus invenitur.*" (PG, 14:1149 C.) Cf. Theodore of Beza, in Quenstedt, *Theologia didactico-polemica* 2 (1696): 120: "*Simplicitatem in apostolicis scriptis summam agnosco: hyperbata, anantopodata, solecismos etiam aliquos agnosco.*" (Quoted by Auguste Lecerf, in *Études calvinistes* [Delachaux et Niestlé, 1949], 140.)

[7] *Contre Celse*, bk. 1, chap. 62 (M. Borret, SC, 132:246–51). Cf. *In Jesu Nave*, hom. 5, no. 16 (GCS, Or. 7, 459).

[8] *Octavius*, chap. 16, no. 5: "*Quo imperitior sermo, eo inlustrior ratio est, quoniam non fucatur pompa facundiae et gratiae, sed, ut est, recti regula sustinetur.*" In Mohrmann, 3:36.

[9] *Adversus nationes*, bk. 1, chaps. 57–59 (CSEL, 4 [1875], 38–41; cf. 562).

[10] *Divinae institutiones*, bk. 5, chap. 1 (CSEL, 19 [1890]: 400–401).

[11] *Epist.* 14 (PG, 46:1052 C).

incultus" of Scripture, says St. Jerome, its *"rusticitas"*, the *"vilitas"* of its words had at first disgusted him.[12] And Augustine in his *Confessions* writes: "When I turned to consider these Scriptures, they seemed to me unworthy to be compared with the dignity of Cicero".[13] So, as we see, some of our modern historians were not the first to have treated the primitive documents of Christianity with a certain scorn, as "minor literature". But once he had been baptized, and even more after he had been consecrated bishop, Augustine overcame his litterateur's repugnance. He did this following the example of his master Ambrose, and even more resolutely than the latter.[14] With fewer hesitations than the learned Jerome, who constantly strives "to navigate between Scylla and Charybdis, between Cicero and the *'consuetudo'* of Scripture, between the linguists and the common people",[15] he makes an effort to "conform his own language to what he calls the *'usus' ecclesiasticus*".[16] In the long run he manages to shape his writings "not only from the ideas of the Old and of the New Testament, but from biblical

---

[12] *Epist.* 22, chap. 30, no. 2 (CSEL, 54:189); *In Jon.* 3:6–8 (SC, 43:100–101). Cf. G. Q. A. Meershoek, *Le Latin biblique d'après saint Jérôme* (coll. "Latinitas christianorum primaeva", fasc. 20, Noviomagi, 1966), 4–44.

[13] Bk. 3, chap. 5, no. 9: "*Cum adtendi ad illam scripturam, sed visa est mihi indignam quam Tullianae dignitati compararem.*" He adds admirably, "*Tumor enim meus refugiebat modum ejus, et acies mea non penetrabat interiora ejus.*" See also, *De catechizandis rudibus*, chap. 9, no. 13 (PL, 40:320).

[14] See above, Chapter Four, 162.

[15] Meershoek, 63.

[16] H. I. Marrou, *Saint Augustin et la fin de la culture antique, Retractatio* (1949), 654. Cf. *De civitate Dei*, bk. 10, chap. 21 (PL, 41:299); bk. 13, chap. 11 (385), etc.

expressions and forms".[17] In his preaching, his syntax turns easily to popular expressions, for he knows that the *"imperitiores"* whom he wishes to instruct need a language that is neither too ornate nor too polished; and so, to make himself understood by all, he adopts "the ordinary and common language",[18] the "words of everyday conversation".[19] "What do we care", he said one day to his audience, perhaps with a little exaggeration, "about the demands of the grammarians? It is worth more for us to use barbarous language that you can understand than stylistic refinements that would leave you with a sense of frustration."[20] In short, whenever necessary, the teacher of rhetoric unhesitatingly abdicates before the pastor of souls.[21]

But these pragmatic considerations, as well founded and important as they might be, still remain on the surface. Jerome and Augustine themselves warn us of this: the extraordinary Christian novelty which had sud-

[17] Joseph Finaert, *L'Évolution littéraire de saint Augustin* (Paris: Les Belles-Lettres, 1939), 17.

[18] *De Genesi contra Manichaeos*, chap. 1: *"non ornato politoque sermone"*, *"communis loquendi consuetudo"*.

[19] Cf. *De doctrina christiana*, bk. 3, chap. 3, no. 7: *"Plerumque loquendi consuetudo vulgaris utilior est significandis rebus quam integritas litterata. Mallem quippe cum barbarismo dici: 'Non est absconditum a te* ossum *meum', quam ut ideo esset minus apertum, quia magis latinum est."* (CCL, 32:81.)

[20] *Enarr. in ps.* 36, *Sermo* 3, no. 6: *"Quid ad nos grammatici velint? Melius in barbarismo nostro vos intellegetis, quam in nostra disertitudine vos deserti estis."* (CCL, 38:371.) There is here a subtlety combined with an assonance which escapes translation. Cf. Lactantius, *Div. inst.*, bk. 6, chap. 21, no. 6: *"Summa Providentia carere fuco voluit ea quae divina sunt, ut omnes intelligerent quae ipse omnibus loquebatur."* (CSEL, 19:563.)

[21] On St. Augustine as a preacher in Latin, see Finaert, especially 37–81. Mohrmann, 1:68–71 and 391–402.

denly burst into the area of Hellenistic culture was bound to give rise to a certain number of original forms of language which in the eyes of stylists and even of average literate people would appear at first as so many uncouth barbarisms and solecisms.

This was noticeable as far back as the first Greek translation of the Hebrew Bible, and much more so with the appearance of the New Testament writings. The Greco-Roman world was overrun by "a tidal wave of creative genius".

> "Behold! I make all things new" (Rev 21:5). We are in the presence of something that resembles the emergence of a new species in the evolutionary process. . . . There was something sudden and extraordinary in this phenomenon of the primitive Church arising from the empty tomb in the land of the Jewish faith, at the beginning of the first century, and spreading like a forest fire from Judea to Samaria, and from there to Damascus and Antioch, thence to Asia Minor, Greece and beyond, driven by a powerful instinct (or by the Spirit of God) toward the capital of the Greco-Roman world, where the head of the Twelve would eventually bear witness and pay for it with his life some thirty years after the crucifixion. "These men who have turned the world upside down have come here also" (Acts 17:6).[22]

"The world", the minds, were turned upside down; the language had to be also. But this could not be a total novelty; the witnesses of Christ had not received, ready-

---

[22] Dom B. Christopher Butler, O.S.B., *L'Idée de l'Église* (Fr. trans., Simone de Trooz, 1965), p. 165. The New Testament "is a collection of astonishing variety in view of its small compass; but this variety is controlled by an underlying unity of exultant, dynamic faith and hope".

made, a revealed language which none of their listeners would have understood and which they themselves might not have understood either. The circumstances surrounding the origin of the Christian language were quite different:

> The prophets uttered the Word; Jesus incarnated it. Still, God did not provide them with any heavenly language, syntax, or grammar; to express themselves they had to strain their ingenuity to twist borrowed words and phrases. Thus, as soon as it appeared in Palestine, the theology of biblical revelation was as halting as Jacob after his struggle with the angel. It suffered from a disproportion between what it was supposed to announce on behalf of God and the means at its disposal for saying something to men.[23]

Under the influence of the gospel, and in proportion as succeeding generations of Christians sought to assimilate its substance, there thus occurred a syntactical and "semantic evolution", which in certain cases took on the appearance of a "complete revolution".[24]

> This linguistic revolution, which, as regards its essential elements, was achieved in the course of a few generations, is the most eloquent witness to the spiritual revolution effected by Christianity in the ancient world. No other sect, no other oriental religion, ever occasioned such a profound linguistic differentiation.

The new religion professed ideas that differed radically

---

[23] Gabriel Widmer, *Théologie et philosophie*, in *Revue de théologie et de philosophie* (1968), 375.

[24] C. Spicq, O.P., *Agapé, prolégomènes à une étude de théologie néotestamentaire*, Studia hellenistica 10 (1955): xii, with a quote from B. B. Warfield.

from the religious ideas prevalent in the Greco-Roman world in which it began to spread; it tended to overturn the very principles of the society it was invading.[25] These innovations, these transformations, were reflected in the language. We find, for instance, certain words which were rare or without any religious connotation purposely chosen to be charged with a new meaning. Such, in Greek, was the word *agapē*, which seems to have come from the popular Greek spoken in Egypt.[26] Adopted by St. John, it even replaced words which had been traditional in Israel, "words with clearly more pronounced religious connections, but too penetrated by the Israelite spirit to speak to all hearts".[27] In Latin the same thing was true of the words "*salus*" and "*salutaris*", which up to then had had only a profane and rather commonplace meaning. For "the scrupulosity of the first centuries, which consciously avoided any contact with pagan religious thought, led from the beginning to the exclusion of words with pagan connotations". Hence there are very few examples of such words taking on a Christian denotation. The "epiphany" of the Lord is a transposition, not of the religious epiphany of Greek divinities, but of the earthly epiphany or "solemn entry of Hellenistic sovereigns" into their cities.[28]

[25] Mohrmann, 1:65, 84–86, 127.

[26] Spicq, 73–74. K. H. Schelke, *Écriture et Parole de Dieu*, in *Exégèse et dogmatique* (Paris: Desclée de Brouwer, 1966), 15. Who can tell the intellectual repercussions, indefinitely prolonged in time, of the revelation of God as Love?

[27] Jacques Guillet, *La Générosité de Dieu*, "*Foi vivante*" 20 (Paris, 1966): 129.

[28] Mohrmann, 1:245–75. For another example, see M. Harl, *Le Guetteur et la cible: les deux sens de* σκοπός *dans la langue religieuse des chrétiens*, in *Revue des études grecques* (1961), 450–68. On the hesitations

These are instances of what the historians of language call "semantic neologisms". In other cases we have new derivatives, formed from classical words, or again (and these are numerous), pure neologisms: "biblicisms" or direct "Christian words"; entirely new words or groupings of words that had become necessary to express ideas, sentiments, institutions or behavior unknown to ancient religions. The list of these terms grew ever longer as the language of theology developed and became more precise, or as the analysis of the human heart transformed by the grace of Christ made further progress.[29] "It became necessary", wrote Frederic Ozanam, "to penetrate more deeply than the ancients had ever done into the depths of the human heart. . . . The ancient Romans had never said, and the Christians were the first to say: *compassio.*"[30] In these different cases an attempt was made first of all to follow as closely as possible the "*idioma Scripturarum*", the "*mos*" or the "*consuetudo Scripturae*".[31] St. Jerome, no doubt following Origen, observes for example that the word "*apokalupsis*", rendered into Latin as "*revelatio*", is "proper to the Scriptures" (i.e., the Septuagint), and "is not found in any of the

---

over the adoption of the word "*sanctus*", see Jean Rolland, *Remarques sur le mot "sanctus"*, in *Revue de l'Université catholique de l'Ouest* (1968), 5–18.

[29] *Richesses et déficiences des anciens psautiers latins* (Vatican City, 1959), 73–74 and 129–34.

[30] *Oeuvres* 2 (1855): 133.

[31] Origen, *In Levit.*, hom. 5, no. 12 (Baehrens, 357). Similar expressions in St. Jerome: *In Ps.* 15, 7 (CCL, 78:375); and in St. Augustine, *Sermo* 46, chap. 12, no. 28 (PL, 38:286). Cf. Augustine, *Retractationes*, prol., 3, where he criticizes the language he used in his early works, written "*adhuc saecularium litterarum inflatus consuetudine*" (Bibl. aug., 12, Bardy, 268).

learned men of this century".³² Had not the translators of the Greek Bible found it necessary to make great efforts *"ut proprietatem peregrini sermonis exprimerent, nova novis rebus verba fingentes"*? Jerome adds that Cicero had had to do the same thing to render into Latin certain philosophical notions drawn from the Greeks. But in addition, and more and more frequently, writers freely took their inspiration from this "use" of Scripture or its translators in order to invent a language that corresponded with their needs. Thus, the neuter word *"salutare"* took on the meaning of a noun and finally came to designate the Savior personally³³—rivalling the word *"salvator"* (and *"salvare"*), a term unknown in Latin, at least that spoken by cultured people, but one "which the Savior made Latin when he came to the Latin people".³⁴ So too, instead of using the verb *"beare"* (to make happy), they created the neologism *"beatificare"*,³⁵ and this through a very sure religious instinct, since the beatitude promised by Jesus was something quite different from the ordinary happiness spoken of by the "man in the street". Tertullian, who made use of common words like *"res"*, *"gradus"* or *"corpus"* to forge a theological language,³⁶ created a new terminology with these kinds of words when, in defining the Catholic

---

³² In fact the word did exist, but it was rare and had a purely profane meaning. *In Galat.*, 1:11–12 (PL, 26:347 C).

³³ Thus in Hilary, *Super Psalmos*, 13, 15 (Zingerle, 82); Augustine, *Sermo* 89, no. 1: *"salutare Dei Jesum Christum"* (PL, 38:554).

³⁴ Augustine, *De Trinitate*, bk. 13, chap. 10, no. 14 (P. Agaësse, Bibl. aug., 16:304); *Sermo* 299, no. 6 (PL, 38:1371). On these words, see René Braun, 487–95.

³⁵ Mohrmann, 1:60–61 and 92–93.

³⁶ Cf. J. Rizetto, commenting on Moingt, *Revue d'histoire ecclesiastique* (1968), 510: "With rather primitive weapons, he managed to affirm the truth of the faith."

Church, a reality whose like the world had not then or ever before seen, he wrote "in a language that certainly no Roman would ever have wished to acknowledge as his own": "*Corpus sumus de conscientia religionis et disciplinae divinitatis et spei foedere.*"[37] Still, it would be difficult to maintain that Tertullian was nothing but a clumsy writer, ignorant of grammar and not very well read; on the contrary, one must admit that he was in the history of language as in that of theology, if not always a creator, at least "the great pioneer, the innovator who introduced the idiom of Christians into Latin literature".[38] As for St. Jerome, expanding on his remark about the word "apocalypse", and appealing to the example of his predecessors, he shows that he was clearly aware of this necessity which sometimes compelled Christians to forge new words: "*Ut autem et nobis fingendorum nominum licentiam praesumamus, rebus quidem novis, ut ait quidam, nova fingenda sunt nomina.*"[39] In addition it is well known—to take one more entirely classical example—how, in spite of verbal continuity, the two concepts of "nature" and "person", in their dogmatic usage, soon no longer carried the same meanings they had in everyday language nor those which a purely natural philosophy would have produced.[40]

[37] Ozanam, *Oeuvres* 2 (1855): 137: "How the Latin language became christianized".

[38] Cf. J. Moingt, *La Théologie trinitaire de Tertullien*, 3 vol. (Paris: Aubier, 1966). Mohrmann, 1:147 and 57: "Tertullian does not hesitate to make use of neologisms in popular style and to introduce into his very artificial and rather learned style certain real slang expressions."

[39] *In Galat.*, 5:26 (PL, 26:452 A). Cf. G. Q. A. Meershoek, *Le Latin biblique d'après saint Jérôme* (Nimegue, 1966), 33–36.

[40] On the introduction of "persona" in the trinitarian vocabulary, see. G. L. Prestige, 143–57. René Braun, 207–42. Cf. M. Nédoncelle, *Prosopon et Persona dans l'Antiquité classique*, in *Revue des sciences*

What was happening to words was sometimes also happening to syntax. With syntax, too, in certain cases, the norms of classical usage had to be violated, whence the criticism often levelled at the early Christian writers, and primarily at the translators of the Bible, that they wrote badly. They did not dodge the reproach, and their reply was finally summed up in the slogan: "Donatus must yield to the Holy Spirit."[41] St. Gregory the Great gave his explanation on this, in very elegant Latin, in the letter-preface accompanying his moral commentary on Job.[42] In the ninth century, Godescalc of Orbais, so intransigent when it came to grammar, again discussed this question. The regularity of human language, he said, can be modified from above. God, who inspired the sacred writers and who likewise guides our pontiffs when they institute the liturgy, can teach ways of speaking which apparently contradict the rules of grammar; but this is so only in appearance, for the Holy Spirit cannot speak *contra artem*, he who is *Ars artium*.[43] Here

---

religieuses 22 (1948): 277–99. *Les Variations de Boèce sur la Personne*, ibid., 29 (1955): 201–38. See also Christiane Morati, *Dogmatique et vie spirituelle*, in *Revue d'ascétique et de mystique* (1969), 13: "Even from the linguistic point of view, in order that the person, the *persona*, which up until the Christian era in Roman language was nothing but the author's mask, might come into being, it was necessary that a God, that God himself, should become incarnate."

[41] See *Exégèse médiévale* 3 (1961): 53–98.

[42] *Epist., missoria*, chap. 5: "*Praepositionum casus servare contemno, quia indignum vehementer existimo ut verba caelestis oraculi restringam sub regulis Donati.*" (PL, 75:516 B.)

[43] *Oeuvres théologiques et grammaticales de Godescalc d'Orbais* (Louvain: Éd. C. Lambot, 1945), 180, 390, 505; cf. 141. Jean Jolivet, *Quelques cas de "platonisme grammatical" du VIIe au XIIe siècle*, in *Mélanges offerts à René Crozet* (Poitiers, 1966), 97.

Godescalc is repeating, almost word for word, an apology which St. Ambrose had once put forward in a long letter addressed to Justus, the Bishop of Lyons: "Many say", observed the Bishop of Milan, "that our authors have not written *secundum artem*, and we do not deny it. For they have not written according to art but according to grace, which is above all art; they have written, in fact, what the Spirit inspired them to say."[44] However, while Ambrose was thinking especially of the terms used in Scripture, Godescalc was here concerned rather with syntax.

At all events, in pleas of this kind we should see something more than ingenious efforts to safeguard the idea of the Scriptures' perfection; neither does one find here merely a sharpened sensitivity to the grandeur and literary beauty of biblical style. The mention of the Holy Spirit was not an idle remark.[45] Godescalc affirms his conviction, a very well-grounded one, that the verbal forms codified through human experience can only stretch or even burst asunder when the echo of a new reality, of a superior order, enters into our understanding. Like Ambrose, he thinks that from this must come a new art. As the Cistercian Gontier said, toward the end of the twelfth century, if no writer should be ignorant "of what he owes to Priscian", every Christian should

---

[44] *Epist.* 8, no. 1.: "*Negant plerique nostros secundum artem scripsisse, nec nos obnitimur; non enim secundum artem scripserunt, sed secundum gratiam, quae super omnem artem est; scripserunt enim quae Spiritus iis loqui dabat. Sed tamen ii qui de arte scripserunt, de eorum scriptis artem invenerunt, et condiderunt commenta artis et magisteria.*" (PL, 16:912 A B.)

[45] Notice the precise allusion made by St. Ambrose to Acts 2:4: "*Et repleti sunt omnes Spiritu sancto, et coeperunt loqui variis linguis, prout Spiritus sanctus dabat eloqui illis.*"

also know "what he owes to his God."[46] He should be ignorant neither of grammar nor of logic; but in certain cases, if he wishes to be faithful to Scripture, he must of necessity transgress these sciences—in order to transcend them. These are authors who are very concerned about speaking a language which is not only correct but refined who say to us—once again following St. Gregory the Great, "*Scientias omnes atque doctrinas ipso etiam locutionis suae more Scriptura sacra transcendit.*"[47]

However, if modifications in vocabulary were often perceived quite soon, even if at first they were not initiated deliberately, the changes in syntax nearly always escaped notice for a rather long period of time.[48] This is because such changes belong to a more subtle order. They put into operation some very delicate psychic mechanisms, involving spiritual attitudes whose roots sink to the deepest level of the personality. So, most of the time, it was only after the event, when the new usage, at first tentative, had finally become fixed, that observers pointed it out and tried to determine its exact significance.[49]

[46] *De oratione*, bk. 1, chap. 1 (PL, 212:106 B).

[47] St. Gregory: *Moralia in Job*, bk. 20, no. 1 (PL, 76:135 C).

[48] So Miss Mohrmann remarks, 3 (1965): 15–16: "Most linguistic modifications occur through a slow evolution which escapes the attention of those who speak"; in conjunction with what she says in 1:22 and 50: "It is not primarily the cultured people who create or transform a language. . . . The real creators (of the Christian idiom) were the Christian communities." These observations prove correct, we think, above all with reference to modifications in syntax.

[49] This is what J. N. D. Kelly, in *Early Christian Doctrines*, 2nd ed. (London, 1960), calls "a pre-reflective, pre-theological phase of Christian belief", and of which he rightly says, "This in no way diminishes their interest and importance" (90).

Now, as we saw above,[50] this is exactly what took place with the formula of the Apostles' Creed, which had to express not only this or that aspect of the Christian faith, or some particular feature of its contents, but its very structure, the fundamental attitude which makes one a Christian, the spiritual reality which lies at the root of all his life, namely, the act of faith itself. We also know already that this privileged formula did not immediately gain exclusive recognition. No doubt, if a few instances of *"in Ecclesiam"* can still be found in the course of the Middle Ages, these are explained by a late contamination rather than as evidence of what certain primitive formulations of our Creed might have been. But in the official creeds of the Greek church, the preposition εἰς has no very special meaning. Now, from this point of view, these creeds are the descendents of more ancient ones, such as that of the Church at Jerusalem, as far as we have been able to reconstitute it from the Catecheses of St. Cyril, where the same preposition is used before the mention of the Church, baptism, the resurrection of the body as well as before each of the three Persons of the Trinity.[51] This is because the expression πίστευειν εἰς— in Latin, *credere in*—followed the trend of the Koine, that debased Greek which tended to multiply prepositions.[52] Naturally, these expletive forms passed over into the corresponding Latin. Thus, we find in St. Augustine

---

[50] Chapter Four, above.

[51] Cf. the Creed that has been reconstituted on the basis of St. Cyril's catecheses (PG, 33:533).

[52] Mohrmann, 1:195: "The majority of the prepositional expressions are explained by the prevalence of the use of the Koine, in which the prepositions εἰς and ἐν, like εἰς and ἐπί, are regularly used interchangeably."

frequent use of *in*, *de* or *per*, which were unknown in classical Latin and which here indicate no special emphasis.[53] But by the insistence with which he comments, in another connection, on the phrase *"credere in Deum"*, the same St. Augustine seems to be warning us not to limit ourselves to these trivial observations.

Certain historians of language have in fact explained to us how this particular expression, *credere in*, was introduced into the Christian language. But even after all their explanations, two questions remain with specific reference to our Creed: why was this expression so quickly abandoned (if indeed it was not set aside from the start) when mentioning the various objects of our belief? And why on the contrary was it always and everywhere maintained when the reference was to faith in the three Persons? There is a contrast here which provides us with food for thought, and one can hardly believe that it was due to mere chance. Even if it did not result from deliberate choice, from a decision immediately aware of the reasons demanding it, this exclusive usage still required some understanding, which was not long in being brought to light. Maintained with regard to the three Divine Persons, and to them alone, the solecism—in terms of classical Latin—constituted by the form *credere in* was found to be a necessary solecism in these three cases. A new form of language had to be invented to correspond with this totally, radically new thing, the faith of the Christians. It could not be explained if one failed to recognize "the creative force

[53] S. Poque, St. Augustine, *Sermons sur la Pâque* (SC, 116), 120. This multiplication of prepositions, whether expletives or not, is one of his most notable deviations from classical syntax. See Finaert, 68–69.

belonging to primitive Christianity", of which it has given us one of the finest examples.[54] The proclamation of the gospel in the power of the Spirit brought about a spiritual revolution which created a new mental structure deep within man, and, by an imperative logic, this latter, despite some hesitations, had to clear a way to express itself. Erasmus had recognized this when he commented on and adopted as his own the traditional explanations: when used in this way, not indiscriminately but as the result of a particular, unique choice, this preposition *in* "adds a certain force to what is said". It specifies a privileged use of the verb "believe". That is why, Erasmus continued, giving the demands of Christian faith precedence over his literary tastes, *"credo in Deum"* is a well-chosen expression even though those who speak polished Latin can hardly bear it.[55]

The fact is that neither the Greek words πίστευω and πίστις nor the corresponding Latin words *"credere"* and *"fides"* were particularly significant in themselves. In Plato's *Republic*, πίστις designated only one of the four states in which the soul may be as regards knowledge, between νόησις (intellection) and διανοία (discursive knowledge), on the one hand, and εἰκασία (simulation), on the other.[56] In ordinary language, πίστις was understood objectively as "pledge", "bond", "guarantee", and subjectively as "confidence" or "fidelity". Such are

---

[54] Cf. Percy, *Die Probleme der Kol. und Éph. Briefe*, 77; quoted by K. Prüm, art. *Mystères, Dictionnaire de la Bible*, suppl., s.v. Bible, col. 216.

[55] *"Sed cur non placet haec sermonis forma, 'credo in Deum', quam Latini emendate loquentes vix agnoscunt? . . . Videtur tamen praepositio nonnihil vigoris addere sermoni"* (loc cit.).

[56] *Republic*, bk. 6, 511 d e.

also, approximately, the meanings of the Latin word *fides* in the oldest known instances of its use. This was "an old word springing from Indo-European roots", which at first had had a "semi-religious, semi-juridical" meaning, but which in the course of centuries had become desacralized. Its usual connotation had become entirely profane, like that of the verb *fido*, which, it seems, had never had any other meaning. It was Christianity that reintroduced them into the vocabulary of religion, where they played a central role.[57] However, even if they could serve to express a religious belief, if they even possessed the proper shades of meaning sufficient to justify their choice in translating the biblical realities of the two Testaments, these words did not suffice in themselves to render "what constitutes the basic originality of the Christian attitude and makes it irreducible to its religious expressions as well as to all its historical influences",[58] namely, faith itself in the Christian sense of the word, that faith which "is not a special kind of faith but simply faith in itself";[59] that faith which, humanly speaking, proceeds from an unprecedented experience of life and which is itself an entirely new life; faith, the notion of which is not merely a generic concept, prior to the specific differences that might produce varying types of belief, but which constitutes an original, irreducible notion:

---

[57] René Braun, 443–44. Cf. A. Meillet, in *Mémoires de la société de linguistique*, 22:218. Ernout and Meillet, *Vocabulaire étymologique de la langue latine* (1932), 220.

[58] André Manaranche, *L'Homme dans son univers* (Paris: Éd. Ouvrières, 1966), 160.

[59] Gerhard Ebeling, quoted by René Marlé, *Recherches de science religieuse* 50 (1962): 20.

What the New Testament calls "faith" does not take on a religious attitude that might apply to various contents— something like an abstract category, like knowledge capable of apprehending a multitude of disparate objects while still remaining "knowledge". Faith, in the Christian sense, has a unique and exclusive character. It is not an all-embracing notion which might be adapted to numerous modalities: Christian faith, Moslem faith, paganism of the ancient Greeks or Buddhism. . . . The word designates a unique thing: the response given by man to God, who has come to him in Christ.[60]

This is precisely what Smaragdus, the Abbot of St. Mihiel, said about the Trinity in the ninth century: "Compared with our faith, no other should be called by that name."[61] This does not mean, or at least does not only mean, that Christian faith is the only true faith, the only one with a fully real object—but that it alone is truly faith; that nothing else is like the Christian reality constituted by this faith; that nowhere else does the formal concept of faith prove true. So, speaking of Christians, Lactantius could write: "*Qui credunt in eum (Deum) ac vocantur fideles*":[62] there were other "believers" besides Christians, but Lactantius distinguished these latter simply by calling them "the faithful". Before the spelling out of the beliefs to which they adhered, the faith of

[60] Romano Guardini, *Vie de la foi*, ("Foi vivante" Paris: Éd. du Cerf, 1968), 23. Cf. Juan Alfaro, S.J., *Foi et existence*, in *Nouvelle revue théologique* 90 (1968): 561–80.

[61] *Grammatica*, fol. 18: "*Ad comparationem fidei nostrae, . . . nulla alia dicenda est fides.*" Cf. Jean Leclercq, *Smaragde et la grammaire*, in *Revue du moyen âge latin* 4 (1948): 19.

[62] *Institutions divines*, bk. 4, chap. 13, no. 26 (S. Brandt, CSEL, 19:324). Cf. Nicetas, on the grace of baptism, "*Ex hoc vero fidelis incipit appellari.*" (Bk. 1, s. 1, no. 12; Gamber, 18.)

Christians was already specified; it was already Christian, in these simple words: *"credere in"*, *"fides"*. In other words, the formal concept of faith, in Christianity, is inseparable from its essential contents; faith and the contents or object of the faith are intrinsically bound together.

Ordinary language certainly knows nothing of such precisions. Not to mention more profane or common uses, it is customary to find this same word "faith" applied to all sorts of religious beliefs. But, as Fr. Irenaeus Hausherr very correctly observes with regard to the notion of spirituality, "too broad a use of words risks provoking dilution of the concepts they stand for".[63] What generates resistance to such "dilution" is not a reflex springing from partiality but concern for rigor in analysis and for phenomenological objectivity. The Buddhist religion, for instance, does not involve, in any of its actual stages, what Christianity calls "faith", any more than it involves what we would call "charity". The spiritual realities which distinguish this religion do not correspond with those we designate by these two words. Nor is this, as some have feared, a question of inventing "discriminatory nomenclature" for "sentiments which everybody experiences"; that would be an odious paradox when talking about charity, which is a unifying force. If charity is nothing but a "human sentiment" like "love, compassion, tolerance, patience, friendship" or even "desire and emptiness, etc.", then it is clear that it should not carry a "sectarian label".[64] But in fact a comparative study of Christianity and Buddhism shows

---

[63] In the collective volume *La Mystique et les mystiques*, by André Ravier, S.J. (Paris: Desclée de Brouwer, 1965), 415.

[64] Cf. Walpole Rahula, *L'Enseignement du Bouddha* (1961), 24-25.

clearly that Christian charity, understood in the precise tenor and full strength of this concept, is one thing, and Buddhist good will, understood in the same way, is something else. That is true no matter what the numerous practical interferences of daily life and independently of all judgments of value or of truth and, a fortiori, of any evaluation of the comparative merits of individuals.[65]

Just as one cannot extend or "dilute" without blurring the reality of notions like faith or charity, so too one cannot without serious damage, in the opposite direction, designate Christian faith by some other word, too readily considered to be its synonym. This was what some humanists belonging to the so-called "Ciceronian school" attempted to do in the sixteenth century. One of these was the Frenchman Christophe Longueil, who when speaking of Christian things systematically substituted "persuasion" for the word "faith". Already inadequate in its application to beliefs, the word entirely misrepresented the act of the Christian who "believes in God". Erasmus was not wrong when, over and above a ridiculous obsession with language which whetted his zest for irony, he went on to denounce with dead seriousness this attempt by our "Ciceronians" on the faith itself.[66] While one cannot of course accuse them of such an attempt, it does happen sometimes that authors discussing the Catholic faith allow their explanations to be based a little too easily on the "contemporary vocabulary" in order to lay down at the beginning a general idea of faith which can be taken as a common denominator for some very diverse realities. "Whether it be Christian or not", some

---

[65] Cf. H. de Lubac, *Aspects du bouddhisme* (Paris: Éd. du Seuil, 1951), chap. 1; cf. *Amida* (ibid., 1955), chap. 12.

[66] Erasmus, *Ciceronianus* (1528). Cf. *Exégèse médiévale* 4:461–62.

might say, "religious faith has for its object truths which transcend the scope of human reason and has for its basis the authority of a transcendent being and has for its goal a supernatural beatitude."[67] It is not certain that such a definition can be fully verified outside of rather rare cases; at least, and this is to its credit, it says nothing that does not apply to the Christian religion; but it leaves out the most fundamental characteristic of faith itself; it overlooks its basic element, which will prove very difficult to recover later on without some inconsistencies.

A new idea of God, a new idea of man, a new idea of the relationships between man and God: this is what was latent in the first act of Christian faith, which had been foreshadowed by Israel. This act, in its newness, was not an idea but reality. It dealt with an encounter, with *the* encounter, in view of which the whole adventure of the created universe had been set in motion. This same encounter which, considered from man's point of view, is called *faith* is given the name revelation when considered from God's point of view. A personal challenge addressed to man by God, revelation calls forth from man an equally personal response: that is what faith is. Thus, a relationship is established which must be called reciprocal and which later on will very rightly be designated as "interpersonal".[68] Reciprocity is so strong that

---

[67] M. L. Guérard de Lauriers, O.P., *Dimensions de la foi* (1952), 1:15.

[68] Cf. René Latourelle, S.J., *La Révélation chrétienne* (Montreal, 1957), 65; M. J. Le Guillou, O.P., *Le Visage du Ressuscité* (Paris: Éd. Ouvrières, 1968), 28: "The primacy of this interpersonal relationship, as well as the absolutely irreducible character of the events which constitute salvation history, have always been kept in mind by Christian thinkers, even though speculative research groped about

in biblical language the same word which we today translate by "faith" and which evokes fidelity on both sides also defines the attitude of each of the two beings thus joined to each other.[69] But if one wishes to acknowledge, as is fitting, the divine initiative in the work of our salvation as in that of creation, one needs to make these statements more accurate by saying that, on God's side, the revelation addressed to man is "personalizing",[70] whereas on man's side, in his response to God's call, faith is discovery and acknowledgment of the Divinity as a personal Absolute. It is precisely in this discovery and this acknowledgment that, as a consequence, man's being attains its full personalization.

> God calls each being by its name. By responding in faith to this divine call, the being becomes truly conscious of itself, for it begins to fulfill the divine idea about it. By calling it by name, God comes seeking it in those depths where being has not yet penetrated and which it does not know. By revealing God to it, faith reveals to it its own true self. "That I may know thee, and that I may know myself!"[71]

---

for a long time before succeeding in elaborating the notion of the person". Paul Toinet, *Existence chrétienne et philosophie* (Paris: Aubier, 1965), 281–82.

[69] "The *fides* and the *fidelitas* of a God who keeps his word—because he keeps what he himself is—is the foundation for the specifically human form of *fides*, this fidelity which rests on the acknowledgment of God as God and on a perfect abandonment of self to God": Hans Urs von Balthasar, *La Foi du Christ*, "*Foi vivante*" (Paris: Aubier, 1960), 27.

[70] Cf. Gal 1:15–16: "*Cum autem placuit ei qui me segregavit de utero matris meae . . . ut revelaret Filium suum in me.*" Compare Phil 3:12: "*Si quo modo comprehendam in quo et comprehensus sum a Christo Jesu.*"

[71] Paul Marie de la Croix, O.C.D., *L'Évangile de Jean et son*

Is this not also what we find when we look at the spiritual history of mankind? We see there the human imagination and human instincts bringing forth an unbelievable profusion of anthropomorphic gods. Then we also see emerging, as a result of personal reflection or mental concentration, the idea of a unity in the Divinity;[72] again, in more mature and critical times, we see the abstract pattern of these gods, or of this Divinity, take shape in the form of ideals and values. But since he is incapable of transcending his own resources, man always remains a prisoner of the narrow notion of individuality which he has projected onto his gods; or, if he escapes from this, it is only to dissolve himself by allowing himself to be absorbed in the divine which he has conceived. Throughout the manifold variety of these attitudes, one misgiving is discerned, but it is powerless to take shape; a yearning for transcendence, but one that always remains ambiguous; a dream, but one which is threatened by the ruin and despair of awakening.[73]

Very different appears to us the trend of thought which originates in Abraham and culminates in the faith of Christ. There has been much speculation and debate

---

témoignage spirituel (1959), 302. Cf. Paul Claudel, *Magnificat*: "You called me by my name. . . . And now, all of a sudden, you are someone!" And in *Ma conversion*: "*It is true!* God exists; he is right there. He is someone; he is a being as fully personal as I! He loves me; he calls me." (*Contacts et circonstances*, 12.) It was not exactly in this sense that the American historian H. F. Muller attributed to Christian revelation "the advent of the human personality". Hence the criticism of his thesis rightly undertaken by Miss Mohrmann, 3:25–26.

[72] Cf. *Homélies clémentines*, 6, 20: "Through allegories your philosophers have caused the faces of the gods to fade into the elements of the world." (PG, 2:212–13.)

[73] Cf. H. de Lubac, *Le Mystère du surnaturel*, "*Théologie*" (Paris: Aubier, 1965); *Sur les chemins de Dieu*, 25–43.

about the features that distinguish Jewish and Christian faith. They have even been contrasted at times.[74] Here the tradition of the Church as well as meditation on the texts must enlighten us. If there really is a difference between the faith of the New Testament and that of the Old, it is not that this faith of the New Testament deviates in the slightest degree from that of the former; rather, it fulfills it, gives it its complete and definitive form.[75] In Jesus Christ, the perfect meeting of God and man, both call and response, revelation and faith are united; in him is perfectly expressed, in a unique Amen, the twofold Yes of God to man and of man to God; the marriage between the Creator and his creation is consummated. In each one of those who believe in him, in proportion to his faith, this marvel is renewed.[76]

We would thus be more truly justified in recognizing in the characteristic formula of our Creed, as well as in many other words translated from Scripture, a hebraism, as Erasmus had observed long ago, rather than an idiomatic expression from the Koine.[77] But this is

[74] See especially Martin Buber, *Two Types of Faith* (English trans., 1951).

[75] Cf. Gerhard Ebeling, in René Marlé, loc. cit.: "The concept of faith which emerges from the Old Testament received only in Christianity its central and decisive significance."

[76] Hans Urs von Balthasar, *La Foi du Christ*, 27–51 and 77–79.

[77] Loc. cit.: "*Summa enim et sacra, ut dici solet, fiduciae speique ancora non est fingenda nisi in Deo. Sed revera sermonis figura fluxit ab idiomate linguae Hebraicae, quae frequenter addit praepositionem* in, *ubi sermo Latinus eam repudiat. Apostoli vero, quanquam graece scripserunt, tamen interdum referunt proprietatem nativae linguae.*" Cf. Mohrmann, 1:47: "Many Greek words borrowed by the Latin are really Hebrew words disguised in Greek." So too F. Gomar, quoted by Lecerf, 142: "It is a pure hebraism, which unquestionably departs from the Greek and Latin idiom; one cannot find a single example of such a construction, either in Greek or in Latin, in any reputable author. The Seventy and

again on the condition that we go beyond the level of philological considerations in order to grasp the doctrinal significance of these words. Furthermore, the Latin Creed is not the only text to enclose within a single little syllable all the power and originality of the faith. If we needed confirmation of the analyses we have been making on this point, we would find one, dating back to the apostolic age, in the Gospel of St. John.

As we have remarked above, the thing that has concealed in our own times from erudite historians the newness of the formula which a fifteen-century-old tradition has never ceased to assert and confirm is the unquestionable fact that in the language used in the first centuries of our era, the words εἰς or *in* were often expletives. Rev. Fr. de la Potterie, in his study of the use of εἰς in John's writings, begins by recognizing this fact. As far back as the third century B.C. the two prepositions εἰς and ἐν tended more and more to be used interchangeably, so that the former in many cases no longer implied any idea of movement. Now, the author of the fourth Gospel uses this word frequently in a variety of contexts. Summing up and completing the observations made by E. A. Abbott, Joseph Huby and M. Zerwick, Fr. de la Potterie concludes, from an exhaustive and minute examination of the texts, that, contrary to what might have been expected, John always makes a distinction between the two prepositions. Whatever the local or metaphorical

---

the Jews who spoke Greek used this hebraism often. So the Apostles, guided by God, used it also as an accepted expression in the Church of God, and the Greek and Latin Fathers followed their example." Cf. Augustine, *Locutiones in Heptateuchum* (CCL, 33:381). "Hebrew idiom has infiltrated the most varied aspects of the language used in the Bible": Meershoek, 66; 24: "The Greek Bible and the Latin Bible both show a Hebrew coloration."

meaning of the phrase containing this word, εἰς in his writings always has a meaning which is both pregnant and dynamic, even if the verb which it complements is not itself a verb indicating movement. The same thing is true of St. Paul[78] and St. Matthew.

These conclusions have a far-reaching effect, given the doctrinal character of some of the passages in question. This is particularly true with regard to the expression that concerns us here: πιστεύειν εἰς (believe in). In the fourth Gospel we find this expression some thirty times.[79] True, it does not always refer to the theological act properly so called, "as will be the case later on for the formula *credere in*"; yet it always implies "an interior movement of adhesion to the one to whom one has given his faith".[80] In none of these texts is it merely a question of "to believe that. . .". In other words, for St. John, εἰς is not an expletive.[81] John also differentiates, as St. Augustine would do systematically to great advantage later on, between this "believe in" and the simple "believe about" (πιστεύειν, followed by the dative, with no preposition). He uses this latter construction rather often, speaking of the Scriptures, of Moses, of the

---

[78] Rom 3:22; 4:24; 10:14.

[79] Thirty-seven times, if we include the first letter of John. John always uses the verbal form, never the substantive πίστις.

[80] Ignace de la Potterie, S.J., *L'Emploi dynamique de* εἰς *dans saint Jean et ses incidences théologiques*, in *Biblica* 43 (1962): 366–87; especially 375–76. See also Heinrich Schlier, *Croire, connaître, aimer d'après l'évangile de saint Jean*, in *Einsicht und Glaube*, Festschrift G. Söhugen (ed. J. Ratzinger and H. Tries; Freiburg: Herder, 1962), 98–111: "The idea of believing, in absolute terms, changes with the expressions believe *about*, believe *that*, believe *in*; our Gospel does not have any general theological term for undifferentiated belief."

[81] Nor does John ever say πιστεύειν ἐν.

"works" of Christ or his words, of Jesus himself or the Father who sent him, insofar as they bear witness.[82] On both sides the usage is constant enough to enable us to discern with certainty that the writer used these forms intentionally. In two places in the Gospel the two constructions are even juxtaposed, so that the contrast is more apparent. This is especially true in chapter 6, vv. 29–30. Jesus says to those around him: "This is the work of God, so that you may believe in him whom he has sent (*ut credatis in eum quem misit ille*)"; they reply to him: "What sign do you show that we may believe you (that we may accept what you say, *credamus tibi*)?"[83] It is to be regretted that many French translations disregard this difference; it is remarkable that the Latin Vulgate, on the contrary, respects it.[84] Finally, let us note that if the verb "believe" followed by the accusative without any preposition is very rare in John,[85] and has for complement neither a personal name nor a personal pronoun, the two formulas we have just been distinguishing (believe in and believe about) can both be applied to Jesus Christ; and thus one

---

[82] So Augustine says, "*Mihi vel illi potius credite qui ait: Quaerite et invenietis.*" To Romanien, *Contra Academicos*, bk. 2, chap. 3, no. 9 (R. Jolivet, Bibl. aug., 4:74).

[83] ἵνα πιστεύητε εἰς ὃν ἀπέστειλεν—πιστεύσωμὲν σοι. Cf. J. H. Moulton, *A Grammar of New Testament Greek* 1:67: "Jesus, who was getting ready to begin his discourse on the Bread of Life, explicitly demands an unconditional faith in his person, while the Jews, carnal as they were, were still asking for signs in order to believe the elementary fact of revelation itself." (Joseph Huby.)

[84] So too the Anglican version of the Bible (Revised Version) and the commentators Wescott and J. H. Bernard.

[85] There are two examples: Jn 11:26 (with *touto*: "*Credis hoc?*") and 1 Jn 4:16 (with τὴν ἀγαπήν: "*credidimus caritati*" as the Vulgate has it. It might be better to use "*caritatem*").

can understand "that John readily goes from one construction to the other, since Christ is at the same time the Revealer whom one must believe and the Truth *in which* one must believe".[86]

Of course, "the identity in Jesus of the object and the witness", this assertion which is at the heart of our faith, has "other bases in the Gospel besides these fine grammatical details".[87] Still these fine details are significant. They throw light on one of the major examples of solecisms, so disagreeable to the ears of the Greco-Roman scholars, mistaken by them at first (and later by certain learned philologists) to be a corruption of the language but which in reality are bearers of the new Christian message.[88]

---

[86] Joseph Huby, *La Connaissance de foi dans saint Jean*, an appendix to *Le Discours de Jésus après la Cène*, new ed., "*Verbum salutis*" (Paris: Beauchesne, 1942), 145–46. For the formula πίστευω ὅτι (*credo quia* . . .), see below, Chapter Ten.

[87] Th. Camelot, *Revue des sciences philosophiques et théologiques* 30 (1941): 151.

[88] The message of Christ, contained in the gospel and formulated by the Church in the first centuries, split wide open certain categories, both profane and religious, of pagan antiquity (and in certain cases, even Jewish antiquity). It will always be thus, and so it must be today as well, with reference to any other language—despite any tendency to some sort of pure "contemporaneity". Eternally new, this message remains eternally "scandalous" and "wonderful". For this reason it is an illusion that makes people demand, for instance, a eucharistic prayer expressed solely in the language of "current" or "everyday life", using only "familiar concepts". *Des prières eucharistiques pour l'Église d'aujourd'hui*, in *La Maison-Dieu* 94 (1968): 137–38.

CHAPTER NINE

THE DYNAMISM OF FAITH

Among the problems of conscience that the Christians at Corinth brought up to St. Paul was one that had to do with the "idolothytes". Was it permissible to eat meats that had been sacrificed to idols? In his reply, the Apostle enlarged the scope of the discussion. He took advantage of this opportunity to consider Christian liberty in its relation to the demands of fraternal charity. We know perfectly well, he answered in substance, that an idol is nothing at all and that there is no god save the one true God; hence nothing prevents us from eating such meats in complete peace of conscience. However, in making use of this liberty as of any other, we have to be careful not to become an occasion of sin to some brother less enlightened or weaker than ourselves. Whatever the circumstances, I should willingly limit the use of my own liberty if in doing so I risk wounding the conscience of my brother.[1]

There we have an example of St. Paul's constant concern. It has often been remarked that he preaches fraternal charity on every occasion, while he hardly ever speaks of loving God but only of believing in him. Here that is not completely the case since, at the beginning of his explanations and precisely in order to lay the foundation for this fraternal charity which he is going to

[1] 1 Cor 8:1–13.

recommend so strongly, he declares: "If anyone loves God, that man is known by him."[2] To speak more accurately, Paul habitually defines man's Christian attitude toward God by faith rather than by love. In this same passage he tells the Corinthians: "For us there is but one God, the Father, from whom all things come and for whom we live."[3] The words καί ἡμεῖς εἰς αὐτόν (Vulgate: *et nos in illum*) might be translated: "for whom we exist",[4] where "we" stands for the whole human race. But this "we", especially if we compare it with the "for us" (Christians) which opens the phrase, seems to indicate also the movement of the believing conscience, that movement which, upon hearing the Word, freely ratifies the destiny inscribed in our very being by the Creator; in other words, the resumption and transformation of the secret movement essential to every creature through the dynamism of faith. When I answer the call that God has made me hear through the preaching of the gospel, I recognize that I am for him (εἰς αὐτόν), and I rush toward him (εἰς αὐτόν). At first I had turned aside from God in order to turn toward idols; by the movement of conversion to which his messenger invites me, I now turn aside from the idols that had seduced me (ἀπὸ τῶν εἰδώλων) in order to turn back to God (πρὸς τὸν θεόν). These are the very words used by Paul in his first Epistle to the Thessalonians.[5] According to St. Luke's account, he expressed himself in the same way in front of the elders of the Church at Ephesus: "You know", he told them when bidding them farewell, "how . . . I called

[2] 1 Cor 8:3.
[3] 1 Cor 8:6.
[4] That is how the Jerusalem Bible translates the passage.
[5] 1 Th 1:9: "*Quomodo conversi estis ad Deum a simulacris*"; 1:8: "*fides vestra, quae est ad Deum* (ἡ πίστις ὑμῶν ἡ πρὸς τὸν θεόν)".

THE DYNAMISM OF FAITH

upon Jews and Greeks to be converted to God (τὴν εἰς θεὸν μετάνοιαν) and to believe in our Lord Jesus (καὶ πίστιν εἰς τὸν κύριον ἡμῶν Ιησοῦν)."[6] In the address he delivered at Jerusalem before Agrippa and Bernice, the construction is similar, with the difference that εἰς or πρός is replaced by ἐπί: "To all I preached that it was necessary to repent and turn back to God" (ἐπιστρέφειν ἐπὶ τὸν θεόν).[7] These prepositions, all of them followed by a noun in the accusative case, are therefore interchangeable as far as Paul is concerned, in this same expression: to turn to God, to be converted to God, to believe in God. On the other hand, the single preposition εἰς will have to be translated, depending on the preceding verb, either as "for" or "to" or "in". But in all these cases we are dealing with the same reality, the same dynamism.

These passages from St. Paul correspond with those from the Johannine writings we examined in the last chapter. They are less numerous, not because Paul, in striving to clarify his thought, really differs from St. John, but because he most often uses πίστις, a word which is fundamental for him, and uses it without any complement. In Paul as in John, the act of faith is certainly "the total behavior, the disposition by which man, through the power of grace, corresponds to the call

---

[6] Acts 20:21. Cf. 1 Pet 1:8 and 1:21.

[7] Acts 26:20: "*ut paenitentiam agerent et converterentur ad Deum*"; 26:18: "*ut convertantur a tenebris ad lucem et de potestate Satanae ad* (ἐπὶ) *Deum*". So too in Acts 15:19: "*qui ex gentibus convertuntur ad* (ἐπὶ) *Deum*" (in St. James' address). Heb 6:1: "*non rursum jacientes fundamentum . . . fidei ad* (ἐπὶ) *Deum*". Cf. Jacques Dupont, *Études sur les Actes des Apôtres* (Paris: Éd. du Cerf, 1967), 421–57: "*Repentir et conversion d'après les Actes.*"

of God revealing himself".[8] It is the act by which he abandons himself to the attraction of God, in an obedience that makes him free.[9] And just as this act is not isolated among many others; just as, as we have seen, it is not a form lacking content, neither does it have a content which could be called purely intellectual; it is not separated from the other two acts that St. Paul also mentions: hope and charity. It includes them implicitly. In a word, it is the *theological act*.

"Nowhere in Scripture", wrote the abbot Joannès Wehrlé to his nephew René, "have I ever found a purely intellectualistic notion of faith; but always the idea of a voluntary and total movement of the human being toward God, expressing itself in an unshakeable confidence."[10] Thus, he observed in writing to Maurice Blondel about the same time, "we cannot even dream of untying the vital knot which binds together in an indissoluble unity the act of the mind and the transport of the heart, knowledge and confidence, intelligence and will."[11] No doubt it will always be legitimate to consider a faith which is "dead"—but on condition that we clearly recognize that it is indeed dead, emptied of what

---

[8] Hans Urs von Balthasar, *La Gloire et la croix* 1 (Paris: Aubier, 1965): 109. Cf. Jacques Dupont, *Études sur les Actes des Apôtres* (Paris: Éd. du Cerf, 1967), 428.

[9] Cf. Heinrich Schlier, *Croire, connaître, aimer d'après l'évangile de saint Jean*, in *Einsicht und Glaube*.

[10] Letter dated April 26, 1903. But also, "who can fail to see that this deep disposition of soul includes infinitely more than the recognition of a limited creed; who can fail to see that it is worth the whole series of revealed truths, since it makes one adhere to the divine, total Reality, such as it is practically constituted in its relationship with humanity, and since this Reality is the Creed in action?"

[11] May 19, 1903.

made it a living reality; and that we do not try to draw from it a definition that would serve as a basis for a study of faith. The dissection of a corpse may certainly be useful to science; but who would dream of forming a real idea of man by studying him reduced to the state of a cadaver?[12] If God's call is a call of creative and saving Love, and if, in fact, "Love alone is worthy of faith", how could this faith, since it is a response to Love, not itself be the response of love, at least an incipient love? God's love for man was manifested in Jesus Christ, and Paul's gospel consists in proclaiming this fact; so, to understand fully the teaching on faith that the Apostle gives in the Epistle to the Romans, we should comment on it by means of the Epistle to the Galatians: "The life I now live in this body, I live in faith in the Son of God who loved me and gave himself up for me."[13]

With different nuances in language, and through perspectives which sometimes differ slightly, Christian tradition in its greatest representatives remained faithful to this dynamic concept, which is that of our Creed just as it is that of our Scripture.

In a formula which joins the two verbs "to be converted" and "to believe", by giving them the same complement, Clement of Alexandria declares in one of

---

[12] Cf. F. Mallet (i.e., Maurice Blondel). *L'Unité complexe du problème de la foi*, in *Revue du clergé français* 53 (1908): 262: Faith, he says, "survives after grace and sometimes coexists with bad will", but "it is never born or revived as a lifeless corpse".

[13] Rom 4 and Gal 2:20; cf. Rom 5:1-11 and Gal 5:6. Cf. Hans Urs von Balthasar in *Dialogue* (Geneva: Labor et Fides, 1968), 42. Also Lucien Cerfaux, *Le Chrétien dans la théologie paulinienne* (Paris: Éd. du Cerf, 1962), 132, note: in the majority of texts from St. Paul "faith, which is the response to the message, includes both intellectual submission (ὑπακούω) and the giving over of one's life to God".

his *Stromata* that he makes use of the Scriptures in order to help any Jew who might hear him "to be converted to the one *in whom* he has not yet believed".[14] In his *Pedagogue*, he draws out the implications of this statement: "Eternity and time", he says,

> are not identical, nor are the impetus of setting out and the final fulfillment. Still, it is one and the same being which is involved in both steps. One can say, for instance, that the impetus is faith, generated in time; that the fulfillment is the taking possession of the promised object, guaranteed for eternity.

To faith thus understood, "nothing is lacking; it is perfect in itself, complete; in its own way it has already grasped, in its impetus, eternal life, it has received the promise and the down payment for it".[15]

A "conversion" followed by "an impetus"; for Clement too, this is faith. Clement is not the only one to draw this teaching from Scripture.[16] But patristic texts afford us two manners of drawing attention to this. Sometimes, as is the case here with Clement, the entire spiritual movement started in response to the call of preaching is summed up in the single word "faith"; sometimes, on the contrary, faith is prolonged by hope or charity or by both of them. In reality, however, the difference is usually minimal, if not purely verbal—at least in the living phases of theological reflection. In the second case,

---

[14] *Deuxième Stromate*, chap. 1, no. 2, 1: ἐπιστρέψαι . . . εἰς ὃν οὐκ ἐπίστευσεν. (Mondésert and Camelot, SC, 38:33.)

[15] *Pédagogue*, bk. 1, chap. 6, nos. 4–5 and chap. 29, no. 2 (Marrou and Harl, SC, 70:162–65).

[16] For Justin and Irenaeus, see above, Chapter Four.

THE DYNAMISM OF FAITH

in fact, hope and charity do not come to join faith as though from outside, in order to bring about a movement that would exceed the power of faith alone; they are represented, rather, as explicitations of what was already implied in faith, like the rising of the sap in the tree, like two fruits of which faith is the fecund root. So at times we see the same author using both methods alternately. St. Paul had already done this when, after speaking of "living in the faith of the Son of God who loved me", he spoke a little farther on of "faith that works in charity";[17] or again, when he exalted, on the one hand, the "law of the faith" by which alone we give glory to God[18] and, on the other hand, enumerated the inseparable trio: faith, hope and charity.[19]

It is in the work of St. Augustine that this dynamism of faith is subjected to the most thorough analyses. We shall say nothing of the Augustinian theory of faith considered in its relationship to authority, i.e., as the necessary basis for social life and for all spiritual education; nor shall we discuss faith as fidelity, which applies to God as well as to man, nor the complex relationships between faith and intelligence. Nor shall we go back

---

[17] Gal 5:6.
[18] Rom 3:27-28 and 4:20.
[19] 1 Cor 13:13. Cf. H. Schlier, *L'Existence chrétienne*, in *Essais sur le Nouveau Testament* (French trans., Paris: Éd. du Cerf, 1968), 157: "Faith is not only the source of hope and charity; it always remains attached to them, it is also the measure of their truth." William of Saint Thierry had said, in his *Speculum fidei* (The Mirror of Faith): "*Sic sibi invicem connexae sunt et conjunctae, ut sint singulae in omnibus, et omnes in singulis.*" And again, "*Ad similitudinem ergo summae divinitatis, sicut fides spem gignit, sic caritas ab utraque, hoc est a fide et spe procedit.*" (Éd. Déchanet, 54 and 56.)

over the threefold meaning of *credere* already brought out in Chapter Four.[20] The only thing important to note here is a certain number of traits which characterize St. Augustine's commentary on *credere in*.

Let us observe first of all that this *credere in* applies to "Christ" as well as to "God".[21] By this, St. Augustine indicates that this Jesus, whom he likes to present as the one who alone leads to the Father, is at the same time something more: more than the way that must be followed, more than the perfect model whom we must imitate, more than the veracious witness who must be believed. Jesus is the Son; he and the Father are one. Augustine is not a rigid biblicist; whether he is interpreting creation, the government of Providence or the divine unity, his thought gives ample space to what we call natural theology; but this does not lead him to blur the traits which distinguish the Christian faith. No matter which Person of the Trinity the context leads him to mention, faith in God is a movement which begins by "conversion": baptism is *"sacramentum conversionis et fidei"*.[22] But this movement of conversion is actually only a beginning. By it a dynamism is set in motion; a journey is begun, which must now be pursued. The believer is not established in a state which he needs merely to preserve; it is not enough for him not to turn back, not to renounce the faith of his baptism. He must go forward, advance. This is what Augustine explains by means of four verbs: to believe in God is to tend

[20] See above, Chapter Five.
[21] See for instance, *De civitate Dei*, bk. 17, nos. 5, 11, 12, 16; bk. 20, no. 30. *In Joannem, tract.* 53, no. 10, etc.
[22] Cf. S. Poque, SC, 116:34–35.

THE DYNAMISM OF FAITH 299

toward him, to move toward him, to progress each day on the path that leads to him and finally to reach him.[23]

Such then is the faith that God requires of us.[24] In each of its stages it is accompanied and upheld by its two sisters, hope and charity. *"Credendo in Deum ire"* means *"credendo diligere"*.[25] The one who believes but does not hope or love may well believe that Christ exists; he does not believe in him. This is the case with the demons spoken of in St. James' Epistle: "They believe and tremble", for they confess Christ but do not love him. They declare this themselves; there is nothing in common between him and them.[26] Does this mean that the movement which brings us to God is something extrinsic to faith? Not at all. If we wish to remain faithful to St. Augustine's language, the language we adopted in distinguishing faith and belief, we cannot say that the demons have faith. Faith belongs exclusively to those who believe in God. Faith is not a powerless reality

[23] *In Joannem*, tract. 29, no. 6 (on Jn 6:29): *"Quid est ergo credere in eum? . . . Credendo in Deum ire, et ejus membris incorporari."* Tract. 48, no. 3: *"Accedere est credere. Qui credit, accedit; qui negat recedit. Non movetur anima pedibus, sed affectibus."* (PL, 35:1631 and 1741.) Sermo Denis 20, no. 13: *"Fratres mei, demus operam cotidie proficiendo in Deum. . . . Attendamus Abrahae fidem. . . . Ut boni filii ad patriam tendamus."* (Morin, 123–24.)

[24] *In Joannem*, tract. 29, no. 6: *"Ipsa est ergo fides quam de nobis exigit Deus."* (PL, 35:1631.)

[25] Ibid. *"Credendo amare, credendo diligere, credendo in Deum ire."*

[26] *Sermo* 144, no. 2 (PL, 38:788). Sermo Denis 19, no. 4: *"Tu dicis, quia unus est Deus. Bene credis; sed et daemones credunt, et contremiscunt. Si ergo tantummodo credis, et non diligis, adhuc cum daemonibus tibi commune est. . . . Filium Dei confitentur apostoli, Filium Dei confitentur et daemones: confessio videtur par, dilectio dispar."* (Morin, 101.) *In Ps.* 130, no. 1 (PL, 37:1704).

which needs some external help in order to become truly operative. It includes within itself hope and charity which are the very names of its own movement; they constitute as it were faith's definition.²⁷ For faith, unlike simple belief, does not come from the intellect alone, as an analysis of the faculties of the human soul might lead one to suppose; it comes from the center of the personality, from the *heart*.

> To believe means to touch through the heart. This woman (suffering from the hemorrhage) who touched the fringe of Jesus' mantle touched him through his heart, for she believed (in him).... "Someone has touched me", said the Lord; "she touched me; she believed in me".... The crowd pressed upon him, but faith touched him.... Believe in him so that you may touch him; touch him so that you may remain in him; remain in him so that you may never be separated from him.²⁸

Thus, for St. Augustine, there is no difference between the impulse of faith and that of charity.²⁹ This impulse which is normally a response to the invitation of the Word and is directed first of all toward the Son, who

---

²⁷ *Sermo* 144, no. 2: "*Ille enim credit in Christum qui sperat in Christum et diligit Christum.*" (PL, 38:788.) *In Ps.* 130, no. 1: "*Hoc est enim credere in Christum, diligere Christum.*" (PL, 37:1704.)

²⁸ *Sermo* Guelferb., 14, no. 2: "*Tangere autem corde, hoc est credere. Nam et illa mulier quae fimbriam tetigit, corde tetigit, quia credidit.... Tetigit me aliquis, ait Dominus: tetigit me, credidit in me.... Turba premit, fides tangit.... Sic credite, et tetigistis. Sic tangite, ut haereatis. Sic haerete, ut numquam separemini.*" (Morin, 487–88.) Cf. *In Ps.* 77, no. 8: "*Credere in Deum ... utique plus est quam credere Deo.... Hoc est ergo credere in Deum, credendo adhaerere ad bene cooperandum bona operanti Deo.*" (PL, 36:988.)

²⁹ Cf. Étienne Gilson, *Introduction à l'étude de saint Augustin* (Paris: Vrin, 1943), 36–37.

THE DYNAMISM OF FAITH 301

is recognized in Jesus, only comes into being through the attraction of the Father, under the inspiration of the Spirit.[30] But just as Augustine is not a pure biblicist, neither is he a pure supernaturalist. He knows that God created man for himself; he knows that the human heart seeks God; that its obscure search is constant; and that it will find rest only in him.[31] God's revelation in Christ comes to meet man, not to set him in motion, but to orient and correct his steps. It shows him the way, teaches him to sacrifice the desires of flesh and blood in order to begin loving as God loves. This necessary turning is at the same time an accomplishment for man. For in the depths of human nature, beyond the aberrations of man's conscience and of his free will, there exists a deep longing, a combined desire for what is good and for happiness which always remains ready to recognize its goal in the disinterestedness of divine love.[32] Periodically in the history of Christian thought, a discussion will bring into conflict the defenders of a natural love and those of an entirely disinterested love; reproaches of egoism and of utopianism are exchanged. Both sides appeal to St. Augustine, and both of them are partly right in doing so. Yet both are also wrong, because they do not understand that their two opposing views would be reconciled if they took the complete doctrine of their master as their foundation. It is on the level of natural love, or rather it is from the root of this

[30] Jn 6:44, etc. Cf. Augustine, *In Joannem*, tract. 26, nos. 2–6 (CCL, 36:260–63).
[31] *Confessions*, bk. 1, chap. 1, no. 1: "*Fecisti nos ad te, Deus, et inquietum est cor nostrum, donec requiescat in Te.*" (PL, 32:661.)
[32] Cf. H. de Lubac, *Le Mystère du surnaturel* (Paris: Aubier, 1963), chaps. 11 and 12.

love, that there arises either, through depravity, the poisonous tree of egoism which "bends" back to the earth; or else, by transfiguration, the stem which bears the flower of pure love.

The African bishop St. Quodvultdeus represents the Augustinian tradition. In the exhortation he addresses to those about to renounce Satan and receive baptism, there is a formula which names neither faith nor love but which defines very well, in its origin and source as well as in its conclusion, the movement that Augustine designates by these two words joined together: "As if all this assembly had only one heart and one soul, (coming) from God and (going) to God, let us all say together with one voice: I renounce...."[33] Faustus of Riez, on the contrary, belongs to that group of semi-Pelagian writers who opposed St. Augustine's teaching on grace; but on the point at issue here he speaks no differently from Augustine. For him, "to believe in God means to seek him faithfully and to enter into him through total love".[34] One should note the power of the expression: "*in eum transire*"; Faustus does not use it by accident; it appears on two different occasions in his treatise on the Holy Spirit and again in one of the sermons which have come down to us under the name of "Eusebius the Gallican".[35]

---

[33] "*Si ergo haec omnis sancta congregatio unum cor et unicam habet a Deo et in Deum, simul omnes una voce dicamus: renuntio.*" *De accedentibus ad gratiam*, no. 3 (PL, Suppl., 3:263).

[34] *De Spiritu sancto*, bk. 1, chap. 1: "*In Deum ergo credere, hoc est, fideliter eum* quaerere, *et tota* in eum *dilectione* transire." (CSEL, 21:102.)

[35] "Eusebius Gallicanus", *Sermo* 10 *de symbolo* 2 (PL, Suppl., 3:583). One of the vehicles of the Augustinian notion of faith transmitted to the Middle Ages was the *Sermo de symbolo* 1, of pseudo-Augustine (*Sermo* 181 de tempore: PL, 40:1190–91). This was a cento of Augustinian formulas. It was quoted by Peter Lombard (*Sent.*, 3, dist. 23) and by his commentators.

St. Caesarius of Arles refers to this same dynamism by the expression *"scintilla fidei"*.[36] It is this dynamism which is manifested clearly by the definition of faith given by William of Auxerre, which most of the great Scholastics later repeated: *"perceptio divinae Veritatis, tendens in ipsam"*.[37] It is this "tending" which Albert the Great uses to characterize faith in his explanation of the threefold *"credere"*:

> Faith is based on the primary Truth; but the latter can be received either through a sign or in itself. If one relies on signs, then one "believes God", i.e., one considers his word to be true. . . . But if one chooses Truth in itself, or rather if one tends toward it, then one believes in God. As for assent without any such tending, this is simply to believe that God exists.[38]

St. Thomas Aquinas also knew that the realization of God's existence, "as an assent to revelation made to us, is entirely different from that which philosophy can provide, because for the believer it is a first real discernment of God and a first step on the path leading to his

---

[36] *Sermo* 43: "*Si qualemcumque scintillam fidei haberent.*" (Morin, 184–85.) Caesarius does not mean by this a beginning of faith but the ardent and efficacious character of true faith. Cf. H. Rochais, in Defensor de Ligugé, *Livre d'étincelles*, introduction (SC, 77 [1961]: 24).

[37] *Summa aurea*, bk. 3, *tract.* 3, chap. 2, q. 1. St. Thomas cited this under the name of Isidore of Seville. It can be found again in Philip the Chancellor, Albert the Great, Bonaventure. Cf. Yves Congar, *La Foi et la théologie* (Tournai: Desclée, 1962), 73–75.

[38] *In 3 Sent.*, dist. 23, art. 7: "*Fides enim innititur primae veritati; haec autem accipitur in signo, vel in seipsa. . . . Si in signo innititur, tunc est credere Deo, hoc est, credere veracem qui dicit. . . . Si autem innititur in seipsa, aut sic quod tendat in ipsam, sic est credere in Deum; aut ut assentiat sine tensione, et tunc est credere Deum.*" (Ed. Borgnet, *Opera* 28 [1894]: 418.)

final destiny in the beatific vision".[39] But Aquinas is not satisfied with repeating the classical schema of the three-fold *"credere"* that the act of faith includes,[40] nor with adopting as his own the formula inherited from William of Auxerre,[41] nor with explaining that faith is essentially adherence to a personal Being, not to concepts or to things, but to Someone.[42] It is not enough for him to distinguish dogmas from mysteries (under different words),[43] or to say that through faith Christ "is received into the heart",[44] or even to compare the adherence of faith with a marriage between the soul and God, quoting Hosea and showing in this union the fruitful seed of all spiritual life.[45] In a number of passages he makes more completely his own the teaching of the Fathers, especially

---

[39] Étienne Gilson, *Introduction à la philosophie chrétienne* (Paris: Vrin, 1960), 18–19.

[40] *De veritate*, q. 14, art. 7, ad 7.

[41] *Summa theologica*, Secunda secundae, q. 1, art. 6. *In 3 Sent.*, dist. 25, q. 1, art. 1, quaest. 1a 1, obj. 4.

[42] *Summa theologica*, Secunda secundae, q. 11, art. 1: "What would seem to be most important, and which in some way has the value of the end, in every act of faith, is the Person to whose word one adheres."

[43] Ibid., q. 1, art. 2, ad 2: "*Actus autem credentis non terminatur ad enuntiabile* (dogma), *sed ad rem* (mystery)." Cf. art. 6: "*Perceptio divinae Veritatis competit nobis secundum distinctionem quamdam. Quae enim in Deo sunt, in nostro intellectu multiplicantur.*"

[44] *In Joannem*, chap. 1, lectio 5, no. 4: "*Hoc est recipere eum, in eum credere, quia per fidem Christus habitat in cordibus nostris.*" (Parma, 10:303 A.)

[45] *Opusculum 7*, on the *Creed*, chap. 1: "*Per fidem anima conjungitur Deo; nam per fidem anima facit quoddam matrimonium cum Deo.*" Hos 2:20: "*Sponsabo te mihi in fide.*" (Parma, 16:135–51; Vivès, 27:203.) This is the classical image. Cf. Ruysbroeck, *Christian Faith*, prologue: "By faith the soul is attached to God as the bride to her spouse." (*Oeuvres*, trans. by the Benedictines of St. Paul of Oosterhout, 5 [1930]: 243.)

that of St. Augustine, on the dynamism characteristic of faith. Faith is ordained toward the goods one hopes for;[46] by means of the *"enuntiabilia"*, the believer's intellect, without pausing at multiple images, tends toward its sole Object, which is the primary Truth.[47] This impulse of faith is also that of charity, two things which cannot be separated, nor, it would seem, even fully distinguished from one another, *"nam credere in Deum est credendo in Deum ire, quod caritas facit"*.[48] Faith tends to God through loving him: *"credere in Deum, id est amando in eum tendere"*.[49] One other important detail should be noted, and it too comes from St. Augustine. This God toward whom faith rushes in a movement which is also, indivisibly, that of charity is already the One toward whom the mind and spirit of man naturally tend, without knowing it, as toward their end; in fact, *"mens nostra solum in Deum fertur sicut in finem"*.[50] This is the knot, as we find in Augustine, that joins the order of creation to the order of revelation, the order of nature to that of grace. The Word who was made flesh is already the one who enlightens all men. The gospel message is an appeal to man's liberty, so that

---

[46] *In Hebr.* chap. 11, lectio 1: " '*Substantia rerum sperandarum*': in his ergo verbis ostenditur ordo actus fidei ad finem, quia fides ordinatur ad res sperandas quasi quoddam inchoativum, in quo totum quasi essentialiter continetur, sicut conclusiones in principiis."

[47] *De veritate*, q. 14, art. 8, ad 5 and ad 11.

[48] *In Rom.*, chap. 4, lectio 1: "*Credere in Deum demonstrat ordinem fidei in finem, qui est per caritatem, nam. . . .*"

[49] *In 3 Sent.*, dist. 23, q. 2, art. 2, quaest. 1a 2: "*Ex hoc vero quod intellectus determinatur a voluntate, secundum hoc actus fidei est credere in Deum.*" Cf. Durand de Mende, *Rationale*, bk. 4, chap. 25, no. 15.

[50] *In Joannem*, chap. 6, lectio 3, no. 7 (Parma ed. 10:409 A). Cf. Augustine, *In Joannem*, tract. 29, no. 6 (PL, 35:1630–31). Cf. above, the argument presented by Paschasius Radbert.

he may ratify through personal commitment what his nature secretly desires, the object of which is made known to him in the manifestation of divine Charity.

There are, however, two characteristics found in St. Thomas which indicate the beginning of a change in orientation which was gradually brought about in the theology of the Schoolmen. On the one hand, the process of conceptual analysis proper to Scholasticism eventually led, by becoming more rigid, to a categorical distinction between the intellect and the will which was reflected up to a point in a certain reciprocal exteriority of faith and charity. No doubt, since faith is an act of the intellect moved by the will, whatever it includes which is accidental to the intellect can still remain essential to it.[51] Still, the supplement which charity brings to it must be said to be accidental *"secundum genus naturae"*, even though it is essential *"prout refertur ad genus moris"*.[52] On the other hand, at least in certain texts, the opposition between "seeing" and "believing"—an opposition which he bases on the words of the Epistle to the Hebrews: *"argumentum non apparentium"*—is understood by St. Thomas in such a way that he seems to consider faith mainly as a sort of imperfect knowledge, midway between opinion and science.[53] Consequently, if he does

---

[51] *De veritate*, q. 14, art. 3, ad 10: *"Fides non est in intellectu nisi secundum quod imperatur a voluntate. Unde, quamvis illud quod est ex parte voluntatis possit didi accidentale intellectui, est tamen essentiale fidei."* Cf. *Summa theologica*, Secunda secundae, q. 2, art. 2.

[52] *De veritate*, q. 14, art. 5, ad 4: *"Ipse habitus caritatis, cum non sit intrinsecus fidei, non potest dici forma substantialis neque accidentalis fidei."* Art. 6, ad 1: *"Id quod fides ex caritate recipit, est sibi accidentale secundum genus naturae, sed essentiale prout refertur ad genus moris."*

[53] Cf. *Summa theologica*, Prima secundae, q. 67, art. 3: *"Imperfectio cognitionis est de ratione fidei; ponitur enim in ejus definitione."*

acknowledge in the spirit of the believer a movement which carries him farther, this movement is no longer, as it was in the texts where he repeated the expressions of St. Augustine, the very impetus of faith. It is now the effect of a desire which urges the believer to seek "something else"; in other words, to go beyond faith so as to attain vision. This vision is the beatific vision, no doubt; but in his explanations St. Thomas sometimes compares it in a way to some kind of knowledge.

> Man's desire can repose in every kind of knowledge, for he naturally desires to know the truth, and when he comes to know it his desire is satisfied. But in the knowledge of faith, man's desire does not repose: faith is an imperfect knowledge; we believe what we do not see; hence the Apostle says that it is the evidence of things that appear not (Heb 11:1). Thus, when one possesses faith there remains in his soul a movement toward something else (*adhuc remanet animae motus ad aliud*): namely, to see perfectly the truth which he believes and to pursue whatever may bring him into contact with this truth.[54]

The intellectualistic concept which underlies these reflections seems rather distant from the idea of a spiritual dynamism which characterized the teaching of the Fathers of the Church, that of St. Irenaeus and St. Gregory of Nyssa even more than that of St. Augustine. In one area of modern Thomism it is affirmed in a more exclusive manner.

---

[54] *Compendium Theologiae*, 2, 1. Needless to say, we are not attempting here to analyze all the Thomist doctrine concerning faith, nor to study the evolution of St. Thomas' thought. See below, 312–13 this chapter. In this same *Compendium*, 1, 1, faith is called "*praelibatio quaedam illius cognitionis quae in futuro beatos faciet*". Cf. *Summa theologica*, Prima secundae, art. 4, ad. 1.

When Calvin, writing his *Institution chrétienne* (1536), got to the chapter on faith, he repeated almost verbatim the essence of the traditional distinctions by contrasting two sorts of faith:

> The first consists merely in holding as true what is affirmed about God and Jesus Christ: *"Si quis credat Deum esse, historiam quae de Christo narratur veram esse arbitretur."* In his eyes this faith *"indigna est fidei appellatione"*, for it does not involve any personal commitment, insofar as it can exist in the most impious of the impious: *"Eam se habere cum diabolis communem."* True faith is something quite different. It is a movement of one's whole being toward God and a trusting and personal abandonment to the One who alone can save: *"Altera est, quae non modo Deum et Christum esse credimus, sed etiam in Deum credimus et Christum."*[55]

The unfortunate thing is that Calvin, ignorant as he was of the teaching of the great Scholastics, should have included them too in the reproaches which he addressed to certain decadent theologians of his time. The *"frigida Parisiensis opinio"* that he criticizes, that *"mortua opinio"*, he also calls *"scholastica fides"*.[56] If he had known the latter a little better, and if he had preserved in his own explanations the intermediary term of *"credere Deo"*, he might perhaps have avoided the unilateral form of his antithesis which, assuming the appearance of a dichotomy, dangerously opened the way to promoters of a "faith-trust" emptied of all doctrinal content. But the young Calvin[57] had merely followed the theory set forth fifteen years previously by Philip Melanchthon in his

---

[55] Alexander Ganoczy, *Le Jeune Calvin, genèse et évolution de sa vocation réformatrice* (Wiesbaden, 1966), 153.

[56] Op. cit., 153, note.

[57] Fr. Congar made the timely observation that Calvin was twenty-seven when he completed his *Institution* and that his early studies had

THE DYNAMISM OF FAITH

Loci communes. Not satisfied with repeating after so many others down through the centuries that *"credere Deum"* does not suffice to constitute faith any more than one would accord to the gospel accounts the same sort of belief one would attribute to the tales of Livy or Sallust, he refused to see in any "unformed faith" anything but *"ficta fides"*, *"simulatio"*, *"hypocrisis"*.[58] Such, he claimed, was this *"sophistica fides"* of the Scholastics, that *"qualitas parisiensis"*, that *"mortua imaginatio"*. True faith was something altogether different; it was faith in the promises, trust in the forgiveness of sins, the expectation of promised salvation, *"non aliud nisi fiducia misericordiae divinae promissae in Christo"*.[59] All of which was legitimate enough, save for that *"nihil aliud"* which turned the believing soul back on itself. This polemical depreciation of the *"credere Deum"* did not develop to the profit of the movement of faith *"in Deum"*, that movement which according to St. Augustine and St. Thomas impelled the believer's entire being toward God. A change in orientation was taking place, the consequences of which would appear later; the direction was no longer toward God but toward man. Yet would man be any more exalted because of this? Does not the only salvation worthy of man consist in God, sought for his own sake and not for salvation as such? Did not the "expectation of salvation" still resemble too closely that "natural desire" which could only be viewed with suspicion by anyone

---

been in law, not theology: *Vraie et fausse réforme dans l'Église* (Paris: Éd. du Cerf, 1950), 311–12.

[58] He does this through an abusive interpretation of 1 Tim 1:5 and of Titus 1:15.

[59] Or, *"Fidem (Scriptura vocat) qua Evangelio, seu promisionibus divinis fiditur"*; *"fidei nomen . . . nempe pro eo quod est fidere gratuita Dei misericordia"*.

who wishes to know nothing but the promises of Scripture? Does not the objectivity of the promise return to a subjective concern for salvation?[60]

No more than we did in discussing "functional" Christology do we ascribe to Melanchthon, or to Luther, whose interpreter he is, the immanentism of the liberals who sought to invoke their patronage. As for Calvin, we are familiar with the correction that he brought about in the Christian attitude, summed up by his "*Soli Deo gloria*". One may, however, consider that in the older doctrine there was not only a more complete understanding of Scripture but also an equal grandeur, a richer synthesis and a more powerful dynamism.

To make use of an analogy drawn from natural understanding, we might say that the movement of faith belongs to the order of foresight, whereas the objective recognition of its intellectual content belongs to that of retrospection. In the former, the mode of knowing is direct and concrete; "one's whole life is projected forward by concentrating on it." In retrospection, analysis discovers and itemizes under an abstract form, without of course ever exhausting it, the treasure of truth that the simple act of foreseeing presupposes and puts into effect. To speak once again using Maurice Blondel's words, we might say that the movement of faith is its pneumatic element, whereas the notions that it implies and the inventory made of them constitute its noetic element.[61]

---

[60] *Loci theologici, De justificatione et fide* (*Corpus Reformatorum*, 21 [Brunswick, 1854]: cols. 160–76). *Explicatio symboli Niceni, De vocabulo fidei* (vol. 23, cols. 454–55). See above, Chapter Three.

[61] Cf. Maurice Blondel, *Le Point de départ de la connaissance philosophique* (*Annales de philosophie chrétienne* [1906], vols. 151 and 152), etc.

Each of these calls for the other. Even if retrospection remains rudimentary, its object is always present just the same, under a more or less implicit form. The unity appears even stronger here than it did when we recognized it between faith and beliefs. It has been expressed by Romano Guardini in a definitive phrase: *"Faith is its content.* Faith is determined by what it believes. It is the living progress toward One in whom one believes. It is the living response to the call of One who announces himself in revelation and who draws man by grace."[62]

If faith, then, is a movement, will this movement end with earthly existence? Is it destined to cease or to continue?

The passage in the first Epistle to the Corinthians which mentions the three theological virtues, contrasting them with various charisms, has been interpreted in contradictory ways. A number of modern commentators think that for St. Paul, while faith and hope must pass away, like the charisms, charity alone will remain. Such however is not the meaning which an unprejudiced reader will draw from the Apostle's conclusion: "In short, there are three things that last: faith, hope and love; and the greatest of these is love."[63] Without deny-

---

[62] *Vie de la Foi*, *"Foi vivante"* (Paris: Éd. du Cerf, 1968), 24. Emphasis ours. Cf. Karl Barth, *Dogmatics*, vol. 4, 1: 820. The believer exists "in an eccentric manner"; he ceases "to be himself".

[63] This is how the Jerusalem Bible renders the passage (1 Cor 13:13). In this versicle, the difficulty lies in the νυνί δέ at the beginning, which can be understood in a temporal sense or in an adversative one (and one will be inclined to take one meaning or the other according to one's translation of the words in versicle 8: ἡ ἀγάπη οὐδέποτε πίπτει). Osty translates it as "at present", but in a note he suggests another translation. On the interpretation of the whole chapter 13 of 1 Cor, see François Marie Lacan, O.S.B., *Les Trois qui*

ing the textual difficulties to be found, one might consider that on this point exegesis has at times allowed itself to be ruled by a theological prejudice, i.e., by an idea of faith which is at least incomplete. In the past an Irenaeus, an Origen—to mention only these two great names—judged differently. "As the Apostle teaches", says Irenaeus, "when all the rest has been destroyed, these three realities remain: faith, hope and charity. For faith, which is directed toward our Master, will always remain firm."[64] And Origen writes: "Today I believe in an imperfect manner; but one day perfect faith will come, and that which is imperfect will disappear. For faith through vision infinitely surpasses our present faith, which can be called, like our current 'gnosis', a faith 'through a mirror and in enigmas'."[65]

Note Origen's expression: faith through vision, διὰ εἴδους πίστις. Indeed, faith is not defined essentially by its obscurity; that is only the present condition for its exercise. In itself it is not "non-seeing". Even now it is in some way a familiarity, a seeing; just as it is a commitment; and in an indivisible manner one can even say it is a knowledge. "I know my own", said Jesus, "and my own know me."[66] "We know", says St. John, "that we have passed from death to life."[67] This was what St. Thomas recognized when he said that "faith is a *habitus*

---

demeurent, in *Recherches de science religieuse* 46 (1958): 321–43.

[64] *Adversus haereses* bk. 2, chap. 28, no. 3 (PG, 7:806 A B). So too Tertullian, *De patientia*, chap. 12, no. 10 (CCL, 1:313).

[65] *In Joannem*, bk. 10, chap. 43, 305–6 (E. Preuschen, 222). Cf. *In Num.*, hom. 14, 4 (Baehrens, 128). Paul Henry, *"Manet autem fides"* (Rome: Pont. Univ. Gregoriana, 1951).

[66] Jn 10:14   [67] 1 Jn 4:14; cf. 5:14–15; 5:18–20.

of the mind by which eternal life has begun in us",[68] or even more when he adopts as his own explanation from the Gloss on the Epistle to the Romans: "In the gospel, the justice of God is revealed from faith to faith, i.e., beginning with faith from the word and ending by faith from sight."[69]

But this "faith through vision" is also vision through faith. It remains a movement because it brings man to the encounter with the thrice-holy God, because it is a movement of love, powered by the attraction of Love. In faith man does not progress toward an impersonal knowledge which some day he may possess perfectly; he is not looking for an equation for the world, even a supposedly divine world. He is not exploring a being whose limits he must discover. The "knowledge of the blessed" of which Scholasticism speaks is not that of which some theologians have dreamed since the days of Cajetan and Bañez; it is not a "scientific" theology like that which is evolving in our schools, but which would eventually satisfy the mind entirely because it would rest on principles based, not on the obscurity of faith, but on the clarity of vision.[70] All these are childish concepts. Indeed, nothing would be more hopeless than the perspective of a science that is complete, in a state that is henceforth fixed.[71] And if theology must remain and grow deeper beyond death, it is not that kind of science—

[68] *Summa theologica*, Secunda secundae, q. 4, art. 1. Cf. H. de Lubac, *Augustinisme et théologie moderne* (Paris: Aubier, 1965), chap. 4.

[69] *Summa theologica* Tertia pars, q. 7, art. 3. *Glossa in Rom.*, 1:17.

[70] Gregory of Valencia in his day criticized this notion of a theological science which would be continued in heaven: *Commentaria theologica*, vol. 1, *In Primam*, 3rd. ed. (Lyons, 1603), 23–28.

[71] Cf. Paul Claudel, in many passages of his works.

not to be despised today, but of which St. Thomas so rightly said, at the moment of his death, that it seemed only straw to him—it is theology in its most ancient and noble sense, which is the movement of faith, adoration, ecstasy in God. That theology will never end because God is inexhaustible.

God is not a spectacle. He freely manifests himself by his Word, and this Word "is never something closed, which could be taken in at a glance like a circumscribed landscape; it is something which is always happening anew, like water from a spring or rays from a light". Hence it is not enough, as St. Augustine said, to have been initiated once unless one is unceasingly inebriated at the fountain of eternal Light.[72] "To anyone who loves, this truth is immediately obvious; the face and the voice of the Beloved are at each instant as new for him as though he had never yet beheld them."[73] Such a one cannot fear that the day might come when he will have exhausted God; he drinks at the source of a knowledge and of a love which, he understands better and better, will eternally surpass him:[74]

> This characteristic of God who, in revealing himself, shows himself to be incomprehensible, is not conditioned simply by the obscurity of earthly faith. This faith therefore cannot simply disappear in the face-to-face vision; on the contrary, it is then, precisely, that the incomprehensibility of God in every perception of God will reach its maximum. It would be ridiculous and contrary to all experience as well as to all true faith to interpret this

[72] Augustine, *In Ps.* 118, 26, no. 6.
[73] Hans Urs von Balthasar, *La Prière contemplative* (Fr. trans., R. Givord, Paris: Desclée de Brouwer, 1959), 23.
[74] Cf. Eph 3:19.

face-to-face vision as a definitive grasping (*comprehensio*, κατάλειψις), after the fashion of an acquired science or a human philosophy. Augustine's axiom, *"si comprehendis, non est Deus"*, applies in heaven as well as on earth.[75]

"God", says Irenaeus, "will always have to teach us, and we shall always have to be instructed about the things of God; the divine riches are 'neverending', just as the kingdom of God is without end."[76] St. John has taught us that "God is light, and in him there is no darkness."[77] We must be careful never to lose sight of that teaching. But we also know, as the Psalmist says, that "he made the darkness his dwelling place";[78] in other words, his light is too intense and too profound ever to be penetrated. Whoever makes progress into it as though into a "luminous cloud" understands better and better that his true knowledge and his true vision consist in "not-grasping".[79] It is thus that he enters and plunges

[75] Ibid. *La Gloire et la croix* 1:389–90; cf. also 429. By the same author, *Théologie de l'histoire* (Fr. trans., R. Givord, Paris: Plon, 1951), 44–45.

[76] *Adversus haereses*, bk. 2, chap. 28, no. 3: "*Ut semper quidem Deus doceat, homo autem semper discat quae sunt a Deo . . . et ut diligamus eum vere semper, quoniam ipse solus Pater, et speremus subinde plus aliquid accipere et discere a Deo, quia bonus est, et divitias habens interminabiles, et regnum sine fine.*" (PG, 7:806 A B.)

[77] 1 Jn 1:5. [78] Ps 17:2.

[79] St. Gregory of Nyssa: *Vie de Moïse*, nos. 162–64, 234–35 (SC, 1 ter:210–13 and 266–69). He proceeds "from beginning to beginning, through beginnings that have no end": *In Cantica Cantic.*, hom. 8 (PG, 44:941 C). Cf. Paul Evdokimov, *L'Orthodoxie* (Neuchâtel: Delachaux et Niestlé, 1959), 175: "The epectasis—tension—of which St. Gregory of Nyssa speaks is an outburst of faith which goes beyond time and even traverses eternity without ever stopping or being fully satisfied."

deep "into the joy of the Lord".[80]

And even the humblest movement of faith secretly introduces us to this end that knows no end.

---

[80] Cf. Mt 25:21 and 23.

CHAPTER TEN

FAITH AND PROFESSION OF FAITH

To conclude, let us now return to the Creed itself. Can it be said, as we have perhaps seemed to be implying up to this point, that it constitutes or at least includes an act of faith?

Strictly speaking, no. While I am reciting the Creed, and by this recitation, I am not making an act of faith. I am stating or proclaiming my faith; we might even say, using two traditional words, that I am "professing" or "confessing" it; or again, employing a somewhat more archaic term, that I am "protesting" my faith, in the primary meaning of the word "protest": one of the meanings—the best one—which gave rise to the name "Protestant". The formula of my Creed, whatever its content, always presupposes as something antecedent to it an act of which it gives an account, and this is the act of faith, properly so called. This act, which is interior and anterior, is that very movement of faith we have just been analyzing. It is my response to the God who calls me, my adherence to the God who reveals himself, my return commitment to the God who gives himself. Before saying outwardly "I believe in God", and so that I may be able to say it sincerely, I must have said in my heart, "O Lord my God, I believe in Thee."

Some well-founded criticisms have been made of certain stereotyped texts of "acts of faith" found in many catechisms or modern prayerbooks. They remind one too much of that "faith of obedience" which breeds rote recitation and religious indifference, and which we have criticized above.[1] "My God, I firmly believe all that you have revealed and that you teach us through your Church. . . , because you are Truth itself. . . ." There is a sort of formal but empty perfection in this. "Actually, a believer might repeat twenty or a hundred times a day all through his life" a formula of this kind, "and yet if he limits himself to this alone, he would remain as ignorant at eighty as he was the day he was born of what God has actually revealed, of what the Church has actually transmitted concerning this revelation, in short, of the faith in which, actually, he can share in the eternal and living truth which is God."[2] Such formulas do at least deserve credit for not only expressing clearly the motive of faith but also suggesting that faith is an act addressed directly to God, that it constitutes our human share in the dialogue instituted by God himself with his creature[3] and that its first expression, which is wholly interior, thus necessarily takes the form, not of a recitation or a proclamation, but of a prayer. It is beginning with this basic prayer—a prayer of response, of thanksgiving—that every other prayer arises in it, every other prayer is already included in advance; without it, any other prayer would be in vain. If, then, the Creed gives us, in more or less developed form, the essential *content* of the faith, the act of faith

[1] See Chapter Seven.
[2] H. M. Féret, O.P., preface to Joseph Comblin's book *La Résurrection* (1953), 11–12. Still, one should suppose that the one who had learned this "act of faith" would also have received enough instruction to know its content.
[3] See Paul VI's encyclical *Ecclesiam suam*.

which the Creed presupposes gives us its *form*—and the very terms in which this Creed is formulated are sufficient to show that this content without this form would be not only vain theory but a lie. In short, I can say *"Credo in Deum"* because first of all I have said *"Credo in Te, Deus meus"*.

In other words, in order to be legitimate, the *objective* language of the Creed must be the manifestation of the *existential* language of the act to which it testifies. Still, just because it is second does not mean that it is any less necessary. The faith of a Christian who addresses God must also, necessarily, be expressed externally. St. Paul reminded the Christians of Corinth of this, quoting the Psalmist whose words he applied to himself and to his brethren in Christ: "Possessing the same spirit of faith of which it is written, 'I believed, and this is why I have spoken', we too believe, and this is why we speak."[4] And to the Christians in Rome:

> The word is close to thee, in your mouth and in your heart; this is the word of faith which we preach. For if you profess with your mouth that Jesus is Lord and believe in your heart that God has raised him up from the dead, you will be saved. It is in fact with the heart that we believe unto justice; and it is with the mouth that we confess unto salvation.[5]

Following St. Paul, all Christian tradition affirms this necessary bond.[6] In the prologue to his little book on *Faith and the Creed*, St. Augustine calls our attention to

---

[4] 2 Cor 4:13; cf. Ps 116:90 (Septuagint version).
[5] Rom 10:8–10; cf. Dt 30:13–14.
[6] Cf. Cyril of Jerusalem, *Deuxième Catéchèse mystagogique*, no. 4: "You confessed the saving confession." (SC, 126:110.)

this fact. "Our faith requires of us the service of both heart and tongue." If we refuse the second, we are unfaithful to God, who at the same time gives to man the chance both to believe in him and to confess him.[7] In the treatise by Paschasius Radbert which we cited previously, we read: "Following the tradition of the Apostles, the three Persons must, all together, be the object of a single confession, in the same sense; and we must all confess them in an intelligible voice";[8] or in the great sermon by Yves of Chartres on the Apostles' Creed: "With faith in the heart, confession on the lips is also necessary. . . . Faith then must be preserved in the heart and proclaimed by the mouth."[9] "Religion's first act", remarked Bossuet, "is to believe, just as its second is to confess."[10] On this point there was no chance of any disagreement between him and Fénelon. It was because of this necessary bond, which from the beginning was recognized everywhere, that the candidate for baptism (or his sponsor) was invited to recite the Creed aloud, in such a way as to be heard by the whole community gathered together.[11]

---

[7] *De fide et symbolo*, chap. 1 (Bibl. aug., 9:18). Also *Sermo* 214, no. 1: "*quod et credere et confiteri debetis*" (PL, 38:1065), etc.

[8] *De fide, spe et caritate*, bk. 1, chap. 6, no. 1: "*In totis sane tribus Personis una confessio est ab apostolis tradita, una proprietas verbi, et omnibus voce intelligibili confitenda.*" (PL, 120:1402 D.)

[9] *Sermo* 23: "*Cum fide cordis necessaria est oris confessio. . . . Est ergo fides et corde servanda, et ore promenda.*" (PL, 162:604 B C.) Cf. *Liber de modo bene vivendi*, chap 1: "*Maneat in te recta fides, sit in te incorruptae confessionis fides.*" (PL, 184:1200 B C.)

[10] *Histoire des variations*, bk. 5, no. 32 (*Oeuvres*, ed. Lachat, 14:205).

[11] Cardinal Garrone, *La Profession de foi de Paul VI* (Paris: Beauchesne, 1969), 8: "Christian faith has never been willing to dissociate the two elements which are the two complementary requirements imposed by the Word of God and by human nature."

FAITH AND PROFESSION OF FAITH

After having turned toward God in an impulse of his whole being to declare his faith to him, the Christian, without turning his thoughts away from the Divine Presence, thus immediately turns to men to confess before them what he believes. As St. Paul just advised us, this second step, quite like the first, is usually necessary for salvation. Moreover, it corresponds with the spontaneous need of the one who, having been regenerated by Christ, is anxious to bear testimony to him. Besides, the Gospel is explicit: "Whoever confesses me before men, I will also confess him before my Father who is in heaven; but whoever denies me before men, I too will deny him before my Father who is in heaven."[12]

Every once in a while unrealistic minds, mistrustful of anything written down, rebel against the formularies proposed by the Church for our profession of faith. A truly living faith, they think, "does not need charters drawn up by theologians in order to propagate, clarify or maintain the distinctive doctrines of Christianity; the free flowering of religious thought under the sanctifying breath of the Spirit of God constitutes a more secure guarantee than a letter inscribed on parchment. . . ."[13] The experience of liberal Protestantism has undertaken, once again, to prove the contrary. Still, the same illusion always keeps reappearing. Today it assumes more radical forms. Faith, certain highly cultivated people object, cannot be expressed in words; if you formulate it, you constrain it, you freeze it. Worse still, by objectifying it you betray it; you are making a worldy reality out of what is divine, you are "stopping the absolute at the level

---

[12] Mt 10:32–33. Cf. Lk 12:8–9.

[13] F. Lichtenberger, article "Symbole" in *Encyclopédie des sciences religieuses* 11 (1881): 763. See above, Chapter Four, on the relationship between "faith" and "beliefs".

of relative formulations", etc. We prefer to place our trust, in all simplicity, in the first Apostles of Jesus rather than in their subtle arguments; we will trust in the martyrs—and in that long line of witnesses from whom we have received the words of our Creed. We realize, of course, that the written word, while a necessary vehicle for us, is always an imperfect vehicle for the mind. We have learned from St. John that "no one has ever seen God", and from St. Paul that "he dwells in light inaccessible". We know full well that God's revelation itself can be received by us only in a human mode; that our intellects can perceive only a refracted ray of the light; that our humble knowledge through concepts is always analogical, inadequate and relative when we are dealing with mystery; that if God's ways are impenetrable to begin with, his inner mystery is even more so. Nor do we overlook the fact that the inevitable mechanism of objectivation always impoverishes the truth that the mind is trying to grasp, and that this truth would indeed be irremediably corrupted if the action of the mind were limited to such a mechanism. But we do not mistake inadequacy for error, or even for inexactness; we also know that a false spiritual dynamism can exist, a morbid fear of objectivation, which leaves the mind without nourishment, norms or direction, exposed to every wind that blows. We are not scandalized by the adaption of the divine light to our human condition. We realize very well that contemplation of the mystery should reduce us to silence; but this silence comes at the end, not at the beginning; it is a silence of fullness and transcendence, not a silence of refusal and emptiness.[14] We distrust,

---

[14] See above, Chapter Seven.

deliberately, a concern for purity whose impossible desires end in accepting words which are very different from the words of salvation. Our faith as Christians then cannot consent to remain "buried in the depths of our conscience like some sterile opinion".[15] It is very important that we should be the disciples, not of a pure dynamism devoid of content, but of a *revealing Word*, whom nothing, not even values, can reduce to the silence of complicity,[16] because the Paraclete "in them whispers irrepressible words to them".[17] The Spirit cannot be separated from the Word, either in himself or in us.[18]

A more common temptation, unaccompanied by considerations of higher criticism, leads the believer to experience a sort of modesty about displaying his faith, about mixing it, so to speak, with his ordinary thoughts and his social relationships; he may think it better to show respect for its sacred character by keeping it hidden within the sanctuary of his soul. That would be to misunderstand both the nature of man and that of Christian faith. A twofold reason imperiously demands that the content of that faith should be expressed externally:

A faith which would forego expressing itself distinctly and in as precise a way as possible would be condemned to remain indecisive and even inconsistent. It is part of

[15] Cf. Mt 25:18.
[16] Cf. Acts 4:20: "As for us, we cannot but speak out concerning what we have heard and seen."
[17] André Manaranche, *L'Homme dans son univers* (Paris: Éd. Ouvrières, 1966), 17.
[18] On the necessity and the rightfulness of stating the mystery of faith, see Stanislas Breton, *Le Paradoxe du menteur et le problème de l'indicible dans les énoncés de foi*, in *Mythe et Foi*, by Enrico Castelli (Paris: Aubier, 1966), 537–46.

man's function to express his convictions, to formulate the certitudes that govern his life.... The formulation of the faith is the very condition of its reality. And because this faith is not merely a jealously guarded secret but something which must be communicated so that it can become the living and ardent bond of the fraternal community—for the characteristic of Christian faith is that it is received and lived in the Church—it must be conveyed in communicable formulas, signs of recognition and junction points of our unity in the love of the Lord.[19]

The twofold aspect or finality of the Creed are summed up in the two words "confession" and "creed" (*symbole*). Both of them are frequently employed, and both have been amply commented on throughout Christian tradition.

A first meaning of "*confessio*" (ὁμολόγησις, ἐξομολόγησις) is avowal, the confession of sins. This does not interest us here. A second meaning, which is found especially in the older translations of the Psalms and in the patristic commentaries, is praise, thanksgiving, in the proclamation of the great divine deeds. "*Confiteri*" is then more or less synonymous with "*benedicere*" (to bless), "*cantare*" (to sing), "*glorificare*" or "*magnificare*" (to glorify); it includes these various nuances fused together.[20] Thus, in

---

[19] Henri Holstein, S.J., *De l'Évangile à la formulation dogmatique*, in *Prière et vie* (1968), 392–93. Cf. Karl Rahner, on "the importance of the formula of faith, objectively exact and which constitutes the ecclesio-sociological basis of common thought and faith", in *Réflexions théologiques sur l'Incarnation* (Fr. trans., G. Daoust, in *Écrits théologiques* 3 [1963]: 99). Paul Tillich: *Dynamique de la foi* (Fr. trans., F. Chapey, Casterman, 1968), 41: "Only in a language community can a man make his faith real."

[20] Louis Bouyer, *Eucharistie* (Paris: Desclée, 1966), 48 and 96–97. Cf. P. Prigent, *La Confession du Dieu créateur dans l'Église ancienne*, in *Foi et vie* (May–August 1959), 33–43.

Psalm 91: *"Bonum est confiteri Domino et psallere nomini tuo, Altissime"* ("It is good to give thanks to the Lord and to exalt thy name, O Most High").[21] It is in this sense that Jesus cried out, according to the Gospels of Luke and Matthew: *"Confiteor tibi Pater quia abscondisti haec a sapientibus...."*[22] We are familiar with the use that St. Augustine in his *Confessions*[23] made of the word in this second meaning, in imitation of Scripture. The third meaning is that of the confession of faith: *"confiteri"* in this case means to attest, recognize and proclaim the object of one's faith. We find it as early as the second book of Maccabees[24] and also in some passages of the New Testament: in the texts from St. Matthew and the Epistle to the Romans quoted above, in the Epistle to the Philippians,[25] in the Apocalpyse,[26] in the first Epistle

---

[21] Still, Jerome here takes *"confiteri"* in the former meaning: *"Bonum est primum agere paenitentiam et peccata sua hominem Domino confiteri, et ... tunc ei psallere.... Confessionem sequitur laudatio."* Tract. in Ps. 91 (PL, Suppl., 2:245). Similar thoughts in Nicetas' sermon *Ad competentes*, edited by Klaus Gamber (Regensburg, 1966), 54–55, commenting on Psalm 135:1: *"Confitemini Domino quoniam bonus...."*

[22] Lk 10:21; Mt 11:25.

[23] Bk. 8, no. 1: *"Deus meus, recorder in gratiarum actione tibi, et confitear misericordias tuas super me."* Bk. 11, chaps. 1–2, etc. "The *Confessions* strive to be a hymn of praise addressed to God by man, the spokesman for all creation." Pierre Hadot, in *Problèmes et méthodes d'histoire des religions* (Paris: P.U.F., 1968), 216. Cf. A. Solignac, introduction to the *Confessions* (Bibl. aug., 15:9–12). Joseph Ratzinger, *Originalität und Ueberlieferung in Augustins Begriff der Confessio*, Revue des Études augustiniennes 3 (1957): 375–92. J. M. Le Blond, *Les Conversions de saint Augustin* (Paris: Aubier, 1959), 6–11.

[24] 2 Macc 7:37.

[25] Phil 2:11: *"Et omnis lingua confiteatur, quia Dominus Jesus Christus in gloria est Dei Patris."*

[26] Rev 3:5: *"Qui vicerit..., confitebor nomen ejus coram Patre meo."*

to Timothy.[27] It is used in the Nicene-Constantinople Creed.[28] It is frequently found in the liturgies of both East and West. For instance, "Lord", says the Coptic liturgy of St. Mark, "we proclaim thy death and we confess thy Resurrection and holy Ascension";[29] and a Roman collect for March 25, celebrating the mystery of the Incarnation: *"Deum verum et hominem confitemur."*[30] "It is faith in the Trinity", says St. John Chrysostom, "which wins for us the grace of forgiveness of sins; and it is confessing that faith that wins for us the adoption as sons."[31] The earliest and most famous of these confessions of faith, the one which is at the very origin of the Church, is that made by Simon Peter on the road to Caesarea; St. Leo the Great praised it in a homily which we read on February 22 when we celebrate the feast of St. Peter's chair at Antioch: *"Primus est in Domini confessione, qui primus est in apostolica dignitate."*[32]

It sometimes happens that the three meanings which we have just distinguished may be combined in a single passage. At least this is what we find in a line from St. Jerome's commentary on Psalm 88:6, *"Et confitebuntur caeli mirabilia tua, Domine"*:

---

[27] Tim 6:12: *"Certa bonum certamen fidei. . . , confessus bonam confessionem coram multis testibus."*

[28] *"Confiteor unum baptisma. . . ."* Cf. Augustine, *Confessions*, bk. 1, chap. 11, no. 17: *"Te, Domine Jesu, confitens in remissionem peccatorum."*

[29] Similar phrasing can be found in the liturgies of St. James and St. Gregory the Theologian.

[30] Or again on October 9: *"Ut studeamus confiteri quod credidit. . . ."*

[31] *Deuxième Catéchèse baptismale*, 26 (Wenger, SC, 50:148).

[32] *Sermo* 4, *in anniv. assumpt. suae*, chap. 2. Ibid., chap. 3: *"Sicut confessores suos in caelestia provehit, ita negatores ad infima demergit."* (PL,

This is also said in Psalm 18: "The heavens declare the glory of God." But, as regards what we read here, that "the heavens confess thy marvels", this is a sign of the penance which we must preach, that penance we received when the Apostles announced it in the confession of the Lord Jesus.[33]

More often, the second and third meanings are found closely associated, or even united into one. For it is in the joy of adoring praise and of thanksgiving that the Christian proclaims his faith before God and men. Thus, *confessio* becomes closely allied to *theologia*, in the sense of liturgical praise and glorification of God.[34] The example of the *Te Deum* comes to mind here: "*Te Deum laudamus, te Dominum, confitemur.*"[35] So too the first part of the anaphora (our present Preface), which is a profession of faith accompanied by praise: "We declare here", says St. Cyril of Jerusalem,[36] "that theology which the angels have handed down to us." Severus of Antioch comments in one of his homilies: "Isaiah heard the Seraphim crying out around the throne, 'Holy, holy, holy is the Lord of hosts!' This perfect theology of the

---

54:150 A C.) Augustine, *Enchiridion*, chap. 96 calls the Creed "*nostra confessio*" (PL, 40:276).

[33] "*Hoc est quod in octavo decimo psalmo dicitur, 'Caeli enarrant gloriam Dei'. . . . Quod autem dicit, 'confitebuntur caeli mirabilia tua', signum est paenitentiae praedicandae, quam nos apostolis annuntiantibus in Domini Jesu confessione suscepimus.*" (PL, Suppl., 2:232–33.)

[34] Cf. Eusebius of Caesarea, *In Ps.* 110, 10 (PG, 23:1345 C). *Histoire ecclésiastique*, bk. 10, chap. 3, no. 2: εἰς εξ ἁπάντων θεολογίας ὕμνος; cf. chap. 4, no. 21. (G. Bardy, SC, 55:80 and 88). See Louis Bouyer, *Le Rite et l'homme*, 146–48.

[35] Cf. Albert Blaise, *Le vocabulaire latin des principaux thèmes liturgiques* (Turnhout: Brepols, 1966), 154.

[36] *Cinquième Catéchèse mystagogique*, chap. 6 (J. Quasten, 101).

Trinity, thus mysteriously sung by the celestial armies, is now understood by those who, having been baptized, confess their faith in the Father, Son and Spirit."[37] The Roman Breviary's hymn for Terce supplies another example:

> *Os, lingua, mens, sensus, vigor*
> *confessionem personent.*

These two lines can be understood as "the public confession of one's faith without affecting the main meaning" of the strophe, which is "that of the praise of God."[38] One might also observe, with J. Jérémias, that the testimony paid by John the Baptist to Jesus in the fourth Gospel, and the "confession" he made about his relationship with the Messiah when speaking to the authorities from Jerusalem, are presented by the Evangelist within and immediately following his Prologue; now this Prologue is understood as a song of praise by which the believing community exalted the gift of God in the Word made flesh; this is therefore a christological hymn which "ends in a personal confession and reaches its climax in thanksgiving, praise and adoration".[39]

Besides, our Creed itself has a doxological character. In its liturgical setting it constitutes a true celebration.

---

[37] *Homélie 90* (*Patrologie orientale* 23:128). The ancient Orient was accustomed to call the monks theologians because they chanted the glory of God.

[38] S. Primont, *Les Hymnes du Bréviaire romain* 1 (Paris, 1874): 103. Cf. G. Q. A. Meershoek, *Le Latin biblique d'après saint Jérôme* (Nijmegen, 1966), 85.

[39] J. Jérémias, *Le Message central du Nouveau Testament* (Fr. trans., F. Refoulé, Paris: Éd. du Cerf, 1966), 76–82 and 88; on page 80 the author calls attention to the analogy with the second article of the Creed, "which says and confesses in a hymn of praise the history of Jesus Christ until the Parousia".

"*Symboli salutare carmen*", said Faustus of Riez.⁴⁰ This is also what St. Ambrose observed when writing to the Emperor Valentinian:

> This is a mighty song indeed; none other is more powerful. In fact, what could be more powerful than this confession of the Trinity, celebrated every day by the voice of the entire people? All vie with each other in giving their full attention to the confession of their faith; they know how to proclaim the Father, Son and Spirit in their song.⁴¹

No wonder, then, that we find in Christian antiquity certain instances of a sort of "communication of idioms", in which the Eucharist and the Creed, the celebration of Mass and the confession of faith exchange their usual respective denominations. When the profession of faith takes on the name of Eucharist (εὐχαριστία), the thanksgiving, which is what the anaphora essentially consists in, is designated as ἐξομολόγησις (in Latin: *contestatio*). This custom, which goes back at least as far as Origen,⁴² is followed by St. Athanasius⁴³ and St. Basil.⁴⁴

One can confess his faith before God or before the other members of the Christian community or outside before whoever is present. These three confessions, moreover, cannot in principle be dissociated from one

---

⁴⁰ *De Spiritu sancto*, bk. 1, chap. 1 (CSEL, 21:102).

⁴¹ "*Grande carmen istud est, quo nihil potentius. Quid enim potentius quam confessio Trinitatis, quae quotidie totius populi ore celebratur? Certatim omnes student fidem fateri: Patrem et Filium et Spiritum norunt versibus praedicare.*" (Epist. 21, no. 34 (PL, 16:1017 C D.)

⁴² *In Ps.* 10:3 (R. Cadiou, 99). Cf. Meershoek, 80. J. A. Jungmann, *La Grande prière eucharistique* (Paris: Éd. du Cerf, 1955), 24.

⁴³ *In Ps.* 9, 1 (PG, 27:84 C).

⁴⁴ *In Ps.* 29, 5 (PG, 29:313 A).

another. It is to God, in reality, that the newly baptized "pronounces the Creed" which had been handed down to him when he recites it aloud before the assembly;[45] and it is always primarily before God that the Christian in any circumstances declares his faith.[46] On the other hand, this faith is always the faith related to the community and which he has in common with it, which binds him to it. Finally, he must always be ready, should the occasion arise, to declare it to anybody. As a disciple of him who was the first Witness, the Christian is a man who, like the Apostle Paul, "bears witness to the gospel of God's grace".[47] "I shall tell you why we fearlessly confess our faith when we are questioned", declares St. Justin in his second Apology.[48] In this case the words "confession" and "witness" take on their full weight and seriousness. "Fight the good fight of faith", says St. Paul to Timothy, "take a firm hold on eternal life in view of which you made your noble confession of faith; I charge thee before Christ who bore his noble witness before

[45] Augustine, *Sermo* 58, 13: "*Reddite symbolum vestrum, reddite Domino, commemorate vosmetipsos. . . .*" (PL, 38:399.)

[46] Karl Barth, *Connaître Dieu et le servir*: "What is said thanks to the knowledge that comes from faith is originally and expressly said to God, not to men." (Fr. trans., Lepp and Brutsch [Neuchâtel-Paris, 1945], 56.) Ibid., *Introduction à la théologie évangélique* (Fr. trans., Fernand Ryser [Geneva, 1962], 100–102), 131.

[47] Acts 20:24. Cf. Jean Mouroux, *Disciple du Christ*, in *La Table ronde* (November 1968), 100–102: "Our confession is then nothing other than the 'solidarity' of faith (the *Mitmenschlichkeit*) which comes about first of all in and with the community, and thereby in the world." Otto Weber, *La Dogmatique de Karl Barth*, Fr. trans. (Geneva, 1954), 238.

[48] *Second Apology*, chap. 4, no. 1 (Pautigny, 156). Cf. Karl Barth, précis of his *Dogmatics*: "To believe means that one is called to make a personal contribution."

Pontius Pilate."⁴⁹ And St. Polycarp echoed him: "Whoever does not confess the witness of the Cross (μὴ ὁμολογῇ τὸ μαρτύριον τοῦ σταυροῦ) is of the Evil One."⁵⁰ Eusebius relates that the man who had denounced the Apostle St. James the Greater "was moved by seeing him bear witness and confessed that he too was a Christian".⁵¹

As persecutions of the Christians multiplied, the use of the word in this precise meaning became more widespread. Tertullian, for instance, in his *Scorpiace*, has the heretics yielding to the world and, defaming the martyrs, say:

> "These simple souls do not know what they must confess, nor where, nor when, nor before whom." —But then, it is not merely simplicity, it is vanity, even more it is lunacy to die for God!⁵²
>
> Some think that the confession does not need to be made here below. . . . But, if the Lord had been speaking of a heavenly confession, he would have spared me the mistake of understanding this of an earthly confession. . . . Whoever is questioned on earth and confesses will take with him the keys to heaven. . . . Persecution is the indispensable element in any confession as in any denial. . . . Persecution is consummated in confession. . . . The Lord has not destined any other place but earth for this confession. . . .⁵³

---

⁴⁹ 1 Tim 6:12–13. The Vulgate is more redundant: "*Coram . . . Christo Jesu, qui testimonium reddidit sub Pontio Pilato, bonam confessionem.*"

⁵⁰ *Epist. to the Philippians*, chap. 7, no. 2 (Camelot, SC, 10:212).

⁵¹ Eusebius, *Histoire ecclésiastique*, bk. 2, chap. 9, 1–2 (Bardy, SC, 31:62).

⁵² *Scorpiace*, chap. 1, no. 7: "*Nesciunt simplices animae quid, ubi et quando et coram quibus confitendum—nisi quod nec simplicitas ista, sed vanitas, imo dementia, pro Deo mori.*" (CCL, 2:1070.)

⁵³ *Scorpiace*, chap. 10: "*Non intra hunc ambitum terrae . . . con-*

In the same way St. Cyprian says of the martyrs who had gone before him: "Having confessed the name of the Lord, they overcame the violence of the magistrates and the fury of the unchained mob."[54] Lactantius declares: "By their glorious confession they obtained the eternal crown as the reward of their faith."[55] St. Augustine, preaching on the Holy Innocents, remarked, "They were capable of suffering for Christ, they who could not yet confess him";[56] and speaking of the martyrdom of St. Cyprian, "Blessed Cyprian confessed Christ. . . . Let us keep his example in our hearts and beseech God that we may not fear men like these (i.e., his judges), may not be silent before them about the faith and hope which are ours. Let us confess Christ without fearing men."[57]

The opposite of "confessing" in such cases is not just keeping silent but "denying", renouncing.[58] There

---

fessionem putant constitutam. . . . —Eripere me debuit ex isto terrenae confessionis errore . . . si caelestem praecepisset.—Quas (claves) hic unusquisque interrogatus atque confessus feret secum. . . . —Persecutionem . . . quae confessionis negationisve materia est. . . . —Persecutio in confessione finitur. . . ." (Ibid., 1087–90.)

[54] *Epist.* 56, chap. 1: *"Nomen Domini confessi, violentiam magistratus et populi frementis impetum vicerant."* (Hartel, CSEL, vol. 3, 2: 648.) Chap. 2: *"Nomen Domini confessos esse"* (649). Cf. Collect in the Roman missal for March 10, *"Gloriosos martyres fortes in sua confessione cognovimus. . . ."*

[55] *De morte persecutorum*, chap. 1 *"Gloriosa confessione sempiternam sibi coronam pro fidei merito quaesierunt."* Chap. 16: *"Novies adversarium gloriosa confessione vicisti."* (CSEL, 27:171 and 189.)

[56] *Sermo* 199, chap. 1, no. 2: *"Illi pro Christo potuerunt pati, quem nondum potuerunt confiteri."* (PL, 38:1027.) Roman missal: *"Non loquendo sed moriendo confessi sunt."*

[57] *Sermo* Guelferb., 28, nos. 6–7 (Morin, 541).

[58] Tertullian, above. Quodvultdeus(?), *De SS. Perpetua et Felicitate*,

FAITH AND PROFESSION OF FAITH

is no escaping the alternative. Confession, witness and martyrdom: in the end they are all one. The Latin text of the Epistle by Clement of Rome mentions the *"testimonium martyrii"*,[59] and Tertullian writes in like manner: *"confessores et martyres"*;[60] the two words are practically pleonasms. Martyrdom is the perfect testimony, the perfect confession. It takes place *"in certamine confessionis et passionis"*.[61] Yet Tertullian did exclaim, *"O martyrium et sine passione perfectum."*[62] Before long, Origen said in a similar vein, "I have no doubt that in this assembly there are a number of Christians whom God alone knows, who, before him and by the testimony of their consciences, are already martyrs, prepared to shed their blood for the name of the Lord Jesus Christ whenever this is required of them."[63]

By the beginning of the third century, occasions for heroically bearing witness to their faith had become so common for Christians that, by a refinement of meaning already suggested in the New Testament,[64] the words *"confiteri"* and *"confessio"* were often used thereafter without any complement; they had become technical terms

---

3 (PL, Suppl., 3:304). St. Leo(?), *De Macchabaeis*, 2 (ibid., 334), etc.

[59] 1 Clem., chap. 5, no. 13: *"Dato testimonio martyrii, sic a potentibus liberavit se ab hoc saeculo."* This expression, explains Miss Mohrmann, is a *"genitivus inhaerentiae"*; i.e., the two words are synonyms, the second being only somewhat more technical: *Études* 3:99.

[60] *De corona*, chap. 2, no. 1 (CCL, 2:1041). Cf. Pseudo-Bernard, *Meditatio in Passionem*, chap. 6, no. 11: *"O beatissimum non latronem, sed martyrem et confessorem!"* (PL, 184:747 C.)

[61] Quodvultdeus, 306.

[62] *Scorpiace*, chap. 8, no. 7, commenting on Daniel 3:16 (CCL, 2:1083).

[63] *In Num.*, hom. 10, no. 2 (Baehrens, GCS, 30:72).

[64] Cf. Karl Rahner, *Le Martyre*, in *Écrits théologiques* 3 (1963): 172.

used in Christian language to designate that bearing witness before men which could lead to death, and which did lead at least to torture or imprisonment.[65] The same thing happened to the word "confessor"; it appears for the first time with this specialized meaning in Tertullian's writings.[66] Not long afterward the ninth chapter of the *Apostolic Tradition* dealt with the "confessors".[67] And before long, finally, through a quite natural process of transfer and objectivation, the martyr's tomb came to be venerated as his "confession", a term that has remained in use to this day.[68]

We know that the "confessors" who had escaped death after suffering for the faith were usually accorded great veneration by the rest of the faithful, but that "some of them abused this and became a nuisance".[69] Whence arose the need for making rules concerning

[65] Once the period of persecutions had passed, St. Avitus of Vienne wrote, *Epist.* Pieper 6: "*Est tamen et aliud sanctitatis genus, in quo, si tempus persecutionis absistat, martyrium quoddam plena confessio queat imitari.*" (PL, Suppl., 3:802.)

[66] Cf. H. Hoppenbrauwers, *Recherches sur la terminologie du martyre de Tertullien à Lactance* (Nijmegen, 1961), quoted by Meershoek, 72, note. In *Ad Scapulam*, chap. 4, we find an even more general sense: i.e., "those who avow". "*Videtis ergo quomodo ipsi vos contra mandata faciatis, ut confessos negare cogatis. Adeo confitemini innocentes esse nos, quod damnare statim ex confessione non vultis.*" (CCL, 2:1130.) So too in the *Acts of the Sicilian Martyrs* (Carthage, 180), the proconsul condemned to death the individuals "*ritu christiano se vivere confessos*". Cf. Hermas, *Simil.* 9, 28 (SC, 53 *bis*:348).

[67] SC, 11 *bis*:64.

[68] By a similar objectification, "*catholica professio*" came to mean, no longer the act of professing the Catholic faith, but the Catholic religion itself (A. Blaise, 602). It is in the same sense that we speak today of the various Christian "confessions".

[69] B. Botte, SC, 11 *bis*:27–28.

them, so that they might not encroach on the rights of the bishops. The celebrated "Letter of the Churches of Vienne and Lyons to Those of Asia and Phrygia", undoubtedly written by St. Irenaeus, contains a lesson in modesty addressed to the Asiatic confessors. The lesson is artfully included in the account of the persecution that had taken place in Lyons and in the report of the feelings of those who had endured it. The Letter goes on to speak of those who had just undergone ordeals that had not proved mortal:

> Not only did they not proclaim themselves to be martyrs, but they would not even allow us to call them by that name. . . . They preferred to reserve that title of martyr for Christ, the faithful and true Martyr. . . . They also remembered the martyrs whom Christ had deigned to take to himself in the midst of their confession, sealing their martyrdom with their blood. As for us, we are humble little confessors. . . .[70]

When, during Hitler's persecution, certain Christians in Germany, tired of the compromises and connivances which were inspired by a faltering faith and which in the eyes of some seemed to be authorized by the Lutheran tradition of entire submission to civil authority, decided to organize resistance in the name of Christ against the pressure of this authority, they turned again to the old word in which, since the beginning, humble Christian self-respect had been manifested: they called themselves

---

[70] Chap. 5, no. 2, Fr. trans., Pierre Nautin, in his book *Lettres et écrivains chrétiens des deuxième et troisième siècles* (Paris: Éd. du Cerf, 1961), 33–34. See in this work the commentary on this passage. Hippolytus calls "martyrs" the Christians condemned to the mines in Sardinia whom Callixtus had met there in his youth: *Philosophumena*, 9, 12 (Wendland, 246).

the "confessing Church", knowing full well the commitment that such a name implied.[71]

Like the act of faith itself, the confession of faith is thus an eminently personal act. Just as it is the person who freely responds to God, so too it is the person who freely testifies, and his testimony reveals the extent of his involvement. But this eminently personal act is never something individualistic. For the Christian it is never a purely "private affair". As we have seen, he received his faith from the Church; it is in the bosom of the Church that he believes; and his faith unites him to all the other members of the Church, his brothers. So, too, he confesses his faith in union with all of them and, as it were, in their collective name. This is underscored by a liturgical practice found in the Orthodox Church. Just as in the Latin liturgy, a moment before they receive the body of Christ, the officiants offer each other the kiss of peace, so too in the Orthodox Church, before singing or reciting the Creed, they proclaim: "Let us love one another, so that with a single mind we may confess the Father, the Son and the Holy Spirit, the consubstantial and indivisible Trinity."[72] In making his sacrifice, the martyr "realizes that he belongs to a community of brethren, in which and in whose name he is giving his witness".[73] The *homologia* or *confessio* might then be defined as "the

---

[71] Cf. H. Bouillard, *Karl Barth* 1 (1957): 156–60. Daniel Cornu, *Karl Barth et la politique* (Geneva: Labor et Fides, 1967), 21–22, 43–45, etc.

[72] A. M. Alchin, *La Contribution de l'Orthodoxie au débat sur Dieu*, in *Contacts* (1968), 121–22.

[73] M. Pellegrino, *Le Sens ecclésial du martyre*, in *Revue des sciences religieuses* 35 (1961): 152. Cf. G. Jouassard, *Le Rôle des chrétiens comme intercesseurs auprès de Dieu dans la chrétienté lyonnaise au second siècle*, in *Revue des sciences religieuses* 30 (1956): 217–29.

common, public adherence, binding one to the one apostolic faith defined by the Church".[74]

This essential requirement of Christian faith which is reflected in the communal character of the *confessio* is understood with difficulty today by a number of cultured believers, who think themselves obliged to keep their distance from the "common run of Christians" and who seem to be afraid that the expression of their faith, or even their faith itself, might be reduced to some common scheme. Such qualms have a long history. The victory of the Christian requirement over this scruple is admirably illustrated in the account given by St. Augustine, in the eighth book of his *Confessions*, of the conversion of Marius Victorinus. Victorinus, the rhetorician, was a learned and venerated old man who had deserved to see his statue erected in the Forum at Rome. Little by little he had become convinced of the truth of the Scriptures, so that he confided to his friend Simplicianus: "Know that I am already a Christian." Simplicianus replied, "I shall not count you among the Christians as long as I do not see you in the Church of Christ." The old man answered, mockingly, "So, it is walls that make people Christians?" This was because he feared the scorn of the pagan intellectuals.[75] But then,

---

[74] H. Schlier, *L'Unité de l'Église d'après le Nouveau Testament* (Fr. trans., René Marlé, in *Unité de l'Église et tâche oecuménique* [1962], 38).

[75] Cf. 1 Cor 1:26–29. Tertullian, *Adversus Praxean*, chap. 3, no. 1: "*Simplices quique, ne dixerim imprudentes et idiotae, quae major semper credentium pars est. . . .*" (CCL, 2:1161.) St. Jerome, *In Galat.*, bk. 3, praef.: "*Ecclesia Christi, non de Academia et Lycaeo, sed de vili plebecula congregata est.*" (PL, 26:400 D.) Cf. D. Bonhoeffer, letter dated 1940: "Ever since its first beginnings, the Church has been made up of ordinary folk, lacking prestige, etc." (René Marlé, 50.) M. Pellegrino, 154: The Christian is not the defender of a doctrinal system

Augustine tells us, he finally began to fear even more that he might be denied by Christ before the angels unless he confessed him before men. So, one fine day he came to find Simplicianus and said, "Let us go to the church; I want to become a Christian." He gave his name as a candidate for baptism. Then the time came for him to confess his faith on the day of the sacrament. At Rome this ceremony took place in a conspicuous place, in the presence of the faithful. "The priests had suggested to him that the rite be performed in private; it was customary to offer this opportunity to persons who they feared to see waver because of timidity; but Victorinus himself preferred to confess his salvation in the presence of the holy assembly." The faithful, who had been informed of all this, crowded around; and after listening in the deepest silence to his confession, each one praised him and hurried joyfully toward him.[76] Thenceforth Victorinus was fully a Christian, a member of the Catholic community.[77]

"proposed to the cultured for their examination", but the witness to a gift (χάρις).

[76] Augustine, *Confessions*, bk. 8, chap. 2, nos. 3–5: "*Habet enim (Simplicianus) magnam laudem gratiae tuae confitendam tibi quemadmodum ille doctissimus senex.*"—"*Ut ventum est ad horam profitendae fidei, quae verbis certis conceptis retentisque memoriter de loco eminentiore in conspectu populi fidelis Romae reddi solet.*" "*(Maluit ille) salutem suam in conspectu sanctae multitudinis profiteri.*" The works of Marius Victorinus have been edited by P. Henry and P. Hadot in *Sources chrétiennes* (68 and 69; 1960). See also Pierre Hadot, *Porphyre et Victorinus* I (*Études augustiniennes*, Paris, 1968, 2 vol.).

[77] Cf. Maurice Blondel, letter to Paul Archambault, October 27, 1925: "At all periods there has been a conflict between the human appearances of Christ and the requirements of faith; and Newman observed that for him as for so many other *intellectual* or *ethical* types, aristocrats by taste and idealists by tendency, the hardest trial was to be seated in the Catholic Church alongside small people, small minds,

FAITH AND PROFESSION OF FAITH

The word which expresses this community aspect of the confession of faith is "creed" (*symbol*).

It was originally a Greek term, σύμβολον. Its basic meaning, rendered by the Latin words *indicium* or *signum*, is "a sign of recognition."[78] Before parting, it was the custom for friends, guests, associates or businessmen to break up some object: a token, seal, emblem, coin . . . and to distribute the pieces among themselves, so as to recognize each other if they ever met again. *Symbolon* or *symbolos* comes from the verb συμβάλλειν: to throw or put together, to join what had first been separated; the fragments of the broken object are fitted together and made one again.

Thus reconstituted, the object is nothing but itself; but the act of putting it together is a meaningful act, a sign of recognition or identification. This sign accredited the

---

small characters, pharisees and the unworthy. How many occasions for scandal, demoralization, almost shame! And, foreseeing these circumstances which will always occur, Christ still told us: Blessed is he who is not scandalized because of me in my most squalid members. As for my poor part, I have suffered acutely because of this impression I have constantly had of the immense disappointment given by the people of Christ, but at the same time and even more strongly do I feel an inner certainty and as it were the touch of the purity, truth and goodness of Christ himself and of his work among us. Note well that there is no question here of duplicity or of subtlety, nor of some idealizing or distorting interpretation of things; no, what I adhere to is not a Christianity reformed and transfigured to conform with my tastes and dreams; it is the concrete, historic continual reality of the incarnate Word, descended to the lowest levels of our wretchedness in order to endure them and to help us to endure them, and thus to expiate, purify, and make divine our poor, deficient and so often repulsive humanity."

[78] Cf. Th. Camelot, *Note sur le mot symbole*, in *Lumière et vie* 2 (1952): 79.

owners of the two halves of the object to each other. To the absent partner whom I do not know, but with whom I have come to an agreement, I send a messenger who bears half of a ring: when we meet some day, this far-off recipient and myself, we will *know* each other by this reconstructed object.[79]

This same basic meaning was specialized by its use in certain mystery cults; the *symbolon* in that case was the sign, a material object or a password, by which the initiated could be recognized. The word then took on a third meaning in military terminology; adding a further precision to *sême*, the *symbolum* became the sign, watchword, insignia which served as a rallying point for the troops and insured their cohesion. In each of these three meanings, as we can see, the essential idea was always that of union, which was the thing sought.

The word first appeared in Christian Latin writing in one of St. Cyprian's letters, where he was speaking of the Novatians' baptismal creed: "If anyone objects that they baptize using the same creed as we do, let him know that the same law of the creed does not apply to us and to these schismatics."[80] Tertullian uses the word *symbolum* only twice, and does so as a metaphor, referring to its

---

[79] Pierre Emmanuel, *La Considération de l'extase*, in *Études carmélitaines* 39 (1960), *Polarité du symbole*, 75. The hospitium, or contract of hospitality, was a freely established convention between two parties (towns or individuals); it involved the exchange of a written document or of some distinguishing mark which was substituted for this; the mark was made in two copies, "so that comparing them would suffice to establish their authenticity". J. Marquardt, *La Vie privée des Romains* (Fr. trans., V. Henry, 1 [Paris: Thorin, 1892]: 230–32).

[80] *Epist.* 69, chap. 7: "*Quod si aliquis illud opponit ut dicat . . . eodem symbolo quo et nos baptizare, sciat . . . non esse unam nobis et schismaticis symboli legem.*" (G. Hartel, CSEL, 2:756.)

original meaning as a seal which guarantees a contract.[81] When speaking of the creed of faith he uses the equivalent word *tessera*, which in classical Latin was the specific name of the object that served as a sign of recognition.[82] Two of Plautus' characters happen to meet: "I am the son of Antidamas whom you are seeking." "If so, let us compare our 'tesserae' of hospitality; here is mine." "Let me see. . . . Yes, it is indeed just like the one I have at home."[83] In the same way, for Tertullian, the handing on of the same rule of faith ("*ejusdem sacramenti una traditio*") assures the bond between the Churches; it is the "*contesseratio hospitalitatis*";[84] by it the Churches in different regions are united to one another, *contesseratae*.[85]

Before long, and in a definitive manner throughout the whole Church, the formula used for the confession of the faith, and thereby for the communion of Christians among themselves, was called the "symbol", or creed. To explain it, some started, for instance, with the image

---

[81] *De paenitentia*, chap. 6, no. 12; *Adversus Marcionem*, bk. 5, chap. 1, no. 2 (CCL, 1:331 and 664). Cf. A. d'Alès, *Tertullien, Symbolum*, Recherches de science religieuse 26 (1936): 468.

[82] Tessera originally meant some square or cubical object, hence a die for casting lots; then it came to mean any sort of token or identification device. Cicero in his *Pro Balbo*, 18, 41, mentions "*tessera hospitalis*".

[83] *Antidamae gnatum me esse. —Si itast, tesseram*
 Conferre si vis hospitalem, eccam attuli.
 —Agedum, hic ostende. Est par probe quam habeo domi.
  (*Poenulus*, vv. 1047–1049. A. Ernout, 5:232.)

[84] *De praescriptione*, chap. 20, nos. 8–9 (SC, 46:113–14, with notes by F. Refoulé). Cf. *Adversus Marcionem*, bk. 4, chap. 5, no. 2: "*Illis (ecclesiis) de societate sacramenti confaederantur.*" (CCL, 1:551.)

[85] Op. cit., chap. 36, no. 4, speaking of the Church of Rome: "*Cum Africanis quoque ecclesiis contesseratis unum Deum Dominum novit.*" (SC, 46:138.)

of merchants, while others used that of soldiers. The first of these was used principally when stress was laid on the care taken to discern the true faithful: they alone possessed the *"sigillum integrum"*, as Optatus of Milevis said, i.e., the *"symbolum catholicum"*,[86] while certain barely Christianized Jews in the early times,[87] or later on various heretics, could never show more than a mutilated, insufficient fragment of the identifying sign. "We call creed [*symbole*]", says St. Augustine, "the text which contains the faith ratified by our society, and the faithful Christian is recognized by his profession, as if by a prearranged sign."[88] St. Ambrose, in his *Explanatio*, developed this image in an original manner; beginning with the presumed equivalence between the Greek *symbolon* and the Latin *conlatio*.[89]

> "Symbol" is a Greek word which means "contribution" (*conlatio*). Indeed, merchants are in the habit of speaking of this contribution (*symbolam*) when they deposit their money; and the amount thus collected through each one's contribution (*conlatione*) is kept whole and inviolable, so that no one would dare commit any fraud with regard to this common contribution or to this operation. And then

[86] *De schismate Donatistarum*, bk. 2, chap. 8: *"Quia soli sigillum integrum, id est symbolum catholicum non habentes, ad fontem verum aperire non possunt."* (PL, 11:961 A B.) The identification tag is here compared with the seal conferred in baptism.

[87] Rufinus, chap. 2: *"Symbolum . . . indicium vel signum idcirco dicitur, quia in illo tempore . . . multi ex circumeuntibus Judaeis simulabant se esse apostolos Christi. . . , nominantes quidem Christum sed non integris traditionum lineis nunciantes."* (CCL, 20:135.)

[88] *Sermo* 214, no. 12 (PL, 38:1072). Cf. *Sermo* 212, no. 1 (below).

[89] On this equivalence, which arose from a certain confusion between the two words συμβολον and συμβολή, see below.

it is the custom among merchants that if anyone does commit fraud, he is expelled from the group as a crook.[90]

The second image, that of soldiers gathered around the same standard, is used all the more frequently, since, according to St. Paul, the Christian is a "soldier of Christ" (*"miles Christi"*)[91] and since it closely resembles that of the *"militiae sacramentum"*, or military oath,[92] which was familiar to Tertullian.[93] The two can even more or less merge, as in the case where the Latin word *"sacramentum"* is used to designate the rule or creed of faith.[94] Rufinus developed the image.[95] The Roman Catechism adopted it, explaining why "the Apostles called 'symbol' the profession of Christian faith and hope". This was because, among other reasons, "they wished to use it as a mark and a watchword which would

---

[90] *Explanatio symboli*, no. 2: "*Symbolum Grace dicitur, latine autem conlatio. Et maxime symbolam negociatores dicere consuerunt, quando conferunt paecuniam suam, et quasi ex singulorum conlatione in unum constipata integra et inviolabilis conservatur, ut nemo fraudem conlationi facere conetur.*" (B. Botte, SC, 25 *bis*:46–47). Nicetas, bk. 5, *Sermo* 1, no. 25 (Gamber, 107).

[91] 2 Tim 2:3. Cf. 1 Tim 1:18; 6:12. Clement of Rome, *Cor.* 37:1–3. Tertullian, *De oratione*, chap. 19 (PL, 1:1183 A).

[92] Ambrose, *De virginibus*, bk. 3, chap. 4, no. 20: "*Quando enim sine militiae sacramento miles in tentorio, bellator in praelio?*" (PL, 16:225 C.) Cf. Augustine, *De civitate Dei*, bk. 1, chap. 35: "*Deum, cujus sacramentum gerunt*" (CCL, 47:33).

[93] F. Refoulé, introduction to the *De baptismo* (SC, 35:49).

[94] Tertullian, *Adversus Praxean*, chap. 30, no. 5: "*Spiritum sanctum. . . , deductorem omnis veritatis, quae est in Patre et Filio et Spiritu sancto, secundum christianum sacramentum*" (PL, 2:196 A). Peter Chrysologus, *Sermo* 58: "*confessionis sacramentum*" (PL, 52:361 B).

[95] *Comm. in symbolum apostolorum*, chap. 2: "*In bellis civilibus haec observari ferunt.*" (CCL, 20:135.)

make it easy for them to distinguish the true soldiers of Jesus Christ from the deserters and the false brethren".[96]

Then again, stress was sometimes placed on the idea of a distinctive sign, *"symbolum est spiritale signaculum"*,[97] and sometimes on that of a unifying bond. "Two men who meet know that they are both Christians if they speak a language that both can understand. The Creed [*Symbole*] is this very language."[98] Thus, it is why Christians recognize one another and why they recognize that they are united: *"Symbolum ergo dicitur"*, says St. Augustine, *"in quo se agnoscant christiani."*[99] The first notion is the one expressed by terms such as "password", or, as Jungmann says, "passport": the creed "was the passport thanks to which a travelling Christian could prove his identity to a foreign Christian community".[100] The second notion was brought out by John Cassian when he said that the "symbol" is "the *Credo* of all the Churches" because "the faith of them all is one".[101] It was stressed even more by St. Peter Damian, who connected the *"sanctorum communio"* to the *"symbolum catholicae professionis"* in a sort of reciprocal causality: for by giving evidence to God of their faith, Christians also manifest and fortify the communion of the Church.[102] It

---

[96] First part, chap. 1, no. 2.
[97] *Explanatio symboli* (PL, 17:1155 C).
[98] Cardinal Garrone, *La Profession de foi de Paul VI* (Paris: Beauchesne, 1969), 13.
[99] *Sermo* Guelb., 1, no. 2 (Morin, 443).
[100] J. A. Jungmann, *La Liturgie des premiers siècles*, 150.
[101] *Conferences*, Nest., VI, 3, 6.
[102] *Liber qui dicitur Dominus vobiscum*, chap. 10: "*Addimus: 'sanctorum communionem', ut, ubi Deo fidei nostrae testimonium reddimus, ibi etiam communionem Ecclesiae, quae cum eo unum est, consequenter adstruamus.*" (PL, 145:239 C D.) Cf. Luther: "*Propter confessionem coetus*

is this same communion that, in a recently discovered sermon, St. Chromatius of Aquilea celebrated, contrasting the reciprocal hostility existing between earthly kingdoms and the unity of all the faithful who, even though subjects of these different kingdoms, do battle for the one kingdom of God in the one army of Christ.[103] It was this same communion, a pledge of gentler manners for the whole universe, that Prudentius has the blessed martyr Lawrence praise before his judge:

> *Confoederantur omnia,*
> *Hinc inde membra in symbolum*
> *Mansuescit orbis subditus;*
> *Mansuescat et summum caput!*[104]

This mutual recognition and this union of Christians with one another, through the bond created by the creed, is just as truly the mutual recognition and union between the Christian and his God. Thus understood, the creed is compared to a pact which demands fidelity. Such was the point of view adopted by Nicetas of Remesiana when he exhorted the newly baptized: "Always keep", he told them, "the pact which you have made with the Lord, namely the creed."[105] This was also one of

---

Ecclesiae est visibilis." Wa, 39/2, 161. (In Kung, *L'Église* 1:65.)

[103] *"Et licet eas (gentes) secundum regnum saeculi discordasse regni diversitas faciat, tamen secundum regnum Dei et unitatem concordiae pari fide comparent uni imperatori, secundum fidem omnes Christo militant."* Sermon on the Acts of the Apostles, ed. J. Lemarié, in *Revue bénédictine* 75 (1965): 138.

[104] Prudentius, *Peristephanon* 2, *Hymnus in honorem passionis Laurentii*, 437–40 (G. Bergman, CSEL, GI, 312).

[105] *"Retinete semper pactum quod fecistis cum Domino, id est symbolum."* (Ed. Burn, 51.) Cf. Tertullian, *Adversus Marcionem*, bk. 4, chap. 16, no. 12: *"Quamdiu intra Israelem erat sacramentum . . ."* (CCL, 1:584).

St. Augustine's points of view; in two of his sermons to the people, he colors the image of merchants in this sense:

> The word "symbol", which is borrowed from Greek, draws its name from an image: merchants are in the habit of establishing between themselves a voucher, the *symbolum*, by which they base their association on a commitment of mutual good faith. Your society deals with spiritual goods; you must be like businessmen looking for a fine jewel: the charity poured forth in your heart by the Holy Spirit who will be given to you.[106]

> Now with the selling and buying of the faith, the kingdom of heaven is offered to you for purchase.[107]

St. Peter Chrysologus took up once more and with great clarity the idea of Nicetas in order to exalt this "pact of life", this "pact of hope" and of salvation, i.e., the creed, "the indissoluble bond of fidelity" between the Christian and his God.[108] Much later still, Erasmus further refined it by using the traditional evocation of the nuptial union between Christ and his Church: "Between bride and bridegroom, by mutual consent, the creed is given so that henceforth it is no longer permissible to violate this pact."[109]

---

[106] *Sermo* 212, no. 1. Cf. *Sermo* 58, no. 13. The reward of faith will be the vision of God, and then we shall no longer need any voucher, any symbol.

[107] *Sermo* 216, no. 3. (S. Poque, SC, 116:174–75: cf. 60.)

[108] *Sermo* 58: "*Accepturi ergo symbolum, hoc est, pactum vitae, salutis placitum, et inter vos et Deum fidei insolubile vinculum, pectora parate, non chartam. . . .*" (PL, 52:361 B.) *Sermo* 59: "*Hoc spei pactum, hoc salutis placitum, hoc vitae symbolum, hanc fidei cautionem mens teneat.*" (365 B.) *Sermo* 57 and 62 (360 C, 372 A).

[109] "*Jam inter sponsum et sponsam ex consensu mutuo datur symbolum,*

Several other explanations of the word "symbol", based on another supposed etymology, were suggested and enjoyed a certain vogue. To tell the truth this derivation served rather to illustrate than to give them a foundation. According to this doubtful etymology, σύμβολον, confused with συμβολή, was translated into Latin as *"collatio"*, with the meaning of "epitome" or "resumé". Hence we find in St. Augustine this description: "The creed [*symbole*] is the rule of faith in summary form, so that it may instruct the mind without burdening the memory, may be stated in a few words, by which many may be won over."[110]

St. Augustine also said to his catechumen: "The time has come for you to receive the creed, which contains in summary all that we must believe in order to attain eternal life."[111] Thus the creed is the *"verbum breviatum"*, the *"breviarum fidei"* (abridgment of the faith), condensing the substance of the Sacred Books, as we saw explained by Cassian[112] and others in the first chapter. St. Ambrose in his *Explanatio* and Rufinus of Aquilea had

---

ne liceat a pacto recedere": Explicatio in symbolum (1541), 13; 15: *"Indissolubili vinculo coït inter Christum et Ecclesiam."*

[110] *Sermo* Guelferb., 1, no. 2: *"Symbolum est ergo breviter complexa regula fidei, ut mentem instruat, nec oneret memoriam, paucis verbis dicatur, unde multum adquiratur."* (Morin, 442.)

[111] *Sermo* 212, no. 1: *"Tempus est ut symbolum accipiatis, quo continetur breviter, propter aeternam salutem, omne quod creditur."* (Ed. and Fr. trans., S. Poque, SC, 116:174–75.)

[112] *De incarnatione Domini contra Nestorium*, bk. 6, chap. 3: *"Symbolum quippe, ut scis, ex collatione nomen accepit."* (M. Petschenig [1888]: 328–29.) See above, Chapter One, 31. Nicetas had already said: *"Pauca quidem verba, sed omnia continent sacramenta. De totis enim Scripturis haec brevitatis causa collata sunt, tanquam geminae pretiosae in una corona compositae."* (Gamber, 121.)

spoken in the same way, comparing the *collatio* and the *indicium*.[113] Faustus of Riez does the same thing.[114] In a very eclectic passage, St. Fulgentius of Ruspe in his turn adopts this explanation and concludes that in the formula of this pact, in this true *"collatio"*, the sum of the entire Christian faith is briefly condensed.[115] It was thus a very widespread tradition that St. Isidore of Seville echoed when he wrote that the faithful come to realize their unity when they sing together the *"verbum breviatum"*.[116] Finally, the same etymology is connected to another closely allied meaning, the only difference being that in this case one proceeded by gathering together the elements composing it. Such was the first sense pointed out by the Roman Catechism: the Apostles, it tells us, "gave to their profession of faith the name creed [*symbole*], either because they composed it by combining the various truths which each one of them had formulated, or. . . ."[117]

Relying on the more concrete image suggested by the word, *"collatio"* is explained in still another manner, or rather with some supplementary details, by Rufinus of Aquilea. This explanation, which was destined for

[113] Rufinus, *Expositio Symboli*, no. 1: *"Verbum enim consummans et brevians in aequitate, quia verbum breviatum faciet Dominus super terram."* No. 2: *"Symbolum enim graece et indicium dici potest, et collatio."* (CCL, 20:134.)

[114] *"Eusebius gallicanus"*, *Sermo* 10, *de symbolo*, 2 (PL, Suppl., 3:583).

[115] *Contra Fabianum arianum*, fragm. 35: *"Est autem symbolum quoddam verum pactum veraque collatio, in cujus brevitate totius credulitatis christianae summa consistit.* (PL, 65:822–63.)

[116] *De ecclesiasticis officiis*, bk. 2, chap. 13 (PL, 83:817 A).

[117] First part, chap. 1, no. 2; see above, 48f. William of St. Thierry, *Aux Frères du Mont-Dieu*, bk. 2, chap. 3, no. 4: *"Ut . . . ea quae cogitationem faciunt, continuo libere concurrant sibi et cooperentur in bonum, et quasi symbolum faciant in gaudium cogitantis."* (PL, 184:347 C.)

FAITH AND PROFESSION OF FAITH

widespread acceptance, was closely connected with the legend which, as we know, Rufinus helped to popularize. *"Collatio"*, he says, *"hoc est, quod plures in unum conferunt"* (what several contribute in order to put it together). These *"plures"* in the case of our creed were the twelve Apostles. "This was, in fact, what the Apostles did with their words, each one having contributed to the whole what he thought."[118] Rufinus alludes here to an old custom, which has always existed: at certain community banquets, or simply for a picnic, each one contributes his share, his portion: *"symbola"*[119] or *"collecta"*.[120] By extension these words could signify the meal itself, as in the Vulgate translation of Proverbs (21:17): *"Quia vacantes potibus et dantes symbola consumentur."*[121] It was also easy to allegorize the idea: thus Aulus Gellius compared the material shares of the banquet with the question which each guest contributed for common discussion.[122] This is also what Tertullian did when in mockery he applied the word *symbola* to the meeting of the Valentinians.[123] Rufinus did the same thing for the Apostles' Creed. Not long afterward Faustus of Riez repeated the image in more explicit terms in his first

---

[118] Op. cit., chap. 2 (CCL, 20:134). In addition, this was only one of the *"multae et justissimae causae"* which, according to Rufinus, led the Twelve to choose this title of creed, or "symbol".

[119] Plautus, *Curculio*, 4, 1, 15. Terence, *Eunuchus*, 3, 4, 1.

[120] Cicero, *De Oratore*, 2:57.

[121] "Pleasure lovers stay poor, he will not grow rich who loves wine and good living." (Jerusalem Bible.) Note that the feminine singular has become, as a result of the confusion with *"symbolum"*, a neuter plural. (In the Vulgate, this is an example of "hapax".)

[122] *Attic Nights*, 7, 13, 12 (F. Gaffiot, 1532).

[123] *Adversus Valentinianos*, chap. 12 (CCL, 2:763). Cf. Ad. d'Alès, in *Revue des sciences religieuses* 25 (1935): 496.

homily on the Creed: "Gathered in one place, the associates would place their contribution in common, in view of the solemn banquet, so as to share in the expense of the meal."[124] Now this sermon was circulated under the name of Eusebius of Emesa, also called "Eusebius the Gallican", to whom considerable authority was attributed,[125] so that this explanation, the most arbitrary of all, was also the most widely popular in the Latin Middle Ages. We find it in Rabanus Maurus, who simply copies a page from Rufinus,[126] as does Magnus of Sens.[127] Yves of Chartres developed it further, but in his own way, evoking by transposition the heavenly banquet which will be shared by all who are united to the "*sodalitium*" of the Apostles.[128]

In the twelfth century, Peter Abelard began his explanation of the Creed with the text of Proverbs, giving a commentary based on "Eusebius of Emesa".[129] Joscelin of Soissons (d. 1152) gives evidence of a position more dependent on the same comparison by his use of a stronger etymological explanation of the word "*symbolum*". He said that the word was made up of the preposition *sun* (meaning "with" or "together") and the noun *bolus*,

---

[124] "*Apud veteres symbola vocabantur, quod de substantia sua collecti in unum sodales in medium conferebant ad solemnes epulas et ad caenae communes expensas.*" (Caspari, 262–63.)

[125] See above, Chapter One, 29.

[126] *De clericorum institutione*, bk. 2, chap. 56 (PL, 107:369 A B).

[127] *Libellus de mysterio baptismatis* (PL, 102:981–82).

[128] *Sermo 25, de symbolo apostolorum*: "*Solent quippe sodales, cum aliquem in sodalitium suum admittunt, symbolum dare, et ita initum fidei pactum confirmare. Ad hanc similitudinem sancti apostoli spirituale sodalitium inter se connectentes, hoc symbolum confecerunt, quo sodalitium eorum intrare cupientes, fidei commercio sibi colligarent et sic caelestis mensae participes secum efficerent.*" (PL, 162:604 C D.)

[129] *Expositio symboli* (PL, 178:619 C D).

which means "mouthful". Thus, each Apostle would have contributed, so to speak, his own mouthful to the banquet; in other words, each one would have uttered his "article", and from all of this would have resulted that *"confra spiritualis"*, that sign of brotherhood which is the Creed.[130] In the following century, Albert the Great repeated this, in the chapter of his treatise "on the Sacrifice of the Mass", which relates the legend about the composition of the Creed.[131] St. Bonaventure[132] and William of Mende[133] reproduced this fantastic etymology only to bring out the idea of the Creed as a resumé that unified a number of statements. As for St. Thomas Aquinas, who is freely eclectic in such matters, he found four reasons that justified the name "symbol" taken as a synonym for "collection".[134]

While they are often not very scholarly in their methods, and sometimes overly studied and subtle, all these old explanations still deserve credit for expressing, each in its own way, one aspect of the Creed's nature, one of its characteristics or purposes. Several of them bring out a fundamental truth, something essential to Catholic con-

---

[130] PL, 186:1480 A B.

[131] Bk. 2, chap. 8, no. 2 (*Opera*, ed. Borgnet, 38 [1899]: 58). For more details, see J. de Ghellinck, 134–35 and 156–57.

[132] *In 3 Sent.*, dist. 25, a. 1, q. 1: "*Dicitur enim symbolum quasi plurium sententia simul composita.*" (ed. Quaracchi, 3:536.)

[133] *Rationale*, bk. 4, chap. 25, no. 6: "*Sicut pueri in festivo convenientes offerre solent bolos, id est frusta carnium et panis, quae in unum collecta symbolum vocatur, id est collectio minutiorum.*"

[134] *In 3 Sent.*, q. 1, a. 1: "*A quatuor collectionibus nomen symboli imponitur: primo, a collectione multorum hominum in unam fidem. Secundo, a collectione praedicantium fidem* [the Apostles]. *Tertio, quia ex diversis locis sacrae Scripturae colliguntur ea quae credenda sunt.... Quarto, omnia beneficia divinitus collata ibi colliguntur....*" See also John of St. Thomas, *Cursus Theologicus* 7 (Paris: Vivès, 1886): 133–34.

sciousness. This is a truth that is always applicable, more opportune than ever at a time when that consciousness is seriously threatened, even among active and influential members of the Christian community.

It is a personal and public obligation, a bond of communion with all the other believers; such is the double reality signified and effected by the confession of faith in the recitation of the Creed. The fact that we say *"credo"* in the singular, and that we say it in common, is deeply significant.[135] These two traits reinforce each other, for if the public commitment produces communion, the support of the community strengthens the commitment. Fr. Karl Rahner observed:

> Courage to believe always comes about in the event of Pentecost, "where many are gathered together". Faith is always an act of confidence in the personal experience of others, a conviction inspired by the Spirit acting in the others, and a personal experience of the Spirit which is given to some for the sake of the others.[136]

This necessary union of all in the same Creed must remain uppermost in the minds of all Christians who undertake the work of theological reflection:

> The inevitable pluralism met with in theology cannot and must not cause the unity of the creed of faith to disappear from the Church, even in its verbal expression. . . . A single creed of the faith (is necessary). . . . In the Church

---

[135] Whatever may be the historical origin of this singular, which we mentioned before. At Nicea and at Constantinople (in 381) the Fathers declared: *"Credimus. . . ."* It would be worthwhile to read some of Karl Barth's reflections on this point: *Dogmatics* (Fr. trans., Fernand Ryser, Geneva: Labor et Fides, 1967), 4/1:123–24.

[136] *La Foi du prêtre, aujourd'hui* (Hanover: Katholikentag, 1962).

which is one we must rediscover unity even in the creed of faith expressed in words.... This has nothing to do with timid and comfortable conformism.... One's personal vision of the faith ... must always be integrated with this ecclesiastical confession of faith and must sincerely adopt that one confession.[137]

Let us complete these remarks by one more. Here everything holds together, everything is interconnected. The Creed, both confession and "symbol", expresses outwardly the act of faith itself. Now this act, which is addressed to God himself in response to his call and his gift, is, as we have seen, essentially a movement *in Deum*. The union of those who profess their faith in common, then, can only be a union of *convergence*. This convergence, like the movement itself, exists only by the power and through the Spirit of the One who said, "When I have been lifted up from the earth, I shall draw all things to myself": and it is by going through him that we are carried to the Father.

> The crystallization of the Church ... is the convergence of those who follow a Person. John understood this very well; he uses ... the verb "to believe toward", and also the verb "to come to". The apostolic group can be explained only as the conjunction of the attraction emanating from the Cross and of the movement of believers going to Jesus to become "his own". All that goes up to Calvary converges; Christ gives us to each other; he is our *vinculum*.[138]

---

[137] Karl Rahner, *Hérésies dans l'Église actuelle?* in *Au service de la Parole de Dieu* (Gembloux: Duclot, 1968), 420–22.

[138] André Manaranche, *Prêtres à la manière des apôtres* (Paris: Éd. du Centurion, 1967), 95–96.